P9-DWA-313

*Hawthorne's
Divided Loyalties*

Hawthorne's Divided Loyalties

England and America in His Works

Frederick Newberry

Rutherford ● Madison ● Teaneck
Fairleigh Dickinson University Press
London and Toronto: Associated University Presses

Associated University Presses
440 Forsgate Drive
Cranbury, NJ 08512

Associated University Presses
25 Sicilian Avenue
London WC1A 2QH, England

Associated University Presses
2133 Royal Windsor Drive
Unit 1
Mississauga, Ontario
Canada L5J 1K5

The paper used in this publication meets the requirements
of the American National Standard for Permanence of Paper
for Printed Library Materials Z39.48-1984.

Library of Congress Cataloging-in-Publication Data

Newberry, Frederick, 1941–
   Hawthorne's divided loyalties.

   Bibliography: p.
   Includes index.
   1. Hawthorne, Nathaniel, 1804–1864—Knowledge—History.
2. Hawthorne, Nathaniel, 1804–1864—Political and social
views.   3. Hawthorne, Nathaniel, 1804–1864—Knowledge—
England.   4. Hawthrone, Nathaniel, 1804–1864—Knowledge—
United States.   5. England in literature.   6. United
States in literature.   7. Literature and history.
I. Title.
PS1892.H5N4   1987   813'.3   85-45769
ISBN 0-8386-3274-2 (alk. paper)

Printed in the United States of America

To the memory of my mother
and
to my father

We of the nineteenth century appear in the world as mediators. . . . We must bind together the past and the future. . . .

Orestes Brownson (1836)

Each settlement of the Pilgrims was a little piece of the Old World inserted into the New.

Hawthorne, "Sir William Phips" (1830)

And England, the land of my ancestors! Once I had fancied that my sleep would not be quiet in the grave unless I should return, as it were, to my home of past ages, and see the very cities, and castles, and kneel at the shrines of its immortal poets, there asserting myself their hereditary countryman.

Hawthorne, "Fragments from the Journal of a Solitary Man" (1837)

Contents

Acknowledgments

G. R. Thompson encouraged me to seek the publication of my seminar paper on "Endicott and the Red Cross" and "The Gray Champion," as well as to extend their application in a dissertation. I am grateful for his early support. Robert C. McLean directed the dissertation and, perhaps more importantly, taught me how to read James. I am indebted to him for his rigor, high standards, and confidence. Virginia M. Hyde helped me to clarify the dissertation's approach to the Puritan tales and *The Scarlet Letter*. I feel especially obligated to her for the depth and clarity of her insight.

As for the considerably revised and expanded book manuscript, Alexander Hammond read all but one chapter, Kathleen McLean read several sections, and Fred D. Crawford read the whole. I thank them for their generous spirit and cogent remarks.

My wife's parents, Don and Shirley Woolery, provided indispensable help during the last stage of composition and throughout the period of revision. Were it only for them, I should feel blessed. So much more inestimable, therefore, my gratitude to Ruth, who typed the manuscript again and again, and without whose sacrifices, strength, and buoyance my work might not have been completed.

My son Darren, no reader yet, contributed in his own inimitably charming way by demanding my attention, no irrelevant matter to consider in relation to a book concerned with the values honored by one generation and inherited by the next.

Note on the Texts

Unless otherwise noted, quotations of Hawthorne come from two sources: *The Centenary Edition of Works of Nathaniel Hawthorne,* ed. William Charvat et al. (Columbus: Ohio State University Press, 1962–), cited parenthetically by volume and page number in the text; and *The English Notebooks by Nathaniel Hawthorne,* ed. Randall Stewart (1941; rpt., New York: Russell and Russell, 1962), cited parenthetically by *EN* and page number in the text.

Hawthorne's
Divided Loyalties

Introduction

One perspective of this study looks forward in time, from the moment in 1821 when seventeen-year-old Nathaniel Hathorne wrote to his mother announcing the lofty ambition to write a literature "equal to the proudest productions of the scribbling sons of John Bull."[1] Not yet having discovered historical warrant to spell his surname as the world would come to know it, having no interest in the work-a-day professions available in the young republic, and having no American example other than Irving's to bolster his confidence, Nathaniel had already decided to become a writer patterned after the literary sons of England. The self-conscious levity in the letter to his mother may qualify the immodesty of youthful ambition, but we no doubt slight what turns out to be a major impetus of Hawthorne's literary enterprise if we ignore the specific English orientation of his vision.

We are aware, of course, that there is nothing initially remarkable or particularly auspicious in Hawthorne's wish to emulate English authors. After all, virtually all American writers in the early national period looked to England for literary models, forms, and sources. From England, more than from anywhere else, came the poets, novelists, and dramatists they read—much to the consternation of nationalistic cultural spokesmen who, long before Emerson's famous peroration in "The American Scholar," called for an indigenous literature based upon native characters, speech, setting, and themes.[2] And, as every student of Hawthorne knows, young Nathaniel was considerably indebted to such authors as Spenser, Bunyan, Milton, Addison, Steele, and Scott. It is hardly surprising therefore that he should want to write and win fame equivalent to the beloved writers of his youth. Nevertheless, the fact that he did win such fame, and decidedly won it while creating distinctively "American" works evincing an unmistakable "American" voice, has perhaps led us too quickly to dismiss the implications of the young man's wish to write up to the mark of the "scribbling sons of John Bull." For they and, more importantly, the literary and cultural traditions of England that nourished them, were seldom excluded from Hawthorne's deepest preoccupations.

The last years of Hawthorne's career comprise the second point of view of this study. England was more obviously at the forefront of his attention during this period than it had been when he first began to write. As consul

15

to Liverpool, he lived in England from July 1853 to January 1858, keeping a voluminous account of his experiences and impressions. In 1859, after sixteen months in Italy, he returned to England for another seven months to see the English version of *The Marble Faun* through the press before returning to the United States. By October 1860, the first essay-sketch on England was published in *The Atlantic*. Drawn from *The English Notebooks*, it was followed by similar pieces during the next three years until the whole, with an addition, appeared as *Our Old Home* in September 1863. These were scarcely the extent of Hawthorne's absorption in English material, however. Before writing most of them, he also composed three separate versions of a romance involving an American's real or imagined claim to an English patrimony. Moreover, after abandoning this project, he tried to incorporate some of its subject matter into a final romance dwelling on an elixir of life.[3]

Over the course of his career, Hawthorne was often preoccupied with England—or, more precisely, with the lost cultural and aesthetic inheritance America experienced in the historical split with the mother country. Not simply for the convenience of writing a romance does he lament, in *The Marble Faun*, the lack of storied and poetical associations in America. As an American, indeed as a Puritan descendant, he felt from the very beginning the lack of native aesthetic traditions and rich cultural continuities offering access and encouragement to a would-be artist. Bereft of the advantages available to the literary sons of England, he had to make do with what he had—or with what he could get away with. He evidently discovered rather quickly, after publishing *Fanshawe* in 1828, that he could not get away with imitating English gothic and sentimental novels. Fortunately, Hawthorne thereafter turned to the model of Scott, without whom he would probably have floundered and never found the voice that we recognize as uniquely his own. For it was Scott who led the way to the historical subjects Hawthorne discovered in the colonial and early national past of New England. And it was Scott who revealed how historical issues had to be studied carefully, no doubt helping to explain the intensive period of historical reading Hawthorne undertook from 1827 to 1830—not only in New England history, as previous commentary has stressed, but also in English history. From Scott, too, Hawthorne must have come to realize more clearly than he might have on his own that with the supposed conclusion of any historical conflict there continue to be cultural repercussions of multiple kinds, waxing and waning over subsequent decades or centuries.

If Scott had a built-in writer's edge because the cultures of Scotland and England were both older and richer in available lore, Hawthorne had a paradoxically narrow advantage in undertaking an examination of a New World environment inhabited by immigrants who brought with them some of the customs and traditions of the Old World but who, for reasons he found worth exploring, did all they could to detach themselves from the ancient continuities. This was Hawthorne's great discovery, to delve into the roots of his own sense of personal and cultural deprivation. After *Fanshawe*, his early works often present a writer intensely aware of how New England Puritans disinherited themselves from the cultural traditions of the mother country. It is as if, in wanting to rid the English Church of its excesses, the Puritans in Hawthorne's fiction are brought up against the fact that they could not meddle with the parts without affecting the whole, which, with all its integrated harmonies accumulated over time, proved fragile indeed. In these works, virtually the entire culture is at stake, not the least constituents of which for Hawthorne's purposes are the aesthetic values encouraged and "nurtured at the rich bosom of the English Church" (1 : 109). Thus, by opposing the Church of England, Hawthorne's Puritans are obliged to oppose the greater part of the traditional culture attached to and largely grown up around it.

In coming to the New World, of course, the Puritans recreated the church according to their own taste. That taste, as Hawthorne presents it, while originally containing something admirable in its simplicity and sincerity, is too stark and severe—certainly too plain, as time goes on and the taste calcifies—to transmit a cultural heritage to future generations without dire results. The Puritans dispense with ancient pageants and ceremonies, exclude festivals and holidays hereditary to the old Church calendar, ban traditional forms of merriment, and persecute those who participate in time-honored customs and rites expressing the joy of living in the world. Quite aside from the primitive conditions imposed by the New World, beauty and art have little if any place among the majority of Hawthorne's Puritans. Church architecture is stripped of traditional aesthetic symbols and images of Christian faith, which Puritans considered idolatrous. Swept away are most expressions of splendor and grandeur, of pomp and ceremony, associated with the English past and with the Anglo-Catholic church so integral to that past. On a scale immeasurably less contested but more damaging in its long-term influence, New England Puritans largely achieve the theological and social reforms sought by Independent forces in the English Civil War.

What kind of home, in Hawthorne's view, is established in the New World as a result of the Puritan victory is a primary concern of this study. The idea of home has significant bearing upon most of those works we now consider Hawthorne's best.[4] His early New England tales suggest that the original Puritans were themselves aware of having lost their traditional "home" values in the howling wilderness. The loss of cultural values associated with home in England, mostly resulting from the narrow character developed from the Puritan errand, is rarely far from the center of Hawthorne's concern throughout his colonial tales. These values, deeply related to art and human sympathy, are special points of regret for Hawthorne—so much so that when, later in his career, he turns his attention to nineteenth-century affairs, he tries to recreate them in a series of works disclosing the partial recovery of the ancient home in England. Such repossessions of English ties, of hereditary continuities disrupted during the Puritan and Revolutionary epochs, are noticeably at stake in such works as "The Old Manse," *The House of the Seven Gables, The Blithedale Romance,* and *The Scarlet Letter.* More cogently than the others, *The Scarlet Letter* concentrates on why the seventeenth-century Puritan experiment failed to establish a cultural environment which, over time, would nurture tolerance, sensitivity, and art.

Both the causes and consequences of the historical process of expelling English cultural traditions may be traced in Hawthorne's narrow-minded Puritans and in the impoverished culture that they pass on to later generations. Acting upon the presumption that they are by analogy the chosen people of God, his "typical" Puritans contain a surfeit of self-righteousness, intolerance, and militant zeal, habitually expressed in acts of persecution. In their severity and bigotry, in their customary grays and blacks, Hawthorne's Puritans basically grow joyless and opposed to art to the degree that they sever themselves from beneficent historical roots. And theirs is the violent, iconoclastic legacy, descending to nineteenth-century America, with which Hawthorne must contend as an artist. To be sure, Hawthorne does reserve a limited amount of respect for the nobility and strength of character evident in a few early Puritan settlers. John Winthrop, Roger Williams, John Wilson, John Eliot, and Simon Bradstreet stand out in Hawthorne's cast of Puritanic zealots not only because they occupy prominent positions in New England history but also because they somehow manage to sustain positions of moderation among the radical Puritan majority. Their powers of conciliation or their lingering tastes for Old World values recede in New England history as the intolerant side of Puritanism, represented especially by John Endicott, increasingly dominates the first century of settlement and becomes *the* Puritan tradition.

Hawthorne's treatment of Endicott, however, is neither simple nor one-sided. For Endicott, too, is one of the early founding fathers who sometimes appears to be applauded for his strength of character. Antagonistic to the best cultural values admired by Hawthorne, and staunchly opposed to the influence of England on Massachusetts Bay, Endicott nevertheless becomes the typal forebear of leaders in the Revolutionary War. Such a view of Endicott depends, of course, upon an understanding of national typology, a political adaptation of biblical hermeneutics current in Hawthorne's time and considerably adumbrated in recent years.[5] Especially as it became codified in George Bancroft's historiography, the political typology of Hawthorne's day posited a redemptive configuration in American history. Where Old Testament figures and events serve as types prefiguring Christ's redemptive role in typological readings of the Bible, political typology offers persons and events in colonial history that foreshadow a secular redemption: independence from England and the establishment of democracy.

The first three chapters of this study are largely devoted to an examination of Hawthorne's use of this typology, with a particular focus on Endicott as the representative "type" in three early tales, "The May-pole of Merry Mount," "Endicott and the Red Cross," and "The Gentle Boy." Even as Endicott seems to be extolled as a typological forebear of American independence, Hawthorne raises serious questions over whether such a configuration of American history is tenable and over whether the sacrifices made under Endicott's brand of Puritanism are either necessary to or worth the cultural loss in the split with England. An analysis of "The Gray Champion" in the last section of chapter 1 emphasizes how Hawthorne casts doubt on the historical necessity for Endicott's restrictive kind of Puritanism. Democrat though Hawthorne was, a typological reading of the historiography in his seventeenth-century tales does not sufficiently explain why he repeatedly dwells on lost qualities incurred in the violent contests between extremist factions in New England history; nor does it explain why he resurrects those lost qualities, reclaiming the best of English traditions expelled through Puritan severity and revolutionary zeal, in works having a nineteenth-century setting. As I have suggested in earlier published essays, and as Michael Colacurcio has unsurpassingly demonstrated in *The Province of Piety*, Hawthorne's historiography adamantly resists a patriotic reading in any way commensurate with the democratic ideology of his time.[6] The thoroughness of his historical knowledge ought to caution us against allying him with his orthodox contemporaries. If we lack that particular knowledge ourselves, we might at least entertain the possibility that Hawthorne's irony counts for something serious enough to approach a revisionist historical purpose.

A more accurate view of Hawthorne's historiography, I believe, must recognize the importance of his placing mediating figures between contending historical forces in seventeenth-century New England. Having slight warrant from his reading that such moderating figures were actually present, Hawthorne nevertheless imagines that these countervailing "types" (always gentle and often enough artists) had to exist. Surely not everyone in seventeenth-century New England was an extremist. And yet, like weaker radical factions such as the Quakers, these potential mediators are overwhelmed by the dominant forces of Puritanism. Their loss proves doubly tragic. For in them existed a bright alternative to Puritanic severity and gloom; in them resided a potential adaptation of the best of Old World culture to New World experience. All the same, whether imagined or not, these figures become positive "types" for Hawthorne himself, their nineteenth-century descendant, who both embodies and looks back to them as cultural predecessors once potentially available to America. Not by coincidence, these typal "ancestors" for Hawthorne the artist are generally associated with England or English cultural values.

Obviously, my point of departure is indebted to the seminal work of Q. D. Leavis, who first recognized in "The May-pole of Merry Mount" Hawthorne's regret over New England's severing itself from English traditions, rites, and pageants.[7] Michael Bell also gives special attention to the importance of England in Hawthorne's historical works, but his approach is either different from or antithetical to my own. Bell argues that "the characteristic tension in Hawthorne's fiction of New England is not between nobility and intolerance, but between Old World values and New World conditions."[8] Accordingly, Hawthorne understands that Puritan nobility and intolerance are complementary elements of historical necessity. Given the harsh environment of New England, Puritans necessarily had to be strong and intolerant in order to survive, the rough New World being fundamentally uncongenial to Old World values and cultural forms. Hawthorne regrets the loss of English splendor and beauty, Bell says, but the loss is the price America had to pay in order to establish its independence. Bell's thesis, a sophisticated expression of national typology and environmental determinism, does not appear to do full justice to Hawthorne's historiography, his critical view of Puritanism, or his need for a cultural tradition unavailable in America. The present study argues that Hawthorne considers the dominant form of Puritanism represented by Endicott, not the New World's harsh environment, to be the primary determinant of America's disinheritance from the rich culture of England. Hawthorne's historical fiction set in the seventeenth century elaborates this position through its treatment of mediating figures—often typal representatives of the author himself, placed anachronistically into Puritan settings—who offer optional paths at moments of historical transition. Such paths, had they been followed, implicitly promised futures less culturally barren and violent than those following upon their displacement.

The burden of Chapter 1 is to show how Hawthorne builds this pattern of lost options into the political typology at work in his seventeenth-century tales. The standard political typology of his day remains an undeniable presence in these tales, of course, and becomes especially prominent when Hawthorne shifts to the eighteenth century in "Legends of the Province–House," which are discussed in chapter 2, and when he recapitulates the entire course of New England history in *The Whole History of Grandfather's Chair*, which is examined in chapter 3. In these works, the worst social and political traits of England are often suggested; but in response, the dominant legacy of the early Puritans—independence, absolutism, and harsh militancy—becomes reanimated in the colonial descendants, leading to the final severing of links with the homeland in the Revolutionary War, the political fulfillment of the typological design.[9] Hawthorne's evocation of this historical pattern is only partial at best, and its function may finally suggest that, rather than subscribing to the democratic ideology that puts forth this design, Hawthorne either subverts it or questions its legitimacy as a historical explanation. While certain characteristics of England and the English are well worth casting aside, others are not. Yet, as Hawthorne conceives, positive and negative qualities are swept out together. The undiscriminating extent of this disinheritance from England is what concerns him. Clearly enough, he accepts the democratic benefits won in the split with England, and yet he just as clearly regrets the loss of cultural and aesthetic values accompanying that split. And he ultimately locates responsibility for the disinheritance in the iconoclastic, extremist mentality of the Puritan mind as it was forged by figures like Endicott, New England's version of Cromwell.

The original Puritan settlers provide Hawthorne the means to examine the initial cultural transition between Old and New Worlds. Having given brief attention to this transition in "The May-pole of Merry-Mount," Hawthorne returns to it again on a full scale in *The Scarlet Letter.* To a limited extent, selected representatives of the founding fathers appear as positive characters, especially when compared to persons in later generations. But I would submit that their best credentials owe less to noble strength of character or "independent" tendencies than to values associated with the "sunny richness" of the mother country (1:230). Thus the "myth of decline" in Hawthorne needs to be realigned on a different axis.[10] Hawthorne's founding fathers are ultimately celebrated not for their rigid independence and resistance to English political hegemony but for their breadth of vision and their retention of Old World values—the real positive pole in Hawthorne's historiography being, in this case, the English or European Renaissance. *The Scarlet Letter* enunciates this point both prosaically and figuratively in the images of Renaissance artistry associated with Hester and Pearl.

The Old World connections linked to Hester are indispensable to understanding her historical and aesthetic function in the novel. Their anomalous presence in Puritan America suggests just how far Hawthorne was willing to go to create an aesthetic typology, an artistic tradition for himself based upon continuities of England's Anglo-Catholic culture in the Puritans' New World experiment. That the tradition eventually recedes and then dies, not unlike the way moderating figures in the seventeenth-century historical tales become overwhelmed by the Puritan majority, shows the degree to which the iconoclasm of Hawthorne's second- and third-generation Puritans (lacking the aesthetic memory of their Elizabethan forebears) succeeds in wiping out nascent proclivities toward art. In *The Scarlet Letter,* Hawthorne explores the historical roots of the barren aesthetic condition in which he finds himself, and he posits the existence of an artistic predecessor such as Hester through whom he could link himself to his native land and, by extension, to England. Hester functions as a type or symbol of Hawthorne's aesthetic tradition, a mixture of New and Old Worlds—as proud and ill at ease in seventeenth-century America as Hawthorne is in the nineteenth century.

Chapter 4 of this study establishes a foundation for this reading of *The Scarlet Letter*. In "Drowne's Wooden Image" and "The Artist of the Beautiful," Hawthorne writes preliminary studies of how the success of American artists depends first of all upon defying the Puritan iconoclastic tradition. Then, in "The Old Manse" and "The Custom–House," he not only defies that negative tradition but also embraces the cultural and aesthetic traditions of England. "The Old Manse" looks backward and forward in Hawthorne's literary canon. In it, Hawthorne imaginatively invests an American place with the ambience of a Catholic abbey and English parsonage, evoking the pastoral golden age from Roman and English literature in his celebration of a historic organicism uniting New and Old World cultures and aesthetics. Knowing that this is by no means the main heritage received by nineteenth-century America from its Puritan ancestors, Hawthorne repudiates in "The Custom-House" the joyless austerity of these ancestors and sets forth, as in the Puritan history tales and in *The Scarlet Letter,* the alternative directions that New England might have taken in the seventeenth century. His adoption in "The Custom-House" of English artists as forebears in preference to his actual Puritan ancestors thus constitutes a profound affirmation of the very art they deprecated. In this period, then, Hawthorne creatively attempts to recover the broken ties between Old and New Worlds—a practice so common in his work that, after he finally encounters English art and culture at first hand in the 1850s, we perceive no novelty when he writes in a letter, "The truth is, I love England so much that I want to annex it."[11]

Hawthorne's experiences in England come under scrutiny in chapter 6. Predictably, these experiences result in divided responses. But as an examination of *The English Notebooks* reveals, the surviving aesthetic wonders in England were more breathtaking than Hawthorne had imagined over the years. His ambivalent loyalties to England and America would seem far more wrenching and profound than the responses of his compatriots, analyzed by Cushing Strout in *The American Image of the Old World.*[12] He never has a harsh word for the traditional cultural artifacts he finds there. And by the last two years of his visit, the harsh criticism of English society that frequently surfaces during his first two years all but disappears. He develops, I am convinced, a respect and admiration for English institutions absolutely at odds with his avowedly democratic sympathies but perfectly in keeping with his appreciation for and idealization of English culture over the years. Despite a good deal of evidence that Hawthorne believed old England was gradually declining and that the future would see the growth of the kind of democratic institutions exemplified by America, there remain persuasive reasons to believe that Hawthorne regretted the prospect.

Positive attitudes toward England so thoroughgoing as those found in *The English Notebooks* are either toned down or omitted from *Our Old Home.* Yet even this published version of his experiences in England betrays such emotions that Henry James was led to say: "It abounds in passages more delicately appreciative than can easily be found elsewhere, and it contains more charming and affectionate things than, I should suppose, had ever before been written about a country not the writer's own."[13] Moreover, quite aside from the content of *Our Old Home,* there is in the very title of the book a loving and reverent evocation of all that England had stood for in Hawthorne's career.

Finally, his divided response to experiences in England illuminates the question of his inability to complete, in the last years of his life, a romance involving an American returning to that ancestral homeland. This question, drawing on *The American Claimant Manuscripts,* is probed in the conclusion of chapter 6. When Hawthorne first began the romance set in nineteenth-century England, he intended to expose the foolishness of Americans who came to England claiming a right to landed estate and aristocratic title, an extension of Robin's ambition in "My Kinsman, Major Molineux," written more than two decades earlier. But his intent became clouded and jumbled with his divided loyalties to England and America, past and present. As he shifted from one to another version of the romance, he could not decide if the American claimant was a fool or a good-but-misguided young man quixotically attempting to reestablish ancient ties between cultures now radically different from one another. Nor could he decide whether or not the protagonist had a legitimate claim on the family inheritance. At issue in these questions, I would suggest, was Hawthorne's awareness that he too was an American claimant, profoundly ambivalent about his lost inheritance. Such ambivalence, this study will argue, dwells as a shaping force in the critical treatment of American history and in the appreciation of England throughout his career.

To the reader who cares less about the background leading to Hawthorne's recovery of an English aesthetic tradition than the manner or method of the recovery itself, the first three chapters might well impose a strain on patience. A word about my strategy may therefore be in order. I should not like to be understood to argue that Hawthorne set out to castigate the Puritan tradition on the one hand while aligning himself with England on the other. Even the unarguably "historical" tales do not suggest such a strict emplotment or ironic intent. What they do suggest is that Hawthorne discovered for himself an essential quarrel with nineteenth-century pieties extolling the political virtues residing in the Puritan errand and continuing in the Revolutionary War period. Patriotic interpretations of seventeenth-century Puritanism and its typological extension to the Revolutionary War are simply too well made, the logic entirely too reductive and the coherence altogether too tight. As a serious historian/artist,

Hawthorne recognized that the historical record was more complex than popular ideology would have it. Indeed, his efforts to become an artist were entangled and even inhibited by a cultural aspect of the Puritan tradition omitted by that ideology. It therefore seems to me that we cannot appreciate how Hawthorne recovers English traditions without first understanding the extent of his critical reevaluation of colonial history, which defines the depth not only of his but also of his culture's need for the recovery.

1

John Endicott as Puritan Type: The Loss of England in the Seventeenth-Century Tales

"The May-pole of Merry Mount"

In Hawthorne's reconstruction of key episodes of seventeenth-century New England history, "The May-pole of Merry Mount" comes first inasmuch as the event it commemorates took place before the main body of Puritans arrived in 1630. The story itself may have been written as early as 1829, prior to the other historical tales treated in this study.[1] Initially, the issues at stake in the tale seem nothing less than what Hawthorne's narrator identifies hyperbolically in the opening paragraph: "Jollity and gloom were contended for an empire" (9:54). The seriousness underlying this allegorical conflict can easily be overlooked because of the stylized pageant depicting the Puritan and non-Puritan contenders. Hawthorne plays unusually loose with the historical facts originating in William Bradford's account,[2] elevating the significance of Endicott's Puritan raid on the Mount Wollaston settlement, which occurred long after the Pilgrim force led by Miles Standish had in fact scattered the Merry Mount revelers and captured Thomas Morton. Probably because the Pilgrims at Plymouth gradually declined in number and influence, eventually becoming absorbed by the Puritans of Massachusetts Bay, they were unsuitable for the historical design Hawthorne had conceived once he seriously undertook the study of history in the late 1820s. A major part of that design, in the words of Q. D. Leavis, "lay in the conflict between the Puritans who became New England and thus America, and the non-Puritans who were, to him, merely the English in America and whom he partly with triumph but partly also with anguish sees as being cast out."[3] In the recurring heart of Hawthorne's configuration of seventeenth- and eighteenth-century colonial history,

25

minor acts, such as Endicott's cutting down the maypole, often have a symbolic function as great as, or greater than, historical events superficially appearing more prominent; for in such "remarkable" events can be found the essential characteristics and impulses giving shape to colonial history as Hawthorne perceives it. Here also can be discovered an index to Hawthorne's view of his own cultural inheritance that emerges from the Puritan victory in the recurring quarrel over transplantation of English traditions and manners.

Paralleling the method of his other "Puritan" tales, "May-pole" focuses on the actual historical conflict between intolerant forces of Puritanism and the Merry Mount faction, which deviates from Puritan piety and authority. The real significance of the contest awaits fuller definition and settlement in the American Revolution, and yet we can hardly fail to sense the proleptic struggle already established between New World authority of the Puritans and Old World customs and traditions.[4] As Leavis recognizes, "the essential truth Hawthorne rightly seized on" was that the Puritans "set themselves in absolute hostility to the immemorial culture of the English folk with its Catholic and ultimately pagan roots, preserved in song and dance, festivals and superstitions, and especially the rites and dramatic practices of which May-Day ceremonies were the key."[5] But the tale also enunciates a secondary focus and subsidiary conflict between Puritan (and even Merry Mount) extremism and the representative party of moderation, Edith and Edgar—the young bride and groom whose wedding is the particular occasion for celebration in the mid-summer's-eve setting.

The primary conflict, entailing a spectacular contrast of colors, textures, and images, illustrates a kind of ritualized pageant corresponding to the rituals plainly exploiting democratic typology in "Endicott and the Red Cross" and "The Gray Champion."[6] Because of the striking visual effects and the amount of attention devoted to them, the contest between the Puritans and Merry Mount revelers tends to divert attention from Edith and Edgar, the central figures in whom an alternate pattern for American development—as the tale presents it—can be found. The Puritan defeat of the revelers, along with the exaggerated and thus essentially counterfeit English past that they represent, is not nearly so crucial as the defeat of Edith and Edgar. In them exists a New World hope for balancing reactionary extremes having begun in the Old World order. Their defeat by an incipient power structure that will essentially define seventeenth-century New England marks the first lost opportunity for a holistic culture in New England history.

Whereas other historical tales written by Hawthorne during this period have opening and closing paragraphs serving as historical frames for inset narratives, "May-pole" avoids this framing device and employs instead a headnote whose content misleads as much as it informs. It reads:

> There is an admirable foundation for a philosophic romance, in the curious history of the early settlement of Mount Wollaston, or Merry Mount. In the slight sketch here attempted, the facts, recorded on the grave pages of our New England annalists, have wrought themselves, almost spontaneously, into a sort of allegory. The masques, mummeries, and festive customs, described in the text, are in accordance with the manners of the age. Authority on these points may be found in Strutt's Book of English Sports and Pastimes. (9:54)

Most readers of the tale respond to the rhetorical nudge and find a psychological allegory in the standoff between the Merry Mounters and Puritans. Accordingly, as one reader has summarized it, the tale is a "psychological fable," an "allegory of the opposition of heart and head, of unbridled sensuality and iron repression."[7] At one level, of course, the tale does work within this formula, positing the need for mediation between the extreme poles of this conventional opposition.[8] As a result, Edith and Edgar are generally seen as a norm, a golden mean—retaining something of youthful mirth and sensuality associated with the Merry Mounters as they seem to shift toward adopting the mature solemnity of the Puritans. Their apparent progression toward a Puritan world view has also been defined as a moral development "from pagan eros to Chrisitan agape" or from the soul's innocence to self-knowledge.[9] In such readings, the couple's mediating function is symbolized by their recognizing the contrived, evanescent gaiety of the revelers before Endicott and the Puritans enter the scene.

If "May-pole" were simply a psychological or moral fable, or even, not so simply, a vital fall from innocence closely paralleling Paradise Lost,[10] the resolution of the sensuality-suppression dialectic would be wholly satisfying. Yet the tale also contains serious cultural implications warning against a tidy resolution of the struggle between heart and head. It is by no means too much to say that "light and darkness are not simply allegorical representations of psychological faculties; they are also forces at work in history."[11] The historical level of the story reveals something considerably more sweeping than the mere reduction of the revelers by morally zealous Puritans. Edith and Edgar, the party of mediation, are defeated as well. This double defeat characterizes the fundamental pattern of New England's seventeenth-century history as Hawthorne envisions it: Puritan extremism overcomes not only extremist opponents but also recessive, synthesizing forces having potential to mediate these extremes. More often than not, lost potential for cultural synthesis implies or underscores a loss of salutary influences out of England's past.

The convenient dichotomy between the Puritans and revelers begins to break down when Hawthorne's careful delineation of the Merry Mounters is scrutinized. Michael Colacurcio is doubtless correct when he says that "the ponderous and prolific moral choice offered—Puritan or Reveller, Gloom or Jollity, even . . . Grace and Nature—is entirely spurious, the product not of moral reality, adequately considered, but of somebody's antique prejudice. A Puritanic reduction masquerading as a perfect dichotomy."[12] Thus the Merry Mounters seem to represent the Old World in conflict with the New, the English past vs. the Puritan present. Their celebrations at Merry Mount apparently follow English models and traditions; and their sources can be found, as the headnote states, in Joseph Strutt's *The Sports and Pastimes of the People of England.* "All the hereditary pastimes of Old England," says Hawthorne's narrator, are "transplanted" at Merry Mount (9:60). Ancient seasonal rites and Church holidays are observed, but not in their proper turn or fashion. Games, sports, dances, and songs, "rich with the old mirth of Merry England," continue without intermission (9:57). The maypole itself, symbolizing the ceaseless rejuvenation of a gala ritual, stands all year decorated with the multicolored foliage of the first three seasons, the prismatic flashes of sunlight refracting even through the ice and frost of winter.

The Merry Mount immigrants therefore bring with them the festive rites and games belonging to the mother country, in contrast to the Puritans, those "most dismal wretches, who said their prayers before daylight, and then wrought in the forest or cornfield, till evening made it prayer time again" (9:60). Unlike the revelers, who strive "to communicate their mirth to the grave Indian" (9:61), the Puritans have "their weapons . . . always at hand, to shoot down the straggling savage" (9:60). In the maypole setting, they wear no colorful costumes but rather "a horse-load of iron armor" (9:61). Their only dance is "round the whipping-post, which might be termed the Puritan May-Pole" (9:61).

To the extent that the Merry Mounters serve as transmitters of the English past, the story implies that New England could not, in fact, reproduce the Old World.[13] As this point has been elaborated, "the revellers represent, not the true gaiety of the Old World, but a hopeless attempt to deny that this gaiety has been irrevocably lost."[14] This interpretation, however, takes it for granted that the revelers are artificial only because their festivities duplicate in America a way of life belonging exclusively to England. But the fact is that the votaries of Merry Mount do not transmit, intact, the cultural values of English festivities but rather a nightmarish version of them undoubtedly meant to confirm the worst fears of the most Puritan of Puritans.

The Merry Mounters actually present a falsified example of "Merry England"—a hyperbolic distortion of Grecian and Roman traditions torn completely out of the cultural context in which they were practiced, distilled, and harmonized in English culture over many centuries. A maypole standing all year would not have been tolerated in England during the 1620s or any earlier period. Neither Charles Stuart nor Laud had any intention of going so far when they encouraged periodic occasions for indulging in sports and pastimes. And so it would appear that the Merry Mounters possess a view of life as unbalanced or distorted as that of the dismal Puritans.

In a series of ironic oppositions, Hawthorne adumbrates the ways in which the revelers have corrupted associations with the Old World. Their connections both with a world of pastoral dream and with the English past seem firmly established but then are abruptly broken. The opening two paragraphs of the tale, for example, evoke Arcadia. Colorful displays of assorted ribbons and floral arrangements lead the narrator to intone, "Oh, people of the Golden Age, the chief of your husbandry, was to raise flowers!" (9:55). Yet in the next paragraph, the harmonious relation between the revelers and Arcadian myth is disrupted: "But what was the wild throng that stood hand in hand about the May-Pole? *It could not be,* that the Fauns and Nymphs, when driven from their classic groves and homes of ancient fable, had sought refuge, as all the persecuted did, in the fresh woods of the West. These were Gothic monsters, though perhaps of Grecian ancestry" (9:55; emphasis added). By introducing the anomalous images of a stag, wolf, and bear, the Merry Mounters convert the scene from pagan idyll and Anglo-Catholic tradition into an unconsciously parodic pageant of the transformation of man into beast. Indeed, such transformation is less reminiscent of classical pastoral, as the text suggests, than it is of Milton's *Comus.* A demonism associated with a Protestant, neo-gothic movement seems to have a hand in the revels of Merry Mount.

After disconnecting the Merry Mounters from the Golden Age, the text next places them more specifically in relation to English traditions. The "Salvage Man," the figures wearing "fools-cap" with bells hanging from their costumes, and those disguised as animals are all modeled parodically after types found in Strutt. Included among the revelers is an "English priest, canonically dressed, yet decked with flowers, in heathen fashion" (9:57). Having been a "clerk of Oxford" (9:57), and having associations with Chaucer's pilgrim, he is aligned with pre-Reformation English religious traditions, a link strengthened by Oxford's unswerving allegiance to Catholic and monarchical loyalties antipathetic to Puritanism which, by the early seventeenth century, had gained a strong foothold at Cambridge University.[15] Years later, Hawthorne will again call upon Oxford's Anglo-Catholic evocations in his treatment of Dimmesdale in *The Scarlet Letter.*

Once having established the revelers' ties to the Old World, however, the text emphatically dissociates them from the cultural norm of England. Like the Puritans, they emigrate to America because "the old world and its inhabitants became mutually weary of each other" (9:59). As exemplified by the leaders at Merry Mount, "Erring Thought and perverted Wisdom were made to put on Masques, and play the fool. The men of whom we speak, after losing the heart's fresh gaiety, imagined a wild philosophy of pleasure. . . . They gathered followers from all that giddy tribe, whose life is like the festal days of soberer men" (9:59). Moreover, the revelers take the extreme position, as repugnant to the Church of England as to the Puritans, of calling the maypole "their religion, or their altar" (9:60). As for the English priest, "the very Comus of the crew" (9:57), Endicott will recognize him as an apostate: " 'I know thee, Blackstone! Thou art the man, who couldst not abide the rule even of thine own corrupted church' " (9:63). Yet the presence of an Episcopal priest is absolutely necessary to establish the Puritans' theological and cultural distance from the Church of England and its traditional endorsement of May Day festivities.

Hawthorne knew from several historical sources that the Reverend Blackstone had nothing to do with the antics at Merry Mount—a footnote in the tale says as much.[16] Indeed, he was sufficiently informed to know, and thus to enjoy the ironical play over the fact, that Blackstone was one of many residents in the vicinity of Plymouth who paid part of the costs for the deputation led by Standish that broke up Morton's enclave at Merry Mount.[17] Still more ironic, he knew that when Blackstone remarried in 1659, Governor Endicott performed the ceremony.[18] From his wide reading in English history, Hawthorne also knew from Thomas Frankland's *Annals of King James and King Charles the First* that, despite Puritan protests, England proclaimed mirthful rites and antics as an integral part of a full life, never as expressions of a philosophy complete in itself.[19] Strutt himself reveals that May Day was not among the movable feasts celebrated in the church calendar. The Merry Mounters thus pervert traditional "festal days of soberer men" in England—events such as "wakes, church-ales, and fairs" (9:59)—by willfully indulging in them throughout the year. Not being countenanced in England, these extremists are not unlike the Puritans: they come to America because "many had been maddened by their previous troubles into a gay despair" (9:59). It is therefore difficult to accept the anachronistic point that the Merry Mounters are Cavaliers and that such a representation issues from Hawthorne's sources. At the very least, they are "untypical Episcopalians."[20] Nevertheless, from a Puritan point of view, it hardly matters that these untypical celebrants indulge in traditional pastimes all year long. One moment is enough.

Even though Hawthorne relied on Strutt for the actual forms of games and ceremonies celebrated in England, he did not find in Strutt the inveterate mode of practicing them found at Merry Mount, "where jest and delusion, trick and fantasy, kept up a continued carnival" (9:57). On the contrary, Strutt specifies the special days and hours reserved for community festivals, pageants, games, and other pastimes.[21] Such time-limited activities deny neither the work-a-day world nor the devotional services on Sunday, as the early seventeenth-century prayer book of the Church of England also shows. Sports and pastimes are interspersed among the normal and often burdensome experiences of life, providing a measure of relief if not a semblance of balance between jollity and gravity.

Clearly enough, the Merry Mounters represent a newly developed extreme seemingly invited by New World opportunity but considerably alien to the cultural heritage of England. They are as incompatible with ancient cultural norms as are the Puritans. Anomalous even in England, the Merry Mounters are bound to become embroiled with the sanctimonious Puritans who oppose any transferal of merry-making activities permitted by the English Church. The larger implications of the struggle are therefore posed in historical terms: "The future complexion of New England was involved in this important quarrel. Should the grisly saints establish their jurisdiction over the gay sinners, then would their spirits darken all clime, and make it a land of clouded visages, of hard toil, of sermon and psalm, forever. But should the banner–staff of Merry Mount be fortunate, sunshine would break upon the hills, and flowers would beautify the forest, and late posterity do homage to the May-pole" (9:62). Hawthorne evidently favors neither side in the struggle, choosing instead to expose the poverty inherent in both artificial extremes. Still, he accurately records the ultimate victory of the "grisly saints" that will cast a shadow over the future course of American history.

Too facile by any realistic measure, the allegorical struggle between Puritans and revelers not only obscures the plight but also the potential of Edith and Edgar. The newlyweds are really left with no choice in the story. Endicott simply overpowers them along with the rest of the Maypolers. Yet, midway through the tale, Edith and Edgar can no longer be identified with the Maypolers, for they have realized, independently and together, that life entails grave responsibilities; but their realization hardly implies an endorsement of the Puritan way. Quite clearly, they will be denied choice and individual expression as much among the captor saints as they surely would have been among their former associates at Merry Mount. They seem to share the narrator's view that, once they "truly loved, they had subjected themselves to earth's doom of care, and sorrow, and troubled joy" (9:58).[22] Yet such a view does not mean that the couple has abandoned gaiety or hope of expressing it in ways, perchance, recalling English customs and traditions. The narrator, a nineteenth-century heir to the very Puritan gloom that wins the day in the tale, does not allow Edith and Edgar any other option except Puritan severity. Behind him, Hawthorne enforces the tragic historical point on the beginning of New England's narrow way. And rightly so. Romance imagination can go only so far in its manipulation of the historical record. The Pilgrims did break up Morton's consortium at Merry Mount and Endicott did cut down the maypole. Traditional English festivities were indeed aborted.

In the concluding line of the tale, the narrator says that Edith and Edgar "went heavenward, supporting each other along the difficult path which it was their lot to tread, and never wasted one regretful thought on the vanities of Merry Mount" (9:67), evidently implying that Edith and Edgar have willingly adopted the rigors of Puritan piety. They have shifted, in other words, from one religious and cultural extreme to another, disregarding the notion that life is a mixture of care and joy, trouble and glee. While this shift measurably satisfies the simplistic "either/or" possibilities with which they are confronted, it fails to honor the text's earlier characterization of Edith and Edgar as more independent and complex than the restricting polarities in the story finally allow them to be. We might hope, along with one reader, "that the 'difficult path' the young lovers take may be something of a middle way" between the Puritan and Merry Mount extremists.[23] It is nevertheless difficult to fathom where we are to find such a hope, considering the utterly grim condition of the couple at the conclusion.

A key word in the last paragraph might suggest support for some hope, but at the same time it also stresses an underlying point in the story. "As the moral gloom of the world overpowers all *systematic* gaiety, even so was [the Maypoler's] home of wild mirth made desolate amid the sad forest" (9:66–67; emphasis added). The revelers' systematic gaiety, not gaiety itself, is the real issue; and their cheerful system opposes, even while resembling, the systematic severity of the Puritans. Neither extreme is desirable or realistic. Edith and Edgar see the futility of the Maypolers' system, but they must wait beyond the story's end to recognize the Puritans'. Thus their potential role as mediators between cultural richness or barrenness is cut off, sacrificed to the Puritan victors who win the typological contest at Merry Mount.

Hawthorne was still brooding over the consequences of that victory fourteen years after writing the story: in *The Scarlet Letter* the narrator inserts a nineteenth-century opinion into the seventeenth-century context of that novel by saying, "we have yet to learn again the forgotten art of gayety" [*sic*] (1:232). The forgotten art lamented in *The Scarlet Letter* is also lamented in the tale's ambivalent counterpointing of traits defining the distinctions between American and English cultures. "The May-pole of Merry Mount," the first tale in Hawthorne's historical chronology, exaggerates the initial American break with the English past. Our sense that the extensive loss of the English past is both radical and unnecessary results from the recognition that Edith and Edgar have been denied their potential to embark upon a middle course that might amount to a sustaining recessive legacy in New England history. If it had not been their "lot to tread" the "difficult path" of the narrow Puritan way, they might have chosen the best forms to retain from Puritan piety and English festivity. And if so, the logic is clear, the nineteenth century might have inherited a tradition quite different from Puritan severity and gloom, one in which a full range of human sorrow and joy could find its time-honored expression in adaptation to New World experience. But Edith and Edgar are not able to fulfill their potential as mediators between extremes. They are the first such lost possibilities in Hawthorne's rueful reconstruction of the Puritanic tradition in American history.

"Endicott and the Red Cross"

If Hawthorne had a specific philosophy of history at the time he wrote "The May-pole of Merry Mount," the particular lines of that philosophy remain obscure in the tale itself. A hint of historical recurrence surfaces in the treatment of the revelers, but, as we have seen, they represent exaggerations of several ancient models to which they are initially equated. A conservative metaphysic of some kind might be discovered in the reactionary Puritans; and yet they too, we realize, are exaggerations of their kindred in England. Something old yet new is thus inherent in both parties, as if the New World itself invited, or just simply allowed, out of its amplitude, an unleashing of psychic extremes prohibited in the Old World. Nevertheless, while the responsibility for America's future falls upon the Puritan victors, the allegorized polarities of the tale do not establish a clear pattern of historical cause and effect. Nor can we find any traces of "progressive" historiography, so popular in Hawthorne's time. It is true that Edith and Edgar apparently make their way toward heaven, thereby potentially conforming to some providential design, at least for themselves. But it would take an unduly austere nineteenth-century reader, to say nothing of a modern one, to endorse the wonder-working providence ostensibly embraced by the newlyweds and, by extension, their Puritan captors. The tale closes on a decidedly dark note, in perfect harmony with the gray and gloomy metaphors applied to the Puritans, even though the concluding moral rhetoric ironically carries the burden of elevating the reader's thoughts to the light of heaven. However much Edith and Edgar may sense their having fallen into time, we have only an ambiguous sense of the actual nature of that time. Surely the methods of the narrow Puritan way, so unattractively presented in the tale, fail to invite even provisional consideration of Puritan teleology as a given of Hawthorne's views of history.

Endicott's role in "The May-pole" scarcely offers an easier subject for interpretation than the elusive historiography. The weight of negative rhetoric and imagery falls on him but this "iron man" (9:66) does soften for a moment near the end of the story. Influenced by the youthful love of Edith and Edgar, Endicott throws a wreath of flowers over their head. Whether this tender response reflects Hawthorne's unexpressed knowledge that Endicott has buried his wife not long before the events at Merry Mount can only be conjectured.[24] Even if his "sympathetic gesture obscures the fact that he has triumphed,"[25] we are still faced with the possibility that

Endicott, like Melville's Ahab, does have his "humanities." And even if he is "the Puritan of Puritans" (9:63) and the "immitigable zealot" (9:65), Endicott, along with his iron-encased retinue, is momentarily let off the hook of our total condemnation, thus throwing the tale open to a welter of interpretations—if, that is, the tale is read in isolation from Hawthorne's other historical tales. When the "May-pole" is placed in a larger context, however, we see that both its historical perspective and Endicott fit into a pattern wherein the worst elements of Puritanism increasingly gain ascendancy in New England and thus darken the legacy inherited by nineteenth-century descendants.

"Endicott and the Red Cross" commemorates the next remarkable event in Hawthorne's chronology of New England history, offering not only another lost mediator caught between extremist factions but also another view of Endicott's Anglophobia. Here, too, as in the "May-pole," Hawthorne plays loose with historical facts for larger purposes. The actual event, the removal of the red cross from the English flag in 1634, probably resulted from the collusion of Roger Williams and John Endicott. Taking the Puritan position that the use of the cross was sacrilegious, yet acting on his own and thus overstepping his authority by causing the cross to be removed from the banner, Endicott was not only held responsible for the deed but also censured by the General Court and prohibited from holding office for a year. The official fear, of course, was that Endicott's behavior would be interpreted in England as an act of disloyalty redounding in sanctions imposed upon the Bay colony. Not wanting England to interfere with their affairs or to threaten the unique possession of their charter, the Magistrates were prompt in castigating Endicott and in publicizing the colonists' readiness to allow the king's banner to fly with the cross intact.[26] What the Puritans did with the holy symbol on their own score was another matter; but the leaders realized that England could have its will in colonial affairs, and so their equivocation over the use of the cross was a small price to pay for carrying on with their enormous measure of autonomy.

Hawthorne knew the basic facts involved with the rending of the cross from several sources.[27] He knew, for instance, that Endicott may not personally have removed the cross from the flag. Yet, just as Hawthorne magnifies Endicott's heroics at Merry Mount, so he credits his ripping the cross from the ensign beyond factual warrant. He also knew that Williams was at least implicated in (and probably behind) Endicott's activities, but instead of conflating them as he does in "Grandfather's Chair," he pits them against one another. He was familiar with at least one piece of historical evidence justifying their disunion.[28] And from Joseph Felt's *Annals of Salem*, he knew that England construed Endicott's part in the episode as an act of rebellion,[29] but the tale says nothing about the proceedings of the colonial officials against Endicott.[30]

Instead, Hawthorne seems to present Endicott as a typological precursor of American independence from England. Certainly this view has become the predominant reading.[31] The basic rationale of the typological interpretation depends upon taking at face value the patriotic rhetoric in the closing paragraph of the tale:

> With a cry of triumph, the people gave their sanction to one of the boldest exploits which our history records. And, for ever honored be the name of Endicott! We look back through the mist of ages, and recognize, in the rending of the Red Cross from New England's banner, the first omen of that deliverance which our fathers consummated, after the bones of the stern Puritan had lain more than a century in the dust. (9:441)

This patriotic outburst indeed rings with praise. From the historical perspective it offers, we have the first real suggestion of Hawthorne's philosophy of history (or of American history). American independence, already half a century removed from Hawthorne's narrator, may be seen as the culmination of a particular historical progression. Looking back through the epochs of New World history, the narrator discovers an instance and a typal figure foreshadowing the American Revolution by 140 years. Because Endicott's deed is the "first omen" of eventual separation from the mother country, others will presumably follow, making up a continuity justifying the Revolution as well as the typological events foreshadowing it. We must remember that the narrator, echoing the familiar historiography and ideology of George Bancroft in his own time, takes it for granted that the Revolution is the end result. He must look back deductively or reductively to discover a "type" prefiguring the founding father "antitypes" of the republic. The noble end requires a noble beginning, and Endicott's rebellious act is offered as a valorized political genesis.

As some readers have observed, the traits of Endicott and the Puritans under his command scarcely deserve the accolade of the concluding paragraph.[32] The Puritans in this tale, as in the "May-pole," are committed to severity and persecution in their insistence on conformity. Whereas this severity was practiced upon non-Puritans beyond colonial centers in "May-pole," it is now brought to bear upon citizens of the Puritan community itself. The conflict between Puritans and recalcitrants in both tales is, for all practical purposes, the same. The broader conflict between England and America suggested in "May-pole" is now pronounced in "Endicott and the Red Cross." Indeed, the opening paragraph of the tale describes how the Puritans who have gathered for a "martial exercise" are preparing for an imaginary invasion of British forces prompted by Charles I and Archbishop Laud, despite the fact that no historical basis exists for the narrator's finding such a motive in this preparatory exercise.[33] Obviously, we can no longer say that "jollity and gloom were contending for an Empire." The jollity disappeared with the destruction of Merry Mount, while the gloom and the militant, persecuting spirit enforcing it remain.

The setting itself must be the grimmest in all of Hawthorne. Once again, a rather static, ritualized pageant unfolds but with an added twist: the grotesque visual effects described in the opening scene come from mirror images reflected in Endicott's breastplate. What we see amounts to a catalog of Puritan forms of punishment labeled, in sober understatement, as "characteristics of the times and manners of the Puritans" (9:434). Prior to this catalog, the diabolic nature of the punishments is suggested in a central image reflected in Endicott's breastplate—the head of a wolf, dripping blood, "nailed on the porch of the meetinghouse" (9:434). This crude image seems as anomalous to a church as the architecture ("with neither steeple nor bell to proclaim it,—what nevertheless it was,—the house of prayer") to which Hawthorne's irony draws attention in order to remind the reader of the Puritans' stark form of religious expression. While the Puritans have rejected aesthetic forms and symbols inhering in the Church of England, they have ample dark symbols of intolerance and violence, epitomized by such implements as whipping post, stocks, and pillory; by such temporary punishments as labeling a man "A WANTON GOSPELLER" for offering "unsanctioned" interpretations of the Bible, and forcing a woman to wear a "cleft stick on her tongue" for having wagged it "against the elders of the church"; and by such lasting marks of misconduct as cropped ears, branded cheeks, and slit nostrils (9:434–35). These forms of punishment may indeed suggest a "penal colony,"[34] one created from the inability of some inveterate English citizens to adapt to the recently constituted legalism of the Puritans' New Israel. It comes as no surprise when the cross in the English flag, the sole Christian symbol in the scene, is eliminated, reducing the setting to gruesome, hellish uniformity.

These signs of civil and religious oppression evidently define the "difficult path" in store for Edith and Edgar after their capture and assimilation by the Puritans. All is not well, even though effectively managed, in New Jerusalem. If England poses a threat from without, some of its emigrating citizens offer potential threats from within the Puritan community, not the least being an "Espicopalian and suspected Catholic," along with a person "who had boisterously quaffed a health to the King" (9:434). Such remnants of Old World allegiances are strictly forbidden at a time when Archbishop Laud and Charles I enforce High Church forms and doctrine. Moreover, as threatened in the earlier tale, the maypole has in fact been replaced by the whipping post, "with the soil around it well trodden by the feet of evil-doers" (9:434). No evidence of Christian love and charity exists before Roger Williams enters the scene, except, ironically, in a woman prefiguring Hester in *The Scarlet Letter*, who wears the scarlet *A* on her breast: "with golden thread, and the nicest art of needle-work; so that the capital A might have been thought to mean Admirable" (9:435). By color and material, the scarlet *A* is associated with the red cross in the British flag; and both in their symbolic function and in their texture they contrast with the metallic, even mechanistic adornment of the Puritans' steel armor, whipping post "engine," and pillory "machine" (9 : 434). This contrast is later highlighted in the one between Williams, a man of the cloth, and Endicott, a man of steel. The woman wearing the scarlet letter is also, we might note, the first instance of Hawthorne's projected version of an artist in a Puritan setting. By no coincidence, she is an outlaw among other culprits who retain loyal ties to England.

Just as in "May-pole," the military power commanded by Endicott dominates the scene; and this power has far-reaching consequences in American history. For the legions of Puritan authority not only overwhelm English patriots but also extend beyond the Salem community to dominate the Indians on the outskirts of the scene. Their "flint-headed arrows"—not without purpose labeled "childish weapons" (9 : 436)—contrast once more with the Puritans' steel armament as a signal historical reference forcasting the red man's doom.[35] These historical references and allusions gathered in the tale's setting bear on the tale's central, ritualized pageant, framing it as a full historical paradigm in which the assault on the red cross foreshadows the English Civil War and regicide. Since one proleptic event may be a harbinger to another, the American Revolution may not lie too far in the future. In the meantime, we might also notice that some sort of literary crucifixion is intimated in Endicott's deed.

Endicott is the principal actor in the ritualized drama. As a "type" of Old Testament militancy, as a patriarchal leader, he is, with his armor and sword, the very image of the regicide figure who will later appear in "The Gray Champion." Endicott's role counterpoints that of Roger Williams, whose entrance on the scene inaugurates the action of the tale. Given the military exercises in progress and all the grisly signs of Puritan persecution surrounding the church, Endicott's greeting to Williams—"'What, ho! good Mr. Williams. . . . You are welcome back again to our town of *peace*'" (9 : 437; emphasis added)—is a broadly ironical play upon the meaning of Salem. When Williams later admonishes Endicott to refrain from demaguery[36] and Endicott retorts, "'Hold thy *peace*, Roger Williams!'" (9 : 439; emphasis added), the timely repetition allows no doubt that Endicott understands peace only in his own tyrannical terms.

As a "fortress" of steel (9 : 436), Endicott contrasts as sharply with Williams as he did with the maypole revelers. Williams wears a "black cloak and band, and a high-crowned hat, beneath which was a velvet skull-cap" (9 : 436). With his "mild visage" (9 : 439), he aptly resembles a "pilgrim, heightened . . . by an apostolic dignity" (9 : 436–37), unlike Endicott or any of the other Puritans. Williams also resembles a pastoral shepherd carrying a staff.[37] His appearance, benevolence, and peaceful counsel prefigure the traits Hawthorne later associates with Governor Bradstreet in "The Gray

Champion." In all his qualities, therefore, Williams represents a gentle though highly recessive side of Puritanism, antithetical to the dominant side represented by Endicott. Hawthorne may have distorted Williams's historical part in the red cross event, but he had considerable justification from Felt's *Annals of Salem* to present Williams as a mediating peacemaker.[38]

Surely Williams functions as a peacemaker in the tale. He enters the scene with a letter from Governor Winthrop containing news of potential threats from England to the colony's autonomy. He also has a further message from Winthrop specifically addressing an informed expectation that Endicott's rash and fiery temperament will need special handling. Williams advises Endicott that " 'the Governor consulted, respecting this matter, with my brethren in the ministry at Boston; and my opinion was likewise asked. And his Excellency entreats you by me, that the news be not suddenly noised abroad, lest the people be stirred up unto some outbreak, and thereby give the King and the Archbishop a handle against us' " (9:438). Endicott nevertheless proceeds to stir up the assembled militia with an incendiary speech, but not before responding to Winthrop's special plea: " 'The Governor is a wise man,—a wise man, and a meek and moderate' " (9:438). These qualities, alien to Endicott's temperament, are the ones Hawthorne typically attributes to Winthrop, no doubt accounting for his selecting Winthrop as governor in the tale instead of the sometimes hotheaded Thomas Dudley, who actually filled the post during the red cross episode.[39]

Neither as fully expressed nor as explicit as Williams's, Winthrop's moderation perfectly conforms to the spirit of his "Modell of Christian Charity" delivered aboard the *Arbella*. We might speculate that Winthrop's political, theocentric views were identical with Endicott's, and yet it would seem amiss to propose that Hawthorne submits Endicott as a radical stand-in for Winthrop.[40] In the charitable spirit lying behind manner and method lies all the difference, to say nothing of political caution. Winthrop's spirit of compromise does indeed seem more in accord with an American political tradition,[41] but that tradition would appear to originate basically in the post-Revolutionary period. Prior to that era, as Hawthorne presents it, the dominant Puritan tradition is characterized by the "uncompromising bigotry" of Endicott (9:69). Why else does Hawthorne relentlessly investigate Puritan history and develop such consummate skill in literary irony if the case were otherwise? Far better to leave matters to such filiopietists as Bancroft.

Accordingly, it seems to me that Hawthorne deliberately aligns Winthrop and Williams in opposition to Endicott. Williams himself seems gifted with Hawthorne's knowledge that not long after the red cross incident he will be banished by the Puritan oligarchy in Boston, and that he will escape to Providence as a result of Winthrop's apparently benevolent warning.[42] Thus it appears altogether fitting that, when Endicott asks a series of rhetorical questions pointing to ostensible Puritan gains in civil rights and liberty of conscience, a "sad and quiet smile flitted across the mild visage of Roger Williams" in response to a cynical interjection by the Wanton Gospeller who says, " 'Call you this liberty of conscience?' " (9:439). Then, Williams also demurs over Endicott's strategy of working upon the anti-Catholic and even anti-monarchical emotions of the assembled crowd.[43] Upon Endicott's calling Charles I a " 'son of a Scotch tyrant,—this grandson of a papistical and adulterous Scotch woman, whose death proved that a golden crown doth not always save an anointed head from the block,' " Williams interrupts by saying: " 'Nay, brother, nay, . . . thy words are not meet for a secret chamber, far less for a public street' " (9:439). Williams must thereafter give up hope of controlling Endicott, who threatens him "imperiously" to hold his "peace" much in the way he threatened the Wanton Gospeller with his sword. Endicott clearly dominates the scene, going on to tear the cross from the flag. Meantime, Williams proves as impotent a mediator as the essentially powerless Edith and Edgar in the "May-pole."

Endicott not only opposes moderate civil authority in the New World and England but also rebels against authority in both environments. He opposes Williams and Winthrop in the New World, Charles I and Archbishop Laud in England. In rending the complex symbol of the cross, he defies a considerable span of Christian heritage, anticipates the regicide of Charles I, and performs a symbolic crucifixion, appropriately at the noonday hour. Roger Williams, as a Christ-like figure already receding in Puritan history, might be seen as a victim of a symbolic crucifixion. As I have argued elsewhere, the allusions in the tale to the *Fairie Queene* imply Endicott's identification with the Anti-Christ figure of the Sarazin fighting against Spenser's Red Crosse Knight.[44] In his attempts to justify extremism because of the demands imposed by a harsh wilderness, Endicott conveniently ignores the evidence that the Indians stand by in subjection, scarcely different from the persecuted colonists. He also overlooks the fact that Williams comes out of the forest with his shoes "bemired" (9:436), no less at peace from the experience.[45] The intolerance and violence of Endicott do not seem to issue from a hostile environment, but rather from an extremist Puritan ideology fully compatible with engrained defects in his character.

Balanced against the irony, historical allusions, and overt commentary that undermine Endicott and his Puritan followers are the opening and closing paragraphs of the tale in which the narrator submits Endicott as a noble founding father of American liberty. The assumption behind this position is that "Endicott and the Red Cross" fits a pattern of national typology evident not only in other works by Hawthorne but also in many native writers of the national period who sought in America's Puritan past the roots of independence and democracy. The early Puritans are usually depicted either as noble founding fathers or as narrow-minded bigots.

Hawthorne's contribution to the convention, as Michael Bell sees it, is his combining the two models in a single figure such as Endicott. Unlike other writers of the period, Hawthorne does not seem altogether satisfied with the results of America's separation from England. Endicott's typological act of self-definition carries with it a necessary loss: "Endicott repudiates England, and to the extent that England represents external tyranny it is well lost. But the loss of England involves as well the loss of certain kinds of passion, gaiety, and humor."[46]

National typology certainly seems to exist in "Endicott and the Red Cross," as it will in "The Gray Champion" and *The Whole History of Grandfather's Chair.* But this typological design can only be construed from the opening and closing paragraphs—the frame of the tale. Otherwise, all the other details, including Endicott's flaming oration, go so far toward countering the frame's nineteenth-century ideology that one must ask whether Hawthorne is repudiating the legitimacy of a typological reading of Endicott's act. Hawthorne's New England audience is certainly familiar with the typological reading, as well as with Puritan excesses, and can be expected to forgive the latter for the sake of the former. But does Hawthorne? The narrator's language in the opening and closing paragraphs is nearly as rash and jingoistic as Endicott's, coloring the reader's judgment by urging him to enlist in a patriotic reading hardly different from the way Endicott's legionnaires abandon thought under pressure of emotional and skillful rhetoric. Furthermore, Endicott's domination of Williams, far gentler in the tale than in some of the historical record familiar to Hawthorne, raises issues that a typological reading does not address. Williams alone presents a winning image of piety, particularly when he turns "his face heavenward in thankfulness" before drinking from the fountain (9:437). When Endicott casts aside the moderating advice of Williams (and, through Williams, the advice of Boston divines sought by Winthrop), does Endicott's behavior express historical necessity or determinism? Endicott evidently acts alone, working masterfully upon the Puritan crowd for approval, and therefore might be considered as a forerunner of later American revolutionaries. Patriotic ideology might so reduce and thus emplot it from the vantage of hindsight. Yet how can Endicott be endorsed or excused for behavior putatively required by the historical situation when in the singularity of his acts he denies the very historical realities acknowledged by everyone else?[47]

It seems more reasonable to conclude that in Hawthorne's version of the historical events there was no "necessity" for Endicott's deed. All the irony in the tale functions to subvert Endicott's heroic credentials advanced solely by the narrative frame. To be sure, this irony does not direct sympathy entirely to the persecuted victims in the tale. Yet these figures have become extremists by virtue of their retention of Old World loyalties or reaction to New World authority. Still, their loss to militant Puritanism appears somewhat insignificant in comparison with the defeat of Williams, the mediating figure between extremes who cannot stand up against the power of Endicott any more than Edith and Edgar could in the "May-pole." Williams's role as mediator reveals a potential alternative to the influence of Endicott's brand of Puritanism on American history; and in light of that potential, historical necessity is obliged to give way. Endicott's opposition to England is finally less important than his victory over Williams. England at this time hardly poses the threat to Massachusetts Bay as imagined by the Puritan majority led by Endicott. No actual form of English oppression occurs in the tale, only Puritan oppression. While there may be some cause to worry over English intervention in the future, Williams and Winthrop and others have enough political sense to realize that acts of defiance will only hasten and perhaps worsen the situation. Thus when Endicott closes his harangue by asking, "'What have we to do with England?'" (9:440), he proves insensible to basic political realities. His question and behavior might very well be associated with a typological dress rehearsal for the American Revolution, but that event lies 140 years in the future. In Hawthorne's chronology, the worst of Puritanism is yet to come, and Endicott is without question the "anti-type" for these worst excesses. The tale requires us to question whether American independence from England is really worth having if someone like Endicott is held up as a model for its origins.

"The Gentle Boy"

Viewed in the order of events Hawthorne chronicles in New England history, "The Gentle Boy" completes the trilogy of tales in which Endicott figures as the epitome of Puritan intolerance and persecution. He makes no direct appearance in this story, as he does so prominently in the "the May-pole of Merry Mount" and "Endicott and the Red Cross," but there is no doubt that Endicott's form of Puritanism has become dominant in New England. The events of the story take place roughly between 1656 and 1664, from the time the Quakers first arrived in Massachusetts Bay to when the Puritans finally bowed to Charles II's pressure and quit executing the Friends.[48] This nine-year period, throughout which Endicott is annually elected governor of the colony, comprises the American context of "The Gentle Boy" upon which Hawthorne focuses. In addition, the larger historical context of the English Civil War, the Protectorate, and the Restoration is included as a background for the Puritan scene. Massachusetts Bay still has something to do with England, despite Endicott's typological activity in the "May-pole" and "Red Cross."

Indeed, the English historical background has crucial significance for the Puritan-Quaker conflict in the New World. The enormous cultural shift brought on by the English Civil War actually parallels a less blatant but no less critical shift under way in New England. In both the Old and New Worlds, a radical form of Puritanism ascends to power. Hawthorne later specifically designates this cultural shift in New England as a split between first- and second-generation Puritanism. "Main-street" (1849) and *The Scarlet Letter,* for example, cogently define this split that Hawthorne begins to suggest as early as "The Gentle Boy" and "Endicott and the Red Cross." The second generation—wearing "the blackest shade of Puritanism"— succeeds the first generation, with Endicott correctly serving as an ignoble carryover to lead it.[49] Hawthorne was aware that after Winthrop died in 1649, no one save Simon Bradstreet was left to contain Endicott's excesses, but Bradstreet was both milder and less influential than Winthrop. Hawthorne's ancestor, William Hathorne, lacked the clout to give substance to his frequent opposition to Endicott, as Hawthorne knew from his reading in William Bentley: "In 1644, Mr. Humphries left Salem, and Endicott's influence increased, and he was elected governor. Mr. Harthorne [*sic*] was often opposed to his political opinions, but Endicott was on the popular side.[50] It was Endicott's hour. At last he could defy with impunity the "meek" and "moderate" policies of Winthrop. His hour lengthened into years, as the second generation chose him for governor in fourteen of the next sixteen elections—an unprecedented reign. It does not seem to matter whether the age demanded him or he created the demand, but there may have been no coincidence in the timing of Endicott's emergence as the major political figure in Puritan history.

The rise in Endicott's political power bears significant relation to Cromwell's ascent in England. The regicide of Charles I, obliquely forecast by Endicott in "Red Cross," is an accomplished fact within the historical frame of "The Gentle Boy." While England experiences a Restoration after Cromwell dies, nothing analogous to that reversal occurs in Hawthorne's reconstruction of seventeenth-century New England. Yet Hawthorne chooses to note that capital punishment of Quakers does not stop until 1664, approximately the time of Endicott's death. "The Gentle Boy" briefly details how a modicum of respite follows the decree of "'the King, even Charles'" that Massachusetts Bay observe religious toleration.[51] Evidently, Endicott's attempt to ingratiate himself to Charles II after the Restoration was as fruitless in effect as it was disingenuous in motive.[52] But prior to this respite, the central characters in Hawthorne's tale—Tobias Pearson and Ilbrahim—have been destroyed, overwhelmed far more brutally than Edith and Edgar in "May-pole" and Williams in "Red Cross." With their destruction, yet another potential alternative to Endicott's dominant form of Puritanism proves ineffectual in shaping the history of New England.

Patterns identical to those already seen in other tales also appear in "The Gentle Boy." First, there are the usual dualisms of oppressed and oppressers, victims and victimizers. Second, there is the potential mediator trapped between contending factions. Ilbrahim, the tale's namesake, represents the innocence of childhood, as well as the basic human need for love, home, and community relations. He is aligned with neither the excesses of the Puritans nor those of the Quakers. Along with the Pearsons, his adoptive parents, he symbolizes domestic harmony, perhaps Hawthorne's favored ideal. Gentleness and sympathy, inherent in such a domestic ideal, are overcome by bigotry and cruelty outside the domestic circle. A gentle victim of Puritans and Quakers, Ilbrahim might well be likened to a child's version of Roger Williams in "Red Cross," a Christ-like figure, and to Dimmesdale, in *The Scarlet Letter,* a man of sympathy and sorrow. Unlike Williams and Dimmesdale, though, Ilbrahim is actually sacrificed. His death has no salutary influence on and performs no tragic redemption for either contingent responsible for it—the Puritans and Catherine, his Quaker mother who abandons him for a self-deluding vision of absolute truth. Only the reader, beyond the constricting theological biases of Puritans and Quakers, might find redemption incarnated in Ilbrahim.

The direct cause of Ilbrahim's death is Puritan cruelty, and within the context of this cruelty and other Puritan extremes events in "The Gentle Boy" must be analyzed. In the opening historical frame, blame rests solely upon the Puritans for the "indecorous exhibitions" of the Quakers: "persecution . . . was at once their cause and consequence" (9:69). Hawthorne does not approve of the Quaker's extravagant acts ("abstractly considered," he says, they "well deserved the moderate chastisement of the rod" [9:69]), but he cannot excuse Puritanic oppression responsible for these acts in the first place. Contrary to the views of many readers of the tale,[53] what appears to be a balance between the Puritans and Quakers is really not a balance at all. The Puritans initiate the violence against the Quakers, against Ilbrahim, and even against one of their own—Pearson, whose human sympathy exceeds what is compatible with his denomination's engrained bigotry.

As for the actual execution of two Quakers in 1659, no abstract considerations arise to justify the Puritans. "An indelible stain of blood is upon the hands of all who consented to this act" (9:69), which anticipates the central legend in *The House of the Seven Gables* twenty years later. Still, the person most responsible for the executions is "the head of the government," Endicott: "He was a man of narrow mind and imperfect education, and his uncompromising bigotry was made hot and mischievous by violent and hasty passions; he exerted his influence indecorously and unjustifiably to compass the death of the enthusiasts; and his whole conduct, in respect to them, was marked by brutal cruelty" (9:69).

This judgment of Endicott seems plainly Hawthorne's, and it is buttressed by reference as well to that of the Quakers as recorded by William Sewall, "the historian of the sect" (9:69). According to the Quakers and Sewall, Endicott experienced a "lothsome disease, and 'death by rottenness'" for his leading role in the persecutions (9:70). While this legend expresses only a vindicative wish fulfillment on the Quaker's part, clearly Hawthorne seized upon this outer sign of inner guilt or sin. Later works such as "The Man of Adamant," "Ethan Brand," and *The Scarlet Letter* reveal how visible signs of guilt become a permanent part of Hawthorne's imagination.

"The Gentle Boy," however, shows that Hawthorne is less interested in what happens to Endicott than in the excessive form of Puritanism having achieved dominance in New England coincident with his leadership. The grisly punishments enumerated in "Red Cross," set more than twenty years earlier in history, offer only a preview of the persecutions inaugurated by Endicott as governor in charge of the Quaker persecutions.[54] Liberty of conscience, a principle advocated by the early Puritans and one for which they came to America, is an idea never affecting Endicott and his followers beyond its self-serving application. They have forgotten or never really understood the meaning of their own fruitless efforts to achieve liberty of conscience in England prior to the Civil War. In a blatantly ironic attack, for example, Hawthorne's narrator says in "The Gentle Boy" that the Puritan minister "in his younger days . . . had practically learned the meaning of persecution, from Archbishop Laud, and he was not now disposed to forget the lesson *against which he had murmured then.* . . . He adverted to the recent measures in the province [penal laws specifically aimed at Quakers], and cautioned his hearers of weaker parts against calling in question the just severity, which God-fearing magistrates had at length been compelled to exercise" (9:79–80; emphasis added).[55] Endicott, whom Hawthorne has already excoriated, is the leading exponent of these "measures."

History has come full circle in "The Gentle Boy." The Quakers are in the position of the Puritans two or three decades earlier, trying to achieve liberty of conscience for themselves and to purify the established church. Only one difference separates them. Whereas New England Puritans had "shunned the cross" of English persecutions and escaped to a "distant wilderness," the Quakers welcome "persecutions as a divine call to the post of danger" (9:68). Most Puritans in England did not shun the cross of persecution: they remained and eventually took up arms against the king and the English Church. Tobias Pearson is one of those Puritans who remained and fought in the Civil War. His experience in the Old and New Worlds illustrates not only the cycle of history in Hawthorne's tale, but also another lost possibility to mediate between contending forces.

Pearson fought "during the first years of the civil war," the narrator says, "as a cornet of dragoons, under Cromwell. But when the ambitious designs of his leader began to develop themselves, he quitted the army of the parliament, and sought a refuge from the strife, *which was no longer holy,* among the people of his persuasion, in the colony of Massachusetts" (9:76; emphasis added). Apparently, Pearson recognized that the Puritans were simply aiming to replace one form of power with another, or that the war would result in the regicide of Charles I, an act not contemplated by Parliament at the outset of the rebellion. A total break in English traditions was in the making. In any event, the war was not "holy"—an opinion held apparently as much by the narrator as by Pearson himself.[56]

It seems certain that Hawthorne drew on Scott's *Woodstock* for Pearson's relation to Cromwell and on both *Woodstock* and William Harris's *An Historical and Critical Account of the Life of Oliver Cromwell* for his opinion on the future Protector's ambition.[57] A soldier of Cromwell's named Pearson, appears twice in this novel. The context of the first appearance is Cromwell's raising his voice to deny having any private ambitions in assuming command of the Independent forces against the king.[58] Pearson reappears when Cromwell urges him to leap a twelve-foot interval atop Woodstock castle. Pearson refuses. Angered, Cromwell then reveals his ambition to hunt down the Crown Prince and thus pave the way for his own assumption of leadership in England: "'Ah, base and degenerate spirit!' said the General: 'soul of mud and clay, wouldst thou not do it, and much more, for the possession of empire!—that is, peradventure,' continued he, changing his tone as one who has said too much, 'shouldst thou be called on to do this, that thereby becoming a great man in the tribes of Israel, thou mightest redeem the captivity of Jerusalem. . . ?'"[59] If Hawthorne needed a source for Pearson's view of the "unholy" cause against the king, he would surely have found it in these lines. Additional references to Cromwell's ambition abound, made by Scott's characters and by the narrator.[60]

Pearson's motives for leaving Cromwell's army have gained little approval from Hawthorne critics. His allegedly disingenuous motives for coming to America, however, are usually mentioned.[61] Hawthorne, it is true, allows the barest reason to doubt Pearson's intentions. "A more worldly consideration had perhaps an influence in drawing him thither; for New England offered advantages to men of unprosperous fortunes, as well as to dissatisfied religionists, and Pearson had hitherto found it difficult to provide for a wife and increasing family. To this supposed impurity of motive, the more bigoted Puritans were inclined to impute the removal by death of all the children, for whose earthly good the father had been over-thoughtful" (9:76). This passage quite obviously represents the viewpoint of the worst Puritans, not of the narrator or of Hawthorne, and the viewpoint exposes not only the superstition and bigotry of the Puritans, but also their hypocrisy. The majority of Puritans came to America with mixed motives. Surely they confirm their own worldly interests when, as the narrator puts it, they "shunned" hardship at home and sought to establish an enclave in the New World. Pearson, on the other hand, did not run away from the persecutions in England; he fought in the Civil War until he found it anathema to his faith.

Led in part by the resurgence of his natural feelings for Ilbrahim, Pearson in fact tries to balance the claims of the physical and spiritual realms. Yet because of the absolutist mentality of both Puritans and Quakers, he is eventually caught between the two realms and suffers from both. No slight shift in Pearson's attitudes is involved in his uneasy balancing act. For at the outset of the story Pearson is one of the elected representatives to the General Court. Accordingly, he must have been among those Puritan leaders who drew up a series of punitive laws against the Quakers and must therefore in turn bear responsibility for the execution of two Friends at the opening of the story. This overlooked detail establishes guilt as a powerful force behind Pearson's reaction to Ilbrahim's admission, over one of the graves, that the executed man lying therein is his father—"the Puritan, who laid hold of little Ilbrahim's hand, relinquished it as if he were touching a loathsome reptile" (9:73)—a guilt not only encouraging him to adopt Ilbrahim but also gradually prompting him, in response to the Puritan community's hostile reaction to the adoption, to identify himself with the Quakers. With Pearson's own part in the executions in mind, we more easily understand his sudden change at the graveside: "his heart stirred with shame and anger against the gratuitous cruelty of the instruments in this persecution" (9:74). But whether for strictly personal reasons or not, Pearson suddenly apprehends that the Puritan campaign against the Quakers is no longer holy, just as the Civil War became unholy for him a decade earlier. He has discovered in himself the very narrowness of Puritanism that he had sought to escape during the English Civil War.

Pearson does not, however, immediately take a stand against the Puritan community. Indeed, up until the fourth section of the tale, he can be aligned with his wife Dorothy, as a model of "rational piety" (9:85), trying to balance the claims of the head and heart. The fact that all their children have died since the move to the New World does not in the least impugn the Pearsons' Christian charity. The "bigoted" Puritans, of course, think otherwise: "Those expounders of the ways of Providence, who had thus judged their brother, and attributed his domestic sorrows to his sin, were not more charitable when they saw him and Dorothy endeavoring to fill up the void in their hearts, by adoption of an infant of the accursed sect" (9:76). Pearson repeatedly suffers from the Puritans' lack of toleration and charity during the weeks and months following his adoption of Ilbrahim, so that he too experiences a measure of what it is like to be their victim; and he "naturally" comes to find it impossible to accept their self-righteous selection of those who evince the visible sanctity of the Elect Nation.[62]

Some evidence in the tale suggests that Pearson has antinomian tendencies and that his adoption of Ilbrahim offers him a welcomed excuse for turning from the Puritans to the Quakers. When Tobias explains to Dorothy the circumstances of his finding Ilbrahim at the graveside, he relates "how his heart had prompted him, like the speaking of an inward voice, to take the little outcast home" (9:75). This allusion to the inner-light doctrine of the Quakers is reinforced after Pearson feels the initial stings of Puritan reaction to the adoption: "they entered also into his heart, and became imperceptible but powerful workers towards an end, which his most secret thought had not yet whispered" (9:77). The most telling evidence of Pearson's readiness to ally himself with the Quakers appears in a somewhat obtrusive afterthought in section four, when the narrator tries to smooth Pearson's transition by saying that at the opening of the story Pearson was "in a state of religious dulness, yet mentally disquieted, and longing for a more fervid faith than he possessed" (9:94). Ilbrahim thus serves as the "original instrument" of Pearson's "incipient love for the child's whole sect" (9:94).

The whole process of Pearson's shift from Puritan to Quaker is fraught with nagging complications, aggravated by the fact that some readers have more or less accepted the Puritan point of view and argued a case for Pearson's essential weakness of character.[63] Not that his adoption of Ilbrahim speaks ill of Pearson—it does not—but in the course of his accepting the Quaker faith, Pearson becomes almost as fanatical as Ilbrahim's mother and thus sacrifices the normal cares and duties of this world for a delusory vision of the next. After all, by the closing section of the tale, the Pearson home is bereft of its former household comforts, and the Pearson lands have lain virtually untended. It would therefore seem that Pearson reacts as extremely to the Puritans as he did to the Quakers when, apparently without being affected, he witnessed the Quaker executions.

One must at least partially question the validity of such a case. Whatever unconscious or "incipient" feelings for the Quakers Pearson might have in the early portion of the tale, the plain fact remains that the Puritan community basically sets in motion Pearson's acceptance of the Quakers. Pearson does not so much seek the Quaker faith as he acquiesces to it in rebellion against Puritan persecution of the Quakers generally, his own former complicity in that persecution no doubt helping his acquiescence. He would seem to accept the Friends largely, if not totally, by default when he also identifies as his own the persecution of Ilbrahim by Puritan children. Not until Ilbrahim is unmercifully beaten by these children, it should be noted, does the tale suggest Pearson's association with the Quakers and his downfall in the world.

A crucial question on Pearson's involvement with the Friends is whether he ever actually embraces Quaker doctrine. In the original version of "The Gentle Boy" published in *The Token* for 1832, a fairly extensive passage, following shortly after the episode in which Ilbrahim is beaten by the Puritan "baby-fiends" (9:92), makes it explicit that Pearson fully accepts the doctrine of martyrdom and temporal self-denial of the Quakers:

At length, when the change in his belief was fully accomplished, the contest grew very terrible between the love of the world, in its thousand shapes, and the power which moved him to sacrifice all for the one pure

faith; to quote his own words, subsequently uttered at a meeting of
Friends, it was as if "Earth and Hell had garrisoned the fortress of his
miserable soul, and Heaven came battering against it to storm the walls."
Such was his state of warfare at the period of Ilbrahim's misfortune; and
the emotions consequent upon that event enlisted with the besieging
army, and decided the victory. There was a triumphant shout within him,
and from that moment all was peace. Dorothy had not been the subject of
a similar process, for her reason was as clear as her heart was tender.[64]

Omitted from the final version of the tale, this passage, according to
Seymour Gross, reveals that Pearson's "conversion was not toward the
dogma of the Quakers, but away from the cruel inhumanity of the Puritans—a desperate and despairing escape, without sweetness or light."[65]
Gross believes that Pearson has been converted (however uneasily), not only
in the original version of the tale but also in the revised version's reduction
of it: "Such was his state of mind at the period of Ilbrahim's misfortune;
and the emotions consequent upon that event completed the change. . ."
(9:94). But why did Hawthorne delete such a definitive passage? As Gross
sees it, "Hawthorne realized that by projecting Tobias's ultimate spiritual
peace into the future he was vitiating, even nullifying, the tragedy which
was still to be dramatized." Moreover, "the original version indicated a
spiritual peace, which is wholly absent from the final one. In revising his
original passage, Hawthorne escaped the predicament of the Miracle Plays:
the audience's knowledge that 'tragic' happenings of this world would be, at
the end, recompensed with Infinite Bliss. The Miracle Plays, therefore, are
never tragedies; but Hawthorne's tale is a tragedy."[66]

This interpretation is sensible. Nevertheless, there is reason to doubt that
Pearson's "change" in the final version reflects an unequivocal transformation to his fully embraced conversion in the original. Hawthorne deleted
the original passage, I would suggest, in order to retain precisely this
doubt. In neither the original nor final version does Pearson arrive at any
spiritual peace. He remains spiritually torn, as Gross also recognizes. Even
though the fines, whippings, and imprisonments suffered by Pearson identify him as a member of the Quakers, there is no proof of unambiguous
devotion to, or enthusiasm for, the Quaker cause or doctrine. He has by no
means become an extremist like Catherine or the old Quaker introduced in
section four. These two deny their fundamental duty to nature and nature's
God, as Hawthorne's narrator sees it. Catherine neglects "the holiest trust
which can be committed to a woman" (9:95) when she abandons Ilbrahim
as the price she imagines God levies for her own spiritual reward. The old
Quaker who visits the Pearsons while Ilbrahim is dying boasts that he once
abandoned his dying daughter upon a sudden revelation to serve God
among strangers. Ironically, Pearson's suffering issues from his taking
parental responsibility for Ilbrahim (a stranger)—that is, from his desire to
be connected to this world. Catherine and the old Quaker rightly suffer for

doing wrong while Pearson wrongly suffers for doing right. He may indeed be guilty of neglecting "temporal affairs" (9:95), but Pearson sets himself apart from extremist Quakers by recoiling at the thought of sacrificing Ilbrahim to prove that he can bear any weight of the cross preparatory to martyrdom and salvation. He shudders at the thought of abandoning Ilbrahim on his deathbed, an act directly analogous to that of which the fanatical old Quaker is still proud (9:98).[67]

Pearson's unsuccessful efforts to balance the claims of this world and the next come to a sudden end with the death of Ilbrahim. Prior to the boy's death, however, Pearson arrives at a crisis of faith unresolved by the story. It is his third crisis. In the first, he abandoned the unholy cause of the English Puritans in the Civil War; in the second, he decided to suffer Puritan persecution in the New World rather than to continue in the role of persecutor. In each case, the issue is how to reconcile faith with the responsibilities and demands of the world. Pearson's successive "falls" are indeed great: from a "cornet of dragoons, under Cromwell" (9:76), from a "Representative to the General Court, and an approved Lieutenant in the train-bands" in Massachusetts Bay (9:77), Pearson ends as a despised, persecuted outcast. Having been a Puritan active in two uprisings—against the king of England and the Quakers in America—and having been an ostensible Quaker, Pearson is, at the end, in a state of irresolution about whether to seek a new faith or to deny the efficacy of faith altogether.[68] He has experienced the extremes of Puritanism and Quakerism, and he finds them repugnant. Hence he serves Hawthorne's purposes very well: for, like the gentle boy, he is a displaced individual caught up in radical forces of history. Unable to balance the demands imposed by these forces, neither can he balance their related dualisms within himself: the head and the heart, the claims of this world and the next. Pearson's story therefore ends on a note of utter isolation and defeat.[69]

This defeat corresponds to another one, the failure of Pearson to build a home in the New World.[70] His children are already dead when the tale begins, as Hawthorne mentions when Ilbrahim first enters the Pearson cottage. With his arrival, the cottage once again becomes a home. Dorothy and Tobias develop an affection for the boy that becomes, "like the memory of their native land, . . . a piece of the immoveable furniture of their hearts" (9:88). This affection, equated later in Hawthorne's work with a nostalgic feeling for "our old home" in England, suggests a necessary cross-cultural connection between Old and New Worlds. But after Ilbrahim is beaten by the Puritan children and Pearson is persecuted by their parents, both the home and cross-cultural possibilities seem futile. Even if the harsh conditions of the New World are responsible for the deaths of the Pearson children, they have no bearing on the death of Ilbrahim or the ruin of Pearson. Just as Puritan persecutions are the "cause and consequence" of Quaker fanaticism, so they are the cause of Ilbrahim's death and Pearson's failure to create a home. That Hawthorne does not favor Quaker extremism in no way exonerates the Puritans. The fates of Pearson and Ilbrahim are virtually determined by the Puritans, and their tragedies are similar: for their gentleness, compassion, and charity, they are scorned and persecuted. Gentleness, as well as moderation, is doomed by the zealous severity of Puritanism. Pearson began to learn this fact while serving under Cromwell and he learns it yet more thoroughly as an official colleague of Endicott. Thus he joins Ilbrahim as a potential mediator who, like Edith and Edgar in "May-Pole" and Williams in "Red Cross," is lost to the possible development of moderation in Puritan history. Hawthorne's historical judgment is unmistakably clear: Puritan intolerance and cruelty are inimical to human sympathies of parents and children alike.

It is no accident that in all of Hawthorne's works there exists not one hopeful presentation of a Puritan child growing up in the New World.[71] The severity of the Puritan fathers is passed on by incremental cruelty to succeeding generations. This cruelty is particularly evident in the children with whom Ilbrahim pathetically seeks to establish friendly relations. The child bears the scorn of Puritan elders with comparative equanimity but loses his will to live when a once-injured child he has befriended and entertained with "romances" (9:91) joins other Puritan children in unremitting persecution of the gentle boy. Ilbrahim's loss to the New World is thus compounded, as will be the case with Pearl, for he is projected as a budding artist. The description of the Puritan boy responsible for the twin loss of gentleness and art illustrates the story's most telling forecast of the New England future. Along with the deformity of his body, "the disposition of the boy was sullen and reserved, and the village schoolmaster stigmatized him as obtuse in intellect; although, at a later period of life, he evinced ambition and very peculiar talents" (9:90).[72] The tale concludes with a suggestion that Puritanism eased its attitude toward Quakers after Charles II proclaimed religious toleration, but the reader cannot forget the ominous proclivities of the children who will comprise the next epoch's leaders. During their mature years, they will all evince "very peculiar talents" by ruthlessly wiping out entire villages during King Philip's War and later condemning their own neighbors to die in the Salem witch trials. Both episodes, on the margin of Hawthorne's concern in subsequent work but deeply implanted in New England history upon which the romancer meditates, are not significantly different from events recorded in "May-Pole," "Endicott and the Red Cross," and "The Gentle Boy," events over which the persecuting spirit of Endicott prevails.

"The Gray Champion"

In the tales considered thus far, England figures directly or indirectly in key episodes in New England history and in the "Puritan Mind" as it is primarily characterized by Endicott. Hawthorne was not simply adhering to the historical record by keeping England within close range of his focus on American Puritanism, for his sources rarely promote England in quite the way or to quite the extent that he does. None of his "May-pole" sources, for example, overtly aligns the revelers with England or suggests that affairs at Mount Wollaston portend a split between two national cultures. And none of his primary sources offers a typological reading of the red cross episode, which Hawthorne both seriously and ironically associates with Endicott's activities in that affair. Prophetically inclined though the early Puritan chroniclers were, they hardly foresaw an eventual schism between New and Old Worlds; and even if they had contemplated a possible separation, they would not entirely have welcomed it. There was no small hope among New Englanders, at least before the Restoration, that with the purification of the English Church the colonies and mother country would be joined in mutually loving relations. The anticipation of future independence from England actually issues from a specific American sensibility of the nineteenth century, one in which the historical record was reviewed in search of causes, germinal tendencies, and continuities which explained, if not justified, the American Revolution.[73]

A typological reading of the historical record was not invented by Hawthorne. Indeed, he came rather late, even if most prominently, to the literary adaptation of the Puritans' self-justifying use of biblical exegesis.[74] This very tardiness ought to suggest a warning against the familiar assumption that Hawthorne employs typology for the conventional patriotic purposes of his contemporaries. The ironic subversion of Endicott's patriotic credentials in "Endicott and the Red Cross," for instance, adequately shows permutations on the familiar typological form. Perhaps even a few nineteenth-century readers, expecting an already conventional endorsement of a noble founder and precursor of American independence, would have had to revise their perception in light of Hawthorne's criticism of Endicott. At the very least, they would have had to recognize how Endicott's qualifications as a Revolutionary antecedent could be upheld only by narrowing their opinion of his moral character, or by seriously questioning the validity of worshiping forerunners of American democracy without reservation. To argue that Hawthorne endorsed both the manly strength and the intolerance of an Endicott as requisites to a Revolutionary character would seem an effort to explain away Hawthorne's irony as well as his moral vision.[75] One really ought to wonder if Hawthorne is not exploiting typology in fairly radical terms, if in fact he is not questioning the validity of constructing the historical record in a typological pattern to begin with.

"The Gray Champion" brings us a step closer to such a conclusion, which can be tested against Hawthorne's full-scale treatment of typology in "Legends of the Province-House" and *The Whole History of Grandfather's Chair.* Excluding the witchcraft mania lying behind "Young Goodman

Brown," "The Gray Champion" covers the last episode in seventeenth-century New England history to which Hawthorne gives concentrated attention—the Boston Rebellion of 1689. The tale loosely relates to the actual event during which Edmund Andros, the first governor appointed by the crown after Massachusetts Bay lost its original charter, was over-thrown when Bostonians learned that William of Orange had acceded to the throne in the Glorious Revolution. Hawthorne distills the episode into yet another setpiece, a striking tableau of contending forces. For the first time, these forces are specifically the British and colonists. Governor Andros, in an arrogant military display of Stuart "tyranny," fails to intimidate an assembly of Puritans upon the sudden intervention of a mysterious "gray patriarch" who repels Andros by announcing, " 'There is no longer a popish tyrant on the throne of England' " and " 'With this night, thy power is ended—to-morrow, the prison!' " (9:16). The tale concludes with the disappearance of this gray champion and the announcement of his putative typological significance. Identified as a "type of New-England's hereditary spirit," the gray champion makes legendary reappearances at the Boston Massacre, Lexington, and Bunker Hill as a "pledge that New England's sons will vindicate their ancestry" (9:31).

These closing lines of the tale obviously reflect a nineteenth-century consciousness of national typology.[76] Boston citizens and the evanescent gray champion are linked to the noble Puritan founders who, perhaps in the manner of Endicott, are identified with nascent American independence. All the typological associations, emerging as they mostly do in the conclusion, seem clearly intended to unify the tale by way of recalling the opening "historical" frame. In it, the narrator's rhetoric is charged with antipathy for the British, no doubt reflecting Hawthorne's deliberate though misleading appeal to the biases of his contemporary nineteenth-century audience. This framing device corresponds to the one found in "Endicott and the Red Cross" and as in the manner of that tale, what falls between the opening and closing paragraphs often stands considerably at odds with the frame in tone, texture, and theme. For other than the rhetorical patriotism and typology urged in the frame, no dramatic or symbolic evidence emerges persuasively to support the Puritans as noble forebears of liberty. In other words, the theme of seminal American democracy or independence is not woven into the fabric of the tale but is instead urged by a narrative tone of voice moralizing in favor of the Puritans to the extent that it denounces the British. Yet this tone differs radically from the ironic one adopted by Hawthorne to observe the Puritans on their own merits.[77]

As in "May-pole" and "Red Cross," Hawthorne stylizes the Puritan and English opponents in an impressionistic clash of religious dogma and political ideology. But within the historical context of "The Gray Champion," the Puritans have had to relinquish their original charter and thus the legal source of their autonomous power, and so it is now the "foreign" Englishmen who command the military forces. Our sense of being introduced to rebels and redcoats a century too soon is at once correct and the weak link in the logic of typology. The British approach King Street with Andros and Edward Randolph[78] in the lead, accompanied by an Episcopal clergyman, that hated emblem of religious "tyranny" for the Puritans. While the British march to the beating drum, the Puritans gather as if the roll of the drum served "less as the martial music of the soldiers, than as a muster-call to the inhabitants themselves" (9:10). Not for nothing, we discern, had Endicott put the trainbands through their exercises. Bostonians also gather around separate parish ministers, and former Governor Bradstreet makes an appearance to complete an almost mirror-image standoff between Puritan victims and English oppressors. Both sides clearly represent unions of church and state. The Puritans are certainly not without their own militants, as their response to the drum suggests. Reinforcing this military dimension of Puritan readiness is a deeply ironic description: "Old soldiers of the Parliament were here too, smiling grimly at the thought, that their aged arms might strike another blow against the house of Stuart. Here also, were the veterans of King Philip's war, who had burnt villages and slaughtered young and old, with pious fierceness, while the godly souls throughout the land were helping them with prayer" (9:11). The beating drum summoning the Puritans to Sunday meeting in "The Gentle Boy" (9:78) serves in this instance to call up an array of aging but equally militant zealots in "The Gray Champion."

Puritan extremism, of course, is not immediately apparent in the dramatized crisis. And if the reader forgets that the Puritans are the heirs and latter-day contemporaries of Endicott, either forecast or witnessed in earlier tales, then there can be little reason to doubt the narrator's invitation to take sides with the Puritans now that they are the victims. The "steady march" of the English soldiers, like "the progress of a machine" that must "roll irresistibly over every thing in its way" (9:12), strikes a fearful chord, further encouraging readers to identify with the oppressed colonists, as the narrator emphatically does by stepping back from the scene and pontificating: "The whole scene was a picture of the condition of New-England, and its moral, the deformity of any government that does not grow out of the nature of things and the character of the people" (9:13). As implicit predecessors of American democracy, the Puritan "religious multitude, with their sad visages and dark attire" seems blameless and downtrodden compared to the British, a "group of despotic rulers, with the high churchman in the midst, and here and there a crucifix at their bosoms, all magnificently clad, flushed with wine, proud of unjust authority, and scoffing at the universal groan" (9:13). With such partisan invective, we might just as well be reading an Anglophobic tract from the middle 1770s. To accept this jingoistic outburst as a serious expression of Hawthorne's loyalties, rather than a parody of patriotic rhetoric, is to discredit the balanced complexity of his mind and style that draws us to him.

Vile though the British are said to be, the Puritans are hardly as innocent as they seem. Disguised by superficial discrepancies, the British and Puritan antagonists ironically share several important traits. The old soldiers among the Puritan assembly have themselves been ruthless oppressors, as intolerant of dissenters within their ranks as are the British now among them. The Puritans also prove themselves as blind or lacking in self-criticism as the English, intimated by the homage paid to their ministers. While they are no less incensed by the Episcopal clergyman "in his priestly vestments" than was Endicott by Blackstone, the Puritans regard their own ministers "with such reverence, as if there were sanctity in their very garments" (9:11). Unconsciously, and surely ironically, they perform obeisance to vestments, blasphemous in Puritan theology. The ministers in their own right are as blind and full of presumption as the Episcopalian priest is said to be. In particular, they pose in parodic self-consciousness as they "looked calmly upwards and assumed a more apostolic dignity, as well befitted a candidate for the highest honor of his profession, the crown of martyrdom" (9:11). Perhaps they, too, as the narrator speculates, might be commemorated for all time the way John Rogers is in Foxe's *Book of Martyrs*.

Puritans also share in the implied apostasy of British oppressors, as seen in their treatment as a mob. They appear to be timid and decorous. But this impression results from their nondramatic, virtually static movements, in contrast to the kinetic energy of the British procession with its "roll of drum," "regular tramp of martial footsteps," "confused clatter of hoofs on the pavement" in the light of a "row of fires" (9:12). The compromised faith of the Puritans is not seen in their overt behavior but rather in their ungoverned speech; and Governor Bradstreet, the only figure in the tale to escape explicit or ironic criticism, provides the clue to the Puritans' essential lack of faith. As the British approach, Bradstreet admonishes the crowd not only to "submit to the constituted authorities," but also to " 'do nothing rashly. *Cry not aloud,*' " he says, " 'but pray for the welfare of New-England, and expect patiently what the Lord will do in this matter!' " (9:12; emphasis added). Bradstreet's admonition, reminiscent of Moses' counsel to the Israelites in preparing for a contest with the Egyptians,[79] is a reminder that to cry aloud might be evidence of despair and that to despair is to lose faith or at least to invite the influence of the devil. Prior to Bradstreet's advice, some in the crowd have already "cried": " 'Satan will strike his master-stroke presently' " (9:11). Shortly after his advice, " 'Oh! Lord of Hosts,' cried a voice among the crowd, 'provide a Champion for thy people!' " (9:13). Additional stress is given to this "cried," as if it alone were not already ample evidence that Bradstreet's counsel has been ignored, when the narrator says, "This ejaculation was loudly uttered" (9:13). Thus it would seem that the Puritans are utterly impatient with "what the Lord will do in this matter" and expect the devil's intervention. Bradstreet's "characteristic mildness" (9 : 12) is not what the volatile Puritans want from their former civil authority. They really want someone very like Endicott to champion the Puritan cause against the House of Stuart, because the crowd has reached that mental pitch wherein piety becomes a zealous readiness to throw off all religious and legal restraints, not dissimilar to the experiences of its veterans of the English Civil War. The prayer for a champion ironically evokes the darkest side of the Puritan character and should properly be associated with the "master-stroke" of Satan. Either an Endicott or his typological descendant, the satanic figure whom Hawthorne casts as the leader of the revolutionary mob in "My Kinsman, Major Molineux," is demanded.

Satisfaction of the demand is provided by the gray champion. As one who has " 'staid the march of a King himself' " (9 : 16), the old patriarch is a more proper reincarnation of a regicide figure than Endicott, whose anti-monarchical ideology finds only symbolic expression. It seems certain that Hawthorne invokes this regicide figure to recall the Angel of Hadley legend, in which William Goffe, an actual regicide who escaped to Massachusetts Bay early in the Restoration, withdrew from hiding and helped thwart an Indian attack in King Philip's War.[80] How much more fitting for Hawthorne to call upon this figure, in what turns out to be a thrice-told tale, for a symbolic reenactment of the event for which he earned his original fame: the deposition—this time by word, not deed—of James II. Evidently, Puritan America can contribute to the old grievance against the Stuarts. Since this deposition is bloodless, the regicide champion appropriately wears a sword but carries a staff. Yet, in light of his bloody credentials and manner in the tale, his staff surely bears no resemblance to the shepherding staff of Christ carried by Williams in "Endicott and the Red Cross." Moreover, inasmuch as Hawthorne's source for the Angel of Hadley legend (Scott's *Peveril of the Peak*) does not endorse the regicide figure, we should be wary of considering him in positive terms.[81]

Just how negative the role of the gray champion is might be further estimated in another extra-textual source for his identity and function, that of Scott's *Waverley*. On the eve of the Highlanders' facing the English and Lowlanders in the war of "forty-five," Fergus Mac-Ivor confides to Edward Waverley that he is fated to die or to be taken captive the next day because, in the haunted manner of his grandsires, he has seen the Blodach Glas—the Grey Spectre—whose ghostly image is that of a Lowlander chief killed by a Mac-Ivor ancestor. Ever since the Lowlander's death three hundred years earlier, the Macs-Ivors have observed that " 'his spirit has crossed the Vich Ian Vohr of the day when any great disaster was impending, but especially before approaching death.' "[82] Mac-Ivor then relates how the specter appeared before him in " 'the clear moonlight.' "[83] He called to him but received no answer, for the specter remained in front of him whichever way he turned. Fearing the specter but summoning courage to force it to give way so that he can cross a bridge, Mac-Ivor said, " 'In the name of God, Evil Spirit, give place!' "[84] The specter responded, " 'Vich Ian Vohr, . . . beware of to-morrow!' "[85] Then it disappeared. Pondering the story, later on, Edward wonders, " 'What, can the devil speak truth?' "[86] It turns out that the specter does speak the truth: Mac-Ivor is captured, sentenced to die, but at the last minute manages to circumvent the sentence—despite yet another appearance of the Grey Spectre fortelling his end.

Hawthorne's Gray Champion performs a function similar to Scott's Grey Spectre. He appears mysteriously, like a specter-ridden evocation of Puritan regicide. He does not so much promise a death defining his real-life role in history as he does a downfall, another revolutionary replacement, of the English monarchy. Like the Grey Spectre, the Gray Champion reappears in history on the eve of momentous occasions, always as an omen of ill-fate. Even in their political-religious associations, the two hoary sires share identities. The Grey Spectre is affiliated with the Lowlanders, who are in turn allied to the Church of England after Henry VIII splits with Rome. Thus the Spectre is antipathetic to the Highlanders, who maintain a stronghold of Catholicism. So too is the Gray Champion anti-Catholic and therefore opposed to the House of Stuart, the beloved representative of the Scottish Highlanders hated by the Grey Spectre.

In their evocation of religious and political tensions between past and present, and in their common use of spectral figures prophesying disaster and change, both Scott and Hawthorne seem to be acknowledging the inevitability or even the need for historical change or progress. Yet it is far from certain whether either writer favors the extensive breach with the past so often entailed in revolution. The Grey Spectre in Scott's work never loses his association with the devil. Hawthorne's Gray Champion likewise retains satanic associations. It is with his emergence, after all, that the Puritans are kindled with "lurid wrath" (9:17), as implicitly demonic as the redhot breastplate of Endicott in "Endicott and the Red Cross" (9:437).

To view the Gray Champion as a mediating figure between past and present would seem problematic at best, even though he intervenes between Puritans and English in the tale and apparently prevents bloodshed.[87] The fear of those frenzied Puritans who assume Governor Andros is the Pope's emissary intent on carrying out another St. Bartholomew's massacre (9:11) is countered by the "wiser class" who "believed the Governor's object somewhat less atrocious" (9:12). Evidently, there are some Bostonians whose epistemology and teleology are less fraught with self-flattery than those of the usual zealots in Hawthorne's Puritan gallery.

Least extreme of all is Governor Bradstreet, the real mediator in the tale. His role parallels that of other mediating figures examined in this chapter. Neither afraid of the proud display of English force nor prompted by it to pose histrionically like the Puritan ministers, Bradstreet instead resembles a shepherd trying to soothe a skittish flock. His "characteristic mildness" surely recalls the "mild visage" of Roger Williams, as do his advocation of moderation and temperate speech. Yet the Gray Champion steps in to replace Bradstreets's moderation, in the same way that Endicott overrules Williams and the moderating advice of Winthrop. It is as if Endicott has risen from the grave to advance once again the militant, revolutionary, and devil-oriented spirit of the dominant side of Puritanism, quite in contrast to Bradstreet's benevolent legalism.

The fact was surely not lost on Hawthorne that Bradstreet, virtually as old as Endicott and one of the earliest immigrants, did not become governor until some years after Endicott's death. Even more certain is Hawthorne's awareness from historical sources that Bradstreet had a reputation for peace and moderation. In his *History,* Thomas Hutchinson notes that Bradstreet was the only commissioner from the four New England colonies who opposed a declaration of war against the Dutch colony of Manhados in 1653 (Hawthorne's ancester, William Hathorne, joined with the commissioners from other colonies in support of this war). Later in the same year, Bradstreet alone opposed going to war against the Narragansett tribe.[88] Even more remarkable for Hawthorne's purposes in "The Gray Champion," Hutchinson records that when the issue over retention of privileges granted by the original charter began to come to a head in 1681, "the governor, Mr. Bradstreet, was at the head of the moderate party."[89] This fact throws into ironic relief the shout from the Puritan crowd in the tale: " 'Stand firm for the old charter Governor!' " (9:12). But the most crucial detail from Hawthorne's sources that reflects specifically on the contest at stake in the story comes from Felt's *Annals of Salem.* Translated from Latin, a portion of Bradstreet's epitaph reads: "He was a man of deep discernment, whom neither wealth nor honour could allure from duty. He poised, with equal balance, the authority of the King and the liberty of the people."[90] Of course, Hawthorne undoubtedly read the original in Salem's Charter Street Cemetary where Bradstreet is buried.

Both in history and in Hawthorne's tale, Bradstreet's moderation is spurned. His attempt to mediate between violent contests in New England belongs to the recessive side of Puritanism, as does the moderation of his fictionalized forerunners in the other tales. Violence and rebellion, the legacy of Endicott, dominate the main events of the century as Hawthorne criticizes their sanctioned role in the political mythology of his day. Violence and rebellion thus appear to be propensities far more inherent in the Puritan mind than are peace and mediation. The real enemy of the dominant side of Puritanism is not the New World wilderness against which the Puritans struggle in order to establish what little they could of Winthrop's "city on a hill." The real enemy in Hawthorne's revaluation of nineteenth-century Puritan typology is Stuart and Hanoverian England. It is to carry on the struggle against the king that the mythic champion appears in the

Revolutionary War. The political myth scarcely belongs to Hawthorne. For the irony in the tale insists too stubbornly on exposing the error at the heart of a typological rendering of American history. As Michael Colacurcio observes, "What Hawthorne's deconstruction of New England's mythic Champion does, most essentially, is beg to be questioned on the question typology always begs: what if it had *not* worked out?"[91] By presenting alternatives to the nineteenth-century reduction of seventeenth-century conflicts, Hawthorne suggests the inadequacy of a typological explanation of American history. The ties with England do get severed, and some of them are certainly well lost, as the portrait of the English in "The Gray Champion," however chauvinistic, suggests. Still, with the split from England comes an irreplaceable loss of cultural continuity never really given a chance to develop, in moderate terms, in the New World. The result, as Hawthorne's New England tales evolve toward *The Scarlet Letter*, is not simply a narrowness of American character but a culture dominated by bigotry, violence, and aesthetic barrenness. And unnecessarily so. There were mediating figures among the Puritans who offered other possibilities. At least Hawthorne projected such figures, who became his positive prototypes in an alternative typological history of New England for a writer who was at once their creator and creation.

2

Puritan Typology and Democratic Ideology: The Validity of Revolution in the Eighteenth-Century Tales

Except for "Young Goodman Brown," "The Minister's Black Veil," and "Roger Malvin's Burial," the subject of Hawthorne's historical tales is the growing tension between England and America that points toward the Revolutionary War. They may not all employ "national typology" in their prefigurations, as do "Endicott and the Red Cross" and "The Gray Champion," but we perceive how such a tale as "The May-pole of Merry Mount" is proleptic. Even "The Gentle Boy," which seems provincially focused on New England's problems of faith and authority, has for its broader historical context the English Civil War and Restoration. As "The Gray Champion" clarifies, the English Civil War and regicide constitute examples for the ongoing mission of America's Puritan Saints against the English Church and monarchy. When Hawthorne views the eighteenth century, Puritan opposition to these institutions becomes the leading impetus of the Revolutionary War.

On the one hand, Hawthorne's proleptic, Revolutionary tales work within a prophetic tradition that looks *forward* to a redemptive end of history. Ultimately, this teleology is implicitly apocalyptic, but its design does not necessarily dictate or imply a political preference for democracy over monarchy. Only the Puritans' opposition to the Stuarts might make it seem so. On the other hand, the tales are written from the vantage of hindsight. Hawthorne wrote them roughly between 1828 and 1839, during the predominantly jubilant, nationalistic period of Jacksonian democracy, which marked the culmination of American efforts to legitimize the Revolution by establishing a cohesive democratic tradition in colonial history.[1] In Fourth of July orations, election sermons, campaign speeches, magazine and newspaper articles, and full-scale histories, political and cultural spokesmen venerated the Revolutionary fathers and linked them to the Puritan founders,[2] giving the prophetic tradition a decidedly political cast.

At stake in these self-justifying attempts to discover a usable past was the meaning of the Revolution itself. Was it an essentially conservative event, a colonial reaction to the crown's abrogation of constitutional rights traditionally belonging to English citizens? Or was it a liberal event, an attempt to overthrow an oppressive and remote monarchical system in order to acquire fuller democratic rights than England allowed? Did the Revolution prepare for the immediate and final fulfillment of the Puritan errand, either in its theological or diluted secular version?[3] Or did it break with the inhibiting traditions of the past, allowing the progressive development of human freedom and improvement? After the ratification of the Constitution, these questions were rarely argued in public discourse until the 1840s. By the 1830s, the prevailing views were liberal and progressive—perhaps nowhere codified so well as in John L. O'Sullivan's *United States Magazine and Democratic Review,* where many of Hawthorne's tales appeared. Democratic consensus obtained to such an extent that no "sustained" history of the Loyalists' wartime experiences appeared until more than a hundred years after the Revolution.[4] Everywhere Hawthorne was most likely to look, he would have confronted an essentially provincial interpretation of the foreground and meaning of the Revolutionary War. If we fail to consider the ideological and rather monolithic implications of this crucial fact, we cannot begin to understand Hawthorne's critical achievement in the eighteenth-century tales.

Despite his admiration for Andrew Jackson and his nominally being a democrat, Hawthorne manifestly refused giving uncritical support to the partisan version of the Revolution. His knowledge of New England history, as broad as anyone else's in the 1830s, precluded unquestioning approval of the Puritans as forerunners of American independence and democracy or as praiseworthy Revolutionary founders. As far as the Puritans were violent and revolutionary, Hawthorne seems very willing to grant their "typic" function, but he knew too much about their intolerance and self-righteousness to view them as seminal democrats. Anyone reasonably interested in New England history for its own sake had to view such figures as John Endicott and Thomas Dudley as antipathetic to democratic ideals, and, less extreme, leaders such as Winthrop and Bradford as theoretically opposed to egalitarianism.

Hawthorne curiously avoids any sustained or direct treatment of the causes, events, and participants of the Revolution itself.[5] Unlike historians and other romancers of his time, he refused to capitalize on the patriotic event most obviously appropriate for the historical lore and legends that he found wanting in the new nation.[6] He does, however, approach the Revolution and even dwells on it in a unique way, especially in terms of its causes and consequences with respect to England. Even when Hawthorne seems to join his contemporaries in the search for patriotic traditions, he invariably casts doubt on the validity of revolutionists' motives and even on the legitimacy of the Revolution itself. His integrity as a critical thinker and as a historian would not permit him to imitate the litany of praise to the Puritan and Revolutionary founders common in his time. Hawthorne could no more anathematize or dismiss the English presence in American history than disregard the dilution or loss of English traditions, first and most severely among the early Puritan settlers and then among the Revolutionary and post-Revolutionary generations. If he was not yet ready to recover these cultural values outright in his eighteenth-century tales, he was certainly prepared to expose the chauvinistic ideology of his day, which not only minimized the importance of older traditions but also exploited more recent Revolutionary legends, through "art," to support itself. Aware of the irony in this latter purpose, Hawthorne brought his own irony to bear upon the very patriotic legends he seems himself to exploit.

Although the contents of Hawthorne's two ill-fated collections of New England tales remain uncertain,[7] there seems to be no question that they contained stories dealing with both the seventeenth and eighteenth centuries. Surprisingly, there are almost twice as many tales set in the eighteenth century as in the seventeenth.[8] The interdependency of seventeenth- and eighteenth-century tales, and the proleptic nature of both groups, appear in "The Battle Omen" (1830), which was Hawthorne's first published tale.[9] The story opens *in medias res,* immediately calling attention to a historical foreground: "THE LATEST INCIDENT of this nature is said to have occurred on a cold, bright evening, during the winter that preceded the first actual hostilities in our great War" (11:235). Two rural youths are walking home after attending a "military meeting" in a nearby village (11:235). While they expect a showdown with England, they are full of laughter, "almost forgetting the threatened ruin of their country, in the stirring prospects which were opened to youthful ambition" (11:236). The first young man can even maintain his cheer when reflecting that, despite an impending war that "may chance to separate two worlds," there are no such oracles in the wind or sky as the Puritan fathers used to perceive prior to disrupting events (11:236). He evidently thinks he is superior to the superstition of his ancestors. The second youth, however, is less complacent in his modernity when he considers, " 'if we had inherited the gloom of [the Pilgrims'] religious faith, the winds in the forest, and the meteors in the sky, would have prophesied also to us' " (11:236).

The rest of the story presents the conversion of these New England sons to the gloomy epistemology of their Puritan grandsires. Accordingly, the two young men actually believe that they hear the omen of the war for which they and other New Englanders have been preparing. However "apocryphal" and lacking in "elevated imagination" (11:237), Puritan superstition is persuasive and invariably self-fulfilling. As "The Battle Omen" closes, the two youths have become duly sober, spiritually united with their ancestors insofar as they can now point to cosmic events to justify their actions. In keeping with the prophetic dimension of the Puritan errand, the

Revolutionary War must occur because the two youths have willed it and justified it in the evocation of their omen. Puritan superstition, as it combines with providential epistemology, meanwhile remains efficacious even in the nominally secular or "enlightened" context of eighteenth-century rationalism.

To turn from "The Battle Omen" to "My Kinsman, Major Molineux" (1832) involves an immense shift in aesthetic richness and intellectual complexity. Both works not only anticipate the Revolution but also conclude with an ambiguous, open-ended forecast of the war's meaning in American history. Perhaps one of Hawthorne's first tales,[10] "Molineux" looks back to the 1730s, when party factions and the colonial movement toward independence may not seem especially relevant to the critical foreground of the Revolutionary period. Within the overall pattern of Hawthorne's seventeenth- and eighteenth-century tales, however, "Molineux" prophesies the colonial movement for independence as much as "Endicott and the Red Cross," but the conception of a predetermined contest with England is far more subtle than in the diatribe of an Endicott.

Whereas Puritan opponents in the earlier three tales are essentially caricatures of Puritan deviants and British oppressors, the ostensible antagonist in "Molineux" is at once symbolic and painfully personal. Major Molineux is both literally and figuratively a kinsman. Literally he is Robin's blood relative, but his filling an "English" post makes him a kinsman of the "English" colonists who wish to depose him. Without in the least discounting the importance of patricide in "Molineux," the fratricidal nature of the American Revolution is more profoundly at issue.[11] Although the Major is merely one of the "inferior members of the court party" (11:208), he still represents the patronage system against which New Englanders often inveighed. Tar and feathering Major Molineux certainly offers a temporary satisfaction of ritualizing colonial anger aimed at the king, and it unmistakably suggests a furtherance of a regicidal motive in Hawthorne's seventeenth-century Puritans. Still, the war toward which the ritual points will not actually be fought against the king, except as an abstraction, a symbol. The real fighting will take place between the high and low on both sides, "Englishmen" all and therefore kinsmen, as Hawthorne's title more broadly suggests. As much as the tale invites mythic, psychological, and historical interpretations of overthrowing authority and (presumably) growing up,[12] Hawthorne also urges us to cast aside such abstract considerations to feel the intensely personal agony brought by civil war.

The British patronage system and depreciated currency suggested in the opening pages point to eighteenth-century political sources for the Revolutionary War;[13] but the ideology and behavior lying behind colonial antagonism to England have their causal motivation in seventeenth-century Puritanism. Although the mob with Major Molineux in its grip seems to be a secular phenomenon, it stages its "counterfeited pomp" in front of the church and the mysterious mansion with the "Gothic window" across the street (11:230, 221), thus indicating quite well the continued theocentric nature of Boston's Puritanical society.[14] For this reason Robin is instructed to wait for his kinsman at the church by the split-faced leader of the mob and to remain there by the kind gentleman, who may indeed be the minister of the church for whom, in part, the mob action is presented in order to determine how well it will "take."[15] The church itself seems innocent when Robin looks into its moonlit interior: ". . . one solitary ray had dared to rest upon the opened page of the great Bible. Had Nature, in that deep hour, become a worshipper in the house, which man had builded? Or was that heavenly light the visible sanctity of the place, visible because no earthly and impure feet were within the walls?" (11:222) Outside, however, its impure *deserters* run riot, fully in keeping with the rebellious tradition of Salem or Boston.

Responsibility for the proto-revolutionary mayhem rests upon the city party, not the country party—which, as Hawthorne presents matters, may fairly be said not to exist at this time.[16] Perhaps one must rely too tenuously upon Robin's example to support such a case, and yet it does seem inconceivable that a country youth, however much lacking in the shrewdness with which he credits himself, could be unacquainted with the political, anti-aristocratic animus pervading Boston unless it has not yet spread to the distant countryside from where he comes. Surely his father would have cautioned Robin if it had. But the only warning the youth seems to have received is that life in the big city is not as innocent or friendly as it is in the country, and thus he carries his cudgel.

Robin's wariness conforms to the romantic dichotomy of cosmopolitan and rural life upon which the tale depends. The religious dimension of the story once again offers helpful clarification. In raising the question of the "visible sanctity" of the Boston church *without* the presence of "impure" worshipers, Hawthorne evidently plays with the issue over which the Boston establishment quarreled with Anne Hutchinson and Henry Vane during the antinomian crisis. Bostonians in the 1730s apparently continue to believe in their sanctity, to such an extent that they feel safe to be led by the split-faced figure who seems nothing less than demonic.[17] Yet they are clearly not sanctified within Hawthorne's romantic figuration of "Nature." That they and all mortals share a Calvinistic depravity begs the question.[18] After looking into the deserted Boston church and feeling weary from his evening's ordeal, Robin recalls the customary ritual of his family in the country. "He pictured them assembled at the door, beneath the tree, the great old tree, which had been spared for its huge twisted trunk, and venerable shade, when a thousand leafy brethren fell. There, at the going down of the summer sun, it was his father's custom to perform domestic worship, that the neighbors might come and join with him like brothers of the family, and that the wayfaring man might pause to drink at that fountain, and keep his heart pure by freshening the memory of home" (11:222). Similar to what Hawthorne will evoke in "The Old Manse," this scene of hospitality and refuge is hallowed by nature, "the golden light that shown from the western clouds" illuminating the scriptures (11:223).

Robin's father, no ordinary clergyman in the dominant Puritan tradition, anticipates Hawthorne's reformulation of Roger Williams in "Endicott and the Red Cross"—an evocation of a recessive potential for peace. He lacks the political savvy of Williams; otherwise he should be expected to know or sense that New England's historical antipathy to England will not entirely fade away, even nearly fifty years after the last of the Stuart kings and the comparative stability under the new charter. Still, he lives in a pastoral sanctuary, "at a long distance back in the country" (11:224). And the dissensions in the Puritan capital are not only covert but also recent, inasmuch as when his cousin, Major Molineux, visited him within the past year or so, he had evidently reported no active or foreseeable trouble among the natives.

Major Molineux himself must be a member of the Anglican Church, but that allegiance presents no impediment to his relations with Robin's father. Unless one wants to risk suspecting that father Molineux is himself an Anglican, we should suspect that his religious tolerance has become more dangerous to the Puritan errand than his ancestors predicted when William of Orange declared the Act of Toleration.[19] He apparently gives his blessing to Robin when the young man departs for Boston to put himself under the "generous intentions" of the Major's patronage (11:225). If the father is not an utter fool, he could hardly expect Robin to get very far in the Court Party without adopting its Anglican faith. The latitude of his permissiveness is therefore extreme, and it may hint at yet another reason for Massachusetts's grievance against England. When its ministers are willing to give up their sons to the unpurified church, New England has come to suffer one of the most pressing threats in its century-long series of tribulations. Our positive sense of father Molineux's ecumenical spirit opens up the possibility of our seeing that neither England's politics nor its church is as threatening as unreconstructed Puritans or colonial deviants believe.

Measured by traditional standards, New England's political, economic, and religious quarrels with England seem completely valid, but its mob violence, spawned in secrecy and carried out in shadows, receives no patriotic approval in the tale.[20] However trivial it may be when viewed from the jolly perspective of the moon,[21] the mob's activity is hardly more than an ignoble conspiracy and hence an embarrassment to anyone interested in typological origins of the American Revolution. Its violence is no doubt inherited from Endicott, but at least that stalwart enacted his defiance of England beneath the rays of the noon-tide sun.[22] The violence in "My Kinsman, Major Molineux," however, seems sneaky, uncomfortably gratuitous, and downright mean, directed as it is at "a head that had grown grey in honor" (11:229). If Major Molineux represents England, then he projects an unswervingly dignified image of the parent country and in no way deserves a "foul disgrace" (11:229). New England's conspirators, on the other hand, appear as wayward demons, versed solely in their ancestors' gloomy knowledge of the devil's ploys: "On they went, like fiends that throng in mockery round some dead potentate, mighty no more, but majestic still in his agony. On they went, in counterfeited pomp, in senseless uproar, in frenzied merriment, trampling all on an old man's heart" (11:230). These proto-revolutionists constitute the very "rabble" that England will call them.

One of the unanswered questions raised by "Molineux" is in what way, if any, the Revolutionary and post-Revolutionary periods will transcend their inglorious origins. Though the tale just barely hints at what American colonists later hail as the holy cause of liberty, it unflinchingly reveals that Molineux (and through him, England) is no common villain but a character of honor and grandeur. It is not likely that the mob, composed of rummies and a prostitute,[23] will feel the slightest regret over the displacement of this regal figure; but the story emotionally and morally urges that someone ought to feel a burden of guilt. Perhaps Robin does, and perhaps that accounts for his wanting to return to his father's pastoral sanctuary. Robin's witnessing of Major Molineux's disgrace has become shameful and agonizing because it is so personal. Beyond Robin are Hawthorne's contemporary readers, who will require further open and ironic assaults on their patriotism before they might acknowledge and accept the guilt of warring with kinsmen.

Criticism of seminal American revolutionists in "Molineux" and sympathetic treatment of the Major as England's representative serve as a prelude to Hawthorne's more daring deconstructions of America's patriotic myth of the Revolutionary period in "Old News" (1835) and "Legends of the Province-House" (1838–39). Usually ignored by critics, "Old News" is a formidable sketch in Hawthorne's historical canon.[24] The work is divided into three sections: the first set during the 1740s, the second during the French and Indian War, and the third during the Revolution. Literally drawing from newspapers of the first two periods, Hawthorne presents an overview of Boston culture when her allegiance to England evolved to its height; but in the last section, he shifts to an "Old Tory" who observes the Revolutionary setting from a Loyalist's point of view. In the sketch as a whole, Hawthorne finds something worthy in the importation of English traditions and criticizes their loss to a continuing gloomy and violent Puritan tradition.

The 1740s do not initially seem dominated by the oppressive influence of latter-day Puritans, but the "rigid hand of Puritanism might yet be felt upon the reins of government" (11:136). Accordingly, Hawthorne finds it impossible "to throw a sunny and joyous air over our picture of this period"

(11 : 135). There are many battle omens recorded in the 1740s, resulting from citizens possessing their ancestors' ability to read the wonder of providence in the midnight sky. Yet these forebodings point no farther than to the French and Indian War. Political disputes are confined to local issues, the colonists focusing their discontent upon Governor Belcher and minor royal administrators. Squabbles such as these suggest nothing of the violence indirectly aimed at the sovereign found in the 1730s setting of "Molineux." Indeed, George II is almost universally held in high regard, as exemplified in the festivities commemorating his birthday. Hawthorne is attracted to this occasion of merrymaking because it contrasts with the otherwise dull, gray life of those times and even of his own. He remarks that "the Revolution blotted a feast-day out of our calendar" (11 : 138). As in "May-pole," Hawthorne would appear drawn to those English customs that might happily relieve the heritage of Puritan gloom.

In the second section of "Old News," such relief insinuates itself. The very appearance of Boston papers in the 1760s, apparently stained with wine, gives token evidence of a metropolis familiar with "fashion and gaiety" (11 : 142). Fancy apparel and wigs in the modes of London, as well as witty essays by Fielding and Smollett, reveal that "newer manners and customs had almost entirely superseded those of the Puritans, even in their own city of refuge" (11 : 143). If in that last phrase there lurks a rueful augury of New England's decline, it would seem to reflect Hawthorne's awareness of traditional Puritan values, not his own. Thus he notes how it is "natural" that an increasingly prosperous colony would assimilate the manners of the mother country (11 : 143). Moreover, at least the merchantile class "still called [England] their own home, as if New-England were to them, what many of the old Puritans had considered it, not a permanent abiding-place, but merely a lodge in the wilderness, until the trouble of the times should be passed" (11 : 143). Hawthorne pointedly deflates nine-teenth-century pretensions to superiority over an English mode of life: "The gaudiest dress, permissible by modern taste, fades into Quaker-like sobriety, compared with the deep, rich, glowing splendor of our ancestors" (11 : 150–51). Of course, "there was no longer an undue severity of religion, nor as yet any disaffection to British supremacy, nor democratic prejudices against pomp" (11 : 143-44).

While quarrels with England are not mentioned during these years when the colonies join the British to resist the French presence in Canada, Hawthorne's positive assessment of the colorful style of life is partly offset by his suspicion of its connections to aristocracy. More germane to the Revolution, however, are Hawthorne's comments on the "somewhat" changed character of New Englanders since the conquest of Louisburg in 1745:

After that event, the New-Englanders never settled into precisely the same quiet race, which all the world had imagined them to be. They had done a deed of history, and were anxious to add new ones to the record. They had proved themselves powerful enough to influence the result of a war, and were thenceforth called upon, and willingly consented, to join their strength against the enemies of England; on those fields, at least, where victory would redound to their peculiar advantage. And now, in the heat of the Old French War, they might well be termed a martial people. (11 : 144).

As in the seventeenth-century tales, "Molineux," "Legends of the Province-House," and *The Whole History of Grandfather's Chair,* Hawthorne seems far less concerned with the issues causing or justifying the Revolution than with the militancy and violence issuing from the dominant New England tradition. As the second section of "Old News" closes, Hawthorne skillfully dodges laying blame upon revolutionists for the loss of English merriment and splendor by discussing the devastation caused by Boston's great fire of 1760. "None will be inclined to lament" the destruction "at this late date," he says, "except the lover of antiquity, who would have been glad to walk among those streets of venerable houses, fancying the old inhabitants still there, that he might commune with their shadows, and paint a more vivid picture of the times" (11 : 153). Obviously, Hawthorne is himself that "lover of antiquity." Nothing in modern life quite matches the English-colonial style. What the fire destroys the Revolution destroys more thoroughly. "Doubtless," says Hawthorne, "posterity has acquired a better city by the calamity of that generation" (11 : 153). But this "doubtless" is freighted with irony, as the enthusiasm for the once-thriving magnificence of Boston indicates everywhere else. In "Legends of the Province-House," we shall see just how poorly modern architecture compares to the splendor of pre-Revolutionary times.

In the last section of "Old News," regret over the loss of English manners and customs derives from a Tory of such inveterate Loyalist principles that he "acknowledge[s] no oppression in the Stamp-act" (11 : 153). His extreme Anglophilism might therefore be patronized by nineteenth-century Americans, inasmuch as it can be taken to express quaint heresies no longer vital to the country's welfare or conception of itself. Well might Hawthorne count on such indulgence during the last years of Jackson's presidency, wherein the success of Revolutionary–democratic principles would seem unquestionable. While elected officials and cultural spokesmen were looking to the past to authenticate liberty and progressive ideology, Hawthorne raised his voice against their self-serving exploitation of history. Liberty and democracy may have been won in ways not so glorious as patriotic hero-worshipers had been codifying for several decades. More than a comparatively simple matter of setting the record straight seems to have motivated Hawthorne, for, along with the political advantages resulting from the split with England, there have been costs in cultural values and morality that no one quite understands or admits but that sooner or later must be paid.

Just as in "Old Esther Dudley" and in the penultimate section of *The Whole History of Grandfather's Chair*, the plight of the aged Tory in "Old News" redounds to the discredit of colonial patriots during the Revolutionary War. The old man, though an "Episcopalian," is a native New Englander. As a captain in a provincial regiment, he fought at the Plains of Abraham and was wounded in that English-colonial alliance against the French. He remains in Boston after other Loyalists have gone to Canada or England in the wake of General Howe's retreat. Boston is his home and he expects the rebellion to subside, followed by a restoration of royal prerogative. In the meantime, Boston's patriots treat him as the mob treats Major Molineux: "Hustled have we been, till driven from town-meetings; dirty water has been cast upon our ruffles, by a Whig chambermaid; John Hancock's coachman seizes every opportunity to bespatter us with mud; daily are we hooted by the unbreeched rebel brats; and narrowly, once, did our gray hairs escape the ignominy of tar and feathers" (11:154–55).

To set in motion a patriotic interpretation of the Revolution that Hawthorne attempts to redress, there appears, already, a book on the "History of the War till the close of the year 1779" (11:157). Another tunnel vision of history appears in "An Oration, on the Horrid Massacre of 1770" (11:157). The old Tory's response to the bias indicated in this title plumbs the depth of Hawthorne's moral reservations over American self-justifications for the Revolution: "When that blood was shed—the first that the British soldier drew from the bosoms of our countrymen—we turned sick at heart, and do so still, as often as they make it reek anew from among the stones of King-street. The pool, that we saw that night, has swelled into a lake—*English blood and American—no!—all British, all blood of my brethren* (11:157; emphasis added). Even from this Loyalist point of view, no blame is cast on either side for causing the massacre. Horror at the bloodshed outweighs partisan efforts to argue which side was originally or primarily responsible.

The Old Tory's anguish over the bloody quarrel of brothers actually represents Hawthorne's lifelong regret over the fratricidal nature of the Revolutionary War. Implicit in the early "My Kinsman, Major Molineux," the point is overt in the late "Septimius Felton," written during the Civil War. When Septimius shoots a young British officer in the aftermath of the Battle of Lexington and Concord, the Briton says to him, "'Come my good friend. . . . Let me down as softly as you can on mother Earth—the mother of both you and me—so we are brothers; and this be a brotherly act, though it does not look so'" (13:27). That Hawthorne reiterated the point in the subsequent "Septimius Norton" manuscript (13:234) and that he even considered making Septimius a distant relative of the British officer, adds poignance to Septimius's feeling that to kill in such a battle is "so like murder" (13:24), and to the young officer's expression that "'it is so like murder—old Cain's work'" (13:235). As we shall see in "The Old Manse," the loss of British blood is indeed an evocation of the Cain and Abel story, possessing, for Hawthorne, all the attending guilt.

Hawthorne implicitly advocates the moral imperatives of moderation and mediation in domestic or political affairs. In "Old News," he no more adopts the extremist monarchical views of the old Tory than he does the absolutist but unspecified views of colonial patriots. Given the regnant, self-righteous assumptions of his largely democratic audience, however, Hawthorne is trying to urge a balanced interpretation of the Revolution. "Americans" who side with England in the war are not evil scoundrels wholly or largely imbued by false principles but "men greatly to be pitied, and often worthy of our sympathy" (11 : 159). Anyone reasonably favoring the slow but gradual improvement of human society, and who also has a proper respect for the past, ought to comprehend that "it was pardonable, in the conservative" of the Revolutionary period, "to mistake the temporary evils of a change, for permanent diseases of the system which that change was to establish" (11 : 159). Although this grants considerable justice to the democratic results of the war, it more forcefully argues for a historical and moral understanding of the Loyalist point of view. As Hawthorne says at the outset of "Old News," "In this world, we are the things of a moment and are made to pursue momentary things, with here and there a thought that stretches mistily towards eternity, and perhaps may endure as long. All philosophy, that would abstract mankind from the present, is no more than words" (11 : 133). It will therefore not do to abstract the Loyalists from their historical time and to stigmatize them from the vantage of nineteenth-century American democracy, any more than it will to glorify colonial revolutionists.

Democracy may indeed be a thought "that stretches mistily towards eternity," but that does not mean Hawthorne approves of revolution to achieve it. He takes a stand against revolution in terms similar to those of Edmund Burke:

> A revolution, or anything, that interrupts social order, may afford op-
> portunities for the individual display of eminent virtue; but, its effects
> are pernicious to general morality. Most people are so constituted, that
> they can be virtuous only in a certain routine; and an irregular course of
> public affairs demoralizes them. One great source of disorder, was the
> multitude of disbanded troops, who were continually returning home,
> after terms of service just long enough to give them a distaste to peacea-
> ble occupations; neither citizens nor soldiers, they were very liable to
> become ruffians. Almost all our impressions, in regard to this period are
> unpleasant, whether referring to the state of civil society, or to the
> character of the contest, which, especially where native Americans were
> opposed to each other, was waged with the deadly hatred of fraternal
> enemies. (11 : 159–60)

How kinsmen can allow their disagreements to lead so far is the irony of Hawthorne's concluding remark on the Revolution: "It is the beauty of war, for men to commit mutual havoc with undisturbed good humor" (11 : 160). Evidently, Hawthorne is not amused but disturbed by America's revolutionary origins. And it would seem just as evident that, through the modest pages of *The New England Magazine,* he tries to alert chauvinistic Americans to the danger of construing either the foreground or events of the Revolution as a heroic colonial enterprise.

By not renouncing "aristocratic" fashions and manners, and by adopting a Tory point of view of the Revolution, Hawthorne seriously questions the official, democratic version of colonial America's conflict with England. The only good word for a colonial revolutionary that conforms to the biases of Hawthorne's time is reserved for Washington, who, the old Tory must concede, is an "upright rebel" and unfortunate "fallen angel" (11 : 157); but the absence of jingoistic applause for other Revolutionary leaders and events suggests Hawthorne's revisionist aims. With these aims in mind, we are prepared for a proper examination of "Legends of the Province-House."

Until recently, the four "Legends" have been essentially ignored by Hawthorne critics.[25] The situation has been worse among Hawthorne biographers, who neglect the "Legends," written during the early phase of Hawthorne's emergence from his "reclusive" years, to focus on his job at the Boston Custom House and his romantic relationship with Sophia Peabody.[26] Certainly those two events garner all the attention.[27] Hawthorne's commitment to the causes and consequences of America's War with England, even in the midst of new and distracting interests, should warn those who minimize the depth and sincerity of his attraction to history. The formidable critical analysis of democratic-progressive ideology found in the "Legends" makes it dangerous to disregard the possibility of Hawthorne's having a reserved loyalty to England.

If this loyalty does not seem particularly obvious in the first reading of the "Legends," the reason can be found in Hawthorne's sophisticated use of the frame narrative. The outer frame involves a narrator who, between the summers of 1837 and 1838, pays three visits to Boston's Province House and retells legends relevant to the Revolution that he hears there. Having an uncertain amount of insight and dissatisfied with modern life, the narrator feels attracted to the splendor of New England life during its eighteenth-century "English" phase. Not so Bela Tiffany, who tells the first three inset legends. Tiffany is a partisan Democrat, an anti-aristocratic purveyor of national typology in support of nineteenth-century progressive ideology. The patriotic level of his stories fully subscribes to the politics of John L. O'Sullivan's *United States Magazine and Democratic Review,* where the "Legends" first appeared. The last of the four legends, even after curious editorial meddling by the narrator, entails an old Loyalist's rebuttal to Tiffany's Anglophobic message. Along with the interplay of Tiffany's complacent democratic biases, the narrator's wavering allegiances, and the old

Loyalist's Anglophilism, Hawthorne introduces characteristic ironies to challenge the rampant Whig historiography prevalent in his time. The feat is for the most part subtle, yet we discredit Hawthorne to a grievous extent by not recognizing his achievement as unique and daring.

"Howe's Masquerade"

The principal event in "Howe's Masquerade" commemorates the final expulsion of aristocratic England from New England and thus the advent of an independent, democratic United States. The political typology of "Endicott and the Red Cross" and "The Gray Champion" is at last fulfilled. Since Endicott ripped the cross from the British ensign in 1634, it has taken a century and a half to carry out the implications of his deed; but with Lexington and Bunker Hill behind them in the context of "Howe's Masquerade," New England's sons, as forecast in "The Gray Champion," have begun to "vindicate" their Puritan ancestors. Sir William Howe, the presiding English dignitary in the Bay Colony, has contrived a gala masquerade in order to ease Loyalists' fears that these same New England sons, led by the outsider Washington, will be successful in their siege of Boston.[28]

Puritan descendants evidently have a lingering investment in a providential design such as gave rise to Winthrop's vision of a city on a hill,[29] but British Loyalists in 1776 most surely do not. The main event in the legend seems ultimately meant to instruct them in the validity of the Puritan errand and to remind us of the gloomy message in "The May-pole of Merry Mount." For with the final loss of the old charter late in the reign of James II, and with a succession of Royal governors for more than eighty years, citizens of Massachusetts Bay have become gradually accustomed to what the narrator calls "vice-regal pomp" (9:240). As in "Old News," something recalling the color and dash of the "May-pole" revelers has been reestablished at Howe's masquerade, perhaps, "the most gay and gorgeous affair that had occurred in the annals of government" (9:243). The participants look to models in England for their costumes: "figures that seemed to have stepped from the dark canvas of historic portraits, or to have flitted forth from the magic pages of romance, or at least to have flown hither from one of the London theatres" (9:243). If for no other reason than the existence of an imported mirth formerly expelled from Puritan America, let alone a "parti-colored Merry Andrew" or a Falstaff who is "almost as provocative of laughter as his prototype" (9:243–44), we ought to expect some sort of change in the course of events consistent with Hawthorne's understanding of the dour Puritanical mind and its continuing survival in the eighteenth century.

Accordingly, Bela Tiffany's legend might seem, in its larger configuration, a virtual reenactment of "The May-pole of Merry Mount."[30] Old

World forms of gaiety have for some time been reintroduced into the New World, affronting the would-be (or should-be) gravity of Puritan heirs. Jollity and gloom are once more contending for an empire. But the stakes of the conflict are now considerably higher than they were in 1629. Despite the efforts of Edwards and other revivalists earlier in the century, *some* New Englanders have become far less ignited by the spirit that inflamed their Puritan forebears, and more tolerant of the English church and English cultural modes that emerged after the new charter.

Climaxing the masquerade is a skit representing colonial leaders in the French and Indian War who are, or soon will be, generals in the American army: Washington, Gates, Lee, Putnam, Schuyler, Ward, and Heath. Their uniforms "rent and tattered by sword, ball, or bayonet" (9:244), these caricatures enact an interview with the British commander-in-chief (Howe), the implication being that all the American leaders put together are no match for one British officer. Were the happy response to this entertainment to issue solely from a pro-English faction, it would scarcely cause any wonder. But Hawthorne's Tiffany somewhat oddly discriminates: the applause "came loudest of all from the loyalists of the colony" (9:244)—which must imply that some unmentioned guests at the masquerade are not full-fledged Tories and may even be rebel sympathizers. What is more, notwithstanding the politicized atmosphere of Boston, they have somehow managed to retain a sense of humor. While some of New England's sons lay siege on the capital of their Puritan grandsires, others enjoy festivities ridiculing colonial leaders. The difference between these descendants seems as great as that between Endicott's legions and maypole votaries. Clearly enough, English forms of gaiety must be enticing. Perhaps Endicott was right after all. Old World forms of jollity are altogether too enticing and must be eliminated root and branch.

The distance separating these good-humored descendants from their grim ancestors becomes clear in the presence of the Reverend Mather Byles. Nephew of Cotton Mather and grandson of Increase Mather, Mather Byles could not have been named for stauncher Puritans. These two Divines had done everything possible to retain the old charter in the seventeenth century and, all efforts failing, to preserve as much of the New England way as possible under the new charter. This much was surely known to Hawthorne.[31] Neither of these Puritan worthies would have considered it fitting to his ministerial role to attend a Loyalist party, let alone to laugh at mock-heroic pantomimes of colonial generals. Yet here is Mather Byles, of their name and blood and Covenant training, whose "Presbyterian scruples had not kept him from the entertainment" (9:245). Having " 'laughed more than beseems [his] cloth' "(9:245), he begs Sir William Howe to cancel a final spectacle for the evening, saying, " 'One other such fit of merriment, and I must throw off my clerical wig and band' " (9:245).[32]

For Hawthorne's purposes, Byles is as requisite to Howe's Masquerade' as Blackstone is to "The May-pole of Merry Mount" and as the Episcopal clergyman is to "The Gray Champion." A good-humored clergyman associated with England is necessary to remind us of the contrasting seriousness with which the Puritans undertook their essentially separatist errand into the wilderness. Sir William Howe is completely ignorant of that seriousness and of its legacy perpetuated in the ministerial training at Harvard and, by the setting of the legend, at Yale. As he says to Mather Byles, " 'if mirth were a crime, you had never gained your doctorate of divinity' " (9:245). Howe does not mean to be ironical but Hawthorne does. Representing an Anglo-Catholic tradition popularly invoked by the tag of Merry Old England, Howe expects a clerical indulgence in humor every bit as thorough in the New World as in the Old. Sir William could hardly be more wrong. A Puritan gloom, heretofore unnoticed amid the prevalent cheer, is present at the masquerade, and Howe is about to learn the meaning of that gloom.

Just as the revelry of the Merry Mounters suddenly concludes with the arrival of Endicott and his grim forces, so the hilarity of Howe's masquers abruptly ends with the onset of a final masque, a revival of Puritan scruple and severity altogether worthy of the somber founding fathers. Immediately prior to the exchange between Sir William and Mather Byles, the aged Colonel Joliffe has been introduced, who has "known whig principles" (9:244).[33] Although unarmed and non-violent, he might as well be Endicott: a "stern old figure, the best sustained character in the masquerade, because so well representing the antique spirit of his native land" (9:244). It is not even necessary to know that he has a "black puritanical scowl" (9:244) for us to sense an imminent evocation of Puritan darkness with which to oppose, yet again, English gaiety. Another sort of masquerade begins, ostensibly orchestrated by Joliffe, to the tune and beat of a "funeral march" (9:246) from (aptly) the Old South Church.

Colonel Joliffe not only knows his New England history but also the historical and typological significance of the Puritan errand. Like Bela Tiffany, Joliffe knows how to make the past "usable," to discover in history those proleptic sources required by ideological demands of the present.[34] His direction of a ritualized procession of Massachusetts's governors results in an unmistakable anti-masque[35] designed at once to comment on the English festivity preceding it and the Boston siege sensibly tightening its pressure on the Province House. Whether for the jollity within or for the military events outside the Province House, the king-resisting figure of Endicott must necessarily lead the procession, even though he does not take his proper chronological place in the lineup of governors. Not for nothing had Hawthorne exaggerated Endicott's belated exploit at Merry Mount or his role in the red cross episode. The archetypal Puritan posed against the Saints' most persistent enemy, Endicott reappears in a sense to wipe out, once and for all, Old World mirth and Royal authority.

Consequently, in terms of a patriotic reading of Joliffe's procession, it does not matter that the "milder" Winthrop (9:247) and Sir Henry Vane accompany Endicott, along with all the later Puritan governors save Bradstreet. The internal struggle over the nature and course of the Puritan errand that they *could* represent is definitely not their function. Even Sir William Howe's unsophisticated interpretation comes close to identifying the purpose of the governors. "'In the devil's name, what is this,'" he asks, "'a procession of the regicide judges of King Charles, the martyr?'" (9:247). They may as well be those judges within Tiffany's nineteenth-century redaction of national typology; for wherever an English monarch appears, out goes the cause of liberty, and wherever there exists a military governor such as Andros or Howe, there resides a symbol of the king who must be killed. Regicide is at the heart of the ritual.[36] Colonel Joliffe therefore identifies the Puritan governors in their typic historical role as "'rulers of the old, original Democracy of Massachusetts'" (9:248).

While this democratic version of the past has the attraction of giving post-Revolutionary meaning to the pre-Revolutionary historical record, it flagrantly distorts the politics of seventeenth-century Puritan history. Joliffe's distillation of those politics disregards a wealth of facts that show Puritanical opposition to democracy;[37] but from the point of view of Joliffe and a nineteenth-century audience, Puritanism might well seem democratic in comparison with Royal and Parliamentary prerogative in Massachusetts Bay during the eighteenth century. Still, Joliffe, like Hawthorne's contemporary audience, construes history for his own moral and political purposes.[38] These require a revolutionary foreground easily adjustable to a configuration of rebellion against British rule culminating in the establishment of democracy. Rewriting the historical record to suit ideological interests of the present is certainly an issue in Joliffe's interpretation of the bloodstain on Sir Henry Vane's ruff: "'he laid down the wisest head in England upon the block, for the principles of liberty'" (9:248).[39] Yet Vane, probably the chief Parliamentary figure against Charles I during the Civil War, had nothing to do with the regicide. He was beheaded in his turn during the early phase of the Restoration for specious reasons not bearing upon the regicide, the details of which Hawthorne knew very well.[40]

Howe seems as ignorant of Vane's role in English history as he is of Puritan governors in New England history.[41] He fails to perceive what Lord Percy and other officers suspect in this Puritan phase of the masquerade, that "'there may be a plot under this mummery'" (9:248). Howe ridicules this possibility, regarding it a mere "'jest'" (9:248). Even after Bradstreet and then all the Royal governors in Massachusetts's history appear in a "spectral march" down the Province House stairs (9:251), Howe fails to understand. He even fails to recognize the image of Thomas Gage, his immediate predecessor and close acquaintance, although Lord Percy accurately identifies him. Only when Howe, and Howe alone, sees beneath the cloak of the final masquer does he recognize himself and finally get the point.

There is indeed a "plot" in Joliffe's masquerade. The masquerade and Bela Tiffany's legend have been carefully designed to legitimize, for them, the recurring Puritanical resistance to Royal authority and to English traditions of mirth. Even though the political conflict with England is apparently accentuated in the legend, the whole of English culture is really at issue. The pageantry, games, and mirth (implicitly approved by the Anglican Church) are therefore not incidental matters but integral to Puritan New England's long-standing quarrel with the Old World. Endicott's zeal with the Maypolers gave warning of as much. It could hardly be made more explicit at the conclusion of Tiffany's legend. As the Old South Church rings a midnight "knell" (9:253) and as a roar of artillery announces that New England's sons have come closer than ever to retaking Boston, the political significance of the Puritan errand reaches its climax. Joliffe's funereal summation accords with the Old South's bell and echoes the gray champion's announced demise of Andros: " 'The empire of Britain, in this ancient province, is at its last gasp to-night;—almost while I speak, it is a dead corpse' " (9:254). Yet Tiffany's final comment finds another implication in the symbolism: "the last festival that a British ruler ever had in the old province of Massachusetts Bay" (9:254).

From any meaningful, New England point of view, the war more or less concludes when Howe vacates the Province House and English revelry finally evacuates, purging Massachusetts of Old World impiety and restoring her to the ancient purity of its founders. These are the typological meanings in Joliffe and Tiffany's filiopietistic rendering of New England history. No doubt Joliffe has more exclusive interest in "liberty" than Tiffany, whose interest in democratic origins can draw upon Jeffersonian and Jacksonian democracy. Nevertheless, both these legend-mongers are at pains to suggest the longevity of New England history, as if the Puritan tradition were the only one relevant to New World experience, or as if the conflicting traditions of England that become influential in the eighteenth century were somehow merely idiosyncratic and godless interruptions in the holy Mission of the Puritan errand.

When Tiffany concludes, Hawthorne's narrator offers no endorsement of the legend's patriotic message. He simply acknowledges the "truth-telling accents" of Tiffany (9:255), which seems to leave open the possibility of a gulf between the manner and substance of the narrative. Still, Hawthorne does allow him an indirect analysis, which might easily, but mistakenly, lend the impression that he is not only naive but obtuse.[42] The narrator clearly finds great interest in the discrepancy between the imagined former splendor of the Province House and the common, mundane circumstances of the present. The legend of Puritan freedom-fighters has apparently made no impression on him. Perhaps he is all too familiar with such cant. In any event, his "gorgeous fantasies" are "woefully disturbed" by cigar smoke and the rattle of a spoon in a whiskey tumbler (9:255). An even worse reality greets his eyes: "the picturesque appearance of the panelled walls, that [of] the slate of the Brookline stage [,] was suspended against them, instead of the armorial escutcheon of some far-descended governor" (9:255). In these quotidian details, the narrator confronts the results of a leveling political democracy and seems to accept them. He pretends to belittle his effort, "to throw the spell of hoar antiquity" over a scene with which everyday life has "aught to do" (9:255), as if history and historical sensibility were finally irrelevant.

It nevertheless remains impossible to discount the narrator's sense of loss, and that loss can be measured precisely because English aesthetic values have not been sustained since the redcoats evacuated the Province House.[43] The partitioning of spacious rooms into cramped apartments, the application of "dingy paint" to paneled wainscoting, the introduction of a "bar in modern style" (9:240), and the recent imposition of other crude eyesores in the Province House suggest a contemporary democratic taste basically inferior to the eighteenth-century English aesthetic responsible for the original architecture and decor. If the narrator does not understand that his sense of loss issues from the onset of political independence and democracy, Hawthorne surely does as he leads the narrator out of the Province House. The narrator manages to transcend the democratic present by recovering one final "thrill of awe" when glancing at the unspoiled, "stately staircase, down which the procession of old governors had descended" (9:255). It is a crucial recovery of what seems personal, distinct, and superior in pre-Revolutionary times, as if the narrator needs to be so equipped before entering "the densest throng of Washington street" (9:255). Not quite consciously, the narrator struggles with two traditions in American history, one Puritan and the other English, and he finds himself dissatisfied with the complete survival of one and the truncation of the other. Perhaps he takes the Revolutionary founders and democracy too much for granted; and yet behind his distaste for contemporary cultural forms lies Hawthorne's regret over the extensive loss of an aesthetic tradition in England's expulsion from America.

"Edward Randolph's Portrait"

The frame of "Edward Randolph's Portrait" begins several months after that of "Howe's Masquerade," but the narrator connects the two tales by contrasting the dissatisfying architecture along Washington Street with the splendor of ante-Revolutionary times. Indeed, a hundred years earlier in Boston, Robin Molineux had seen precisely what the narrator here imagines: the "irregular, and often quaint architecture of the houses, some of

whose roofs were broken into numerous little peaks; while others ascended, steep and narrow, into a single point; and others again were
square; the pure milk-white of some of their complexions, the aged
darkness of others, and the thousand sparklings, reflected from bright
substances in the plastered walls of many" (9:221). Contemporary architecture in the "Legends" registers how one loss of England's influence defines
the generally low appearance and condition of urban life in nineteenth-
century America. In addition, we are encouraged to consider how something akin to English aristocratic taste accounts for the narrator's reaction to
contemporary democratic forms expressed in the prevalent architecture.

The sociopolitical dimension of his perspective emerges when the narrator says that, prior to the Revolution, "the buildings stood insulated and
independent, not, as now, merging their separate existences into connected
ranges, with a front of tiresome identity,—but each possessing features of
its own, as if the owner's individual taste had shaped it,—and the whole
presenting a picturesque irregularity, the absence of which is hardly com-
pensated by any beauties of our modern architecture" (9:256–57). The
cramped and enervating similarity of Boston's architecture suggests the
kind of uniformity in democracy that de Tocqueville found so paradoxical
among a people priding themselves upon their individualism. Not even the
Old South Church, whose historical and architectural distinction must cast
it in relief to the other buildings on the street, can alter the narrator's mood.
Indeed, the relentless moral tolled by the Old South's clock expresses only
another version of the regularity and sameness already depressing the
narrator. "'Only seven o'clock,' thought I. 'My old friend's legends will
scarcely kill the hours twixt this and bed-time'" (9:257). He is a bored
young man in a boring town; and, anticipating Hawthorne's self-projected
narrator in "The Custom-House," he looks to history as a kind of unction
for his spirit.

These opening remarks appear directly opposed to the narrator's earlier
stated purpose of seeking out Bela Tiffany in the Province House, "hoping
to deserve well of my country by snatching from oblivion some else un-
heard-of fact of history" (9:256). If the narrator expects "to deserve well"
of his country, the inset legend of Edward Randolph's portrait should
confirm the democratic principles of his contemporaries, who must necessarily include Hawthorne's readers in the *Democratic Review*. Yet how can
this potential confirmation be reconciled with the frame in which the
narrator clearly believes that English aristocracy offered a superior example of individuality and style before the Revolution than American democracy offers afterward?[44] Even if the narrator is a marginally unsuspecting
turncoat, his discontent cannot be taken casually. And unless the legend is
meant to instruct the narrator in a better keeping of democratic faith, as
much as it portends to endorse the biases of a democratic audience, then we
perhaps should be alert to the possibility that "to deserve well" of one's

country may not require giving lip service to its pieties. Thus, in preparing for yet another demonstration of conflict between England and America, we should be sensitive to hints of a more complex view than the patriotic and filiopietistic.

Tiffany's legend of Edward Randolph's portrait, set several years before "Howe's Masquerade," focuses on the controversy in 1770 over the replacement of provincial troops at Castle William with "a garrison of regular troops in the pay of the crown."[45] Once again, an event that might typify the cause for the Revolutionary War occupies Hawthorne's interest far more than the war itself.[46] Perhaps Hawthorne believed, somewhat like John Adams, that the Revolution had already been achieved in the minds of New Englanders prior to the eruption of violence in 1775.[47] The legend therefore concentrates on Lieutenant-Governor Hutchinson's decision to grant approval for the king's troops to occupy Castle William in place of the provincial garrison. Once British troops occupy New England soil, it will be only a short while before an event such as the Boston Massacre will lead to revolution, a causal argument suggested in the closing lines of the legend. As should be expected, the patriotic Tiffany casts Hutchinson as a Royalist villain for signing the orders, hence justly deserving a "peoples' curse" for siding with the king against New England's liberty (9:267). What compels notice, however, is the prolonged amount of time it takes Hutchinson to sign the orders; and it would seem that more than a dramatic literary ploy lies behind his lengthy hesitation.

As the legend opens, Hutchinson has the orders lying before him while he gazes "thoughtfully" at the "void blackness" of a portrait later revealed to be that of Edward Randolph (9:258). The unrest of the colony hardly warrants Hutchinson's apparent distraction: "It was scarcely a time for such inactive musing, when affairs of the deepest moment required the ruler's decision; for, within that very hour, Hutchinson had received intelligence of the arrival of a British fleet, bringing three regiments from Halifax to overawe the insubordination of the people" (9:258–59). If Hutchinson is the loyal English governor that he is supposed to be, why does he contemplate an indiscernible portrait? And why does he fail to sign, immediately, an order that he would seem unable to countermand?[48]

Tiffany does not help us find a satisfactory answer to these questions. His chief interest lies in the possible connection between Hutchinson and Randolph, the eighteenth-century figure who, as Francis Lincoln depicts him, " 'obtained the repeal of the first provincial charter, under which our forefathers had enjoyed almost democratic privileges' " (9:261–62). Hutchinson recognizes Randolph's " 'lot to taste the bitterness of popular odium,' " but he scoffs at the notion that a people's curse instilled a misery horribly revealed in Randolph's face when he died (9:262), regarding it as a fanciful exaggeration of Cotton Mather. Yet his ad hominem argument begs the question of whether Randolph deserves his dishonorable colonial reputation, and Hutchinson is more than adequately informed to appreciate some merit in New England's point of view. By the time of the Castle William crisis, Hutchinson had already published the first volume of *History of the Colony and Province of Massachusetts-Bay* (1764), in which he had shown how Randolph worked against native New England interests, how he made himself obnoxious during the Andros regime, and how he was more or less vilified by the people.[49] We should therefore suspect an uneasy squirm in Hutchinson's supercilious defense of Randolph. His assertion of a rational historicism over imaginative moral truth may in fact be Hutchinson's obstinate way of expelling a premonitory dread of a people's curse being revivified. He has already, manifestly, brooded upon Randolph's cursed fate as a possible prefiguration of his own.

As a native New Englander and reader of Cotton Mather, Hutchinson knows that in Puritan teleology and typology the errand of the Saints is a continuing one, magnifying in its intensity at certain moments in history. He has had firsthand acquaintance with the rebellious, king-resisting spirit of latter-day Puritans ever since he became lieutenant-governor in 1758. He has felt the radical effects of that spirit during the Stamp Act crisis when, as a result of his efforts to enforce the Act, his house was ransacked and a considerable number of historical documents, in addition to some of the manuscript of his history, were destroyed by a mob.[50]

Since the recall of Governor Bernard in 1769, Hutchinson has reconvened the colonial assembly dismissed by the former governor and has, for nearly a year, engaged in one dispute after another with the majority of its "patriotic" members. One of these disputes actually lies behind Hawthorne's tale. Prior to Bernard's departure, a conflict arose over quartering approximately one thousand of the king's troops at several locations in Boston, as well as at Castle William.[51] Hutchinson must have recognized the implications, for he later admits that the colonial opposition to accommodating the troops "was not only unpleasing and troublesome to the governor, but it contributed much to prejudice the people, in general, against him."[52]

Hutchinson was consequently equipped with the experience and the sensitivity to realize that a renewed effort to quarter troops at Castle William would meet further colonial resistance and, this time, would result in prejudice against himself. Violence was not only possible but likely. Accordingly, whether for personal or political reasons, when General Gage wrote to Hutchinson asking for his estimate of the "expediency" of garrisoning troops at Castle William, Hutchinson "gave his opinion that it was not expedient." Nevertheless, by order of the king a few weeks later, Royal troops were sent to replace the provincial force at Castle William; and, by order of the secretary of state, Hutchinson was instructed "that he do not fail, so far as depends upon him, to carry the order into execution."[53] The mandate was clear, even though Hutchinson scrupled over the possible abrogation of colonial rights in the exchange.[54] He personally supervised the substitution of garrisons as quickly and quietly as possible, and then he met colonial spokesmen to discuss the fait accompli. The ensuing outburst was not what Hutchinson had foreseen and what he had tried to forestall through his wary methods. Still, when Hutchinson wrote about the episode, he highlighted its importance in what is surely the most terse paragraph in the *History:* "This was one of the most difficult affairs to manage, that happened during the lieutenant-governor's administration."[55]

He was really caught between personal belief and public duty. This awareness must figure into Hawthorne's initially presenting Hutchinson in a distracted state and then in an overly affected pose of resolve and action. As a crown-appointed official, he finally has no choice. People's curse or no, he must categorically take the position that " 'the rebuke of a king is more to be dreaded than the clamor of a wild, misguided multitude' " (9:263). It would seem better to force the moment to its crisis than to dodge it. Enough of legalistic maneuvering, evasion, and foot-dragging on the part of these disloyal colonials.[56] " 'It is time, after years of tumult, and almost rebellion, that his majesty's government should have a wall of strength about it' " (9:263). Out of torn allegiance and frustration over an order he does not personally approve, Hutchinson desperately resorts to the "show of strength" strategy of Andros in "The Gray Champion."

Nothing quite so disastrous as the Boston Rebellion might come of the regarrisoning of Castle William, but Hutchinson does know that he has been squeezed into complying with a serious political blunder. His bravado, so unlike the smugness of Howe, admits as much. So does his formality. As ready sympathizers to their kinsman, Alice Vane and Francis Lincoln are given no hint of Hutchinson's personal worry. Their entreaties simply receive the stiff and hard-headed response of the lieutenant-governor in the king's employ. Not even Lincoln's reminder that the loyalty of the people may still be intact—as when, in " 'brotherhood,' " they fought with British soldiers " 'side by side through the French war' " (9:263)—can penetrate his uncle's official veneer. Hutchinson decides on the exchange of troops, requires Lincoln (as captain of the provincial garrison) to be present in the evening for the ceremonial exchange, and hastily leaves the room.

The opening scene is not quite over, inasmuch as Alice Vane is privileged with a closing remark of extremely melodramatic gravity. Earlier, we have learned that she is an "ethereal creature, who, though a native of New England, had been educated abroad, and seemed not merely a stranger from another clime, but almost a being from another world (9:259). Whether her artistic taste and talent have anything to do with her other-worldliness, she is one of Hawthorne's earliest examples of an artist whose talent is essentially misplaced in America.[57] More than likely, "the rude atmosphere of New England had cramped her hand, and dimmed the glowing colors of her fancy" (9:259). Perhaps this dimming effect explains Alice's preliminary fascination with the blackened portrait of Edward Randolph. Once she hears the gothic fables associated with it and with the wretched manner of Randolph's death devolving from New England's curse, Alice is clearly scheduled to restore the portrait in some manner.[58] " 'Such arts are known in Italy,' " she says (9:261). Our interpretation of the legend, however, will hinge on whether any foreign agency is necessary to teach a good New Englander anything about magical powers, either divine or demonic.

For the restoration of the portrait, Alice may indeed require foreign techniques; but for the moral or spiritual aspect of the restoration, she has all the inherent qualities she needs. She has, "in spite of her foreign education, retained the native sympathies of a New England girl" (9:263). Acquainted as she is with the king-resisting spirit of New England history, Alice has imbibed the full import of the Puritan errand, both its beatific urge and its habit of uncovering the inhibiting work of the devil. If she possessed Hawthorne's irony, she would thoroughly represent her creator's understanding of the devil-pointing side of Puritan history. As it is, she duplicates Hawthorne's method well enough. Turning to the portrait of Edward Randolph before the first scene closes, Alice calls for all the satanic and gothic influence that Puritan epistemology could summon: " 'Come forth, dark and evil Shape!' cried she. 'It is thine hour!' " (9:264). Her plea seems a far cry from the expectations of frenzied citizens in "The Gray Champion," and yet both the psychological and typological effects will be virtually the same. The final purpose of her art, very unlike Hawthorne's but identical to that of Joliffe or Tiffany, will be to support the narrow biases of her Puritan heritage.

Hutchinson by no means resembles Andros, the specter of Catholicism associated with the Stuarts no longer figures in New England's fear of the mother country, the king's troops do not march in the streets, and so there is no dramatic need for a champion to intervene and to prevent the lieutenant-governor from signing the order to regarrison Castle William. Nevertheless, the closing scene of the legend resonates with ironic hints of how the Castle William episode, like the Boston Rebellion in "The Gray Champion," offers another example of the devil's meddling in the Puritan errand.[59] In "The Gray Champion," the Puritans see the British and the monarchy itself as the devil personified, while Hawthorne's irony suggests the champion's ties with Satan. In the present case, it only remains to be seen whether Alice Vane's summoning the demonic spirit of Edward Randolph will result in our accepting, any more than in "The Gray Champion," New England's identification of the devil's emissaries.

The sedate setting of Hutchinson's chamber in the Province House barely manages to tone down the passionate historical antagonism of the gathering in the closing scene. A few selectmen of Boston are there, "plain,

patriarchal fathers of the people, excellent representatives of the old puritanical founders" (9:264). Giving regenerated support to them is Francis
Lincoln, now formally designated the Captain of Castle William. Also
present are "members of the Council," clearly representing the Royalist (or
Loyalist) faction in the colony,[60] who are "richly dressed in white wigs, the
embroidered waistcoats and other magnificence of the time, and making a
somewhat ostentatious display of courtier-like ceremonial" (9:264). Accompanying this contingent is the major of the British army who will soon
replace Captain Lincoln and the provincial force. The contestants obviously hint at Roundheads and Cavaliers whom Hawthorne is so per-
sistently fond of evoking in revolutionary contests, and we cannot help
sensing a revivication of the English Civil War.

Hutchinson still has not signed the order, as if he must wait for one of the
selectmen to caution him, "'Think, sir, while there is yet time, that if one
drop of blood be shed, that blood shall be an eternal stain upon your
Honor's memory'" (9:265). For the moment, Hutchinson has forgotten
New England's curse upon Randolph. He therefore seems immune to the
insinuated bribe of his deserving "honorable mention" in a future patriotic
history of New England should he not sign the order (9:265). He has not
forgotten that his mansion has been sacked by a mob, or that a reactionary
mob mentality seems to prevail around Boston. In such circumstances, all
law-abiding citizens should want "'to flee for protection to the King's
banner'" (9:265).

But this law and order issue suddenly takes on deeper historical and
typological significance, and it does so through what appears as common
figurative language. The British major blurts out, "'The demagogues of
this Province have raised the devil, and cannot lay him again. We will
exorcise him, in God's name and the King's.'" Captain Lincoln responds:
"'If you meddle with the devil, take care of his claws!'" (9:265). The
essential dispute that brought on the English Civil War in 1642 has plainly
been revived. But from a Puritan or Bancroftian point of view, we are not
encouraged to wonder whose side is God really on or which party is in
league with the devil.

The patriarchal selectman cautions Captain Lincoln, "'let not an evil
spirit enter into your words.'" After all, God has seen His covenanted
people through previous trials, and He will no doubt do so again, which is
the apparent message of the selectman's continuing remarks: "'We will
strive against the oppressor with prayer and fasting, as our forefathers
would have done. Like them, moreover, we will submit to whatever lot a
wise Providence may send us,—always, after our own best exertions to
amend it'" (9:265–66). Except for the last phrase, it might well seem that
we have the renewed voice of mediation here—indeed, an echo of the
policy advocated by Bradstreet in "The Gray Champion." But in the concluding phrase, there echoes every indication that, once again, New En-

glanders will not "'accept patiently what the Lord will do in this matter'"
(9:12), as the lieutenant-governor readily perceives: "'And there peep
forth the devil's claws,' muttered Hutchinson, who well understood the
nature of Puritan submission" (9:266). What Hutchinson faces in the selectman's policy statement constitutes the threat of an Endicott, slightly
updated and softened by an eighteenth-century observance of decorum
and reason, but no less a menace for all that. Since Endicott's death in 1665,
Jeremiads had pronounced backsliding as the treacherous norm of New
England life; but when push comes to shove between England and the Bay
colony, latter-day Puritans rush to embrace the militant God of their fathers—and with Him, the devil. All of which brings us to Alice Vane's
unveiling of the portrait of Edward Randolph as a final means to dis-
courage her uncle from signing the order for regarrison.

Alice's restoration of the portrait, we must understand, does not reveal
Randolph as he may have been depicted by the original artist but solely as
he has been imagined after New England's "curse had wrought its influence
upon his nature" (9:267). Since the Puritan mind believes in the existence
of witches and the devil, New Englanders are able to find them, label them,
and then leave it to gossip and legend accumulated over the years for their
"acquiring an intenser depth and darkness of expression" (9:267). It is a
self-fulfilling practice, surely, but it is also very effective, even upon an
Enlightenment figure such as Hutchinson, who has previously contemplated the blackened portrait and who now sees the "'terrors of hell'"
revealed in the face of Randolph (9:267). Apparently, Hutchinson's meditations have resulted in the discovery that Randolph is indeed the "'blasted
wretch'" that Cotton Mather calls him (9:13).[61] Not for nothing, we realize,
does the blood of Cotton Mather flow in Hutchinson's veins (9:262). The
selectman's interpretation of the portrait, entirely predictable from a Puritan descendant habituated to reading the wonders of the visible and
invisible worlds, simply nudges Hutchinson to be further enticed by a
Puritan way of seeing: "'For some wise end . . . hath Providence scattered
away the mist of years that had so long hid this dreadful effigy'" (9:267).
Hutchinson is supposed to read the personal message of this providential
sign and mend his ways.

From his historical knowledge, from the comments of Alice Vane and
Francis Lincoln earlier in the day, and from the nudging of the selectman,
Hutchinson is actually set up not only *to see* the portrait but also to recognize that the hellish torments in its features result from Randolph's having
trampled on a people's rights and that an identical fate awaits him should
he sign the order. To be sure, he has no conscious insight into the motives
behind his manipulation. In fact he has enough rationality to charge the
manipulation to Alice: "'your painter's art—your Italian spirit of intrigue—your tricks of stage-effect'" (9:268). Yet neither Alice's betrayal
nor the gothic devices will cover Hutchinson's case.[62] If they could, we

should expect everyone on the scene to be equally affected by the portrait. But who, except for Hutchinson and the New England contingent, perceives the devilish aspect of the portrait? When Alice lifts the black veil concealing the apparently refurbished portrait, "An exclamation of surprise burst forth from every beholder" (9:266). But only Hutchinson's observation produces a "tone of horror" (9:266), while nothing of what the "British" faction sees is ever mentioned. Indeed, no reference to that faction exists. This omission is no mere oversight. Nor can it be fully explained in terms of aesthetic economy. Not everyone present is the kind of "beholder" Hutchinson has become.

Of the British contingent, only Hutchinson perceives the ghastly portrait and feels that it will drive him mad, because only Hutchinson is psychologically vulnerable to its analogical message and only he is a native New Englander on the verge of selling his birthright. The New Englanders on the scene, faithful Puritans all, immediately adjust to the undescribed portrait or to Hutchinson's response to it. What essentially takes place in "Edward Randolph's Portrait," I would argue, is the manner by which Puritanical evil, assumed by someone like the Reverend Hooper, is unveiled to show itself to someone like Goodman Brown, who believes he sees it. Hutchinson is beguiled into apprehending the devil and into accepting the power of latter-day Puritans to evoke the devil. The "native" New England part of him cannot be thoroughly expelled. From a native point of view, his heritage dictates his belief. As a descendant of Anne Hutchinson and as a kinsman of Cotton Mather, it is, as it were, in his blood to believe.

From Bela Tiffany's point of view, Hutchinson shakes off these influences and signs the order for the exchange of troops despite his opportunity to remain true to his heritage. As a result, he will suffer a worse fate than Randolph, as he realizes on his deathbed in England. It is far worse to be "choking with the blood of the Boston Massacre" (9:269), far worse to know on this side of the grave that one has failed to enlist in the steady march of the Saints toward liberty and democracy, the eighteenth-century version of the "city on a hill." Francis Lincoln, curiously present at his uncle's death (did he side with England after all?),[63] reinforces the power of New England to know and name the devil's advocate when he "perceived a likeness in [Hutchinson's] frenzied look to that of Edward Randolph" (9:269). Tiffany's closing question, then—"Did [Hutchinson's] broken spirit feel, at that dread hour, the tremendous burthen of a People's curse?" (9:269)—seems at least anti-climactic. What else could Hutchinson feel in a legend so patriotically contrived? He has been instructed to follow his native instincts; he has seen the devil of his fathers as a consequence of his failure to obey; and so, yes, he feels the curse—and, as an apostate native son, wholly deserves to.

However much Hutchinson may be a captive of both England and Massachusetts Bay,[64] there is no possibility of compromising with New

England's absolutist mentality. The natives will have matters their own way, either peacefully or, in the case of resistance, violently through mob action. The stupendous self-righteousness would seem too much for Hutchinson to bear. Thus he detects the "devil's claws" lurking beneath the surface of the selectman's policy of prayer and fasting and humiliation. The threat that New England will "amend" these acts of piety through its "best exertions" shows that nothing is really very different from the mentality that gave rise to the mob in "My Kinsman, Major Molineux." He therefore rebels against New England's presumption to divine guidance and the incipient mob mentality lurking in it. In terms of who will win the Revolutionary War and who will be made an anathema in that patriotic cause, Hutchinson probably should know better.[65] But in terms of a proper response to the dominant provinciality of the New England mind, Hutchinson comes about as close to a sensible, rational decision as we might imagine in the circumstances.

Bela Tiffany would certainly not agree. To him, all New Englanders of good conscience should offer prayers of thanksgiving for the righteousness of their ancestors' cause against the tyranny of England. In the end, therefore, the reader of "Edward Randolph's Portrait" must consider the displacement of English aristocrats by American democrats. If we sense a certain complacency in Tiffany's legend, we are probably attuned to Hawthorne's intent. For Tiffany's filiopietistic and anti-aristocratic message is told from the snug fireside on a stormy winter's night, a year after president Jackson leaves office, and it is stimulated by the alcohol from a hot whisky punch. Apparently, the ends do justify the means, especially when the heroes and villains seem so easy to distinguish. While the details of the legend are new, they are submitted in support of what had become by the time of their telling a common article of faith. Yet when we consider the earlier aristocratic leanings of the narrator and his response to the legend, we correctly see a discrepancy between the frame and Tiffany's tale, which lends further credibility to Hawthorne's irony in the legend itself. The narrator asks Tiffany if the portrait of Randolph still survives in the Province House. He wants to see it, literalistic dullard as he seems to be. Like Hutchinson, he has not been properly schooled in keeping better faith with New England's pieties. As we leave him, he is wending his way home, alone, through snow drifts, left out in the cold. This condition, whether he knows it or not, more than adequately suggests the proper response to self-serving, patriotic interpretations of history.

"Lady Eleanore's Mantle"

If the narrator cannot be cured of some high-toned ways of thinking after "Howe's Masquerade" and "Edward Randolph's Portrait," perhaps he

needs stronger medicine for what seemingly ails him. As "Lady Eleanore's
Mantle" opens, the narrator appears more attracted than ever to the taste-
ful style of the former English inhabitants of the Province House. He
credits Bela Tiffany and himself with drawing attention to the old mansion
through publication of the previous two tales, "almost as effectually . . . as if
we had thrown down the vulgar range of shoe-shops and dry-good stores,
which hides its aristocratic front from Washington street" (9:271). The
image seems innocent enough, but it cannot quite conceal the wish to
destroy the undistinguished and indistinguishable democratic buildings of
modern Boston. Yet his flirtation with the English aristocratic past in America more prominently surfaces in the feast Thomas Waite has arranged in
gratitude for his increase in business. The narrator responds to the occasion by imagining sumptuous feasts given by Royal governors in the eighteenth century, with their "bewigged, and powdered, and embroidered
dignitaries, who erst banquetted at the gubernatorial table, and now sleep
within their armorial tombs on Copp's Hill, or round King's Chapel"
(9:272). Waite's banquet falls short of the "real thing," but it lends enough
vicarious aura of luxury to satisfy a would-be democrat with uncertain
aristocratic tastes or pretensions.

Joining Tiffany and the narrator in their feast is an old man whose
recollections reach back to pre-revolutionary events and "whose attachment
to royalty, and to the colonial institutions and customs that were connected
with it, had never yielded to the democratic heresies of aftertimes. The
young queen of Britain has not a more loyal subject in her realm—perhaps
not one who would kneel before her throne with such reverential love—as
this old grandsire whose head has whitened beneath the mild sway of the
Republic, which still, in his mellower moments, he terms a usurpation"
(9:272). The allegiance of this seemingly anachronistic figure obviously
harmonizes with the narrator's aristocratic conception of the feast.
Hawthorne may very well stop "just short" of "explicitly adopting, in politics and narrative technique, the 'Tory' point of view,"[66] and yet, in going
that far, he alerts careful readers to the danger of taking for granted a
democratic meaning in any of the "Legends." The appearance of an old
Loyalist in the frame of "Lady Eleanore's Mantle" is perhaps the most overt
caution thus far in the series.

Although his "obstinate," monarchical "prejudices" (9:272) are extreme,
the old Loyalist resembles the narrator in his being lonely and feeling out
of step with the times. No self-righteous isolate, he seeks human contact,
though it might lead to accepting "a cup of kindness" from such unlikely
partisans as "Oliver Cromwell or John Hancock; to say nothing of any
democrat now upon the stage" (9:272–73). Displaced himself, the narrator
drolly hints at causes for the old Loyalist's displacement in Anglo-American
history: Cromwell, the English revolutionary Puritan who deposed a King;
Hancock, the colonial leader who helped in the successful revolution

against the crown; and Martin Van Buren, the "democrat now upon the stage." The old Loyalist looks to England, to the continuation of the monarchy in the person of the "young queen," as if he expects a restoration on this side of the Atlantic. One is therefore prompted to reflect on the wrenching mixture of affection, hope, and loss he must have felt when news of Victoria's coronation reached America, only two or three months prior to the frame's setting—and thus a mere few weeks prior to Hawthorne's composition of the story.

During the summer of 1838, when the depressing effects of Van Buren's banking and monetary policies were dominating both the domestic and foreign sections of American papers, news of Victoria's coronation on 28 June took precedence as soon as London papers arrived in New York and Boston in late July.[67] Boston papers did not go as far as the New York *Hearld,* which, on 25 July, featured a full front page of illustrations and a lengthy account of events throughout the coronation day, and then, on 27 July, featured a special report by an American correspondent. Yet Boston papers were neither as technologically equipped to provide illustrations on short notice nor as advanced in their layouts. In almost all cases, their formats comprised a front page of customary ads, with news, poetry, and occasional fiction occupying the subsequent three pages.[68] More often than not, the daily papers devoted nearly a full page to the coronation.[69] Even a belated weekly did as much.[70] Outlying papers followed suit.[71] Obviously, there was abundant material for Anglophiles and Anglophobes alike. Yet the Anglophobic view is not really represented. The accounts, almost exclusively quoted from London sources, are uniformly laudatory and, with one exception, include positive expressions of editors in prefatory notes.[72] Overall, then, Hawthorne (in Boston at the time) and his old Tory would scarcely have missed the full and widespread treatment of the coronation in the papers and, later, in papers sent up from New York.

Despite these American tributes to England's monarchy, there was some commentary to suggest that citizens of the republic were in no danger of giving up their democratic principles.[73] Hawthorne's principled readers in the *Democratic Review* would have taken the jocular, deferential hint of Hawthorne's narrator to view the old Loyalist as simply quaint, mere window-dressing for the legend that follows. But this is surely not the case. Why does a craftsman as careful and clever as Hawthorne choose to introduce the old Loyalist at this particular point in the series? The timing undoubtedly facilitates the old man's narration of the last legend, so that "Lady Eleanore's Mantle" and "Old Esther Dudley" can be told in one sitting, as if in counterpoint.[74] All the same, something else is involved in Hawthorne's strategy.

While "Edward Randolph's Portrait" backs up five years from "Howe's Masquerade," "Lady Eleanore's Mantle" goes back another fifty years to the smallpox epidemic of 1721. Historical progression has now been radically reversed, and we have to wonder how any event as remote and seemingly nonpolitical as the smallpox episode can have any significant relation to the Revolutionary War setting in the first and last legends. Bela Tiffany's account of Lady Eleanore certainly offers no clear explanation for a causal relation, but the old Loyalist functions as a reminder of the Revolutionary context from which, superficially, "Edward Randolph's Portrait" and "Lady Eleanore's Mantle" have withdrawn. His "own actual reminiscences went back to the epoch of Gage and Howe, and even . . . Hutchinson" (9:272). The association of Hancock with the old Loyalist further suggests that the Revolution is the manifest subject of the "Legends" and that the causal relation we habitually expect to find in history does in fact exist. Further, the mention of Cromwell among all the Revolutionary War figures must necessarily enlarge the context of revolution. Obvious or not, something about the Puritans and the English Civil War will have a bearing on the legend of Lady Eleanore and, in turn, of the American Revolution. The prospect should make us wary once again of complacent democratic pieties.

Bela Tiffany presents the legend of Lady Eleanore from a democratic bias, with the addition of "suitable adornments" from the narrator (9:273). In outline, the legend reveals an allegory on pride.[75] Lady Eleanore Rochcliffe, having lost her family in England, comes to Boston to place herself under the guardianship of her distant relative, Governor Shute. She has a "harsh, unyielding pride, a haughty consciousness of her hereditary and personal advantages," which amount to a "monomania" (9:273–74). Before she can step from her coach, Jervase Helwyse, who had fallen in love with Lady Eleanore in London, prostrates himself beside the coach for her use as a footstool. She complies with his self-abasement, placing a foot on his back and a hand in that of Governor Shute. The moment bristles with future democratic significance: "never, surely, was there an apter emblem of aristocracy and hereditary pride, trampling on human sympathies and the kindred of nature" (9:276).

As if wanting her to atone for this emblem, Jervase presents Lady Eleanore with a cup of communion wine several days later at a magnificent ball given in her honor. Taking a " 'sip of this holy wine' " will show that Lady Eleanore has not withdrawn " 'from the chain of human sympathies' " (9:280). Unlike the old Loyalist in the frame, Lady Eleanore refuses the cup, and then, shortly after some wine spills on her mantle, Jervase frantically entreats her to get rid of the garment before it is too late. She also refuses this plea. Subsequently, the smallpox breaks out, first striking the aristocrats who attended the ball and then invading the lower orders of society. Bostonians interpret the mantle as the agent of the dreaded disease, symbol of Lady Eleanor's pride. Jervase has a final confrontation with the lady, now stricken with the ugly marks of the pox, and he takes the mantle in order that it be burned, along with an effigy of Lady Eleanore, in a mob scene concluding the legend. Rumor has it that, after this ritual by fire, the pestilence wanes.

Lady Eleanore's arrival in Boston coincides with the tolling bell of the Old South Church for a funeral. As in "Howe's Masquerade," this tolling forecasts the death of something English and decidedly non-Puritan. Two similar forecasts issue from a Doctor Clarke, "famous champion of the popular party" (9:275). After Lady Eleanore treads on Jervase, Clarke remarks: "'I could well nigh doubt the justice of the Heaven above us, if no signal humiliation overtake this lady'" (9:276). Later, at the ball, as much out of place at that affair as Colonel Joliffe is at Howe's masquerade (and perhaps equally as knowing about events to come), Clark prophesizes: "'Wo to those who shall be smitten by this beautiful Lady Eleanore'" (9:282). The lady herself confirms Clarke's wish to trust in God's justice when Jervase is confronted by her "blasted face": "'The curse of Heaven hath striken me, because I would not call man my brother, nor woman my sister. I wrapt myself in PRIDE as in a MANTLE, and scorned the sympathies of nature'" (9:287)

Despite the egalitarian/democratic message patently evident in the allegory's formula, the presence of nagging details inconsistent with both the message and the formula argue against our accepting the colonists as innocent victims of English aristocratic pride. Lady Eleanore, for example, does step on Jervase, but, as she is perfectly aware, the young man's obsequious behavior deserves nothing less: "'When men seek only to be trampled upon, it were a pity to deny them a favor so easily granted—and so well deserved'" (9:276).[76] The colonial witnesses to the act are scarcely less culpable than Jervase, even if not so extreme in their abjectness. They "were so smitten with [Lady Eleanore's] beauty, and so essential did pride seem to the existence of such a creature, that they gave a simultaneous acclamation of applause" (9:276). Thirty years after the inauguration of the new charter and ten years before the onset of the Great Awakening, these Puritan descendants have willingly conceded to the visible attractions and superiority of English aristocracy and, implicitly, the royal court. Their ancestors might as well have stayed home instead of migrating to New England's Canaan. Endicott might never have walked the narrow path of King-resistance. Clearly, the echoes of sixty years of Jeremiads warning against a backsliding people have not been heeded and might almost as soon fade out.

If Lady Eleanore has too much pride, Jervase and the Bostonians of 1721 initially seem to have too little. They have indeed been smitten by the splendor of rank and privilege; and in this lowly condition, which they seem less unable than unwilling to correct, they expose, by any conventional measure of their own, a state of sin almost unprecedented in New England history. It is one thing to be under the subjection of an external pride but quite another to be so flattered by and to pay such tribute to it that pride becomes a possession of one's own. The curse in the first instance begins to look less perilous than its being welcomed in the second. Which is sin and which is punishment become questions too snarled and problematic to answer with any assurance.[77] Before the last echoes of the Jeremiad utterly fade out, however, one certainty does remain. If the sinful state of an untoward generation is not in itself punishment enough, a visitation of divine retribution can be expected.[78]

Added to the scourge Lady Eleanore deserves for her pride, New England deserves as much or more for indulging in that pride. The logic is that of a convenanted people in decline, exemplified by repeated historical instances in which New Englanders interpreted natural disasters as signs of God's displeasure and then appointed special days for fasting and prayer as evidence of repentance and of intent to reform. Conviction of their sinfulness was essential. In "Lady Eleanor's Mantle," however, the colonists lack such conviction. They are curiously blind to their lapse into aristocratic pride, which suggests on the one hand the dangerous extent of their failure at Puritan piety but accounts on the other for their virulent reaction to Lady Eleanore once the pox begins to take its toll on them. Within conventional Puritanism, New Englanders would certainly deserve the pox for not having suffered and resisted the influence of pride. In this sense, then, the pestilence would amount to a double humiliation.

Unlike "Howe's Masquerade" and "Edward Randolph's Portrait," however, the legend strikes no resounding notes of the Jeremiad or national convenant. A faint echo can be heard in Doctor Clarke's prophesy, but it applies to Lady Eleanore alone. Nor is there a note sounded on the democratic typology so evident in the previous two legends. The silence on these matters, as well as the absence of any New England clergyman, is indeed suspicious. Conceivably, the silence is meant to alert us to something else—to the possibility that, while the theology and politics of the Jeremiad and errand are by no means insignificant, the actual history of the smallpox epidemic does not largely concern itself with either except by way of some unusual difference.

As a matter of historical record, which Hawthorne knew, prominent members of the Boston clergy fundamentally underplayed the rhetoric of the Jeremiad during the smallpox epidemic. Rather than concentrating on the pox as a retribution for a people's sin, the clergy, led by Cotton Mather, shifted its interest to focus on a recently proposed method of inoculation to ward off the full effects of the pox. Boston's medical men, except for Zabdiel Boylston, refused to sanction or to practice the method, and eventually, through their influence, all ranks of society rose up against it.[79] That the clergy and physicians should in effect exchange roles over the issue of inoculation may seem as odd to us as to a writer of one of Hawthorne's sources for the smallpox episode: "The clergy, who were generally in favor of inoculation, supported it by arguments drawn from medical science; while the physicians, who were as much united against it, opposed it with arguments which were chiefly theological, alleging that it was presumptuous in man to inflict disease on man, that being the prerogative of the Most High."[80] Odder yet may seem the response of most Bostonians. Without taking the lead of their ministers, a considerable number of them were reluctant to cast off the Jeremiad view of disasters.[81] Several contributors to James Franklin's Boston *Courant* called the epidemic a divine judgment "on the country's provoking evils of profaneness, idleness and luxury."[82] Hawthorne was familiar with this view and with the anti-ministerial, or anti-Mather, reactions of the populace. In the treatment of the smallpox episode in *The Whole History of Grandfather's Chair*, grandfather says, "Many, who thought themselves more pious than their neighbors, contended, that, if Providence had ordained them to die of the small-pox, it was sinful to aim at preventing it." And some "flatly affirmed, that the Evil One had got possession of Cotton Mather, and was at the bottom of the whole business." After all, people's memories were not so short that they failed to recollect how Mather "had led them astray, in the old witchcraft delusion" (6:102).

If Mather saw inoculation as a homeopathic procedure to afflict a small measure of God's judgment upon a people by way of warning against the full wrath they no doubt deserved,[83] the people of Boston failed to perceive the subtlety. One is inclined to believe, considering how acrimonious and spiteful the "war of words" became in the *Courant* and numerous pamphlets, that the greater number of Bostonians would still have taken Mather to be a quackish intruder and have held to the view that inoculation itself was either a dangerous means to spread the pox or an interference with God's providential design.[84]

Prominent as Boston's ministers were throughout the epidemic, they did not appear in the guise of old Testament prophets familiar to their flocks in previous crises. In their efforts to defend inoculation, especially through the "war of words," they alienated most citizens. The result, as Perry Miller describes it, was that "What had been risked and what had not been regained was the covenant conception itself. Spokesmen for that national philosophy could never again authoritatively contend that what the people suffered was caused by their sins and that repentance alone, as directed by hierophants, could relieve them. The clergy themselves had introduced another method, and so brought a fatal confusion into the very center of their mystique."[85] A corollary result, as Hawthorne shows in *The Whole History of Grandfather's Chair*, was outright disrespect and even violence leveled at ministers, the bomb thrown into Mather's house being the most notorious case (6:104).

One implication of this diminution in ministerial leadership and of the guiding conception of the national convenant is present in "Lady Eleanore's

Mantle." A secular figure such as Doctor Clarke, political "champion of the popular party," fills the vacancy. In his *History*, Thomas Hutchinson presents a physician named John Clarke, who was Speaker of the House at the time of the epidemic. Clarke was an associate of Elisha Cooke, Jr., the principal fomentor of interference with Governor Shute and England's colonial policies.[86] No Winthrop who believes that the basic ills of society are internal, the essential sins or limitations of the citizens themselves, Hawthorne's Clarke looks to England as the major threat. This outlook was also present in the smallpox epidemic in 1721, as Hawthorne was aware. The method of inoculation Cotton Mather initiated in Boston was one observed in Turkey and written up in two separate articles of the *Transactions* of the Royal Society.[87] At approximately the same time that Mather and Boylston began experimenting with his homeopathic method in Boston, Lady Mary Wortley Montagu had her daughter inoculated by the identical method in London, and accounts of this appeared in Boston newspapers.[88] Among the arguments in the press against inoculation were those aimed at these foreign sources.[89] Within an allegory so transparently opposed to English aristocracy as Bela Tiffany presents it, we may have the seminal idea for Lady Eleanore in the person of Lady Wortley.

The method of inoculation subscribed to by Lady Wortley and advanced by Mather was not the Jenner method discovered in 1796, in which cowpox was used as the inoculating agent. In 1721, veins of the inoculee were actually opened for the introduction of pus from a suffering victim. If this procedure helps to explain why many Bostonians legitimately worried that it would spread the disease, it also suggests the reason for the reaction against a "foreign" practice, especially as it was advocated by supposed or presumptuous leading citizens. The reaction against Cotton Mather was often expressed in satires and diatribes on his vanity for appending D.D. and F.R.S. to his name on title pages and public communications. The F.R.S.—Fellow of the Royal Society—was particularly singled out because it was a foreign honor of which Mather was indubitably proud.[90] Although the clergy generally had suffered a loss of respect for a number of years and Mather's reputation had been noticeably edging toward eclipse, this latest expression of resentment was by far the most denigrating.[91] More widespread examples of Anglophobia developed later in the 1720s, specifically during the interim of Governor Shute's abrupt departure from America and William Burnet's arrival in Boston for his abbreviated term as governor in 1728. By this time, New England ministers had recovered some of their former prestige, but not before Cotton Mather, speaking for a number of ministers, asked the government to convene the first synod since the new charter, the appeal being approved by the Council but denied by the elected members of the General Court.[92] The secular world was growing. Not even the Great Awakening could interrupt its growth for long.

What Hawthorne registers in "Lady Eleanore's Mantle" is probably the last time in New England history when latter-day Puritan ministers, calling upon the theocratic conventions of the Jeremiad and covenant, could have summoned influence weighty enough to restore a declining people to the original errand. The difference between this possibility and the legend's narrow concern with English aristocratic pride shows at once how necessary and yet how hopeless such a restoration really was. With too few exceptions, the people would not be inoculated to save themselves, not when the medical effort was being led by the clergy who, as social superiors, were advocating a foreign technique for immunization and cure. Instead, as the legend insinuates, they would be encouraged to rebel from political motives held by such persons as Clarke, whose chief interest is the leveling of aristocratic pride.

Clarke's wish, of course, is granted, and then some. For the pox *is* the great leveler.[93] It afflicts the high and low, proud and meek without discriminating. And during an intermediary phase of the epidemic, the pox-as-leveler seems almost to serve the good office that Camus would later extol in *The Plague:* "it compelled rich and poor to feel themselves brethren, then" (9:283). But this fraternity is short-lived, as the epidemic spreads and claims even more lives. "There is no other fear so horrible and unhumanizing, as that which makes a man dread to breathe Heaven's vital air, lest it be poison, or to grasp the hand of a brother or friend, lest the gripe [grip] of the pestilence should clutch him" (9:283). The dead become, "enemies of the living" and are buried unceremoniously (9:283). Familiar leaders and procedures for maintaining social order are abandoned. "The public councils were suspended, as if mortal wisdom might relinquish its devices, now that an earthly usurper had found its way into the ruler's mansion" (9:283). The result Winthrop warned against finally does occur, the degeneration from aristocracy to democracy to mobocracy. In the mob scene that concludes the legend, a less jingoistic audience than Hawthorne's would have recognized a forecast of a leveling plague of more recent date, the Reign of Terror.

In "Lady Eleanore's Mantle," pox-as-pride moves by degrees to pox-as-revolution.[94] The English Civil War once again becomes a paradigm that recurs like a bad dream. Major Molineux is no more a scapegoat king than Lady Eleanore. She arrives in Boston under escort of anachronistic "cavaliers" (9:274), her bearing likened unto a queen,[95] her mantle symbolizing the monarchical robe of state; and her effigy eventually gets burned in another symbolic regicide. The reference to Cromwell in connection to the old Loyalist in the frame makes the intimations of the English Civil War and the regicide of Charles I unmistakable. Each of the "Legends" thus far agrees on this cross-cultural relationship of revolution.

All of this proleptic revolutionary activity goes forward without the guiding light of the clergy and includes no colonial pretense to comply with the national convenant. The theology and violence of the dominant Puritan tradition headed by Endicott have been torn apart, leaving only violence. The danger of this split was always present, as Hawthorne's seventeenth-century tales were at pains to indicate. By 1721, during a period of change, unrest, and the pox itself, the colonists at large seem so utterly confused over their allegiances to native and English institutions that the only predictable outcome will be social madness.

Madness is in fact a central concern of the legend, represented in three almost inseparable stages: the division of sympathy and pride, the state of pride-as-pox, and the condition of pox-as-revolution. Herein are contained the full symptoms of Boston's infection, latent when the legend begins because each or a combination of each had become an actual or symbolic part of Puritan history in both America and England. Lady Eleanore has the first symptom as indisputably as she lacks the third. Diagnosis remains uncertain in the case of the second. She does contract the pox, but it seems unfitting to discover ready-made disease in her pride when that rigorous logic belongs to Puritan New England's tradition of self-diagnosis. She may come to accept something very much like the Jeremiad yoking of pride and pox, but that moral lesson is not the only, or even the most significant, element of the legend. Instead of Lady Eleanore, then, we should look elsewhere for the full embodiment of the plague that is madness, whether duly chastened or not, and the only candidate who can be both vehicle and tenor of all its symptoms is Jervase Helwyse, the self-proclaimed "banner-bearer of the pestilence" (9:285).

According to Doctor Clarke, Jervase fell in love with Lady Eleanore while serving as "'secretary to our colonial agent in London,'" but "'her scorn has driven him mad'" (9:276). The response of Captain Langford to this information, however, arrives much closer to the source of Jervase's madness: "'He was mad so to aspire'" (9:276). Not that Jervase is deranged because he failed to recognize his inferiority to Lady Eleanore and thus keep his distance, which is Langford's proud meaning, but because he was so susceptible to her English pride that he ignored the traditional Jeremiad values of his native land. Perhaps her pride did not seem so alien or extreme in proud old England; and there was, after all, her extraordinary personal beauty to lend attraction to the pride in the first place. But from the vantage of his Puritan ancestors, beauty itself should have warned Jervase against being infected by the aristocratic lady. The women of Babylon also had their attractions, since the devil always comes in the guise most alluring to one's weakness. In this regard, we should no doubt spell Jervase's last name to read as it pertains to his London fall—Hell-wise—as Colacurcio has suggested.[96]

Back in Boston, however, Jervase demonstrates a divided response to Lady Eleanore. Upon her arrival, he initially bows to her superiority while

Bostonians look on in attitudes flirting with that pride that is supposed to be England. But he soon becomes mindful that he now walks on the turf of his grandsires and hence, at the ball, he offers her the wine from a communion cup. The gesture surely has its high moment. Lady Eleanore has already rebuffed everyone at the gala except four representative male attendants.[97] No reader would want to deny that she needs to share a cup of sympathy with everyone present and thereby join that magnetic chain of humanity so valued by Hawthorne. Yet how, given her allegorical role, can Lady Eleanore possibly accept the cup? She *is* England. Will England readily lower itself to accept such a cup from offspring willing and even anxious to imitate the habits of the mother country? Or will England, after all the strife with Puritans in the seventeenth century, drink from a cup belonging to the Old South Church, scarcely a better reminder than a sword of that very strife?[98] Why bother? As suggested by the presence of an Episcopal clergyman at the ball, the English Church is thriving in Boston—Puritan children have returned to the fold from which they never officially separated.[99] Why encourage them to retrieve the convenant values they have compromised? Seen in this light, Jervase's offering is absurd, as mad as his infatuation with Lady Eleanore.

In refusing the cup, Lady Eleanore in effect informs New Englanders that the problem of pride is not so much hers as theirs. What, she finally intimates, are they going to do about it? She is unaware of course that in New England's conventional terms pride is pox. There can be no flirtation with the disease, which is to say that there can be no immunity produced by inoculation. Once a little pride is introduced into the system, contagion will be let loose. Still, noticeably, English pride is not the specific problem in and of itself, as long as it is confined to England. In New England, however, pride becomes the vehicle of a self-infected epidemic whose distemper will seek revenge on its putative source. Lady Eleanore has no way of anticipating the moral implicit in this rationale when she refuses the communion cup. Nevertheless, Jervase does warn her when he exclaims, " 'It may not yet be too late! Give the accursed garment to the flames!' " (9:281). In his madness, he has apparently come to the ball in the double guise of conciliator and avenger.

Jervase is the crucial figure to understand in the legend, despite the political connotations lying behind the figure of Doctor Clarke.[100] It is he who is most torn between sympathy and pride, most infected by pride-as-pox, and most symbolically representative of pox-as-revolution. As the tenor of insanity and pestilence, Jervase is also the chief suspect as vehicle. His actions and language at the ball are highly suspicious, particularly when we think of him as the scorned lover. He would seem to have more specific knowledge than clairvoyance that Lady Eleanore's mantle is in some way infected with pox, and thus he pleads for her to burn it. Her refusal simply

draws from him a saddened prophecy further indicating his special knowledge: " 'Alas, lady! . . . We must meet shortly, when your face may wear
another aspect' " (9:281).

After the pox reaches epidemic proportions, Bostonians take Jervase's
cue, contriving the story that "the contagion had lurked in that gorgeous
mantle. . . . Its fantastic splendor had been conceived in the delirious brain
of a woman on her death-bed, and was the last toil of her stiffening fingers,
which had interwoven fate and misery with its golden threads" (9:284).
This "dark tale" (9:284) is an obvious fabrication,[101] as much a product of
hindsight as the belated opinions of Lady Eleanore's having seemed "wild
and unnatural," revealing a "feverish flush and alternate paleness of coun-
tenance" at the ball (9:278), as if at that event she were already suffering
the onset of the pox. But prior to news that the pox has erupted, the people
have believed more accurately that the mantle "had been wrought by the
most skilful artist in London" (9:274) and that Lady Eleanore's appearance
at the ball was one of "exceeding beauty" (9:278). Nonetheless, super-
stitious rumors always manage to achieve their malicious ends, especially
when directed by a frenzied people who never do acknowledge their
complicity in pride. Even Jervase seems to believe one of them. When he
enters Lady Eleanore's chamber, he sees the mantle and soliloquizes:
" 'there hangs her mantle, on which a dead woman embroidered a spell of
dreadful potency' "(9:286).

Aside from the apparently insurmountable argument that Jervase does
not literally have the pox, this last utterance would seem to clear him of
setting the disease in motion. He believes someone else is responsible.
Nevertheless, he is decidedly insane at this point, a " 'wretched lunatic,' " as
Doctor Clarke concludes (9:285). He has definitely come to the Province
House to worship Lady Eleanore once again, expecting (strangely—but
then, madly) to find her beauty unmarked by the pox. Thus he has entirely
forgotten his prophecy at the ball. It is therefore no surprise that in his
insanity and loss of memory he should fix upon the macabre tale of a dying
witch who has woven disease into the mantle. Surely he could not deface
the image of his love.

Yet that is precisely what he seems to do. Beginning in his allegorical role
as the scorned lover of pride and continuing in his embodiment of New
England's conception of pride-as-pox, Jervase is the only sure link to Lady
Eleanore, whose pride must be lowered to suit thematic demands on
several levels: moral, political, allegorical, and historical. Through a transformation of all these levels to the literal, it would appear that he communi-
cates his own disease to Lady Eleanore, thereby making manifest the
Jeremiad vision that no one wants to apply to himself. Jervase does not
communicate the pox to the mantle through the spilled communion
wine,[102] for if the wine were infected, he would not be "[pressing] the silver
cup of wine upon" Lady Eleanore while at the same moment pleading with

her to burn the mantle in an effort to save her (9:281). Instead, Jervase more plausibly infects the mantle by touching it. At the ball, we should notice, Lady Eleanore is unaware of his abject presence until she becomes "conscious that some one touched her robe" (9:279). This seemingly inconsequential contact acquires resonance when the four men attending Lady Eleanore—Captain Langford, the Virginia planter, the Episcopal clergyman, and the private secretary of Governor Shute—seize Jervase and throw him out. Thereafter, the logic is clear: these four aristocrats "were the foremost on whom the plague-stroke fell" (9:283). Since the Province House servants also touch Jervase, we need look no further for a logical explanation for the pox first striking Boston aristocracy.

Jervase's peculiar immunity to the ravages of pox does not preclude his being the primary carrier. More design is at work than Jervase realizes when he declares, "'Death will not touch me, the banner-bearer of the pestilence'" (9:285). And more irony is at play than Doctor Clarke realizes when he provides the rationale for Jervase's immunity: "'Madness, as I have noted, has that good efficacy, that it will guard you from contagion'" (9:286). While his madness may exempt Jervase from the pustules and scars of pox, it ironically exposes his advanced case of pride which, morally, instigates the original contagion every bit as much as does that of Lady Eleanore. His is the dangerously unconscious form of pride that must seek out and destroy the rationalized cause for its existence. Thus Jervase simply projects back upon Lady Eleanore the very Jeremiad conception of pride-as-pox in which he is unwittingly implicated.

No doubt Lady Eleanore is a worthy recipient of New England's projection, but only up to a certain point. The most staggering irony in the legend is that she alone becomes conscious of pride and acknowledges some proximate version of the Jeremiad, at least as it applies to herself. "'The curse of Heaven hath striken me,'" she tells Jervase, "'and therefore has nature made this wretched body the medium of a dreadful sympathy. You are avenged—they are all avenged—Nature is avenged. . . .'" (9:287). Would that Bostonians had followed her lead to discover in it an *exemplum* of their own most pressing condition and need, but her humble testimony and atonement are lost on them. Rather than adhering to their moral tradition and looking to themselves as the first step toward expiation, they blame Lady Eleanore's aristocratic pride as the sole cause and consequence of affliction. Thus the lady learns New England's best lesson on individual depravity and God's impatient wrath, while the natives madly ignore it and go on to stage a proto-revolutionary revolt. For them, the enemy is now strictly external or, better, is England alone.

There is on the one hand nothing really new in this self-righteousness. In Hawthorne's Puritan drama, New England always knows its enemies are of the devil and responds to them according to the narrow presumption of its sanctity. The finger of guilt points at someone else—Maypolers, Quakers,

Indians, and, above all, England—except during the witchcraft episode when the confusion caused by internal finger-pointing effectively results in a rededication to discover outside agents. On the other hand, however, something new does emerge in "Lady Eleanore's Mantle." The Puritan treatment of social or theological deviants in the seventeenth- and eighteenth-century tales discussed thus far is conducted more or less in harmony with the covenant, errand, and Jeremiad. We may not agree with the sociology and theology lying behind the impetus to persecute the Maypolers, antinomians, or Quakers, but we can surely understand how that activity fits into a rigorously integrated system that defines a society and holds it together. Coherence and meaning and purpose in society do finally matter to most people, and yet these are precisely the elements missing in "Lady Eleanore's Mantle." The covenant, errand, and Jeremiad have been forsaken for the pursuit of secular politics.

Such a shift might not seem all that bad if one prefers to wear democratic blinders and only wants to see 1776 waiting ahead, but Hawthorne's essential point is how the fallacy of first assuming that the Revolution is wholly sanctified leads to the further error of reductively finding proleptic events in history to give it causal justification. These are the very fallacies of Bela Tiffany, who might just as well be George Bancroft or any other democratic/Whig historian of Hawthorne's time. Through daring ironies and contradictions, Hawthorne shatters the tidy democratic formula of Tiffany. Lady Eleanore's aristocratic pride may be leveled in 1721, as England's will be in 1783. Yet, as we have seen, the lady is no more alone in possessing pride than she is in suffering a scourge for the possession. Her story, however, comes to an end with her owning up to a communitarian ideal which, although perhaps more resonant of the nineteenth century, is supposed to echo the covenant's binding integuments of love first spoken by Winthrop aboard the *Arbella*. This confession properly concludes the democratic allegory. The rest is excess, but in that excess lies the logic of Hawthorne's daring indictment of a revolutionary mob, which ignores the conventional rhetoric of the Jeremiad and blames England for its own ills, and which denies the integuments of love, in whose meaning alone resides any hope for a society to rally together in times of peril. For a moment, back at the ball, Jervase (and through him, New England) seemed to understand the need for the bond of sympathy and love. Yet, as it turns out, he was only paying lip service to the covenant's rhetoric. He is much more in character as a leader of the mob, whose unexpiated pride and mutual mistrust constitute the madness of revolution.

No incidental by-product of this madness is the destruction of Lady Eleanore's mantle, symbol of aristocratic pride but also symbol of the very finest of Old World art. Woven "by the most skilful artist in London," the envy of Boston's ladies even before Lady Eleanore arrives, the mantle has those "magical properties" (9:274) belonging to all art worthy of the name.

Nothing like it has ever been seen in New England, since Hawthorne has not yet created Hester Prynne, whose transmission of Old World art to seventeenth-century New England will provide the fictive genesis of an aesthetic tradition in America. Yet in the eradication of the mantle, Hawthorne is already preparing for the unhappy fate of art under Puritan iconoclasts.

The mantle's beauty, in the minds of New Englanders, cannot be divorced from aristocracy, monarchy, and the Church of England. Fairly or not, art becomes symbol of something other than itself, and any true appreciation of art must perforce be as idolatrous as Jervase's worship of Lady Eleanore's beauty (9:279). The mantle must be destroyed just as the lady's beauty must be made ugly; and its "magical properties" must necessarily be converted to the devil's "dreadful potency." To a Puritanical mind susceptible to and fearful of beauty's infection, art itself becomes a pox, not made by God's hand or inspiration. Puritans in the English Civil War, on this assumption, demolished art work in most churches throughout England. Even though it lacks the religious fervor of its ancestors, the revolutionary mob in "Lady Eleanore's Mantle" follows this tradition. The fallout, for the nineteenth century, is the plain regularity of contemporary architecture and the remodeled Province House. Mob violence, in the name of purging the tyrannical and infectious corruption of anything English, performs a sweeping act of tyranny never consciously equaled by England. Unable to separate the best from the worst of English influences, New Englanders do all they can to destroy both in the name of purgation. The burden of "Lady Eleanore's Mantle" and of the "Legends" as a whole is to show how this excess vents itself in fratricidal and regicidal fury. Whether England is the originating source of aristocratic pride finally does not matter very much. What matters most is New England's overreaction to the contagion.

"Old Esther Dudley"

After moving back in time in the first three "Legends," we now come forward to where matters stood at the end of "Howe's Masquerade." Investigation of self-blinding and frenzied causes of revolution seems complete. With the concluding mob scene in "Lady Eleanore's Mantle" leading to the wartime setting glossed in "Old Esther Dudley," we should expect a treatment of the revolution's consequences. But in a significant and easily overlooked way, hints of political or ideological consequences have been provided all along in the "Legends" frames. Bela Tiffany has accepted nineteenth-century America without question. The narrator, however, has not been nearly as satisfied with contemporary life. Perhaps he has read too much Scott, for he reveals many signs of the historical romanticist preoccupied with bygone splendor. Perhaps, again, he has read just enough to begin a study of how America lost the cultural inheritance from England that attracts him.[103] His antiquarianism might therefore reflect an interest in historical continuity and change comparatively free of political reference or utility. While he has certainly not escaped the prevailing, ideological urge to reduce the past to a configuration justifying the present, his democratic politics and his desire to "deserve well" of his country seem terribly naive compared to Tiffany's.

Yet following the legend of Lady Eleanore, definition of the narrator's politics suddenly assumes a startling clarity, and the possibility of his transcending an ideological appropriation of the past seems lost. We are to believe that not only the narrator and Thomas Waite but also the old Loyalist "bestowed no little warmth of applause upon the narrative" (9:288). Unanimous approval from an audience having such divergent political philosophies must denote ambivalent or flexible meanings in the legend. Nonetheless, the narrator's response is most curious. Clearly, the story has produced a transformation in him: "For my own part, knowing how scrupulous is Mr. Tiffany to settle the foundation of his facts, I could not have believed him one whit the more faithfully, had he professed himself an eye-witness of the doings and sufferings of poor Lady Eleanore" (9:288). Evidently, the narrator has failed to see how unreliable are the eyewitnesses within the legend itself. He has not seen all that we and, to be in character, the old Loyalist have seen. Whereas he inquired about the existence of the portrait after the legend of Edward Randolph, he no longer requires evidence to authenticate the narrative, leaving such literal matters to "sceptics" (9:288).

The narrator is decisively not the ironist responsible for the anti-colonial nuances woven into Tiffany's legend. His editorial "adornments" have apparently been limited to nostalgic details of Lady Eleanore's magnificent procession into Boston, the beauty of the lady and of her mantle, and the sumptuous elegance of the ball. His fascination with these details, extensions of his previous interest in the pomp and ceremony associated with the Province House, he now implicitly repents. It would seem Tiffany's allegory has successfully reminded the narrator of his Puritan and Democratic origins. It has certainly worked a cure on his earlier aristocratic pretensions and English romanticist tendencies. He therefore takes the allegory on pride the way his ancestors once took the Jeremiad. Unlike Jervase Helwyse, he will not worship at the feet of aristocratic beauty and madly divide his loyalties. He will reject aristocracy, pride, individuality, taste, and art, recommitting himself to the errand of his Puritan fathers as it evolved toward the ideals of the Revolutionary founders.

Something along these lines must account for the narrator's rather blatant change in attitude. His conversion perfectly coincides with the finale of Tiffany's three legends, so that in a structurally important sense it comes at the right time. The old Loyalist will narrate the legend of old Esther Dudley; and even though his "blood was warmed by the good cheer" of the bottle (9:288), nothing less than a bold rebuttal to Tiffany's democratic catechism should be expected from this unregenerate monarchist. Re-armed with New England's traditional loyalties, the narrator should be safe.

As the frame setting shifts from "Lady Eleanore's Mantle" to "Old Esther Dudley," it does not appear that the narrator will have cause to worry. However, the old Loyalist's memory stretches back sixty years to the time of the Revolution, and for this reason, in conjunction with his having sup-ported the losing side in the war, he has an emotional stake in the narrative. Indignant at certain points in his narrative, the old Loyalist shakes his fist at his audience. At other moments, his "intellect would wander vaguely," or he would "cackle forth a feeble laugh, and express a doubt whether his wits . . . were not getting a little the worse for wear" (9:291). The narrator *seems* to want to make us think the old man is senile, and we ought to be suspicious. Clearly he contradicts himself, first associating with and then dissociating from the aged Anglophile. Something must indeed be troubling in the old man's story.

A further hint of this trouble appears in an apologia. For the narrator, as editor, has had no small problem in casting the old man's legend to suit a nineteenth-century audience. "The old loyalist's story required more revi-sion to render it fit for the public eye, than those of the series which have preceded it; nor should it be concealed, that the sentiment and tone of the affair may have undergone some slight, or perchance more than slight metamorphosis, in its transmission to the reader through the medium of a thorough-going democrat" (9:291). Affected by the old man's legend, the narrator is no fool. He cannot possibly submit the story to John L. O'Sul-livan's *Democratic Review* without editing it, or without lending the impres-sion that he has edited it, to reassure contemporary readers that its Tory politics have been safely manipulated within a context of democratic ide-ology.[104] Beyond that, if we apprehend an urgent need in his confessing to be a "thorough-going democrat," we are forewarned that the old Loyalist's politics may survive their very omission from the legend of old Esther Dudley and that they do indeed have a "pensive influence over the mind" (9:291).

The reason for the narrator's edginess about his democratic audience becomes evident at the outset of the legend. General Howe, alone at "the hour of defeat and humiliation" (9:291), lingers a few moments before vacating the Province House. His vanity, so marked in "Howe's Masquer-ade," has been checked. In these private moments, he seems an altered man. "Fierce emotions" struggle in him because he has lost Boston to New England's sons, and because he would have preferred a "warrior's death . . . within the soil which the king had given him to defend" (9:291). Conforming to a long tradition among military leaders, his feeling reflects immeasurably less individual pride than a patriotism shared with a larger community, for he broods not only upon himself but also upon the histor-ical implications of his departure: "the sway of Britain was passing forever from New England" (9:291). Evocative of the earlier symbolic loss of the maypole, such a serious realization adds to the intensity of Howe's guilt.

This privileged glimpse of Howe has the effect of clearing away the charged rhetoric of the Revolutionary War, allowing an Englishman's loy-alty to stand forth undemeaned. Any reasonably objective reader would be obliged to recognize that Howe continues to be deeply "faithful to his trust" (9:292) and that there exists something admirable in his unswerving dedi-cation. He may represent the wrong side, but he and his side have princi-ples conceivably no less honorable than those of New England. Considering that "America" hangs in the balance, we are invited to consider that there but for fortune might stand Washington or Adams or Hancock whose patriotic feelings would be no greater than Howe's.

That dignity obtains in being loyal to the King's cause may well be the essential point of the legend. If the stubborn Tory in "Old News" can acknowledge the nobility of Washington, then surely, Hawthorne suggests, nineteenth-century democrats should be able to discover nobility in Howe or, failing that, in a pathetically loyal old woman. Esther Dudley's entrance upon the scene of Howe's meditations seems to fulfill this purpose.

Having the surname of one of the first royal governors, Joseph Dudley, who in New England's view had been a traitorous henchman of Andros, scarcely promises to elicit an immediate democratic sympathy for Esther Dudley; but the name harkens back farther to a member of Winthrop's original migrants and the third Puritan governor, patriarchal Thomas Dudley. Thus, for longevity and sustained influence, there could hardly be a more hallowed name than Dudley in the minds of New Englanders, no matter how much it has "fallen into poverty and decay" (9:292). Hawthorne seems to count on this traditional respectability for the purpose of understanding and even sympathizing with shifting allegiances during the course of New England history.

The first words of Esther Dudley therefore resonate with historic anoma-lies. "'Heaven's cause and the King's are one,'" she says. "'Go forth, Sir William Howe, and trust in heaven to bring back a royal Governor in triumph'" (9:292). The faith of the Puritan fathers has doubled back upon itself, returning to the monarchy and Church of England from which it unofficially separated. Moreover, the Puritan errand and its inherent ty-pology have undergone a Royalist conversion. New England's "province of piety" apparently does not constitute an exclusive claim to the side on which God really fights. Esther's faith in the English monarchy and in the legit-imacy of the royal prerogative in the colonies is even greater than Howe's. As she first appears, "leaning on a gold-headed staff" (9:292), she suggests, more fully than all the nudging metaphors linked to Lady Eleanore, the queen of state with her scepter. Legend has it that "she had entered the portal of the Province-House . . . in the train of the first Royal Governor, and that it was her fate to dwell there till the last should have departed" (9:293). To an extent far outreaching anyone else, Esther represents the sway of monarchy in New England, beginning with the new charter and ending with the Revolutionary War. Her "antique magnificence of attire" (9:292) typifies this span of history. So do her inflexible views.

Not even Howe, moved to tears by Esther's devotion, can persuade her to leave the Province House. Practical politics and military strategy dictate a hasty retreat for Howe, but Esther refuses to go. Hers is loyalty heedless of pragmatic argument. Who better than she to safeguard the key to the Province House until a visionary Royal governor returns? Anticipating the forward-looking democratic ideology espoused at the end of the legend, we are supposed to recognize that Howe's impatience with Esther's "obstinacy" has some merit. As Howe leaves the old woman, he "deemed her well-fitted for such a charge [of the key], as being so perfect a representative of the decayed past—of an age gone by, with its manners, opinions, faith, and feelings, all fallen into oblivion or scorn—or what had once been a reality, but was now merely a vision of faded magnificence" (9:294). But here we should wonder what has happened to Howe's patriotism during the last few minutes with Esther. His mixture of foresight and hindsight have come to sound like an odd yoking of Bela Tiffany's democratic idealism and the narrator's former aristocratic nostalgia. With several years of war lying ahead, and with Howe serving as a leading general in the fighting, how are we to believe that the old Loyalist who tells the legend would present Howe in the act of essentially recanting his Tory principles? Evidently, we have encountered an example of the narrator's taking an editorial liberty with the old Loyalist's story to satisfy the requirements of a "thorough-going democrat." Howe may very well see the practical necessity of escaping Boston, but he should be one of the last to judge Esther Dudley as "the very moral of old-fashioned prejudice" (9:294).

Structurally, Howe's judgment of Esther and his betrayal of aristocratic principles are instrumental in setting up the legend's thematic conflict between past and future.[105] His prescience in seeing American democracy on the verge of replacing English monarchy initiates the means by which Esther Dudley can be cast as a quaint but ineffectual and pathetic creature. As we shall see, she and her monarchical cause will profit from this casting, but not enough to redress the Whig historiography within which she ironically functions. Meanwhile, however, we should understand that in her degraded role as faith's last stronghold she corresponds to the old Loyalist sixty years later. Just as Esther looks forward to the return of a Royal Governor, so the old Loyalist thinks of the American republic as a "usurpation" and devotes himself to Queen Victoria. Given his insinuated expectation of America's being restored to the monarchy, it is inconceivable that the old man would downgrade Esther by saying, "If Hope ever seemed to flit around her, still it was Memory in disguise" (9:294). For such a judgment, we can only be indebted to the narrator's ticklish apprehension of his progressive-minded audience.

Were Esther Dudley the "old fool" that Howe calls her (9:294), she would amount to nothing more than a trivial character in a tale producing nothing but a trivial point, but the legend began with a fairly dramatic and serious presentation of British patriotism. The shift whereby Esther and her aristocratic faith are relegated to an outmoded past might therefore direct us to consider whether the effort to trivialize the old woman is Hawthorne's prime subject. Surely more than half the legend dwells on this effort. What begins as the narrator's "more than slight metamorphosis" of Howe is soon taken up by Boston's rebellious patriots. Yet in their trivializing Esther, we can imagine no discrepancy between the old Loyalist's story and the narrator's edited version. Nothing less might be expected from ardent republicans in the midst of war. We might indeed expect a good deal more. With this thought in mind, we should be able to fathom how Hawthorne manages to elevate Esther and her ties to the aristocratic past, while at the same time seeming to confirm the progressive ideology of American democrats.

After the British retreat from Boston, the magistrates permit Esther to stay at the Province House, "especially as they must otherwise have paid a hireling for taking care of the premises, which with her was a labor of love" (9:295). Yet beyond their tight-fisted Yankee economics, "they were well content that the old gentlewoman, in her hoop-petticoat and faded embroidery, should still haunt the palace of ruined pride and overthrown power, the symbol of a departed system embodying a history in her person" (9:296). To them, she is simply a relic of the past, old and infirm, unquestionably no threat. Thus citizens can afford to patronize her and perhaps even congratulate themselves that, "amid all the angry license of the times, neither wrong nor insult ever fell upon her unprotected head" (9:295). Supernatural fables and stories about Esther's life in the mansion proliferate. In the process of trivializing her, Bostonians gradually take her somewhat to heart. She seems like nothing more than the harmless idiot whom many small towns conventionally adopt as one of their peculiar own, if for no better motive than to be entertained by stories naturally accumulating around such figures. The Revolutionary War is in progress, after all, and levity is at a premium.

Still, lest we should disregard it as a casual ornament, the story about Esther most often reiterated concerns a magical mirror through which Esther summons the former governors, beautiful ladies, and aristocratic ceremonies of the Province House—"in short, all the pageantry of gone days" (9:295). The fact that people embellish and repeat this story in one form or another suggests that it has an unconscious value superseding

mere entertainment at Esther's expense. People require more than levity
from a town fool during these times of "angry license" and "rude mob[s]"
(9:295, 297). British forces have been expelled and Esther Dudley can be
exploited by a people's wish to demean the aristocratic past, but every time
Bostonians imagine the old woman's calling forth the departed system, they
are also implicitly reminding themselves of a stability altogether lacking in
their wartime lives. *They* create the stories and *they* repeat them ritu-
alistically, as if the former routine of the colony were carrying on as usual,
before all havoc broke loose and the future became completely uncertain.[106]

Esther is not wholly the living anachronism she seems to be, certainly not
the trivial character Bostonians want to believe she is. They actually need
her far more than they would be able to admit because she evokes the
traditional connection between past and present during a confusing transition in history. The point is underscored as Esther herself becomes s
storyteller to Boston's children, who spend entire days eagerly listening to
tales about what the narrator, with his audience in mind, mistakenly calls "a
dead world" (9:297). That aristocratic world is obviously not dead for the
old Loyalist, and the past is surely never dead for Hawthorne—not as long
as someone can remember it and, more difficult, bring it to life, which
Esther has the skill to do. "When these little boys and girls stole forth again
from the dark mysterious mansion, they went bewildered, full of old
feelings that graver people had long ago forgotten, rubbing their eyes at the
world around them as if they had gone astray into ancient times, and
become children of the past" (9:297).

The children believe that they sit on the lap of such dignitaries as
Governor Belcher, playing with his fancy waistcoat and pulling the curls of
his wig. Such is the power of Esther's "romance" art, the effect of which—in
tone and language—anticipates Hawthorne's theory of romance in "The
Custom-House": "Thus, without affrighting her little guests, she led them
by the hand into the chambers of her own desolate heart, and made
childhood's fancy discern the ghosts that haunted there" (9:297). Esther
may lack a "proper reference to present things" and she may be "partially
crazed" (9:298), but these opinions intended to belittle her cannot obscure
the fact that she is an artist of considerable gifts.[107] What she offers the
children is a version of the past excluded from their education, just as
Hawthorne offers his "Legends" as a historical criticism omitted from the
democratically sanctioned historiography of his time. It is as real and
significant to America as the Puritan or democratic version that they have
no doubt been taught. And it can be omitted only at the expense of
distorting American history to advance an ideology like that of John L.
O'Sullivan.

Esther's artistic power clearly issues from her faith in America's English
past. If her stories are not entirely disconnected from Tory politics, they

differ from those of Bela Tiffany in their focus upon a past for its own sake, not for its utility as a figuration in a providential design whose significance lies waiting ahead somewhere in time.[108] Compared to Bostonians' hopes for an amorphous democratic future, Esther's faith increasingly conveys an impression of solidity and dignity, so that when she is met by townspeople, "it was really an affair of no small nerve to look her in the face" (9:295). She maintains a pride and superiority to which the colonists continue to defer. Behind her back, however, the trivializing continues, such as when, one evening near the war's conclusion, Esther keeps " 'jubilee for the King of England's birth-day' " (9:298). An old man must explain the holiday, which only a few years earlier was universally celebrated. Knowing that colonial generals have been winning the war, the spectators can afford to scoff: "the people laughed aloud, and would have thrown mud against the blazing transparency of the King's crown and initials, only that they pitied the poor old dame, who was so dismally triumphant amid the wreck and ruin of the system to which she appertained" (9:299).

Although the old Loyalist would probably not credit this crowd with pity, the more interesting facet of the passage is the transition from laughter to pity. Obviously, we have come a fair distance from the laughing mob in "My Kinsman, Major Molineux." Whereas only the narrator has sympathy for the dignified yet fallen Major, the people at large take pity on Esther, casting aside their normal mud-slinging propensities. A twofold advantage obtains in this mass response. On the one hand, Bostonians might be seen as rather decent human beings, content to be deferential despite their confidence in having won the war against the crown. Such sportsmanship would flatter the biases of Hawthorne's readers. On the other hand, the crowd's pity also seems to elevate Esther unintentionally.

Through this double orientation to pity, the substance of the last scene comes into proper focus. As the victorious colonists led by John Hancock preside over the ritualized death of Esther Dudley, they appear to express benevolent respect for the old woman and her monarchical loyalty, but they have basically come to gloat. Ironically, Esther takes Hancock to be the returning Royal Governor and thanks heaven for justifying her prophecy and faith. Hancock corrects her impression in a skillful display of diplomatic manners: " 'in reverence for your gray hairs and long-kept faith, Heaven forbid that any here should say you nay. Over the realms which still acknowledge his scepter, God save King George!' " (9:301). Although his generosity of spirit certainly *seems* genuine, we ought to expect some ultimate act of condescension for which his gentle mockery is preparing her. Esther certainly reacts with horror to his words, no longer deceived by Hancock's rich dress, "stateliness of gait," and other tokens of "gentle blood, high rank, and long accustomed authority" (9:300). Face to face with a traitor, "the monarch's most dreaded and hated foe" (9:301), she begs for death to take her quickly. Before she dies, however, she unconsciously performs a symbolic last act against historical change by dropping the key to the Province House. Consequently, Hancock will not receive her blessing on a continuation of authority antithetical to English tradition. Another, less stalwart implication may also be suggested. As the representative of historical continuity, Esther would paradoxically appear to concede the death of the tradition she has faithfully attended. However much we may doubt the old Loyalist's responsibility for conveying this implication, Esther seems to grant the apocalyptic end to America's English tradition, confirming in her behavior the rhetoric of Hancock and future Whig historians.[109]

For a moment, Hancock himself appears sensitive to Esther's pain and rejection. Thus he performs a final obeisance to the fallen English system, by "lending her his support with all the reverence that a courtier would have shown to a queen" (9:301). Perhaps he merely indulges in another act of mockery. Yet his act may also reveal a latent reverence for aristocratic superiority and historical continuity to the survival of which Hancock, rather than a commoner like Sam Adams, owed his being elected Massachusetts' first governor by a traditionally subordinated people "in plain civic dress" (9:300).[110] Inasmuch as some form of "reverence" for Esther is attributed to Hancock on four occasions in the scene, English influence is not quite as dead as he or anyone else would like to think. Nevertheless, Hancock cannot allow his reverential gesture to Esther to speak for itself. If he could, with Esther subsequently dying on his arm, we might well come away from the legend with a sense of political ambiguity somewhat favoring the colonists. But Hancock is in the spotlight; and in an age super-charged with political rhetoric, he cannot let the occasion go by without making a speech. By anybody's standard he simply says too much:

> Your life has been prolonged until the world has changed around you. You have treasured up all that time has rendered worthless—the principles, feelings, manners, modes of being and acting, which another generation has flung aside—and you are a symbol of the past. And I, and these around me—we represent a new race of men, living no longer in the past, scarcely in the present—but projecting our lives forward into the future. Ceasing to model ourselves on ancestral superstitions, it is our faith and principle to press onward, onward! Yet . . . let us reverence, for the last time, the stately and gorgeous prejudices of the tottering past! (9:301)

Hawthorne very likely never penned a broader irony than the one in this passage.[111] That O'Sullivan and his contemporaries evidently failed to perceive it indicates the regrettable degree to which Hancock's progressive ideology succeeded in trivializing and finally murdering any desire to consider the efficacy of England's role in American history. No satirical mirror held up to ideologues to view themselves as caricatures will be effective. Clearly prefigured in Hancock, their pride and condescension, as enormous as Lady Eleanore's ever were, are too self-blinding to permit it.

Esther's inability or refusal to transmit the key of historical continuity therefore proves significant. Although Hancock will expropriate the key anyway and continue to exploit selected elements of English traditions long enough for colonial minds to be thoroughly indoctrinated in democratic/ progressive ideology, the death of England's province in America is in fact symbolized here. Monarchy has literally been expelled. Aristocratic venera-tion for tradition, pageantry, and class privilege, understood from En-gland's perspective, has also been expelled. Disrespect for and indifference to art are implicated in these expulsions. To argue that most people's lives will continue just the same, or that the government of the United States will usually reflect traditional political ideas rather than new ones, begs the larger question of what English traits will be forsaken.[112] To be sure, embedded in Hawthorne's irony on Hancock resides the belief that an absolute breach with the past is impossible. But, comparatively speaking, a considerable departure from the monarchical past, and from the con-ceptual need for continuity, is achieved in the Revolutionary setting of "Old Esther Dudley." Beginning with "The May-pole of Merry Mount," most of Hawthorne's Puritan and colonial tales have rehearsed the final Puritanical banishment of England resulting from the Revolutionary War. What con-cerns Hawthorne is not so much the purification of England's political system and aristocratic establishment as the repudiation of such cultural products as art and a regard for history divorced from the teleology normally accompanying them. Human minds and social experience be-come statically inbred as a result.

Thus our sense of loss in "Old Esther Dudley" comes nowhere near being balanced by a sense of gain. We are merely left with Hancock's vague and bloated progressive notions, which ultimately seem meant to degrade the history Esther has symbolized. But we have already learned that Hancock's "foot now trod upon humbled Royalty" (9:301), reversing the aristocratic trampling upon colonists in the previous three legends but also echoing the mob's "trampling" on the heart of Major Molineux.[113] A scapegoat king or queen like Major Molineux and Lady Eleanore, Esther rises in our estima-tion because we know that her version of the past must be considered as part of the complexity that always is history. A democratic society-in-the-making might exclude this complexity on pain of creating a provinciality amounting to cultural incest, but a historian like Hawthorne comes along sooner or later to resurrect an officially expunged history, if for no better reason than to expose an ideology's dependence on self-flattery.

We may not be the only ones who sense the loss of Esther Dudley. Conceivably, the narrator feels it too. He might also recognize the self-serving implications of his tailoring the old Loyalist's narrative to appease his readers' ideology and his own reconstituted democratic faith in the aftermath of "Lady Eleanore's Mantle." We can be reasonably certain of one thing. Unless the old Loyalist is as much an ironist as Hawthorne, he would never allow Hancock to have the redundant last words of the legend: "'We will follow her reverently to the tomb of her ancestors; and then, my fellow-citizens, onward—onward! We are no longer children of the Past!'" (9:302).[114] Instead, consistent with his lifelong allegiance, the old Loyalist must surely have concluded with Esther's dying words: "'I have been faithful unto death. . . . God save the King!'" (9:302). Still, considering the narrator's manipulation throughout and Hawthorne's ironic direction of it, a more perfect conclusion than the one we have could hardly be imagined. Hancock puts a "gouty shoe" into his mouth for a second time (9:300), but he no more discerns the impediment to his progressive-minded cant than do his successors in Hawthorne's time.[115]

Whether the narrator may be identified with one of these successors remains problematic. If he is the "thorough-going democrat" he claims to be, then surely he is a target of Hawthorne's irony; but it would seem possible to argue that the narrator's political pose constitutes the most useful rhetorical device by which Hawthorne can disclaim any serious attraction to the English past or to the Tory point of view, and then set out to subvert the disclaimer. It does not necessarily follow that the narrator is totally unconscious of this ploy. Indeed, from the view of the "Legends" as a whole, his awareness seems to develop in a circular pattern: from his original and shallow romantic interest in aristocratic splendor, to his being brought to his Puritan senses after the allegory on aristocratic pride in "Lady Eleanore's Mantle," and then to his return to the discontent which led him to seek out legends involving English aristocracy in the first place. By the end, he hardly appears to be the jejune romantic he was at the start. He seems to understand the historical and political source for the poverty in American cultural life that essentially troubles him at the beginning of the "Legends." Accordingly, the dark tones in the final frame setting might suggest the narrator's having acquired some depth of insight.

From Hancock's inflated optimism, the frame shifts to the virtual hope-lessness of the narrator. The lamp and fire have all but died.[116] The old Loyalist's enthusiasm has disappeared, "as if all the lingering fire of his soul were extinguished" (9:302). His spiritual demise, specifically equated to the death of Esther and "the glory of the ancient system" (9:302), obviously bears upon the intervening sixty years, during which time his own faith in a restoration has gone unrewarded. Doubtless, the narrator sympathizes with the significant loss of historical continuity felt by the old man. Whatever the unmentioned responses of Bela Tiffany and Thomas Waite might be, the narrator fails to offer the slightest hint of trivializing the old Loyalist. His faith has been made a by-word in the history of America as told by progressive democrats like O'Sullivan and George Bancroft—or as tolled by the bell of the Old South Church, whose knell rings again at the close of "Old Esther Dudley," more than adequately suggesting that the Puritan tradition survives the death of English kings and aristocrats, for the Puritan past has been upgraded to serve the typological interests of the democratic present.[117] Not all of America's past is dead, only the English part of it.

The narrator is aware of this suggestion and thus he struggles with the historiographical problem of how history is made and unmade to suit special interests of the present. The gloom in the last paragraph includes his guilt or disgust for aiding the ideological cause against the English presence in American history. No other satisfactory explanation can account for his turning on Bela Tiffany "to lay hold of another auditer," or his deciding not to enter the Province House "for a good while hence—if ever" (9:303). He has heard enough of the party line. This is not to say that the narrator has been converted to the old Loyalist's monarchical point of view, but it is to say that the story of Esther Dudley has sufficiently unsettled his attempt to be as democratically complacent as Bela Tiffany. As we leave him, he is despairingly caught between factious extremes of Democrat vs. Tory, progressive vs. conservative. If he should continue to live in America, where O'Sullivan will invoke God's blessing on manifest destiny while Bancroft carves in stone the providential design of American history, his only hope for intellectual balance will depend on discovering a self-critical irony such as Hawthorne's, which permits a measure of mediation in the division of one's loyalties.

3

The Typology of Violence in *The Whole History of Grandfather's Chair*

The Whole History of Grandfather's Chair was originally written for children,[1] but it illuminates Hawthorne's preoccupation with the historical conflict between England and America in ways more subtle and less patriotic than books in the juvenile genre conventionally reflect. The book deserves serious attention, inasmuch as its moral and political attitudes are every bit as divided and complex as those already seen in Hawthorne's tales, not to mention the use of narrators and audiences almost as sophisticated as those in "Legends of the Province-House." Although many critics have felt free to draw upon passages in the *Whole History* to support arguments focused on Hawthorne's more "serious" fiction, only one fairly adequate examination of the work and its relation to others in Hawthorne's canon exists.[2] Nina Baym has also tried to redress this neglect, arguing that the *Whole History* is "Hawthorne's most extended historical statement; it provides a coherent view of Massachusetts' history from the founding of the Bay Colony to the Revolution; it fits very well with the whole of Hawthorne's historical writing preceding it."[3] I would further suggest that paradoxically, through the tenor and vehicle of myth in the *Whole History*, Hawthorne could not prevent himself, as it were, from demythologizing American history by showing once again the inadequacy of a typological pattern to explain it.[4] Accordingly, conventional posturings against the tyranny of England are noticeably toned down, if not in the end wholly checked, while commentary on independently or democratically minded Puritans is more than balanced by criticism of their intolerance and violence.

The *Whole History* has two narrators: an outside narrator who occasionally intervenes but who basically establishes the settings for Grandfather to tell the inside narrative of New England's history. Perhaps influenced by Samuel Goodrich's Peter Parley series, the *Whole History* probably owes more to a children's history by Scott, *Tales of a Grandfather: A History of Scotland*. But unlike Scott, who only adopts the persona of a grandfather in the dedication of the book to his grandson, Hawthorne creates almost full-fledged characters out of Grandfather and his grandchild audience—Laurence, Clara, Charley, and Alice. The children's responses to Grandfather's narrative are in fact significant extensions of its chief conflicts into the nineteenth century. Epitomized especially by Laurence and Charley, who are by temperament and sensibility benign antagonists, one of these conflicts is between "ideal principle" and "adventurous action" (6:72).[5] Charley is invariably associated with bold, even if mindless, activity, while Laurence is identified with moral integrity and shadowy reflection. Laurence indeed has the same predisposition for the moody precinct of romance art as Hawthorne himself will later define it in "The Custom-House." He urges Grandfather to tell his fireside history when the atmosphere is just right: " 'when we talk about old times, it should be in early evening, before the candles are lighted. The shapes of the famous persons, who once sat in [Grandfather's] chair will be more apt to come back, and be seen among us, in this glimmer and pleasant gloom, than they would in the vulgar daylight' " (6:74).

The *Whole History* is divided into three sections. "Grandfather's Chair" covers what is strictly the "Puritan" period of New England history, from the settlement of Salem and Boston to the governorship of William Phips in 1692, which draws to a close the authority of the original charter brought to the New World by Winthrop. "Famous Old People" takes up Phips's brief term as governor and then proceeds through events conducted under all the royal governors prior to the outbreak of the Revolution. "Liberty Tree" then covers the Revolutionary period. On a patriotic level, conforming to the popular historiography of Bancroft (who was Hawthorne's superior at the Boston Custom House during the composition of the *Whole History*), Grandfather submits the early Puritans and their descendants as types who prefigure the revolutionary anti-types during the Revolutionary War. This level of the narrative, by no means predominant, obviously results from the old man's desire to foster pride in the children for the idealistic spirit and bold action of the main figures who anticipate and bring to fruition American independence and democracy. Thus, while Scott's *Tales of a Grandfather* eventually hopes "to show the slow and interrupted progress by which England and Scotland . . . gradually approximated to each other, until the last shades of national difference may be almost said to have disappeared,"[6] the *Whole History* leads toward disunity and separate national identities.

Support for a typological configuration of American history appears several times in the text. On Endicott's motive in the red cross episode, Grandfather says that " 'a sense of the independence of his adopted country, must have been in that bold man's heart' " (6:24). Contrary to conditions in the Old World, "democracies were the natural growth of the new world" (6:33). The Boston Rebellion in 1689 is depicted as a democratic upsurge against the "absolute despotism" of the royal-appointed Governor Andros (6:53). The siege at Louisburg in 1745 is " 'one of the occasions, on which the colonists tested their ability for war, and thus were prepared for the great contest of the revolution'" (6:119). The spirit of independence belonging to Puritans becomes reanimated upon England's imposition of the Stamp Act (6:150–51). And even though George Washington has no claim to Puritan origins, he appears as the "great Deliverer" (6:124), who, in the exegetical tradition, encapsulates at once the type and anti-type of Moses and Christ the redeemer. But in relation to New England's inherent tendencies toward democracy, Samuel Adams is presented as the redemptive anti-type of the early Puritan types: "'He was as religious as they, as stern and inflexible, and as deeply imbued with democratic principles'" (6:173).

On the patriotic level of Grandfather's narrative, these excerpts suggest that a typological design in American history is fully established, a progress toward democracy well-deserving the children's pride. Yet on another level, a moral one, many of the characters and events Grandfather summons from the past caution against both the existence of the design and the possession of overweening pride in America's revolutionary origins. One of Grandfather's chief aims, we note, is to teach something about people and history not available in children's school books (6:11). Thus, along with the few events attributed to an evolving pattern of independence and democracy, other episodes do not at all validate the nobility or morality that supposedly dwell in the motive for independence. Grandfather does not seem to stress these episodes, as if he bears in mind the tender years of his audience; but in their incremental frequency and length, they reveal how Grandfather exceeds the bounds of what he considers a proper patriotic history for his grandchildren to hear. Sometimes mindful of trespassing these bounds, he apologizes. Apology is indeed an integral part of the narrative, for the glowing events in New England history associated with democratic typology appear only sporadically compared to dark and shameful events. At times glossed in their details, these darker events challenge the justification for a progressive historiography. Just as in the tales, considerable doubt is cast on the validity of a typological reading of American history.

Grandfather's habit of endorsing a typological reading on the one hand and then pulling back from that endorsement on the other echoes the familiar pattern already witnessed in the seventeenth- and eighteenth-century tales. In Richard Brodhead's view, the method shows a "play of opposed attachments" characterizing Hawthorne's art:

> Hawthorne's imagination is so organized that antithetical impulses fuel and release one another in it—so organized that an impulse, once activated, moves both to express itself and to activate an opposite one. . . . The consequence is that Hawthorne can fully occupy positions without becoming fully committed to them, since each of his positions, once embraced, calls up another one that reverses it."[7]

Grandfather is a suitable character through whom Hawthorne can project give-and-take attachments, but with this advantage: the reader is invited to locate the division in Grandfather, not Hawthorne, as if Grandfather's mind were less ambivalently organized than his creator's. As a benefactor of democracy, Grandfather has essentially accepted the conventional typological formula without question and he readily advocates it to the children. Yet he also knows a wealth of historical information that either deconstructs the typological design or that poses a countervailing pattern to it. Venerably wise though he is, Grandfather is not quite conscious of how the greater number of events in his narrative are antithetical to a patriotic design. Thus he clings to the typological pattern despite tenuous and infrequent evidence that might support it, no doubt completely in accord with the selective habits of Hawthorne's nineteenth-century audience. It was enough for this audience, charged with John L. O'Sullivan's nationalistic fervor and acquainted with George Bancroft's providential historiography, to discover token hints of a typological scheme to legitimize a tendency toward independence and democracy.[8] Such a tendency will conveniently satisfy those adult readers who have been taught that history and teleology are the same. If parents can accept the ideological marriage of the sacred and profane, how might their children be expected to make finer discriminations or to question the accuracy of a received hagiography? With the ironic criticism of democratic ideology behind him in "Legends of the Province-House," Hawthorne appears to have this question in mind as he sets out on the delicate task of writing a children's history.

In the development of Grandfather's history, no mediating figures like those in the seventeenth-century tales appear between extremist factions in Puritan times or between colonial natives and British in the eighteenth century. Nevertheless, the obvious need for mediation surfaces again and again in the narrative, as a result of Grandfather's general inability to decide whether characters are heroes or villains. What at first appears to be his equivocation finally amounts to his strength. Owing to his sensitive perception of wrongs or rights in otherwise noble or ignoble events respectively, and his enormous capacity to sympathize with both sides in a conflict, Grandfather unconsciously becomes the moderating figure of his own narrative. Repeatedly evident is his humane morality, which is not lost on the eldest grandchild, Laurence, whose own disposition to mediate between extremes singles him out as the most likely inheritor of Grandfather's benevolence and poise among all the descendants. As we shall see, Grandfather and Laurence are preeminently associated with the namesake of the *Whole History*, Grandfather's chair, one of whose several symbolic functions is that of mediation.

The oaken chair now occupied by Grandfather serves as the central prop and unifying device for the *Whole History*, an antique brought over to the New World aboard the *Arbella* in 1630. During the next 150 years, nearly all the Massachusetts Bay governors sit in it, along with many other persons of note or notoriety. Events taking place beyond the vicinity of the chair are told, at least metaphorically, within its hearing. However fanciful this device might seem to an adult reader, it satisfies the grandchildren's apparent need for a unifying thread in the narrative to the point that, when direction seems to have gone too long astray, they demand that Grandfather draw the connection to the chair. Their desire reflects the need to have history made coherent and personal, relevant to what they know in their immediate experience. For them the chair is a familiar artifact taking on special life as symbol, allowing them to imagine a world beyond their experience as told by Grandfather. Nevertheless, Grandfather's digressive habit satisfactorily alerts us to a deconstructive impetus asserting itself in the narrative. The implication is clear: the complexity of history resists a coherent design under pain or penalty of somebody's imposing one.

Even the forced use of the chair as a unifying device suggests a similar imposition. For the people who sit in it and the events to which it bears witness are as appropriately disparate as history always is until someone gives it an order that always necessitates omission or risks distortion. But as a symbol, the chair can function in the dialectical capacity of nominally unifying the narrative on the one hand while actually subverting that unity on the other through the number and complexity of its incoherent associations. To understand this double role of the chair, it will be necessary to pay careful attention to its description, to its original purpose, and to the people and events associated with that purpose. We will discover that the chair has a crucial bearing on the transmission of culture from Old to New World, on the structure of Grandfather's narrative, and on the merits of a democratic typology in American history.

"Grandfather's Chair"

The chair is initially described as "very large and heavy," with "a back that rose high above Grandfather's white head. This back was curiously carved in open-work, so as to represent flowers and foliage, and other devices, which the children had often gazed at, but could never understand what they meant. On the very tiptop of the chair, over the head of Grandfather himself, was the likeness of a lion's head . . ." (6 : 10). Nearly three hundred years old, the chair originally belonged to the Earl of Lincoln in whose park the oak was cut to make it and whose coat of arms forms one of the curious devices over which the children puzzle. The Earl gives the chair to his daughter, the Lady Arbella, in token of her marriage to Isaac Johnson. As Hawthorne knew from several sources, the young couple emigrates to Massachusetts Bay, along with Winthrop, aboard the ship named in the lady's honor.

All these details are redolent with suggestions, perfectly in keeping with Hawthorne's overall picture of first-generation Puritans. The sturdiness of the chair, its connection to the English aristocracy through its coat of arms, its lion's head traditionally associated with the monarchy or power of state, and its transplantation in the New World—all of these symbolize a continuity between Old and New Worlds in a way entirely appropriate to the first-generation settlers, who could count among their number several leaders who had given up their estates and a degree of their power in coming to Massachusetts Bay. The strength of their commitment to the Puritan errand is transferred to and symbolized by the oaken chair. Yet there is more than just strength here, for the elaborate carvings represent a taste for decorative art and finery possessed by the wealthier of the first-generation Puritans. Hawthorne will enlarge upon the transmission of this traditional taste in his treatment of Hester's needlework in *The Scarlet Letter*.

The chair, then, suggests a blend of qualities—a marriage, as it more literally emblemizes from the moment the Earl presents it as part of his daughter's dowry. This literal marriage, however, is short-lived. Within a month of her arrival in Salem, the Lady Arbella, who has "a gentle and sweet expression on her face, but looking too pale and feeble to endure the hardships of the wilderness," dies (6:15); and within another month Isaac Johnson dies of a broken heart and is buried in Boston, his name thereafter designating the town's cemetery plot. The death of this couple is a fitting omen for Hawthorne's view of New England history. There will be no lasting harmony between contending qualities or factions that very soon develop among the Puritans. The couple do not have the constitutions to shape a new civilization in the wilderness. They have the delicacy represented by the flowers and leaves carved in their marriage chair, but they lack its substance. More ominously, they lack the heart of an Endicott, which is, predictably from Hawthorne, "bold and resolute as iron" (6:17).

The fate of Lady Arbella and Isaac Johnson is as melancholy as Clara, the eldest granddaughter, suggests (6:19). One has to wonder why Grandfather, and Hawthorne himself, chose to begin the narrative with a death, a dashing of hope, rather than with an optimistic episode. Why not first things first: Endicott's cutting down the Maypole? That the New World is not a new Eden and that there must be death in it—as Laurence suggests—is hardly as profound as Grandfather pretends. Nor does the idea address the questions of why death, and these particular deaths, come first in the narrative. Anyone so well acquainted with New England history as Grandfather and Hawthorne knows that Endicott's wife died before the Lady Arbella. It would seem that Endicott's role as a founding patriarch would be strengthened, with his wife dead and yet his resolution to build a city on a hill undiminished. This would be heroic resolution indeed, reinforcing the notion that the environment had more to do than anything else with forming the stern Puritan character. But Grandfather seems to want to make the point that the New World was too rough for the delicacy and refinement of an aristocratic lady—and perhaps too rough for the gentle kind of love shared by Isaac Johnson and Lady Arbella. The chair, which partly stands for delicacy and refinement, will thereafter have no owner or occupant who has these traits.

Grandfather's narrative therefore begins on a sour note, with the figure of Endicott, as usual, "punish[ing] some idler or evil-doer, by ordering him to be set in the stocks or scourged at the whipping-post" (6:17). Loomings, indeed, in the New English Canaan. Many of the early Puritans, even Endicott, receive considerable praise for their boldness and piety, of course. In keeping with Bancroft's history, to which he refers the children, Grandfather presents the growing prosperity and independence of Massachusetts, its confederation with other New England colonies for mutual defense, and the honorable names of Winthrop, Bellingham, Dudley, and Endicott as they take their turns as governor and sit in the chair, which by now has become the chair of state. Still, this admiring, filiopietistic overview does not stand undiminished. For Anne Hutchinson and Roger Williams, unquestionably more suitable to a tradition of democratic idealism than their persecutors, also sit in the chair before their banishment. Except for his treatment of Lady Arbella and Isaac Johnson, Grandfather devotes more attention to Hutchinson and Williams than to anyone else in the first generation, and he gives them an even-handed treatment. They take their place in relief against Grandfather's otherwise positive account of Puritan virtue. From a nineteenth-century point of view, at least, the compromise of Puritan virtues would appear to be no serious impediment to the process of valorizing the founders' nascent principles of liberty and democracy.

Yet further omens echoing the Puritans' bigoted treatment of Williams and Hutchinson are in store. Concurrent with the regicide of Charles I and the assumption of power by Cromwell, Grandfather's chair "had the misfortune to break its leg" (6:35). The timing of such an event within the narrative's world of signs and types results from no coincidence, any more than does Grandfather's phrasing. The chair obviously does not break its own leg; someone, something, is responsible. The injury nevertheless seems to have been inflicted from out of the blue, suggesting some causality larger in dimension than any normally inflicted by an individual. So it is. The injury coincides with the official end to the first generation of Puritans as Hawthorne will later define it. Just as the old reign in England concludes with the death of Charles I, so does the first era of Puritan experience end with the death of Winthrop, who has served as elected governor for nearly half the first twenty years of settlement. These details are omitted from Grandfather's account, just as Bancroft's estimate of Winthrop's importance is omitted: "his lenient benevolence could temper, if not subdue, the bigotry of his time."[9] A shift in the affairs of New England takes place in the wake of Winthrop's tempering influence, a shift at once toward severity and worldliness. As if Endicott is not a worthy successor to Winthrop, the chair "ceased to be the seat of the governors of Massachusetts; for, assuredly, it would have been ominous of evil to the commonwealth, if the Chair of State had tottered upon three legs" (6:35). After Winthrop's death, the chair experiences a fall corresponding to the historical transition. It is sold at auction, "knocked down to a certain Captain John Hull" (6:35).

Here begins the period of historical decline familiar in Hawthorne's view of the seventeenth century. The new era coincides with the rise of the Jeremiad sermon honoring the founding patriarchs and castigating their descendants for an increasing worldliness.[10] During the era, John Hull mends the chair, takes his seat, and counts the immense fortune he amasses after being granted nearly one out of every twenty pinetree shillings he mints for the colony. In an amusing, satirical account, Samuel Sewall (later one of the witch trial judges in Salem) receives much of Hull's fortune by marrying his daughter, whose ugliness he supposedly fails to see and whose dowry he most judiciously never mentions during the courtship. The parallel is clear between the chair's degradation and the backsliding from the upright piety of the earlier generation, not to mention a regression from the marriage of the heart signified by Lady Arbella and Isaac Johnson.

In the absence of more moderate temperaments such as those of "Winthrop, and other wise men of Massachusetts" (6:24), Endicott's radical intolerance and persecutorial spirit now find full expression. Alluded to in "The Gentle Boy," but specifically named here, he presides as governor during the Quaker persecutions. Grandfather seems intent on assigning responsibility. He is also intent on something else. Whereas he has refused to describe the fate of Anne Hutchinson, because "the end of her life was so sad" the children "must not hear it" (6:28), he now itemizes the horrors of the persecutions as if in his review of Puritan vices he cannot manage full control of his tongue: Quakers "were thrown into dungeons; they were beaten with many stripes, women as well as men; they were driven forth into the wilderness, and left to the tender mercies of wild beasts and Indians" (6:40). The most telling indictment of Puritan inhumanity, however, occurs in the sympathetic treatment of Mary Dyer, who sits in Grandfather's chair not long before her execution. The children—appalled and incensed at the cruelty, probably not needing to be told that the Quaker persecutions were "'one of the most mournful passages in the history of our forefathers'" (6:41)—expect by way of warning other shameful events to come.

The narrative moves immediately to another dark episode in New England history, John Eliot's apostolic efforts to Christianize the Indians and the frustration of those efforts owing to the prevailing bad faith of the

Puritans. As Grandfather says, overlooking the good efforts of Roger Williams,

"I have sometimes doubted whether there was more than a single man, among our forefathers, who realized that an Indian possesses a mind, and a heart, and an immortal soul. That single man was John Eliot. All the rest of the early settlers seemed to think that the Indians were an inferior race of beings, whom the Creator had merely allowed to keep possession of this beautiful country, till the white men should be in want of it." (6:43)

Because Eliot is the one Puritan deeply interested in catechizing the Indians, the only one who clearly believes that the Indians may descend from the lost tribe of Israel and that God has therefore "'destined us to deliver the children from the more cruel bondage of ignorance and idolatry'" (6:47–48), his mission meets with predictably limited success. The larger Puritan community has other objects on its mind:

Occasionally, perhaps, the governor and some of his counsellors came to visit Mr. Eliot. Perchance they were seeking some method to circumvent the forest people. They inquired, it may be, how they could obtain possession of such and such a tract of their rich land. Or they talked of making the Indians their servants, as if God had destined them for perpetual bondage to the more powerful white man.

Perhaps, too, some warlike captain, dressed in his buff-coat, with a corslet beneath it, accompanied the governor and counsellors. Laying his hand upon his sword hilt, he would declare that the only method of dealing with the red men was to meet them with sword drawn, and the musket presented. (6:47)

Grandfather's message is as clear as the historical record, explaining the reason that Eliot's feat of translating the Bible into an Indian tongue will prove largely for naught. King Philip has correctly seen the larger measure of Puritan designs on the landscape. He therefore refuses to become a "praying Indian" but takes up arms, which leads to the slaughter of whites and the decimation of his race during the war named after him.

The broad outline of Puritan relations with Indians is already known to Grandfather's audience. Prior to the narrative on Eliot's translation of the Bible, Laurence exclaims, "'I have seen it in the library of the Athenaem; and the tears came into my eyes, to think that there were no Indians left to read it'" (6:44). His sense of loss emerges again at the conclusion of Grandfather's account. Charley, however, also knows something about the historical record but has a predisposition toward Indians altogether at odds with his older brother's. He blurts out, "'I would have conquered them first, and then converted them'" (6:44). Grandfather's reply pinpoints the essential blame for the vanishing American: "'Ah Charley, there spoke the very spirit of our forefathers!'" (6:44). The subsequent account of Eliot's "'disinterested zeal for his brother's good'" (6:49) is lost on Charley, who wants to know details of the battles during King Philip's War, and who proves deaf to Grandfather's point that no participant in the war "'did any thing a thousandth part so glorious'" as Eliot. The narrator steps in to report: "'let Laurence be the apostle,' said Charley to himself, 'and I will be the captain'" (6:50). The pugnacious boy's preference, which concludes the chapter, suggests a Puritan militancy surviving in the nineteenth century. The moral implication is fairly transparent: some people never will learn anything from history.

No doubt less salutary than earlier manifestations of violence aimed at British oppression, Puritan militancy leveled on Indians is nevertheless akin to them. As a result, doubt is cast on the Puritans' self-righteous assumptions. Charley's narrowness, insensitivity, and militancy are the very traits Pearl will combat in the children composing the second-generation Puritans in *The Scarlet Letter*. Just as Hawthorne suggests the horrible deeds for which these children will be responsible later in the seventeenth century, so he suggests the fate of Indians in the nineteenth century, as whites move west animated by the unextinguishable spirits of many an adult version of Charley. The tolerant and loving spirit of Laurence will not likely prevail in the nineteenth century any more than Eliot's did in the seventeenth. However admirable their lives and sensibilities, however worthy their examples for a moralized fable, Eliot and Laurence represent the recessive side of the Puritan tradition, overwhelmed time and again by the dominant side whose basic credentials are the numbers and power of its supporters.

The last three chapters of "Grandfather's Chair" focus on the period from 1685 to 1692, bringing to a unified conclusion what might properly be termed the Puritan eras of New England history. One of the central events during these years is the "Boston Rebellion," which Hawthorne had treated in "The Gray Champion." Here the rebellion is downplayed in favor of elevating the patriarchal Bradstreet, "'the last of the Puritans'" (6:54), who assumes leadership until Sir William Phips arrives in 1692. "'There was no other public man remaining to connect the ancient system of government and manners with the new system, which was about to take its place. The era of the Puritans was now completed'" (6:55). Commemorating the close of this era, Grandfather's chair suffers another injury, once Bradstreet no longer occupies it. Just as the chair's initial injury after Winthrop's death becomes ominous, so it does in this second instance, and in similar terms. Phips, who will next occupy the chair, parallels Hull in his connection with money: He wins his title and appointment for discovering sunken treasure and sharing it with the crown. Just as the persecution of

Quakers begins shortly after Winthrop's death, so the persecution of witches begins after the end of Bradstreet's moderating influence.

Before the political curtain can be drawn on the Puritan era, something else must be noted beyond the injury to the chair. Laurence suddenly feels what seems a baffling change of heart. He declares his sorrow over the last of the Puritans: " 'for, though they were so stern, yet it seems to me that there was something warm and real about them. I think, Grandfather, that each of these old governors should have his statue set up in our State House, sculptured out of the hardest of New England granite' " (6:55). Compared to the anticipated political fortunes of New England under the crown, the Puritans begin to look attractive, despite their intolerance and persecution of Williams, Hutchinson, Quakers, and Indians. "Stern" is, after all, a decidedly mild description of those Puritans responsible for the many cruelties enumerated in Grandfather's narrative. The full Puritan record, then, becomes summarily whitewashed, its blemishes sacrificed to the typological configuration culminating in American independence already familiar to Laurence.

There is no arguing against the occasional references to political typology in "Grandfather's Chair," but the Puritan excesses far outnumber and outweigh these patriotic utterances—so much that we really ought to be tempted to think that, rather than a typology of success, a typology of failure emerges from the narrative. Instead of the dark episodes interrupting a typological design, as the case ought to be, the typological references interrupt a movement toward increasing intolerance and violence. The reversal gains special prominence because no overt discrimination is made among the Puritan patriarchs who are supposed to serve as democratic types. We discover moderates such as Winthrop and Bradstreet, along with the benevolent Eliot, lumped with extremists such as Endicott and Dudley——as if idealism and bigotry, moderating legalism and persecution, must necessarily be yoked and identified as twin constituents of a single "Puritan" character. The actual treatment of characters and events in Grandfather's account, however, suggests the existence of two distinct Puritan types, the extremist model basically dominating its increasingly recessive counterpart. Doubts over the legitimacy of a typological design result from a reaction to this dominant form of Puritanism. Such doubts, already cast up in "Grandfather's Chair," deepen when Grandfather resumes his narrative in "Famous Old People."

"Famous Old People"

Although the administration of Sir William Phips marks the beginning of England's political hegemony in New England, the major event taking place during his rule—the Salem witch trials—suggests that history does not readily lend itself to the convenient order of political terms-in-office. Grandfather now designates this episode as " 'the saddest and most humiliating passage in our history' " (6:79). Having no discernible connection to English rule, the witchcraft delusion results from defects within Puritanism itself, a latter-day extension and distortion of the original piety and superstition of the founders. It is also persecutorial, worthy of an Endicott but more immediately associated with Cotton Mather—" 'the chief agent of the mischief' " (6:94)—who, as an influential spiritual leader, might have been able to prevent the executions were it not for his belief that the devil could assume visible shape and exert his influence in the physical world. Like "Grandfather's Chair," then, "Famous Old People" starts off with death, only now not attributable to a frail English temperament confronting the rugged wilderness of the New World, but to the Puritanical character of the people who have grown up in an environment now cleared of savages and forests. However bold and strong, they are narrow by any psychological measure, less hemmed in by woods than by dogma, the original wilderness now seeming to have reproduced itself in the entangled subtleties of their theology and the darkness of their minds.

In the ominous introduction to "Famous Old People," Puritanical narrowness recurs during the smallpox epidemic in the 1720s. Despite Cotton Mather's attempts to introduce inoculation, the people reject such interference in the affairs of God, and Mather's home escapes the violent threat of an unexploding bomb. Death goes on. Indeed, except for cursory treatments of successive royal governors taking office amidst the regal pomp of state and for an imaginative recreation of Master Ezekial Cheever's old-fashioned school, "Famous Old People" produces a virtually unrelieved record of suffering and death—and not without comment. At the conclusion of New England's part in the war between England and France, the peace treaty of 1697 restores all possessions to the original holders. To Laurence's observation that " 'all the fighting had been in vain' " (6:88), Grandfather replies " 'Far worse than in vain, . . . for no treaty could restore the thousands of lives that had been sacrificed' " (6:88). Thousands indeed die trying to sail up the St. Lawrence to take Quebec in 1711. More die in 1745 when New Englanders capture the French fortification at Louisburg in Nova Scotia. Laurence wants to know if any " 'real good' " was gained in the conquest. Upon being asked whether Parliament's million dollars of gold and coin sent to New England for its expenses and reward was not sufficient, Laurence says, " 'The mothers of the young men, who were killed at the siege of Louisburg, would not have thought it so' " (6:118). Grandfather, as usual, agrees with the boy's humane view: " 'No, Laurence, . . . and every warlike achievement involves an amount of physical and moral evil, for which all the gold in the Spanish mines would not be the slightest recompense' " (6:118).

Despite this judgment of war, Grandfather reactivates political typology through the colonists' preparation " 'for the great contest of their revolution' " (6:119). It would seem that a backward glance over historical roads does indeed reveal a meaningful design through the selectivity of one's focus. Still, while Grandfather imposes the typological design, he goes out of his way to lead the children to a moral judgment of individual events composing it. For the events always involve bloodshed, sometimes even the disruption of domestic harmony, Grandfather's highest value. The narrative of the French and Indian War offers a clear example. Grandfather does not submit details of battles, but he purposely mentions how George Washington held the defeated forces of General Braddock together in 1755. Grandfather's purpose, the external narrator reports, results in the intended effect: "At the mention of this illustrious name, the children started, as if a sudden sunlight had gleamed upon the history of their country, now that the great Deliverer had arisen above the horizon" (6:123–24). This gleam lasts but a moment, however. Immediately after this patriotic reference, Grandfather begins what he considers the most interesting event of the war—the total destruction of the Acadian culture in Nova Scotia—and then imagines the condition of the thousand Acadians brought to Boston as part of a policy of dispersal. Except for the smallpox episode, this tale amounts to the longest one in "Famous Old People." After presenting the misery of the Acadians, Grandfather pictures their entering the Province House and discovering Governor Shirley meditating in Grandfather's chair. Their fate should have taught Shirley, Grandfather moralizes, "that the poor man's earth is sacred, and that armies and nations have no right to violate it. It should have made him feel, that England's triumph, and increased dominion, could not compensate to mankind, nor atone to Heaven, for the ashes of a single Acadian cottage. But it is not thus that statesmen and warriors moralize" (6:128).

Conforming to the Anglophobic bias of national typology, this passage would appear to cast England as the villain, with the fate of the Acadians foreshadowing the threat posed by later English policy to the colonists. But such a reading is inconsistent with other portions of the narrative in which French fleets sail into Boston harbor and raise in the minds of the colonists the double specter of defeat and Roman Catholicism, or those in which New Englanders attack French garrisons in Canada and Nova Scotia. Three thousand Massachusetts men actually carry out the campaign against the Acadians, fulfilling an English policy. As "Englishmen"—a term Grandfather repeatedly applies to them—the colonists are no less concerned with the French than England is. The children's response might be our best clue here: they do not accept Grandfather's nudge, do not, in other words, blame England. They respond to the Acadians' homeless situation as still another and yet worse catastrophe in the ongoing account of wars.

Still more war is yet to come prior to the Revolution, especially the decisive battle on the Plains of Abraham in which General Wolfe dies as the English win a certain victory over Montcalm's forces. "Though he was a man of peaceful thoughts, and gentle spirit," Grandfather's eyes "kindled" when he relates the "glorious" death of Wolfe (6:133). Young Charley, ever the militant, does not need Grandfather's cue to exclaim, "'Oh, it was a good death to die!'" (6:133). Nor does Laurence, who ignores Grandfather's lapse into the glory of a military death. In line with his previous moral and religious identification with Apostle Eliot, Laurence remains silent—"for his heart burned within him, as the picture of Wolfe, dying on the bloodstained field of victory, arose to his imagination; and yet, he had a deep inward consciousness, that, after all, there was truer glory than could thus be won" (6:133). The slack in Grandfather's antiwar message is thus taken up by the external narrator, who delivers Laurence's telling summation of the French and Indian War: "'So, now, at last, . . . New England has gained her wish. Canada was taken!'" (6:134). Not the colonies, not America, not England—but New England. Until now, the underlying if unspoken issue—Catholicism—has remained fairly obscure; but here the real reason for New Englanders' fear of the French clearly emerges as the Catholic faith. This fear, more than a reductive, anticipatory fear of old English policy, largely explains the provincial squint in "Famous Old People."

The chief events reported in "Famous Old People" therefore concern repeated wars between England and France that extend to the New World and cannot be separated from the self-interests of New England. While the preparation for the Revolution served by one of these wars is mentioned, considerable anti-war sentiment and commentary are posed against it. The external narrator and Grandfather, either together or separately, will not allow the martial music to be played without interjecting their own discordant notes. The martial strain triggered by an event in the nineteenth-century context offers a case in point. A "tumult and uproar, passing through the street" turns out to be "a procession of the boys of Boston, in honor of Old Tippecanoe" (6:86–87). Appropriately enough, young Charley has gone off to join the rally for General Harrison's election to the presidency. Grandfather sighs, "'Ah, well! . . . Boys are the same in every generation—always aping their fathers—always taking a mimic interest in grown men's affairs'" (6:87). This observation leads Grandfather to imagine that schoolboys in 1696 imitated, through miniature war games played in the snow, New England's effort to recapture Fort Pemaquid from the French. Laurence, who sees the potential significance of such imitation, says, "'The grown people . . . might have taken this for a satire upon themselves.'" Grandfather concurs: "'Yes; the great game of war is easily shown to be ridiculous'" (6:87). Hence in this vein he thinks snowballs would be fitting weapons to use to settle national disputes—the great advantage being, as Laurence says, "'that peace would come whenever the snow melted'" (6:88).

This playful anti-war episode prepares for the most serious one delivered in the *Whole History*. After relating the disastrous loss of life in the effort to sail up the St. Lawrence to conquer Canada, Grandfather reflects that "'the old moral and religious character of New England was in danger of being utterly lost'" (6:96). To Laurence's comment that it would have been "'glorious . . . if our forefathers could have kept the country unspotted with blood,'" Grandfather replies, "'Yes, . . . but there was a stern warlike spirit in them, from the beginning. They seem never to have thought of questioning either the morality or piety of war'" (6:96).

Such martial spirit lies in the nature of those early Puritans, like Endicott, who achieve dominance. Inherited by subsequent generations, the spirit reveals itself over and over again until, by the eighteenth century, it becomes a chief surviving trait of the Puritan faith. In the first two books of the *Whole History*, Grandfather makes a few gestures to wed the militant spirit, first with religious faith and then with political faith in democracy. He knows the direction of his narrative, after all; and, predisposed to tell providential history, he would like to connect the early Puritan patriarchs with the political fathers of the Revolution. It would seem as natural to seek a coherent scheme for history as to create a tidy continuity for one's narrative. But, as we have seen, Grandfather cannot really manage to draw the typological pattern except through repeated violent contests that expose the decadence of the combatants. Thus he has a problem at the conclusion of "Famous Old People," when events in the narrative have led up to the outbreak of the Revolution: how can he offset the overall negative portrait of the Puritans and their descendants and unite them with the Revolutionary patriots under the salutary banner of democracy?

Grandfather's dilemma might be compared to the outside narrator's. Even more than Grandfather, the narrator is supremely conscious of the discrepancy between the ideals and the actions of the Puritan founders and their offspring. His introduction to "Famous Old People" identifies the rift:

This Epoch presents enough of military and worldly adventure to please our little friend Charley, in whom we discern the traits, which may hereafter render him a man of power among actual affairs, and in all the business of life. Laurence, in whom we represent a more ideal nature, probably feels a greater sympathy with the unworldly Pilgrims, and especially with the Apostle Eliot, who joined to their high excellence a spirit of love, that scarcely any other man of his day possessed. Perhaps, in a third Epoch, we shall find in individuals, and the people at large, a combination of ideal principle and adventurous action, that may attract the interest both of Laurence and Charley. (6:72)

The ensuing attitudes of Charley and Laurence surely bear out the narrator's claim. Charley continues to express the fiery Puritanical temperament. His sole interest is warfare. To his lack of sympathy for the Acadian exiles, as for the Indians, he adds insensitivity to blacks held in slavery (6:109). Laurence, meanwhile, steadfastly identifies with the downtrodden and victimized—an accumulation of historical sacrifices he will be challenged to balance against the political independence and democracy achieved in the Revolution. The challenge to Laurence accords with the one faced by us all: we too might wish to synthesize the dialectic of "ideal principle and adventurous action," no matter how radically out of balance, no matter what degree of moral qualification might need to be ignored. The narrator anticipates the possibility of reaching such a synthesis when he says in the third installment of the *Whole History* that "perhaps" a "combination" can be found.

"Liberty Tree"

The narrator somewhat oddly claims in the preface to "Famous Old People" that each volume of the *Whole History* can be read "independent of our preceding volume" and that each "may be read in disconnection with the past" (6:72), the result, perhaps, of Hawthorne's strategy to publish the individual numbers separately and then to gather them in one volume.[11] Grandfather, on the other hand, finds himself at no loss to assert an overall historical design as he takes up his narrative once again in "Liberty Tree," the Revolutionary period of the *Whole History*. Directly after relating the circumstances accompanying the imposition of the Stamp Act, he says:

> ". . . it was really amazing and terrible to see what a change came over the aspect of the people, the moment the English Parliament had passed this oppressive act. The former history of our chair, my children, has given you some idea of what a harsh, unyielding, stern set of men the old Puritans were. For a good many years back, however, it had seemed as if these characteristics were disappearing. But no sooner did England offer wrong to the colonies, than the descendants of the early settlers proved that they had the same kind of temper as their forefathers. The moment before, New England appeared like a humble and loyal subject of the crown; the next instant, she showed the grim, dark features of an old king-resisting Puritan." (6:150-51)

Once again the Puritan religious and political cause against royal authority in the seventeenth century, culminating in the Parliamentary War and the regicide of Charles I, equates with the colonial cause against George III. It does not matter that religious issues are no longer essentially at stake. Backsliding, imposition of religious tolerance by royal command,

and sectarianism experienced over the last eighty years have effectively precluded any possible unification of the colonies around religious issues. In such a void, however, political self-interest can magnetize the minds and hearts of colonists with an intensity amounting to religious fervor.

Political fervor in the Revolutionary War serves as the typological successor of Puritan piety. In much the same way that Grandfather offers serious qualifications to Puritan piety in the seventeenth century, so he presents serious qualifications to the supposedly democratically-minded colonists (particularly those of Massachusetts) in the eighteenth century. The people who invade the Province House and destroy Governor Hutchinson's papers and artwork receive more severe treatment than in "Edward Randolph's Portrait." They are a "mob," "rough figures" and "idle people . . . who were ready for any kind of mischief" (6:154). Grandfather's listeners, as well as the reader, are nevertheless invited to overlook these negative images and consider instead a historical perspective, "a moment when a loyalist and an aristocrat, like Hutchinson, might have learnt how powerless are kings, nobles, and great men, when the low and humble range themselves against them" (6:157). But taking such a perspective is not easy, for Grandfather seems almost as interested in an objective eighteenth-century observer's viewpoint as in a nineteenth-century ideologue's, one who, knowing the political results, might readily excuse activities of a "drunken multitude" (6:159) as minor compared to the overall political importance of the Revolutionary cause. Commenting on the Hutchinson mob, for example, Laurence says that " 'if the people acted in this manner, they were not worthy of even so much liberty as the King of England was willing to allow them' " (6:159). Grandfather quickly sees that he has gone too far in describing the mob and tries to recover the essence of his point and logic: " 'It was a most unjustifiable act, like many other popular movements of that time. . . . But we must not decide against the justice of the people's cause, merely because an excited mob was guilty of outrageous violence' " (6:159).

Once again, Grandfather exposes an ambivalent perspective. Details in his narrative often do not jibe with the noble democratic message. Readers, as well as Grandfather's young audience, are therefore put to the test through accumulating expectations developed from periodic references to the narrative's typological design. We increasingly become restless over how long we or they can sustain anticipation of noble and heroic deeds performed against the villainy of the crown. Our tension produced by such suspension becomes more acute when we learn that Grandfather's chair, now in the benevolent care of Hutchinson, suffers a third serious injury at the hands of the mob. That the chair is subsequently placed in a Boston coffee house and then in a barber shop, wherein it can be used by the democratic many rather than by the aristocratic few, does little to offset the recognition that every injury to the chair thus far has been associated with mob violence, at least partly iconoclastic in nature. At the outbreak of the Revolutionary War, therefore, American history seems even further removed from a harmonious marriage of qualities originally symbolized by the chair.

Grandfather is not oblivious to a need for harmony, a mediation—however contrary to the historical record—between the colonies and mother country. He claims that until the very moment of the Boston Massacre, "the angry feelings between England and America might have been pacified. England had but to stretch out the hand of reconciliation, and acknowledge that she had hitherto mistaken her rights, but would do so no more. Then, the ancient bonds of brotherhood would again have been knit together, as firmly as in old times" (6:169). Hawthorne's regret over the breach between England and America is just as evident here as in the early tales and, as will be seen, in *The Scarlet Letter* and *The English Notebooks*. The depth of this regret is once again revealed through Laurence, who has a dream in which he reconstructs the impending eruption of the Boston Massacre: "Lawrence dreamed that he was sitting in our great chair, at the window of the British Coffee House, and beheld the whole scene which Grandfather had described. It seemed to him, in his dream, that if the town's people and the soldiers would but have heard him speak a single word, all the slaughter might have been averted. But there was such an uproar, that it drowned his voice" (6:172). This dream conforms to Hawthorne's method of recreating a historical confrontation whose outcome might have shifted in a different direction from the one it took should there have been the mediating agency of a figure such as Laurence. The violence of contending historical forces might have been dispelled, thereby opening a way for language, a word, to work its healing and unifying power. Potential mediation of this kind, of course, lies at the heart of the seventeenth-century tales. In the present instance, it once again suggests that pivotal moments in historical clashes are potentially open, influenced less by moral imbalances than by accident.

Grandfather's account of the Boston Massacre seems reasonably balanced—colonists possess the noble cause, but their behavior degrades them. The ensuing bloodshed clearly brings the narrative up to the point at which Grandfather, if he intends to bring off an affirmative patriotic reading of Revolutionary events, must yoke democratic ideals with honorable character and action. This necessity explains the interlude provided by chapter 6, wherein Grandfather opens a volume and undertakes to show the children a gallery of Revolutionary portraits. Earlier in this "Liberty Tree" section, the narrator reported that "kind old Grandfather had made [Laurence] a present of a volume of engraved portraits, representing the features of eminent and famous people of all countries" (6:146). The universality implied in this volume contrasts with the provinciality of colonial portraits in chapter 6, headed by Samuel Adams, whose face and character at once liken him to the Puritans. Grandfather seems to have forgotten his previous narrative, and so too have the children, since none of them questions the link between Puritans and democracy. The typological design is simply taken for granted. The assumption is not without cause, of course. Grandfather has earlier asserted the typological connection between the Puritan founders and the Revolutionary fathers. Yet, as even the usually dependable Laurence forgets, Grandfather's depiction of the Puritans has not revealed any practitioners of democratic values, with the possible exception of Apostle Eliot—who is posed as a saint compared to his contemporaries. The typological design is obviously being forced, at the expense of the "facts" Grandfather himself has related—and related, apparently, with considerable care.

Clearly, Grandfather's knowledge of the details contained in the historical record often fails to conform to the popular nineteenth-century configuration he gives them by depending on Bancroft's "overruling Providence" (6 : 175) to link the Puritan founders to those of the Revolutionary era. Both in number and concentration, recorded events tend heavily toward darkness, persecution, violence, and death. It is not a narrative the children expect from their kindly Grandfather. Laurence often appears profoundly troubled, and he broods. Clara frequently tries to prevent Grandfather from recounting further tales of suffering and warfare and asks to hear brighter tales. Little Alice weeps openly. Even Charley wants to hear stories of bold actions disconnected from the agony produced by them. The bulk of Grandfather's narrative has nothing to do with colonial relations with England—nothing, that is, to do with a typological conflict between New and Old Worlds leading to American independence. Consequently, the greater part of the narrative deconstructs the very order and design Grandfather tries to give it.

Furthermore, Grandfather knows that the "noble" founders, whether Puritan or colonial, were not uniformly noble any more than their opponents were uniformly ignoble. He conscientiously tries to be fair. The conflict between England and American, for example, involves no unanimous division between the English and colonists. After presenting the portraits of such Revolutionary worthies as Hancock, Franklin, Warren, Otis, Quincy, Knox, and Green, Grandfather shows the children many members of Parliament who supported colonial grievances or a temperate colonial policy. He goes even further, standing aside from his own colonial sympathies to identify with the predicament of colonial Loyalists :

You must not think that there was no integrity and honor, except among those who stood up for the freedom of America. For aught I know, there was quite as much of these qualities on one side, as on the other. Do you see nothing admirable in a faithful adherence to an unpopular cause? Can you not respect that principle of loyalty, which made the royalists give up country, friends, fortune, everything, rather than be false to their king? It was a mistaken principle; but many of them cherished it honorably, and were martyrs to it. (6:177–78)

Grandfather is so absorbed in the predicament of the Loyalists that he devotes an entire chapter, "The Tory's Farewell," to their departure from Boston in 1776. The chapter is as sympathetic to its subject, Chief Justice Oliver, as critical of him and other Royalists who must give up their homeland and who will find themselves, despite their loyalty, unaccepted aliens in England. Grandfather's point, of course, is quickly understood by Laurence, who remarks: "'the misfortunes of these exiled tories . . . must have made them think of the poor exiles of Acadia.'" Even Charley momentarily forgoes the desire to hear about Washington's exploits in order to concede, "'They had a sad time of it, I suppose'" (6:196).

As in "Old News" and "Old Esther Dudley," this sympathetic portrait of an old Tory, along with the sympathy for the Loyalists elicited from the children, adds something of an unexpected twist to the patriotic motif. Preceding the portrait is Grandfather's refusal to narrate anything about the battle of Bunker Hill—he sends the children instead to a diorama for an animated reenactment. He then devotes a six-page chapter to an account of Washington's successful siege of Boston, followed by an equal number of pages to the old Tory, effectively redirecting the children's and the reader's attention to the consequences of war and thereby softening potential fanfare over Washington's triumph. These same pages, in turn, precede the penultimate chapter wherein Grandfather's narrative of the Declaration of Independence and Revolutionary War takes up less than three pages. Such limited coverage of accustomed patriotic material is abbreviated history indeed and utterly anticlimactic to a nominal pattern of political typology. There appears no flag-waving, no shouting, no celebration of any kind. The war is simply brought to summary conclusion, and then Grandfather parades before the children's eyes the maimed and wounded soldiers returning home to Massachusetts. Thus a clear sense of the expense to life and limb dominates, while scarcely any sense is conveyed that either a colonial victory or a typological fulfillment has been achieved. Grandfather never says a word about the Articles of Confederation or the Constitution, for example, which one might reasonably expect to follow earlier hints of democratic typology. Yet he does give attention to Shays Rebellion, suggesting the weakness of the Articles of Confederation, or an undiminished spirit of revolution. Again, one suspects that another design, more prevalent than democratic typology, is at work—one that involves recurrent and perhaps unnecessary violence.

Many of these peculiarities in Grandfather's coverage might be explained by the provincial focus. The *Whole History*, not at all strange to say, is from beginning to end concentrated on Massachusetts. Once Washington's army frees Boston from British occupation, Massachusetts no longer plays a primary role in Revolutionary events. And where Massachusetts is not concerned, neither is national typology, which depends on the Puritans as typal ancestors of Revolutionary leaders. Shays Rebellion *does* take place in Massachusetts and, according to the logic of Grandfather's account, its rebellious violence typifies Puritan history more fully than the rational proceedings of the Constitutional Convention. The provincial focus also underlines Grandfather's returning to Samuel Adams, who winds up in possession of Grandfather's chair. Hawthorne elides the problem, confronted in "Old Esther Dudley," of Hancock's having been elected the first governor of the State of Massachusetts. Grandfather simply skips to Adams, the second governor, whose Puritan heritage evidently completes the pattern of democratic typology and unifies the *Whole History*.

But with no sounds of fife and drum to proclaim democracy, let alone independence, and with no tribute paid to the Revolutionary or constitutional fathers, the conclusion of Grandfather's history ought to seem as unsatisfying to the reader as it is to the children. The reader can for once identify with Charley, who abruptly asks, "'And what next?'" Grandfather simply replies: "'That is all'" (6:204). In a way, Grandfather is right. His narrative really presupposes a historical structure woven from providential design and typological fulfillment. Accordingly, with the close of the Revolutionary War and the inauguration of constitutional democracy, history more or less achieves its prefigured aim. All that remains is the unpredictable interim before the second coming, the teleological heart of Puritan typology and soteriological history. We might readily excuse the children for their impatience with the notion that the zenith of human affairs has already been achieved, that everything subsequent to the Revolution, including their own lives, must logically be anticlimactic. Their imaginations, at least, tell them otherwise.

Since the facts of history have nothing further to offer by way of bringing Grandfather's narrative to a satisfying conclusion, fancy or imagination may provide one. This point, at once literary, historiographical, and moral, is made by Laurence, who wants Grandfather's chair, "'After its long intercourse with mankind,'" to reveal "'lessons of golden wisdom'" (6:204). And so, what is declared to be "all" is never quite everything. When facts give out, imagination or metaphysics takes over. Hence Grandfather's dream, the concluding chapter of "Liberty Tree" and the *Whole History*.

Grandfather's dream, in which the chair speaks to the old man, raises several issues, most prominent of which may be the reassertion of a typological design for the *Whole History*. "'In the days of the Stamp act,'" says the chair, "'I whispered in the ear of Hutchinson, bidding him to remember what stock his countrymen were descended of, and to think whether the spirit of their forefathers had utterly departed from them'" (6:207). What better imaginative authority to reinforce historical structure, let alone narrative unity, than the actual witness to all the events Grandfather narrates? The chair seems not only to approve of the typological configuration, but also to buttress its Puritan origins by mentioning seventeenth-century revolutionists whose occupancy of the chair Grandfather failed to mention: Hugh Peters, instrumental in the Parliamentary War and executed after the Restoration, along with the regicide judges, Whalley, Goffe, and Dixwell. These are British figures, to be sure, but their Puritan roles against Charles I can now be seen as foreshadowings of anti-Loyalist activity during the Revolutionary era. Grandfather's chair also claims to have " 'capered upon my wooden legs, with joy,' " when Simon Bradstreet was called upon to replace Governor Andros after the Boston Rebellion (6:207).

Even though the chair resurrects the preexistent typological design in Grandfather's account, we also recognize that justice, truth, and love—the chief ingredients of happiness the chair mentions to Grandfather—have only intermittently been evident in the narrative and rarely connected to those figures ostensibly typifying an evolving continuity of democratic principles. Nearly all the characters are extremists of one kind or another, repetitive acts of persecution and violence highlighting their behavior as much as they occupy the center of Grandfather's narrative. A concluding reference to Lady Arbella, after a long hiatus, raises once again the values of love, marriage, harmony, and art, which events in the narrative have never really evinced. These values, originally associated with England, seem entirely lost as Puritans quarrel first among themselves and then with the mother country, and as their descendants finally fight against and separate from England.

To stress the severity and violence of Puritans and their descendants, as Grandfather surely does, is not to take sides with England in the colonial conflict. Independence and democracy won by the colonies are not in dispute here. Nor is the legitimacy of the political cause against England. What is in dispute is whether national typology offers a valid configuration of American history and whether there are worthy models among the Puritans exemplifying the idealistic principles of Revolutionary leaders. While Grandfather nods in affirmation to both these propositions, he (and Hawthorne, who manipulates him) goes out of his way to denigrate potential evidence in their support. The inconsistencies and contradictions in Grandfather's narrative, I would suggest, substitute for the irony Hawthorne employs so extensively in the seventeenth- and eighteenth-century tales. The result is a countervailing pattern of intolerance, bigotry, and violence encroaching upon and all but obliterating what typological design exists.

This latter pattern concerns Hawthorne because it impinges on the nineteenth century, affecting not only the fictional persons of Laurence and Charley but also Hawthorne himself. Laurence's sensitivity and his qualms over the basic militancy of the Puritan legacy may fail again to offset the narrow and fiery extension of that legacy already demonstrated by his young brother. The conflict of values in the two boys is essentially a projection of the fratricidal nature of English and American relations over the past two centuries. No childish cuteness is at play when the chair complains to Grandfather that it is sore from Charley's having run into it with a wheel barrow. This fourth major injury to the chair, occurring this time outside Grandfather's history, now becomes a sign of ominous events when latter-day Puritans like Charley reach adulthood in the nineteenth century.

The nineteenth-century setting of the *Whole History* really ends on a rather bleak note, quite aside from the cold January weather. We are left with a sense that the large conflicts of history have overwhelmed basic values that could promote human happiness. Democracy has been achieved, but the cost has been great. Without being quite conscious of it, Grandfather has concentrated on the cost, as his sympathy shifts between absolutist contestants who allowed no margin for compromise. Lost in the course of the struggle between Old and New Worlds was the role of mediating or synthesizing extremes, the role that Grandfather resuscitates and performs in his own narrative. American democrat and patriot, he no doubt feels happy to be rid of English domination and the worst traits of English culture that led to that domination. But grandfather is also aware, the text suggests, that the best of English culture was lost along with the worst, especially as the best was personified in Lady Arbella and Isaac Johnson, in addition to those few early Puritans whose habit of moderation became a recessive legacy within Puritan extremism.

4

The Recovery of English Traditions in "The Old Manse" and "The Custom-House"

With the completion of *The Whole History of Grandfather's Chair*, Hawthorne concluded a decade of writing that often looked to New England's past for its best subjects and that primarily focused either on the tension between the Old and New Worlds or on the development of an extreme form of Puritanism opposed to the cultural and aesthetic values of England. The large majority of Hawthorne's best tales, as we now judge them, were written during this period, but Hawthorne had little reason to believe from their example that he could make a living with his pen. He received small and often delayed payment for the stories as they appeared in periodicals or yearbooks; and the 1837 edition of *Twice-told Tales*, in which many of the stories were collected, was not a financial success.[1] Financial considerations, particularly after his engagement to Sophia Peabody, led him to accept a position at the Boston Custom House from 1839 to 1841, and then to join the Brook Farm enterprise for several months in 1841.[2] Except for the *Whole History* and *Biographical Stories* (1842) (which brought little money to Hawthorne), "John Inglefield's Thanksgiving" (1840), and "A Virtuoso's Collection" (1842), he was unable to write during this period.[3] Following his marriage to Sophia and his move to the Old Manse in July 1842, Hawthorne began another, although less productive, period of creativity.

Considering earlier historical works marginally involved with the decay of Old World aesthetic values in the New World, and also considering Hawthorne's frustration and fear over his failure to earn a living as a writer, it now seems appropriate that during the years at the Manse he began to focus on the problems of being an artist in America. "Drowne's Wooden Image" and "The Artist of the Beautiful" (written as companion pieces and published in 1844)[4] present the best of Hawthorne's early attempts at self-projection into artist figures who must contend with the anti-art legacy of New England Puritanism. Both artists in these tales, Drowne and Owen Warland, successfully complete an imaginative work of art. Yet in the resolution of the stories, each character ceases artistic creation, perhaps reflecting potential if unacceptable alternatives for Hawthorne himself. "Drowne's Wooden Image" and "The Artist of the Beautiful" serve as pivotal works in Hawthorne's career, revealing on the one hand the inherited cultural bias against art with which Hawthorne was at odds, and anticipating on the other hand the strategy he later adopts in "The Old Manse," "The Custom-House," and *The Scarlet Letter.* Both reflect the burden of England's aesthetic traditions having been expelled from Puritan and Revolutionary America. But they also suggest, more cogently than does "Passages from a Relinquished Work," Hawthorne's conscious process of recovering those very traditions.[5]

In "Drowne's Wooden Image," Hawthorne focuses on a native artist whose career precedes the final separation of colonial America from England. Far more seriously than is Alice Vane or the artist in "The Prophetic Pictures," Drowne is submitted as a prototype: "the first American who is known to have attempted,—in a very humble line, it is true,—that art in which we can now reckon so many names already distinguished, or rising to distinction" (10:307). Having attained a modest reputation for carving figureheads and other decorative works imitating real-life models, Drowne is suddenly commissioned by Captain Hunnewell to create a work utterly unlike anything he has done before. He does create it—a beautiful woman—out of a passion overtly equated to Pygmalion's. From the first obscure hints of the image taking shape in the wood until it fully emerges, the painter John Singleton Copley pronounces it an imaginative triumph, resulting from "'the very spirit of genius'" (10:313). But other Boston observers are not as receptive as Copley, suggesting one reason for Drowne's usual carvings having achieved nothing more than mechanical imitation: "The bigots of the day hinted that it would be no matter of surprise if an evil spirit were allowed to enter this beautiful form, and seduce the carver to destruction" (10:315). Beyond the allusion to the Pygmalion myth, the specter of Puritan demonology clearly survives in pre-Revolutionary times.

By giving actual shape to his ideal, Drowne transgresses the conventional rules of verisimilitude. Yet he is not alone in being seduced by the imaginative reality of his artwork. When Boston citizens see the beautiful image in the company of Captain Hunnewell on the street, they all believe "'Drowne's wooden image has come to life!'" (10:316). So perfectly crafted is the art that young men feel the world is a dark place in her absence. Not so their elders. Accordingly, "the aged, whose recollections dated as far back as witch-times, shook their heads, and hinted that our forefathers would have thought it a pious deed to burn the daughter of oak with fire" (10:318). In the end, of course, Captain Hunnewell sails away with the imaginative creation, leaving Drowne with a lifeless physical image. A rumor circulates to the effect that a beautiful foreign lady had sought aid from the captain and that it was she who sailed away with him after serving as a model for Drowne's work. Although this opinion is absolutely wrong,[6] everyone in Boston save Copley can take comfort in Drowne's not having violated the officially sanctioned aesthetic of mimesis after all. Drowne subsequently reverts to that aesthetic, mechanically carving "blockheads" (10:320) deservedly modeled after local citizens; and he ultimately becomes a deacon in the church from whose anti-imaginative doctrines he never again deviates.

The fate of art in the eighteenth-century setting of "Drowne's Wooden Image" scarcely offers a positive American example to which Hawthorne can link his own work and aspirations. The iconoclastic Puritan tradition still exerts firm restraints on imaginative art. Romantic or not, true art must really go elsewhere for its reception or its very life. Hence the embodied spirit of Drowne's imagination is escorted aboard the aptly named *Cynosure* by Captain Hunnewell, who, as a "cavalier" (10:318), opposes Boston's Puritanic survivors in a historical analogue dating back to the English Civil War. Hinting by contrast at Puritan iconoclasm in the seventeenth century, this perspective on England's allegiance to art surfaces again in a forecast of the later eighteenth century beyond the story's time frame. With the outbreak of the Revolutionary War, Copley will side with the Loyalists and eventually go to England, where he will earn his fame as an artist. Despite Drowne's single great achievement, America is left bereft of art while England carries on its aesthetic continuities. Still, the depth of Hawthorne's desire for artistic antecedents in America who defied the plain style aesthetic of the Puritan tradition can be measured by his disregarding the historical case long enough to allow Drowne his one imaginative success.

The nineteenth-century descendants of Drowne's audience presented in "The Artist of the Beautiful" differ in no essential way from their forebears. They have little if any conception of beauty, and they certainly fail to understand Owen Warland's desire to give spiritual embodiment to the "Beautiful Idea" (10:450). Only when Owen keeps the town clock and people's watches regulated to utilitarian perfection does he receive praise. Only when he engraves "in the plainest possible style, omitting a variety of fanciful flourishes" (10:455) does he satisfy the inherited Puritan aesthetic. In terms of the imaginative artist embedded in his nature, Owen is an exile among his practical, no-nonsense contemporaries, represented by the malicious and nearly blind Peter Hovenden and the good-natured pragmatist, Robert Danforth.

Owen's wish "to spiritualize machinery" in the form of a butterfly whose beauty "should attain to the ideal which nature has proposed to herself, in all her creatures, but has never taken pains to realize" (10:465–66) conforms to the highest aim of art as Emerson viewed it, involving nothing less than externalizing the spirit of creation, which is divinity itself. Perhaps Peter Hovenden recognizes Owen's wish (in traditional Puritan terms) as a sacrilegious intervention into the mystery of God's creativity. For, evidently, something far more than utilitarian principles is at stake when Hovenden discovers an incomplete version of Owen's butterfly and says, "'Owen! there is witchcraft in these little chains, and wheels, and paddles!'" Thus he resorts to the iconoclasm of his Puritan ancestors: "'See! with one pinch of my finger and thumb, I am going to deliver you from all future peril'" (10:456). While Hovenden believes that an evil spirit dwells in the mechanism, we understand that Owen is right: Hovenden is the "'Evil Spirit'" (10:457), not only of Owen but also of the development of beauty and art in America. Even Annie Hovenden, the mistaken source of Owen's dedication to art from whom he expects the nourishing power of sympathy, reveals a trace of her father's Puritanic spirit when she inadvertently destroys another version of the butterfly.

Owen, of course, finally succeeds in creating a spiritualized mechanism, his own growth evolving, along with his creation, in stages paralleling those of a natural butterfly.[7] When he gives the artwork to Annie as a belated wedding present, he is met by Peter Hovenden, Robert Danforth (Annie's husband), and the emblem of their marriage's creativity, an infant son. The three generations literally presented in this audience clearly stand for the past, present, and future; and hence their combined response to Owen's butterfly suggests the status of American art over a long period of history. As a result of their shared affection, tolerance, and degree of latent imaginative capacity, Robert and Annie manage to sustain the creative life of the butterfly. But the closer the unimaginative and iconoclastic Peter Hovenden approaches the fluttering creature, the more enervated it becomes until its spirit verges on perishing. This affliction on art from the accumulated bigotry of the past has little chance of being offset in the future, as typified in the Danforths' child, whose supposed innocence and "childish faith" cannot compete against dark influences inherited from Grandfather Hovenden (10:474). Thus, "with his grandsire's sharp and shrewd expression in his face" (10:475), the child snatches the butterfly out of the air and destroys it. Within the story's world of symbol and allegory, the prospect for American art seems no better in the future than it was in the Puritan past.

Owen's indifference to the destruction of the butterfly apparently suggests his newly won ability to transcend ordinary values of the material world, as opposed to Drowne, who sinks back into those values and thrives in typical Yankee fashion. Even though the butterfly represents "the intellect, the imagination, the sensibility, the soul, of an Artist of the Beautiful" (10:471), its external life ostensibly has less import than the internal spirit of its creator. Owen, we are urged to believe, "had caught a far other butterfly than this. When the artist rose high enough to achieve the Beautiful, the symbol by which he made it perceptible to mortal senses became of little value in his eyes, while his spirit possessed itself in the enjoyment of the Reality"(10:475). The logic of this romantic, transcendental notion surely leads to the elevation of the artist, within whom Platonic ideals can be savored for all their private worth. But whatever Hawthorne's sympathy with this idea may be, it also offers a convenient refuge for any artist whose successfully realized work fails to elicit an appreciative audience.[8]

"The Artist of the Beautiful" shows how far Hawthorne was tempted to go in framing the cultural and historical relation of art and audience in America. Like "Drowne's Wooden Image," the story actually reflects Hawthorne's worst doubts about making his living by creating genuine art. Sensing the high call of art, Hawthorne entertains fantasies reminiscent of those written by the desperately impoverished Poe: Drowne has sufficient finances to divorce any thought of acquiring gold from his art; and Owen receives an inheritance allowing him to give away freely "a gem of art that a monarch would have purchased with honors and abundant wealth" (10:473). The solutions in these stories are ambiguous, however. Hawthorne, like Melville, did not want to write merely to sell or wholly for himself, and thus he could not finally endorse the successful, anticlimactic fate of Drowne or the transcendental escape of Owen. But he could identify with Drowne and Owen's confrontation with a culture largely unappreciative and even suspicious of art, owing to Puritan iconoclasm and severed English continuities. As incomplete self-projections of Hawthorne, Drowne and Owen foreshadow the self-projected narrators in "The Old Manse" and "The Custom-House" who far more critically confront their culture and its Puritan origins. Unlike Drowne and Owen, the narrators in both of these works dedicate themselves to an ongoing creation of art, and their purpose reflects Hawthorne's strategy to seek out artistic predecessors in the Old World. Rather than reflecting on the lack of aesthetic and cultural continuities in America, Hawthorne subtly asserts them in his own voice as if they had never been broken; and in so doing he takes the first definitive step toward creating an American tradition of art for himself.

"The Old Manse" and "The Custom-House" have a curious distinction in Hawthorne's canon: both serve as loosely autobiographical prefaces to works that overshadow them, particularly "The Old Manse." In "The Custom-House," of course, Hawthorne courts more attention to the preface by giving a fictive account of how the materials for *The Scarlet Letter* tale came into possession of the author. (Also, he offers the now famous moonlight setting for romance, which scholars interested in generic definitions have exploited for its relevance not only to *The Scarlet Letter* but also to Hawthorne's other romances.) Even though references to the old Manse appear several times in "The Custom-House," the relationship between the two prefaces has not been appreciated as fully as it should be.[9] The remainder of this chapter explores the way England or English cultural models lie at the center of Hawthorne's concern in both prefaces, helping to prepare for yet another concentration on Old and New World conflicts when Hawthorne returns to the seventeenth century in *The Scarlet Letter*. "The Old Manse" has less to do with the stories in *Mosses from an Old Manse*, written before it, than with "The Custom-House" and *The Scarlet Letter* that follow. Both are very much about Hawthorne's own house of fiction, devoting as much attention to why Hawthorne cannot write as to how he manages to write to begin with. These prefaces are therefore crucial for establishing why and how Hawthorne discovers his "novelistic" voice in *The Scarlet Letter* and later works, a process inescapably connected to Hawthorne's looking beyond America to England for an artistic spirit and tradition to carry out his resolve to be an American writer worthy of the scribbling sons of John Bull.

"The Old Manse"

Hawthorne wrote "The Old Manse" between 1845 and 1846 as a prefatory piece for his third collection of tales. Containing an obvious pastoral version of Hawthorne's life from 1842 to 1846, it begins less than a year after he left Brook Farm and only weeks after he married Sophia and moved into the Manse, an old residence built by the Emerson family on the outskirts of Concord. The entries in *The American Notebooks* covering these years confirm that, during good weather at least, Hawthorne actually believed he was enjoying a real-life pastoral, transcendental in character and opposed to the communitarian pastoralism promised at Brook Farm. The joy of an extended honeymoon is evident in all four years. References and allusions often equate Hawthorne and Sophia to Adam and Eve, the Manse environment to Eden. A full, prelapsarian consciousness of innocent, abundant sexuality often highlights the entries. Spiritual regeneration, perhaps the chief end and value of the pastoral since Virgil, is suggested time and again—and one gathers that this regeneration results as much from sex as it does from the bucolic landscape. When, therefore, Hawthorne advises in the preface that men plant a seed, he is hardly speaking about agriculture alone. Among the bountiful harvests produced during the Manse years is the Hawthornes' first child, Una, whose name carries with it pastoral associations of Spenser.

The overall diagraming of the "Manse's" pastoral geography seems largely indebted to classical and Renaissance models, particularly those of Virgil and Sidney, which Hawthorne blends with his own variations.[10] In graphic terms, there are two concentric circles involving separate zones or stages, each having its own components. The outer zone has two separate areas, no doubt distinctive for America, divided between east and west. To the west stretches the realm of frontier or wilderness, the realm inviting Natty Bumppo and Huck Finn, the territory most interesting to readers such as Richard Slotkin or Leslie Fiedler. This area owes little to Virgilian or Renaissance models but contains at once a Christian and Romantic design. Hawthorne gives brief but important attention to this zone, to which we shall return later. Primarily, focus rests on the outer zone of conventional society to the east, an urban world of flux and accident with all the complexity, pressure, and questionable values the pastoralist wishes to escape. This is real, corrupt civilization. Here we might easily find conflict and war.

The inner zone of Hawthorne's pastoral configuration has features both Arcadian and classical, a middle landscape of natural harmony, undisturbed seasonal cycles, fertility, and tradition. Here lie perennial values: brotherhood as opposed to fratricide, fruitful husbandry as opposed to sterile nihilism, cultural and natural continuity as opposed to nervous programs for change or radical iconoclasm. Harsh New England winters have no place within this mixed scheme of Edenic, classical, and Renaissance elements—winters much lamented in *The American Notebooks*. Predictably, Hawthorne becomes the farmer in Virgil's *Georgics*—planting, tending, and harvesting his garden, picking up windfalls in his orchard. Nature is beneficent, as is the god Saturn who appears at the autumn feast gorging upon "vegetable children" (10:15). Lest any doubt remain about the classical origins of this orderly scheme, Hawthorne extols the honey bees, to which creatures Virgil devotes the last book of the *Georgics* as representatives of a harmonious social system, both domestic and political.

At the center of these concentric circles lies the Manse itself, serving not only as the sacred shrine within an Arcadian formula but also as an enduring symbol of historical continuity. For Hawthorne clearly gives the Manse historical signification far greater than its years or setting deserve, and by so doing he expresses once again his absorbing interest in English cultural models antedating those in America. The Manse is evidently no mere house, fictional or otherwise.[11] Instead, it calls to mind "one of the time-honored parsonages of England" (10:4). In keeping with the sense of continuity and tradition inside and outside its walls evoked by this English metaphor, Hawthorne originally considered entitling the preface "Wall-Flowers from an Old Abbey" but thought such a title was "too fine."[12] But an English abbey-parsonage, either predating or existing separately from Puritanism, is the first and ruling historical image of the Manse, as if layered with time-honored values that America really was unable to offer— the very legendary associations over the lack of which Hawthorne laments in prefaces to *The House of the Seven Gables* and *The Marble Faun*. Hawthorne's justification for the use of the Manse in the title of *Mosses* is therefore significant: "the word is not exclusively Scotch, but antique English as well."[13]

Reinforcing the image of the Manse-as-Abbey, especially in its religious dimension, is the description of the Manse's former occupants: "A priest had built it; a priest had succeeded to it; other priestly men, from time to time, had dwelt in it; and children, born in its chambers, had grown up to assume the priestly character" (10:4). These men are really Puritan (and the descendants of Puritan) ministers, clergymen and pastors—titles appropriate to New England divines that Hawthorne assigns to them after first labeling them priests. The superimposition of an abbey-parsonage and priests on a Yankee setting represents Hawthorne's new strategy to reforge broken links with English cultural traditions. Hawthorne knew his New England primer and history too thoroughly to ascribe these anachronistic and anomalous terms to the meeting ground of Puritanism-Unitarianism-Transcendentalism without an overriding purpose:[14] to enlarge the historical import of the Manse in order to gain access to traditions of Christianity and pastoralism not only coexisting with but preceding the rise of Puritanism. In a deep sense, he reintroduces the very cultural constituents that his Puritan ancestors took such considerable pain to exclude. Having created an enlarged time frame, Hawthorne provides himself a stable backdrop to which he can juxtapose elements of American history. Given the support for art in the Anglican and Catholic traditions, the Manse conceived of as an English abbey-parsonage implies the kind of setting in which Hawthorne would not have to take "shame to [himself] for having been so long a writer of idle stories" (10:4), an impious occupation to his Puritan ancestors who, as imagined in "The Custom-House," condemn him for sloughing the work of God in this world (1:10).

Whatever shame Hawthorne does feel has far less to do with his being a writer than with his writing only short fiction. For, as so many commentators have stressed, he hopes to "light upon an intellectual treasure in the old Manse, well worth those hoards of long-hidden gold, which people seek for in moss-grown houses. . . . I resolved at least to achieve a novel, that should evolve some deep lesson, and should possess physical substance enough to stand alone" (10:4–5). Both his hope and resolve will go unsatisfied, postponed until the discovery of the fictional treasure—the scarlet letter enclosed within Surveyor Pue's parchment—in "The Custom-House." What Hawthorne feels when he first enters the Manse is anathema to creative work. But he has not yet conceived of the Manse as an English abbey. The Manse's study, which affords "snug seclusion to a scholar," and where Emerson wrote *Nature*, stifles him. The reason is predictable, and yet, except for "Passages from a Relinquished Work," Hawthorne had not previously made his grievance over the anti-aesthetic views of his ancestors so plain. The study's walls are "blackened with the smoke of unnumbered years, and made still blacker by the grim prints of Puritan ministers that hung around. These worthies looked strangely like bad angels, or, at least, like men who had wrestled so continually and so sternly with the devil, that somewhat of his sooty fierceness had been imparted to their own visages" (10:5). Evidently, Hawthorne is preparing to confront the Puritan tradition over the matter of art.

Accordingly, to give the study an atmosphere within which art and life itself might flourish, Hawthorne covers the blackened walls with a "cheerful coat of paint, and golden-tinted paper-hangings"; and he replaces the "grim prints" with "one of Raphael's Madonnas, and two pleasant little pictures of the Lake of Como" in northern Italy (10:5).[15] Canceling the aura of the Puritan past, these alterations suggest reversals of history resonant with European Catholic traditions, thereby supplementing the idea of enlarging the narrow confines of the Puritan influence on American history. The pastoral setting, the metaphoric English parsonage, the association of priest and Puritan minister, and the Italian source and setting of the pictures—all of these suggest Hawthorne's attempt to extend the context of the Manse beyond the parochial boundaries of Concord, of New England, and of America herself. He thereby establishes a universalized framework within which to explore, among other issues, the historical relations of England and America.

Nature herself, as the pastoral setting in part suggests, becomes the universal framework absorbing the patterns and twists of history. Hawthorne locates the Manse, as a tentative English symbol fixed in space, in the center of this framework. Nature and history revolve around the Manse while simultaneously interpenetrating its interior zone. As the pastoral garden and orchard partially encircle the Manse, so does the adjacent Concord River, "the river of peace and quietness" (10:6). The river, in its eternal flow, offers a stable reality transcending the artificial or mechanistic purpose for which industrializing Americans might use it: "From the incurable indolence of its nature, the stream is happily incapable of becoming the slave of human ingenuity, as is the fate of so many a wild, free mountain-torrent. While all things else are compelled to subserve some useful purpose, it idles its sluggish life away, in lazy liberty, without turning a solitary spindle, or affording even water-power enough to grind the corn that grows upon its banks" (10:6–7).[16] The river and the writer are very much at one, especially in their non-practical, non-Puritanic idleness.

Beyond the inner pastoral circle, however, lies the outer circle of turbulent civilization. At one time in history, the Manse presented a vantage point for the battle of Lexington and Concord in 1775. The clergyman who then lived in the Manse "saw the irregular array of his parishioners on the farther side of the river, and the glittering line of the British, on the hither bank. He awaited, in an agony of suspense, the rattle of the musketry. It came—and there needed but a gentle wind to sweep the battle-smoke around this quiet house" (10:6). With the smoke enveloping the Manse, the house becomes located historically, a setting of peace and pastoral stability from which to examine the violence and warring disruptions of the external world.

Once he establishes the relation between the Manse and the Revolutionary War, Hawthorne widens his vision to take in landmarks of the battle. The only one that stands out is a granite obelisk, nearly twenty feet in height, commemorating the dead of Concord. Hawthorne's commentary on the obelisk deserves close attention, for he not only questions the insular, patriotic motives of the descendants who raised it but also, alluding to the occupation of Cain in the biblical account, criticizes Emerson's "embattled farmers" for spilling the blood of their English brothers. The obelisk "has grown up from the soil that was fertilized with British blood." Moreover, it is a fitting symbol for the provincial villagers to erect, "in illustration of a matter of local interest, rather than what was suitable to commemorate an epoch of national history" (10:8). These descendants, Hawthorne adds, "might rightfully claim the privilege of building a memorial" (10:9); yet he has already hinted at their disregard for the national dimension of the war and at their narrow-minded dismissal of the British blood that is, meta-phorically at least, interfused throughout the obelisk and, by genealogical extension, throughout the villagers themselves.

As we might expect from the historical tales, Hawthorne is greatly ab-sorbed by the larger historical implications of the war, those involving the cutting of blood ties with the mother country upon the political birth of the United States. His political loyalties notwithstanding, he continues to worry over the violent separation from England as an event bristling with moral and cultural repercussions. Evidence of this worry is furnished in his treatment of a grave "marked by a small, moss-grown fragment of stone at the head, and another at the foot—the grave of two British soldiers" (10:9). This grave is a "humbler token of the fight, yet a more interesting one than the granite obelisk" (10:9). It becomes still more interesting after Hawthorne hears the legend about it from James Russell Lowell:

A youth, in the service of the clergyman, happened to be chopping wood, that April morning, at the back door of the Manse; and when the noise of the battle rang from side to side of the bridge, he hastened across the intervening field, to see what might be going forward. It is rather strange, by the way, that this lad should have been so diligently at work, when the whole population of town and country were startled out of their customary business, by the advance of the British troops. Be that as it might, the tradition says that the lad now left his task, and hurried to the battle-field, with the axe still in his hand. The British had by this time retreated—the Americans were in pursuit—and the late scene of strife was thus deserted by both parties. Two soldiers lay on the ground; one was a corpse; but, as the young New-Englander drew nigh, the other Briton raised himself painfully upon his hands and knees, and gave a ghastly stare into his face. The boy—it must have been a nervous im-pulse, without purpose, without thought, and betokening a sensitive and impressible nature, rather than a hardened one—the boy uplifted his axe, and dealt the wounded soldier a fierce and fatal blow upon the head. (10:9–10)

This legend serves as a paradigm representing the entire Revolutionary War, especially its fratricidal nature, despite Hawthorne's awareness that its "circumstances cannot altogether be reconciled with probability"(10:9):

The story comes home to me like truth. Oftentimes, as an intellectual and moral exercise, I have sought to follow that poor youth through his subsequent career, and observe how his soul was tortured by the blood-stain, contracted, as it had been, before the long custom of war had robbed human life of its sanctity, and while it still seemed murderous to slay a brother man. This one circumstance has borne more fruit for me, than all that history tells us of the fight. (10:10)

As in "Molineux," "Old News," and "Legends of the Province-House," Hawthorne worries over the war between brothers, particularly if that war was an outcome of "a nervous impulse, without purpose, without thought."[17] While there appears no further explicit comment on the war or the colonial separation from England in "The Old Manse," the evocation of the English abbey-parsonage suggests Hawthorne's desire to reestablish at least one link of the former ties severed during the Revolutionary period.

Another historical link Hawthorne would like to reestablish involves Indian life also predating the Puritan migration. His sensibility is far more excited by humble artifacts of the Indians—"spear and arrow-heads, the chisels, and other implements of war, labor, and the chase, which the plough turns up from the soil"—than it is by battles and chaos in history (10:10). These artifacts, "so different from the productions of civilized machinery," Thoreau teaches him to identify, and they in turn prompt an evocation of an Indian village, which summons "to life the painted chiefs and warriors, the squaws at their household toil, and the children sporting among the wigwams; while the little wind-rocked papoose swings from the branch of a tree" (10:11). Another epoch of history is thus added, this time one of a pastoral Indian community in harmony with nature, to the widening circle of associations upon which Hawthorne sympathetically meditates within the Manse.

By telescoping the vistas of time and space in these consecutive strata, Hawthorne creates historical connections for the Manse as he does for the arrowhead. The method is the same, even though Hawthorne suggests that the arrowhead, being a more ancient relic, has greater value because it represents a life superior to that of the nineteenth century. The aboriginal vision thus permits a comparison of past and present. "It can hardly be told whether it is a joy or a pain, after such a momentary vision, to gaze around in the broad daylight of reality, and see stone-fences, white houses, potatoe-fields, and men doggedly hoeing, in their shirt-sleeves and home-spun pantaloons" (10:11). Although the observation of incessant labor in the fields seems no less pleasant to him than to Thoreau in *Walden*, Hawthorne counters the nostalgic temptation to glorify primitive life by recalling the Manse and associations of time now attached to it. "But this is nonsense. The old Manse is better than a thousand wigwams" (10:11). With this reminder of the Manse comes a narrowing of the historical view, a return into focus of the Manse itself, leading the reader back to the house through the orchard and garden.

Hawthorne himself calls attention to the expanding-contracting structure of time and space in the work: "What with the river, the battle-field, the orchard, and the garden, the reader begins to despair of finding his way back into the old Manse" (10:15). Seemingly casual, then, the digressions on locations around the Manse are actually designed to enhance its historical ramifications. The technique achieves two aims: it locates the Manse in a historical "space," and it prepares the context by which the subsequent discoveries in the house can be fixed, compared, and evaluated.

Once inside the Manse again, on this occasion in its upper floors, Hawthorne creates a historical perspective extending back to a time when England and America were united. "Happy the man who, in a rainy day, can betake himself to a huge garret, stored, like that of the Manse, with lumber that each generation has left behind it, from a period before the Revolution" (10:16). The Manse therefore houses influences of the Old and New Worlds, its library containing works of both Catholic and Puritan divinity. Yet the prospect of finding an "intellectual treasure" in this library soon results in disappoinment. Among the theological folios, quartos, and smaller volumes, Hawthorne searches for "any living thought, which should burn like a coal of fire, or glow like an inextinguishable gem, beneath the dead trumpery that had long hidden it. But I found no such treasure; all was dead alike" (10:19). While the older volumes may once have warmed their audiences, the "frigidity of the modern productions, on the other hand, was characteristic and inherent" (10:20).[18] Since the theological works from both the distant and the recent past possess no vitality and do not warm his sense of history, Hawthorne tosses them aside as "accumulations of, for the most part, stupendous impertinence: (10:19).

The "blighted" little volumes, the "mouldy thought," and the lack of nourishment in the religious volumes contrast with the life-sustaining reality of the orchard and garden.[13] Apple trees "offer their fruit to every wayfarer—apples that are bitter-sweet with the moral of times' vicissitude" (10:12). Summer squashes proclaim beauty, reality, and purpose in life: "Gazing at them, I felt that, by my agency, something worth living for had been done. A new substance was borne into the world. They were real and tangible existences, which the mind could seize hold of and rejoice in" (10:15). But not all writing from the past is dead: "Nothing, strange to say, retained any sap, except what had been written for the passing day and year, without the remotest pretension or idea of permanence" (10:20). As in "Old News," old newspapers and almanacs do retain vitality because they are real and tangible; and yet, at the same time, they reproduce for the imaginative eye distinct images of their recorded epochs. The perusal of these documents stimulates a series of associations that, through memory, "opens the door to the past."[20]

In the first half of "The Old Manse," history interacts with the work's setting in an intricate pastoral structure having elements of both the Arcadian and classical formulas. The area nearest the Manse, the orchard and garden, is the pastoral land, an Arcadian zone that consecrates and protects the central location—often the dwelling of a holy man devoted to enduring virtues. The Revolutionary War represents one facet of the outer area of turbulence; the downfall of traditional Indian life (once in organic harmony with nature) at the hands of American colonists represents another. Both these disruptive historical campaigns are appropriately located at a distance from the Manse and its surrounding garden and orchard. Other constituents of the pastoral formula also surface in "The Old Manse." A sacred stream or spring flows adjacent to the pastoral inner circle.[21] The Saturnian element of the conventional pastoral appears in Hawthorne's festive invocation of Saturn commemorating the autumn harvest.[22] And, in semi-autobiographical manner, Hawthorne stands for the poet-sojourner who, in the standard Renaissance Arcadian plot-line, methodically wanders back and forth from the outer circle to the inner shrine, gaining sustenance from the latter in order to reenter the outside world, while selecting pertinent worldly experiences to hallow inside. These movements of the poet-sojourner evoke the traditional meaning of the pastoral structure; in Walter R. Davis's words, "the three parts of the pastoral setting represent gradual purification toward the center: from the turbulent, heroic, and sometimes 'subnatural' world with all its complexities and accidents, to the simple natural world that includes the outer world's elements purified, to the supernatural center where the human and the divine meet."[23]

One complexity that Hawthorne faces in using this pastoral design is that to some extent he must *create* the sacred center. The author achieves this creation in the first half of the preface by associating architectural and spiritual traditions of England and the Continent with the New England house. Such translation of Anglo-European culture to America reverses the course of its expulsion begun in Puritan times. More specifically, intimations of cultural traditions preceding the rise of Puritanism serve Hawthorne's purpose of promoting lasting values that contrast with the topical ones of the outer circle beyond the Manse and garden.

The second half of "The Old Manse" begins with Hawthorne's enlargement of the idea of the Manse as a sacred receptacle of time and human values. In this instance, he recalls fundamental values fostered by primitive experience in nature, a romantic and Arcadian condition analogous to Eden. Accompanied by Ellery Channing, Hawthorne rows up the Assabeth River, a tributary of the Concord and thus linked to the pastoral inner circle. On the bank of the river, in the heart of the woods, the two wayfarers reenact the organic relation of American Indians with nature: "Our fire, red-gleaming among the trees, and we beside it, . . . all seemed in unison with the river gliding by, and the foliage rustling over us" (10:24). Freedom obtained in the woods allows a "return within the system of human society, not as a dungeon and a chain, but as a stately edifice, whence we could go forth at will into statelier simplicity" (10:25). The "stately edifice" most immediately refers to the Manse as abbey-parsonage, a social institution having historical value. Hawthorne thus attaches this early primordial experience in the woods to the solid reality of the Manse, past and present joining once again in an essential union.

Grounded in historical continuity and in values derived from an organic relation between man and nature, the Manse contrasts with transient ideas held by contemporaries occupying the outer circle of the pastoral scheme: "how gently did [the Manse's] gray, homely aspect rebuke the speculative extravagances of the day! It had grown *sacred*, in connection with the artificial life against which we inveighed; it had been a home, for many years, in spite of all; it was my home, too;—and, with these thoughts, it seemed to me that all the artifice and conventionalism of life was but an impalpable thinness upon its surface, and that the depth below was none the worse for it" (10:25; emphasis added).

The Manse finally becomes established as the historical and spiritual foundation of society—as home and as parsonage. Hawthorne prays that "the upper influences might long protect the institutions that had grown out of the heart of mankind" (10:26). This prayer must be interpreted in conjunction with the pastoral literary convention, especially in light of the seasonal cycle upon which the work as a whole is structured, for the prayer has significance only in contrasting relation to "the dusty glare and tumult of the world" at large (10:28). That this prayer comes near the end of summer complements the Saturnian reign over Arcadia and parallels Hawthorne's paean to early autumn following shortly thereafter: "I recline upon the still unwithered grass, and whisper to myself:—'Oh, perfect day!—Oh, beautiful world!—Oh, beneficent God!' And it is the promise of a blissful Eternity; for our Creator would never have made such lovely days, and have given us the deep hearts to enjoy them, above and beyond all thought, unless we were meant to be immortal. This sunshine is the golden pledge thereof. It beams through the gates of Paradise and shows us glimpses far inward" (10:27–28). The culmination of the pastoral structure is now complete as the human and divine join together in the Arcadian circle.

These latter words of Hawthorne, reminiscent of the sensual yet spiritual flights of Jonathan Edwards, suggest that the ultimate historical experience offers a preview of heavenly experience—a point that will acquire even greater significance in "The Custom-House." With this fleeting glimpse of the image of divine things, Hawthorne has built "The Old Manse" toward a climactic evocation of faith. The Arcadian territory surrounding the Manse consequently evokes Bunyan's "Enchanted Ground, through which the pilgrim travelled on his way to the Celestial City" (10:28).

Seeing the Manse as a symbolic repository of history and faith pemits an acceptance of the bittersweet effect of time on man's life, an acceptance indicated by the equation of ripe apples to the autumn of human life:

There is no feeling like what is caused by this faint, doubtful, yet real perception, if it be not rather a foreboding, of the year's decay—so blessedly sweet and sad, in the same breath.

Did I say that there was no feeling like it? Ah, but there is a half-acknowledged melancholy, like to this, when we stand in the perfected vigor of our life, and feel that Time has now given us all his flowers, and that the next work of his never idle fingers must be—to steal them, one by one away! (10:26)

This is the irony of time and part of the irony of history—that when nature and humankind are most poised, most hearty, decay sets in, reversing the process of life and leading to death. While nature comes full circle again in the spring, human life has only the possibility of spiritual rebirth. The pastoral itself involves a degree of spiritual rebirth in this world, an opportunity to recover a harmony lost in the usual chaos bewildering human experience. Hawthorne does not, however, extend the pastoral sentiment to the utopian or millennial notion of achieving heavenly rejuvenation in this life. For him, the golden age is finally reserved for the past, whether in terms of his actual experience at the Manse later translated into pastoral literary conventions or in terms of the Judeo-Christian idea of Eden. If he learned nothing else at Brook Farm, he learned to dispense with hopes of attaining heaven on earth. Spiritual rebirth must ultimately take place in a world beyond this one, not in history. Immersed as he is *in history,* Hawthorne refuses to posit a metaphysic of evolution, progress, or American destiny, thus placing himself in stubborn opposition to leading American historians, novelists, and poets of his time.[24]

Having established the spiritual and historical values of the Manse as a center for the pastoral formula, Hawthorne turns his attention to its antithesis, the outer circle of comtemporary degeneration to which he must return. Contemporary decadence has already been suggested in the "frigidity' of modern religious books that Hawthorne virtually ejects from the Manse. A further hint of modern decadence exists in the "speculative extravagances of the day"—an allusion to reformers and fringe-Transcendentalists on the outskirts of the Manse's perimeter. Hawthorne sees negligible value in "any definite idea" and "in any angular or rounded truth . . . dug out of the shapeless mass of problematical stuff" that concern these groups (10:25). He continues to stress the tangible and simple, the true reality having grown out of "the heart of mankind" or nature, ideas that will eventually lead Hawthorne to admire ancient institutions surviving in England when he goes there.

When he returns to his contemporary social scene, Hawthorne measures the ideas and "morbid activity" of idealistic reformers against the substantial realities accumulated within and without the Manse. These reformers, defined as "hobgoblins of flesh and blood," flock to Emerson, "a great original Thinker," and make it difficult for anyone "to view the world precisely as it exists" (10:30). Self-ordained visionaries, they see life as a "labyrinth" and therefore look to Emerson for "the clue that should guide them out of their self-involved bewilderment" (10:30). Evidently unable "to view the world precisely as it exists," they nevertheless concoct various schemes to transform the labyrinthian world, flattering themselves as "important agents of the world's destiny" (10:31). Their ideas and schemes, having been cultivated by the "heady" influence of Emerson (10:31), actually demonstrate a "false originality," leading Hawthorne to conclude, "This triteness of novelty is enough to make any man, of common sense, blaspheme at all ideas of less than a century's standing; and pray that the world may be petrified and rendered immovable, in precisely the worst moral and physical state that it ever yet arrived at, rather than be benefitted by such schemes of such philsophers" (10:32).

This conservative desire to respect only aged ideas is, of course, expressed in a humorous tone. All the same, in light of the conclusion of "The Old Manse," it reinforces Hawthorne's concern throughout the preface with retaining experiences and values having stood the test of time in face of mutability or revolutionary change. Consequently, the three-year stay at the Manse seems like a "fairy-land" where there is "no measurement of time" (10:33).[25] But, in perfect keeping with the pastoral, Hawthorne must return to the actual tumultuous world where time is measured. As a result, the closing pages of "The Old Manse" focus on his move from the Manse to Salem, where he will work in the Custom House. Elements in this shift suggest a view of history at once countering and complementing earlier portions of the preface that endorse a metaphoric layering of time and experience upon the Manse.

After having enlarged the vista of time and distilled three-years' tenure at the Manse into a one-year cycle, and after having created the Manse as a historical emblem of permanence in the midst of contemporary novelty and change, Hawthorne concludes the work with a reminder of how the disruptive world interrupts his idyllic life, how it comes close to undermining his creative efforts to fashion that experience into a work of literature, and even how it pointedly defiles the very pastoral spirit of his essay. Preceding his departure and the arrival of Samuel Ripley, the Manse's owner, "Carpenters . . . appeared, making a tremendous racket among the outbuildings, strewing the green grass with pine-shavings and chips of chestnut joists, and vexing the whole antiquity of the place with their discordant renovations. . . . All the aged mosses were cleaned unsparingly away; and there were horrible whispers about brushing up the external walls with a coat of paint—a purpose as little to my taste, as might be that of rouging the venerable cheeks of one's grandmother" (10:33).[26] The mirth in the passage should not detract from the sober judgment against remodeling antiquity.[27] It must be remembered that Hawthorne's own alterations to the Manse's interior have added to its antiquity and range of historical associations. Several years later, in the closing pages of *The House of the Seven Gables,* Hawthorne would seem to speak through Holgrave on the necessity of permanence and gradual change in relation to Judge Pyncheon's country house: " 'But I wonder that the late Judge . . . should not have felt the propriety of embodying so excellent a piece of domestic architecture in stone, rather than in wood. Then, every generation of the family might have altered the interior, to suit its own taste and convenience; while the exterior, through the lapse of years, might have been adding venerableness to its original beauty, and thus giving that impression of permanence, which I consider essential to the happiness of any one moment' " (2:314–15). Hawthorne's own retouchings of the Manse's interior parallel Holgrave's idea of balancing the claims of the past and present. Ripley, on the other hand, acting through his carpenters, tries to erase and disguise the effects of time on the Manse altogether. Like other progressive reformers in the outer circle, he wants to remake the world anew, not unlike his Puritan ancestors, who did all they could to rid themselves of English cultural models having withstood the test of time.

"The Old Manse" does not disclose the intervening months between Hawthorne's move to Salem and his appointment by Polk to the Surveyorship.[28] But Hawthorne acknowledges the irony in the transition when he says, "Providence took me by the hand, and—an oddity of dispensation which, I trust, there is no irreverence in smiling at—has led me, as the newspapers announce while I am writing, from the Old Manse into a Custom-House! As a storyteller, I have often contrived strange vicissitudes for my imaginary personages, but none like this" (10:33–34).[29] The exact nature of his particular vicissitudes Hawthorne details in "The Custom-House." Whether he anticipated that his position as Surveyor would not turn out well is difficult to say. Surely the qualitative changes from the comfortable rusticity of the Manse period to the commercial activity of the Custom House struck him as antithetical. On the other hand, the main function of the Renaissance pastoral is to strengthen the poet-sojourner with values sanctified in the central shrine, thereby permitting him to reenter the outer world. Hawthorne surely recognized that his real-life pastoral was over, just as surely as he knew that his literary output was insufficient to support a growing family.

He was also well aware that the tales collected in *Mosses from an Old Manse* would "afford no solid basis for a literary reputation" (10:34). While his works were sought and readily published by magazine editors, he had not produced a great number during the Manse years, and he was scarcely the richer. What he had hoped to write but could not was a novel, something solid "that could stand, unsupported, on its edges" (10:34). He had not discovered the "intellectual treasure," the subject to inspire a novel, during the comparatively tranquil honeymoon years at the Manse. We now see, however, that he made initial discoveries potentially useful to the creation of a novel. The first discovery, reflected in "Drowne's Wooden Image" and "The Artist of the Beautiful," was the difficulty of creating art in a culture lacking aesthetic traditions. The second, expressed in "The Old Manse," was a technique whereby he could place Old World continuities in an American landscape layered with legends reaching back in history beyond European settlement. Nevertheless, as his early Puritan tales suggest, what happened after European settlement most interested Hawthorne—the loss of those English cultural values that he somehow needed to reclaim in order to be the kind of writer he wanted to be and, in turn, to win a respectable literary reputation. When he found the inspiration to write about the artist Hester Prynne, in a context of transition between Old and New Worlds, he discovered the "intellectual treasure" missing from the Manse. For through Hester, Hawthorne could reclaim a tradition of Old World art upon which he could draw for support.

"The Custom-House"

In "The Custom-House, Hawthorne focuses on the state of contemporary affairs in a world far beyond the inner circle of the Manse, but his criticism of urban-commercial life achieves added force from both overt and implied contrasts with his life at the old parsonage. If the pastoral atmosphere of the Manse offered a natural and traditional setting for creative work, then Salem's life of money and commerce presented the opposite. Seven references to the Manse appear in "The Custom-House," key reminders of the communal virtues conspicuously lacking in the government's house of custom.[30] Primitive nature, the domesticated garden, the organic stability of the orchard, and the spiritual, historical, and aesthetic values associated with the Manse are notable for their absence from Salem's contemporary scene. The *custom* of modern Salem elevates material values above all else, as if reality and history revolve solely around day-to-day trading on the Merchant's Exchange. Yet, despite its materialism, Salem does not prosper, the signs of its having declined being apparent almost everywhere.

Building on the contrast between the Manse and modern Salem, Hawthorne's "Custom-House" presents nineteenth-century antagonists of English cultural virtues affirmed at the Manse. *The Scarlet Letter* charts Hawthorne's probing analysis of the early loss of these virtues in seventeenth-century Boston, immediately after the initial British emigration when the best traditions of England might have been transplanted and nurtured. The tragedy in this lost potential is bound up in the promise of the New World, offering as it did opportunity for the settlers to lay the foundation upon which the United States would be built. In Hawthorne's view, the American Puritans arrived quickly at a historic moment of deci-

sion: they might look to history to learn to live graciously in whatever
harmony could exist in the world; they might vitiate the freedom by
instituting a severely narrow code of morality and conduct that could
cripple future generations. As the seventeenth-century tales reveal,
Hawthorne thinks they chose the last of these courses. "The Custom-
House" illustrates the nineteenth-century consequences of that choice in
ways more personally confining than those found in "Drowne's Wooden
Image" and "The Artist of the Beautiful."

The structure of "The Custom-House" preface is bifurcated, a division
reflecting the two-storied structure of the Custom House itself. In the
lower "story," Hawthorne probes modern Salem—essentially a wasteland—
and the Puritan ancestors whose dogmas and Anglophobia gave narrow
direction to it from the start. In the upper story, with the imagined discovery of Surveyor Pue's manuscript, Hawthorne creatively assembles aesthetic
and historical traditions that he claims as his heritage, one that transcends
the narrow legacy of the Puritans and their modern descendants. The
structure and theme of the preface center upon an exchange of ancestors,
as Hawthorne repudiates the New England Puritans and adopts the English Surveyor Pue who comes to represent a cultural and aesthetic tradition dating back to the Renaissance and beyond. This is the same cultural
heritage associated with the Manse, the periodic references to which recall
the perennial values connected to the old abbey-parsonage—continuities in
nature, history, and art. But Hawthorne cannot recover such continuities in
the hostile milieu of nineteenth-century Salem or in his own ancestral past.
With the help of Surveyor Pue, on the other hand, he does establish
connections with an English heritage that prepares him to deal with the
issues of cultural inheritance and disinheritance in *The Scarlet Letter*. Supplemented by remarks on "Main-street," a sketch contemporaneous with
"The Custom-House" and related to "The Old Manse," the following discussion focuses on the lower story of Hawthorne's Custom House experience and the thwarting influence it has on him before Surveyor Pue comes
to his aid in the upper story. These three works together compose a kind of
triptych revealing the radical nature of Hawthorne's myth of decline:
instead of affirming the Puritan patriarchs, upon whom the myth is based,
Hawthorne discovers his cultural antecedents in England, the old home
denied by the Puritans but reaffirmed by their nineteenth-century descendant.

The Lower Story

"The Custom-House" begins by revealing the shortcomings of the pastoral outer circle, thus recalling the related shortcomings of that realm in
"The Old Manse." Hawthorne self-consciously notes, with feigned wonder,

that "an autobiographical impulse should twice in [his] life have taken possession of [him]" (1:3). But where the "deep quietude" and domestic harmony highlighting the Manse experience had a positive effect upon him (1:3), "The Custom-House" never duplicates such optimism. It does, however, reproduce criticism of contemporary life beyond the Manse's inner circle. In the earlier preface these criticisms are brief, drawing into relief the hallowed aspects of the Manse; in "The Custom-House" they persist until the very last pages. Criticism begins with an analysis of the Custom House exterior, representing the vagaries of American government and the dubious fortunes of Salem. "Over the entrance hovers an enormous specimen of the American eagle, with outspread wings, a shield before her breast, . . . a bunch of intermingled thunderbolts and barbed arrows in each claw" (1:5). This ominous portal-piece hardly welcomes the populace to share communal security in the federal home. As further commentary on the eagle indicates, the Custom House and the American government it represents, along with the citizens who rely on that government for their livelihood, are satirized for their laziness, sensuality, and banality. Treating these citizens, especially his fellow officers, with sustained humor and irony therafter, Hawthorne allows only one contemporary figure to recover a measure of dignity. Scarcely any wonder, then, that the regional press went after Hawthorne for having viciously attacked his former colleagues.[31]

Hawthorne's attack was surely a vengeful reaction to his being dismissed from the surveyorship, under the shadow of scandal, when the Taylor administration took over the spoils system in 1849.[32] But his revenge on the Whigs, while certainly of biographical interest, is not the most significant issue in the piece.[33] The opening attack comes directly after the first reference to the Manse, affirming its importance as a center of tradition, both domestic and communal. The peace and security it calls to mind oppose the menace of the war-like eagle, perched over the Custom House. An unnatural world of tooth-and-claw replaces the peace and benevolence associated with nature at the Manse. Indeed, among those depending upon the commerce of the Custom House is "the germ of the wrinkled-browed, grizzly-bearded, careworn merchant, . . . the smart young clerk, who gets the taste of traffic *as a wolf-cub does of blood*" (1:6; emphasis added). This degraded moral condition of merchants logically results from nature's having been transmuted, an appetite for gold narrowed into an obsession. In "The Old Manse," Hawthorne gives away fruits from the orchard, or he barters them for a few necessities. On this simple economic level, commerce exists as a natural activity serving community purposes. On the mercenary level pictured in "The Custom-House," however, commerce has devolved into menacing competition.

Complementing the low moral condition of the merchants are the foibles of the Custom House officers,[34] all but one of whom Hawthorne finds repulsive or empty. The treatment of the officials is patently not a panegyric on, or sympathetic picture of, the outer-circle denizens—although some readers think so.[35] "These old gentlemen—seated, like Matthew, at the receipt of custom," are "not very liable to be summoned thence, like him for apostolic errands" (1:7). Even when they sleep they are indirectly damned, a surprising fact at first glance considering Hawthorne's prescription in "The Old Manse": "The world should recline its vast head on the first convenient pillow, and take an age-long nap" (10:29). But the naps taken by guests at the Manse differ radically from those taken by officials in the Custom House. Whereas sleep instilled formerly by the pastoral setting provides a necessary antidote to the morbid activity of the nineteenth century, sleep in "The Custom-House" signifies a kind of death-in-life, a complacent, intellectual, and spiritual torpor. Those in "The Old Manse" who submit to slumber are "world-worn spirits" whom Hawthorne feels obliged "to give . . . rest—rest, in a life of trouble" (10:29). The officers in the Custom House, on the other hand, relinquish consciousness owing to their lack of imagination and gumption, their lethargy paralleling the dwindling business of Salem's port. While the pastoral avenue of the Manse leads to the Celestial City, "neither the front nor the back entrance of the Custom House opens on the road to Paradise" (1:13).

Plainly, most of the officers have lost their souls because their work and performance are useless—"corrupt"—and because they accept "Devil's wages" from the mercenary spoils system (1:39). The famous old Inspector, for example, might just as well have his name crossed off the list of mankind: "He possessed no power of thought, no depth of feeling, no troublesome sensibilities; nothing, in short, but a few commonplace instincts, which, aided by the cheerful temper that grew inevitably out of his physical well-being, did duty very respectably, and to general acceptance, in lieu of a heart" (1:17). The young accountant at the Custom House is no less devoid of a moral center. He reveals "a new idea of talent" (1:24). Yet, as the subsequent discussion shows, his talent relates to the biblical definitions of money, weights and measures, or *talent* as in the parable of Matthew 25:14–30. "His gifts," as Hawthorne ironically names them, are "emphatically those of a man of business; prompt, acute, clear-minded" (1:24). Raised in the Custom House since childhood, he resembles the young merchants who acquire a taste for business as the wolf cub does for blood. His world is like that of Peter Hovenden, "a perfectly comprehended system" of facts and figures, and as a consequence he represents "the Custom-House in himself; or, at all events, the main-spring that kept its variously revolving wheels in motion" (1:24). With this mechanistic allusion, we are obviously far removed from the Concord River at the Manse, which will not provide power for New England machinery.

The only character to receive a measure of Hawthorne's affection is Old General Miller, who distinguished himself at the Battle of Lundy's Lane in the War of 1812. Yet, despite vestiges of his New England hardihood and humor, General Miller shares some inferential guilt with the other officers, primarily because he has been accepting "Devil's wages" for years. To his credit, however, Miller seems to comprehend the discrepancy between his former stature and his present ignoble position as Collector. Hawthorne is certainly aware of this, and he suggests that the old General deserves a dignity and honor in keeping with British tradition but anathema to American democracy: "If, in our country, valor were rewarded by heraldic honor, this phrase ['I'll try, Sir!'] . . . would be the best and fittest of all mottoes for the General's shield of arms" (1:23–24). Since Miller does not have this Old World armorial symbol of his status, and since he appears dimly conscious of the depth to which he has fallen in the Custom House, Hawthorne favors the General's habit of denying the disreputable surroundings by withdrawing into his memories of the past. "It might be," Hawthorne says, "that he lived a more real life within his thoughts, than amid the unappropriate environment of the Collector's office" (1:23). General Miller thus escapes the censure Hawthorne directs at the other officers because his interest in history and his distaste for the Custom House have some correspondence to Hawthorne's own.[36]

The description of General Miller opens a historical dimension closely paralleling Hawthorne's discussion of Salem and his own ancestors. Fort Ticonderoga presents the most appropriate analogue for the General: both have shared heroic moments of the nation's history; both still hint at "features of stubborn and ponderous endurance"; and both exhibit the irrevocability of time in their romanticized states of ruin and decay (1:22). The tight chain of metaphoric associations connecting the two also relates to Salem. Having been the first strictly Puritan settlement in the New World, a preeminent community in Puritan times second only to Boston, and once having boasted a renowned port of trade, Salem, like General Miller and Fort Ticonderoga, formerly commanded the spotlight of history but has since, except for an annual month or two of flourishing trade, suffered from shifts of commercial centers and from the decaying effects of its own history.

The degeneration of Salem follows a mythic pattern of decline, beginning with Hawthorne's familiar attribution of nobility to the first Puritan epoch and proceeding to subsequent epochs of decadence. As we have seen in the previous chapters, this historical perspective, a secular version of the Puritan concept of backsliding, pits the earliest Puritan patriarchs against the moral and manly degeneration of their heirs.[37] To be sure, the logic of the myth requires a subtle discrimination between the "narrow Puritan"— the bigot and tyrant—and the "founding father"—the true heroic model singled out for adulation.[38] As expressed in the colonial tales and *The Whole History of Grandfather's Chair,* Hawthorne rarely finds the latter type. Governors Winthrop and Bradstreet, Roger Williams, and John Eliot are noteworthy exceptions to typically oppressive Puritans, and all are treated as

potential mediating figures who fail to check the influence of more dominant "founding fathers" such as Endicott, John and William Hathorne, and
Cotton Mather, who define the reactionary mainstream of Puritan history.
The legacy of this dominant but cruel and iconoclastic mainstream clearly
impinges upon Hawthorne the artist in the nineteenth century. Thus, while
he works within a scheme of historical decline, it can hardly be said that the
decline issues from a pervasive nobility of character in the Puritan founders
or in their immediate descendants.

As "The Custom-House" and "Main-street" demonstrate, Hawthorne's
interest in the decayed and degenerated condition of Salem involves his
refutation of the basic assumption underlying the myth of decline—the
myth of the noble founding father—at least insofar as the myth has its roots
in New England. In "The Custom-House," Hawthorne confronts the assumption by imaginatively addressing his own ancestors. His purpose
seems nothing less than to resolve the negative influences inherited from
the Puritan past. He comes to Salem, he says, because of "the deep and aged
roots which [his] family has struck into the soil" (1:8). He recognizes that
the gradual decline of Salem parallels the dwindling social prominence and
worldly success of his own family, but the true onus of the fall proves to lie
not on himself, the artist, but squarely on the ancestors themselves. The
"dusky grandeur" of his first American ancestor, an "original Briton," has
stood out in Hawthorne's imagination since his childhood, as if he grew up
sensing the inadequacy of the present in relation to the past (1:8–9).
Indeed, the figurative presence of this "first ancestor" still "haunts [him],
and induces a sort of home-feeling with the past, which [he can] scarcely
claim in reference to the present phase of the town" (1:9).

Hawthorne's dissent from the myth of decline becomes clear in his
treatment of this Puritan forebear. The ancestral Hathorne "was a soldier,
legislator, judge; he was a ruler in the Church; he had all the Puritanic
traits, both good and evil. He was likewise a bitter persecutor; as witness the
Quakers, who have remembered him in their histories, and relate an
incident of his hard severity towards a woman of their sect, which will last
longer, it is to be feared, than any record of his better deeds, although these
were many" (1:9). What the better deeds of this ancestor are, Hawthorne
does not say; his evil traits, however, have had damaging historical consequences. Hawthorne goes on to admit that the son of the first ancestor
also had an evil influence on history, having "inherited the persecuting
spirit, and made himself so conspicuous in the martyrdom of the witches,
that their blood may fairly be said to have left a stain upon him" (1:9).
Accordingly, Hawthorne "take[s] shame upon [himself]" for the curse these
two ancestors may have incurred (1:10). By accepting this shame, he
engages in an act of familial repentance that unequivocally demonstrates
his negative judgment of them and their deeds.

Perhaps the most damning feature of these ancestors' effect on New

England, and thus on Hawthorne's career, was their abhorrence of art. Seeing himself momentarily through their narrow vision, he says, "Doubtless, . . . either of these stern and black-browed Puritans would have thought it quite sufficient retribution for his sins, that, after so long a lapse of years, the old trunk of the family tree . . . should have borne, at its topmost bough, an idler like myself. . . . 'What is he?' murmurs one gray shadow of my forefathers to the other. 'A writer of story-books! What kind of business in life,—what mode of glorifying God, or being serviceable to mankind in his day and generation,—may that be?'" (1 : 10). This famous passage, often cited as evidence of Hawthorne's guilt over being an artist,[39] actually shows that it is not for himself that he "take[s] shame" but explicitly for his ancestors—a cultural issue he explores further in *The Scarlet Letter*. Thematically and structurally, the confrontation actually lays the groundwork for Hawthorne's rebellion against his great-grandsires' contempt for art.

If his art deals with anything akin to his ancestors' concerns, it addresses the recurring moral and spiritual problems faced by man, although in a manner considerably divergent from Puritan dogma. Aware of this, he can vouch with determination and independence, "let them scorn me as they will, strong traits of their nature have intertwined themselves with mine" (1 : 10), "traits" that Hawthorne implicitly draws upon when turning against the iconoclastic heritage of his Puritan ancestors. When he goes on to state that the ancestral spell of Salem has a magnetic hold on him but that the connection is "unhealthy" and "should at last be severed," Hawthorne is obviously preparing to purge the worst influences exerted by the Puritan past in order to affirm the primacy of his art. After working at the Custom House and while writing the Boston-based story of the scarlet letter, he discovers that Salem no longer figures as "the inevitable centre of the universe" (1 : 12). This does not mean that he wishes to deny utterly, or succeeds in denying, the past. It does mean that he defines himself as an artist by challenging and renouncing the austere Calvinistic heritage of his forebears. The shift to Boston in *The Scarlet Letter* shows clearly that Hawthorne's historical concerns transcend self-centered obsessions with his family. Enlarging the scene far beyond his individual patrimony, he evidently cares not only about the Puritan heritage commonly shared by most New Englanders but also about the richer British heritage that, although it helped nurture them, the Puritans came to deny.

One dimension of this larger view appears in "Main-street," a capsulized chronology of Massachusetts Bay history focused on Salem, which Hawthorne wrote while shaping the early chapters of *The Scarlet Letter* and which he originally planned to include in the novel. It expresses his continued attraction, during the Custom House period, to the natural continuities in culture so central to "The Old Manse." Hawthorne's version of the myth of decline is diagramed graphically if narrowly in "Main-street," emphasizing the impact of the Puritan patriarchs' entrance into a "pastoral" American scene.

As far as American experience is concerned in "Main-street," the myth of decline originates with the displacement of ancient Indian culture, one version of a Golden Age existing in long continuity and in organic harmony with the natural environment: "the ancient and primitive wood, . . . ever-youthful and venerably old. . . . The white man's axe has never smitten a single tree; his footstep has never crumpled a single one of the withered leaves; which all the autumns since the flood have been harvesting beneath. Yet, see! along through the vista of impending boughs, there is already a faintly-traced path, running nearly east and west, as if a prophecy or foreboding of the future street [Salem's Main Street] had stolen into the heart of the solemn old wood" (11:50). This condition exists at a time before "the noon-day marvels which the white man is destined to achieve" appear on the scene, marvels that will include a "Museum, where . . . a few Indian arrow-heads shall be treasured up as memorials of a vanished race!" (11:51). It also exists at a time when the great Squaw Sachem and Chief Wappacowet walk in the forest's shade, "holding high talk on matters of state and religion, and imagine, doubtless, that their own system of affairs will endure for ever" (11:51).

But then, in one of the most bitter of Hawthorne's historical reversals, Indian culture is not only displaced but also essentially erased from the historical memory of the Puritan conquerers. Third generation descendants regard their grandparents' accounts of Indian life and early Puritan relations with the Indians as a "vain legend" (11:71), a "fable" (11:72). "Nothing impresses" these later generations, Hawthorne criticizes, "except their own experience" (11:72). What they know about Indian culture does not compass anything beyond what they see and ridicule:

> . . . a drunken Indian, himself a prince of the Squaw Sachem's lineage. He brought hither some beaver-skins for sale, and has already swallowed the larger portion of their pride, in deadly draughts of fire-water. Is there not a touch of pathos in that picture? and does it not go far towards telling the whole story of the vast growth and prosperity of one race, and the fated decay of another?—the children of the stranger making game of the great Squaw Sachem's grandson! (11:72)

This account of the destruction of native American culture, with its own "high talk on matters of state and religion," corresponds to the effect of the Puritans' iconoclastic renouncement of their own Old World culture. Except as a self-flattering hagiography of their own origins, history means nothing.

The first generation of Puritans experienced a brief moment in history when an Edenic spirit could be projected onto a new world. But by over-throwing the native Indians, clearing the forest, settling up "noon-day marvels" clustered around Main Street, and establishing a devout yet grim mode of religious piety, it prepared the way for the moral, and ultimately the material decay of its own descendants:

> In truth, when the first novelty and stir of spirit had subsided,—when the new settlement, between the forest-border and the sea, had become actually a little town,—its daily life must have trudged onward with hardly any thing to diversify and enliven it, while also its rigidity could not fail to cause miserable distortions of the moral nature. Such a life was sinister to the intellect, and sinister to the heart; especially when one generation had bequeathed its religious gloom, and the counterfeit of its religious ardor, to the next; for these characteristics, as was inevitable, assumed the form both of hypocrisy and exaggeration. . . . The sons and grandchildren of the first settlers were a race of lower and narrower souls than their progenitors had been. The latter were stern, severe, intolerant, but not superstitious, not even fanatical. . . . But it was impossible for the succeeding race to grow up, in Heaven's freedom, beneath the discipline which their gloomy energy of character had established. (11:67–68)

The intolerance and gloom of the first generation gives birth to the fanaticism of the second, resulting in Quaker persecutions and Indian massacres. Superstition rampant among the second and third generations spawns the witchcraft delusion. This background gives rise to political crusades in the eighteenth century, and to the worship of money and commerce in nineteenth-century Salem.

Taken together, "Main-street" and "The Custom-House" seem like grown-up versions of *The Whole History of Grandfather's Chair* without the forced democratic typology. The brief chronology of Puritan life recounted in "Main-street" progresses to a focus on the witchcraft episode near the end of the seventeenth century and then concludes with the Great Snow of 1717. "The Custom-House" subtly resumes that chronolgy in allusions to the growing prosperity of the town during its shipping heyday in the eighteenth century. "Main-street" has already forecast this prosperity: "The scenes to come were far better than the past" (11:81). But considering Salem's mid-nineteenth-century condition, this forecast is two-edged:[40] the logic of decline, set in motion before the original Puritans had built their "noon-day marvels," is completed in Hawthorne's portrayal of Salem in "The Custom-House." The wharf is dilapidated, the warehouses have decayed, and the ships now moor in Boston and New York harbors. Similar to commentary in "Legends of the Province-House," wooden houses, "few or none of which pretend to architectural beauty," cover the "surface" ("landscape" being a term entirely too rich for the impoverished aesthetics of the locale); and the once thriving Main Street runs "wearisomely" from "Gallows Hill and New Guinea [the jail] at one end" to "the alms-house at the other" (1:8). Salem has undergone both a spiritual and material decline from its earliest years when Hawthorne's ancestors walked in the gloomiest ways of God. And certainly Hawthorne has come a long way from the Manse and its avenue leading to Paradise.

Modern Salemites follow the negative precedent set by their ancestors in "Main-street," being concerned solely with their own experience and having little, if any, historical memory. The notable recollections of the old Inspector comprise the succulent details of his former dinners. The "chief tragic event of the old man's life" appears to have been a goose that "could only be divided with an axe and handsaw" (1:19). General Miller, although a historical symbol of some distinction, remembers events only as far back as the War of 1812.

Clearly enough, modern Salem and the Custom House have become casualties in the backwash of historical and contemporary events. No less clearly, the entire range of circumstances at the Custom House has a demoralizing effect on Hawthorne. Having deftly contrasted the ancient virtues of the Manse with the negative values of the Custom House, Hawthorne has shown the mindless commercialism and the lack of historical memory in its officials. Old jokes, old snores, and old meals merely deaden one's spirit. Commerce and trade (the obsessive materialism of the present), along with their recorded transactions, have no lasting value; commodities carry Hawthorne's name stamped on their crates to places where he hopes it "will never go again" (1:27). On this first story of the Custom House, therefore, he finds nothing aesthetically or historically appealing.

Yet, beguiling to many critics, Hawthorne observes that, after fraternizing at the Manse with intellectuals like Emerson, Thoreau, Channing, and Hillard, he came to the Custom House with every intention of mixing with men having common-sense values: "Even the old Inspector was desirable, as a change of diet, to a man who had known Alcott. I looked upon it as an evidence, in some measure, of a system naturally well balanced, and lacking no essential part of a thorough organization, that, with such associates to remember, I could mingle at once with men of altogether different qualities, and never murmur at the change" (1:25). These lines have been read as an affirmation of everyday reality, the grub-a-day world of work and masculine camaraderie.[41] Yoked with a reference to Brook Farm and with a catalog of Concord's intelligentsia, the passage covers nearly five years of Hawthorne's life prior to his arrival at the Custom House. It should be clear, however, that Hawthorne counterpoints only a small part of his experience at the Manse with these government servants. Concord's elite transcendentalists do not in any sense relate to the *central values* enshrined at the abbey-parsonage, but rather to the outer circle of the pastoral diagram in "The Old Manse." Hawthorne's apparently ingenuous expectation of interacting for any length of time with Custom House workers, without murmuring at the change, is surely not to be taken seriously. Julian

Hawthorne noticed long ago that a "delicate flavor of irony" punctuates Hawthorne's announcement of any "murmur."[42] Indeed, the author does nothing but murmur.

The Upper Story

As a result of his finding only a negation of the values associated with the Manse on the first story of the Custom House, Hawthorne's decision to contemplate history anew seems almost inevitable, recalling the similar circumstances and choice of the narrator in "Legends of the Province-House." He therefore ascends to the second story where, in the process of examining historical documents, he will further repudiate the bigotry of his ancestors, set the positive pole of the myth of decline in England, and associate himself with an aesthetic tradition utterly at odds with the vapid contemporary world. When he suddenly announces, "But the past was not dead" (1:27), Hawthorne begins a transition leading to the composition of *The Scarlet Letter.* A more significant line in Hawthorne's works could scarcely be found.

The ascent to the second story in "The Custom-House" parallels the ascent in the Manse. Just as the books and tracts in the old house are frigid and fail to activate Hawthorne's historical sensibility, so too the written documents stored in the Custom House have no historical importance and no deeply engrossing features. To begin with, these papers have the inferior trait of recording only "the former commerce of Salem," perhaps the statistical "memorials of her princely merchants"—New England's ironic version of European "aristocracy" (1:28). In addition, the "founders of the greater part of the families which now compose the aristocracy of Salem might here be traced, from the petty and obscure beginnings of their traffic, at periods generally *much posterior to the Revolution,* upward to what their children look upon as long-established rank" (1:28–29; emphasis added). More than merely looking down his nose at these upstarts (Hawthorne's American ancestry dated to 1635), Hawthorne pursues a historical perspective larger than the memory of one or two generations, and he looks for cultural matters transcending a family's rise to economic fortune and social rank. The loss of pre-Revolutionary documents once stored in the Custom House but removed by the British during the War of 1812 suggests an ongoing consequence of severed ties with England—an interruption of the historical record impinging upon the cultural memory of a people. "It has often been a matter of regret with me; for, going back, perhaps, to the days of the Protectorate, those papers must have contained many references to forgotten or remembered men, and to antique customs, which would have affected me with the same pleasure as when I used to pick up Indian arrow-heads in the field near the Old Manse"

(1:29). In such a momentous framework of historical loss, Hawthorne encounters Surveyor Pue's documents on the scarlet letter.

Significantly, the antiquarian papers of Surveyor Pue are British documents, enclosed by a parchment—signed and sealed by the appointee of George II, Governor Shirley. They record a brief history of Hester Prynne that basically predates the Protectorate. From among the Governor's parchment and Surveyor Pue's sheets of foolscap emerges the scarlet letter, eliciting Hawthorne's immediate fascination: "My eyes fastened themselves upon the old scarlet letter, and would not be turned aside. Certainly, there was some deep meaning in it, most worthy of interpretation, and which, as it were, streamed forth from the mystic symbol, subtly communicating itself to my sensibilities, but evading the analysis of my mind" (1:31). Here exists the "treasure of intellectual gold" eluding Hawthorne in the Manse (10:34). By calling it a "treasure" in "The Custom-House" (1:29), he once again connects the two prefaces, but this time the treasure leads to a novel.

The scarlet artifact does not immediately lead to the novel, however. Unlike the imaginative response he has to artifacts in "The Old Manse"— whether Indian arrowheads or the Manse itself—and unlike the creativity he achieves in tales written at the Manse, Hawthorne's response to the scarlet letter is blunted and partial, a result directly attributable to the Custom House setting. Hawthorne misses the "invigorating charm of Nature, which used to give [him] such freshness and activity of thought, the moment that [he] stepped across the threshold of the Old Manse" (1:35). His imagination is a "tarnished mirror": "So little adapted is the atmosphere of a Custom-House to the delicate harvest of fancy and sensibility, that, had I remained there through ten Presidencies yet to come, I doubt whether the tale of 'The Scarlet Letter' would ever have been brought before the public eye" (1:34).

Only after leaving the Custom House can Hawthorne write *The Scarlet Letter;* and only after leaving can he write *about* the Custom House—a fact having important implications on a proper understanding of the famous moonlight passage concerning the theory of romance writing. In this passage, Hawthorne at one point seems to claim that instead of working on his romance of Hester Prynne, instead of trying "to fling [himself] back into another age," he ought to have engaged in a "wiser effort": "to diffuse thought and imagination through the opaque substance of to-day . . . ; to spiritualize the burden that began to weigh so heavily; to seek, resolutely, the true and indestructible value that lay hidden in the petty and wearisome incidents, and ordinary characters" in the Custom House (1:37).[43] To write in such a manner upon such subjects would presumably require ignoring the oppressive materiality preventing Hawthorne from writing in the first place. It therefore seems a serious mistake to accept at face value Hawthorne's apparent wish to transcribe the book of life spread before him, whose pages are "written out by the reality of the flitting hour" (1:37).

In "The Old Manse," he had been able to capture the "indestructible value" of the Manse and to transcribe the "flitting hour" within the perennial rhythms of nature. Even if the Custom House will not lend itself to the same kind of treatment,[44] Hawthorne does, after all, find a way of writing about the reality of the Custom House by revealing its spiritual emptiness, by showing the absence of "true and indestructible value" in the events he experiences there. His account of the Custom House does "diffuse thought and imagination through the opaque substance of to-day," but that process reveals only banality, a fact quickly perceived by his fellow Salemites. Because of their furor over his treatment of Custom House officials, Hawthorne wrote a preface to the second edition of *The Scarlet Letter* in which he wryly but steadfastly defends the accuracy of his portrait. Toward the end of this preface, he says with pregnant irony, "The sketch might, perhaps, have been wholly omitted, without loss to the public, or detriment to the book; but, having undertaken to write it, he [Hawthorne] conceives that it could not have been done in a better or kindlier spirit, nor, so far as his abilities availed, with a livelier effect of truth"(1 : 1–2).[45]

So radically different from the Manse, the world of the Custom House clearly proves inimical to artistic work and to the cultural values Hawthorne holds dear. But he is not the first to suffer from its stultifying atmosphere. According to his fictional version of the historical Jonathan Pue, the former surveyor was compelled to record his antiquarian research on Hester Prynne because it "supplied material for petty activity to a mind that would otherwise have been eaten up with rust" (1 : 30).[46] Hawthorne thus connects his artistic plight, in a fictionalized historical lineage, to that of Surveyor Pue—an Anglican and representative of the Crown, "illuminated by a ray of the splendor that shown so dazzlingly about the throne" (1 : 33).[47] This monarchical illumination accompanying Pue's commission as surveyor apparently offers some compensation, some status conferring dignity, to balance the monotony of the job itself. But no such regal regard or satisfaction obtains in Hawthorne's "democratic" position: "How unlike, alas! the hang-dog look of a republican official, who, as the servant of the people, feels himself less than the least, and below the lowest, of his masters" (1 : 33). As Hawthorne sees it, the lack of dignity in his appointment follows the basic lack of respect held by nineteenth-century American culture for its authors. Not even the writing of Burns or Chaucer, also former Custom House officials, would have brought any distinction to them had these authors been in Hawthorne's American shoes (1 : 26).

Hawthorne therefore joins contemporaries such as Irving, Cooper, and Poe in a tradition of American writers who deplore the cultural neglect or trivializing of professional writers. Adopting with ironic resignation the point of view of his culture, he says: "I know not that I especially needed the lesson, either in the way of warning or rebuke; but, at any rate, I learned it thoroughly; nor, it gives me pleasure to reflect, did the truth . . .

ever cost me a pang, or require to be thrown off in a sigh" (1 : 27). In light of his personal history, of his struggle to support himself as a writer, this statement must be taken as a sarcastic regret,[48] as the references to Burns and Chaucer imply. By invoking these two authors, popular in their own times and possessing literary reputations clearly transcending their nearly forgotten positions as Custom House officers, Hawthorne prepares for the indispensable connection to Surveyor Pue. As we have seen, the scarlet letter and Surveyor Pue's manuscript have awakened Hawthorne's imagination and sense of history, breaking the stultifying routine of the Custom House. When the ghost of Surveyor Pue enters the scene (corresponding to the entrance of Hawthorne's Puritan forefathers), he offers Hawthorne a new genealogy: "With his ghostly hand, the obscurely seen, but majestic, figure had imparted to me the scarlet symbol, and the little roll of explanatory manuscript. With his own ghostly voice, he had exhorted me, on the sacred consideration of my *filial* duty and reverence towards him,—who might reasonably regard himself as my *official ancestor*,—to bring his mouldy and moth-eaten lucubrations before the public (1 : 33; emphasis added).

In taking up this task, Hawthorne explicitly repudiates his Puritan forebears and adopts the Anglican surveyor as an ancestor wholly to his liking.[49] The inclusion of Burns and Chaucer as artist-ancestors who also served in Custom Houses aligns Hawthorne with an artistic tradition antithetical to insular American Puritanism, a tradition extending back through the Renaissance to the Middle Ages, which affirms the cultural importance and legitimacy of the literary profession Hawthorne had, from the outset, been struggling to follow. Accordingly, the myth of decline in Hawthorne does not finally establish New England Puritanism as its positive genesis. To the extent that the decline begins with the Puritans, it begins with their separating themselves and their posterity from English cultural traditions that, among other things, create a proper "atmosphere" to nurture the very author who helps transmit them. As early as "Passages from a Relinquished Work" (1832), Hawthorne had prepared for the ancestral substitution found in "The Custom-House." The aspiring artist in that work, who wants to escape from the "stern old Pilgrim spirit of [his] guardian," must contend with the same ancestral distrust of art that concerns Hawthorne in "The Custom-House." "There is a grossness in the conceptions of my countrymen," the young man asserts; "they will not be convinced that any good thing may consist with what they call idleness; they can anticipate nothing but evil of a young man who neither studies physic, law, nor gospel, nor opens a store, nor takes to farming" (10:407). The youth, intent on becoming a wandering storyteller but having no artists in New England to encourage him by way of example, looks to England for his model: "I had the example of one illustrious itinerant in the other hemisphere; of Goldsmith" (10:408). In the Puritan tradition, art is idleness or idolatry—or both. American writers necessarily had to look to England or the continent for their models and spiritual encouragement.

Hawthorne is aware that, in the mother country, the crown and wealthy aristocrats had traditionally been patrons of artists and that a comparatively stable political continuity helped to insure the longevity of the patronage. As an artist in a politically appointed post, Hawthorne was temporarily "enjoying" a version of such patronage. But as the ghost of Surveyor Pue warns him, "it is not in your days as it was in mine, when a man's office was a life-lease, and oftentimes an heirloom" (1:33). The warning turns into a fact. Hawthorne gets dismissed from his post, after General Taylor takes over the new Whig administration. Thinking that as an artist he was above the mundane squabbles of party politics,[50] he had not expected to be turned out of office. But, using the guillotine as a metaphor for the workings of the spoils system and the presidential "revolution[s]" (1:43) taking place every four years, he wryly observes that his "own head was the first that fell!" (1:41).

General Taylor's election proves to be a blessing in disguise for Hawthorne—a "remarkable event" as he calls it (1:40), echoing Increase Mather. Because of the dismissal, Hawthorne no longer has to fear being transformed into "such another animal as the old Inspector" with his inveterate sensuality; he can henceforth "live throughout the whole range of his faculties and sensibilities" as he had at the Manse (1:40). The three years at the Custom House correspond to the three years at the Manse, but they have antithetical value: they are years "too long," Hawthorne asserts, "to have lived in an unnatural state, doing what was really of no advantage nor delight to any human being" (1:42). Only as an artist, not as a surveyor at the Custom House, can Hawthorne perform a service to mankind, an obligation dear to the ancestral Puritan ghosts who cannot fathom how storytelling might be a "useful" calling.

When Hawthorne turns to composing *The Scarlet Letter*, he keeps his promise to Surveyor Pue, the figurative "ancient predecessor' and surrogate forefather who, like Burns and Chaucer, leads to Hawthorne's resurrection as a literary man. *The Scarlet Letter*, Hawthorne's most sustained treatment of Puritan history, analyzes the English-Puritan transplantation in the New World and criticizes the provincial rigidity and intolerance accompanying that difficult settlement. Since this renewed excursion into Puritan history constitutes Hawthorne's's last full-scale study of it, *The Scarlet Letter* can properly be seen as a monument with epitaph to the subject. Like the escutcheon image closing the novel, the tone is dark and brooding, "A FIELD, SABLE" (1:264). In "The Custom-House," Hawthorne worries about this tone: the story has, he confesses, "a stern and sombre aspect; too much ungladdened by genial sunshine; too little relieved by the tender and familiar influences which soften almost every scene of nature and real life, and, undoubtedly, should soften every picture of them"

(1:43). The implied contrast here is with the Manse experience: the somberness "is no indication," Hawthorne says, "of a lack of cheerfulness in the writer's mind; for he was happier, while straying through the gloom of these sunless fantasies, than at any time since he had quitted the Old Manse" (1:43). Such happiness results, I would argue, from Hawthorne's having found in Surveyor Pue, as he had in the Manse, a means of becoming connected to a tradition of art beyond the boundaries of his native land, a means of transcending the dark, confining legacy of his Puritan ancestors by reclaiming the very Anglo-Catholic aesthetic from which they effectively disinherited themselves.

5

Disinheritance and Recovery of English Traditions in *The Scarlet Letter*

The English Frame

Although Hawthorne's indignation over being dismissed from his post is embedded in "The Custom-House," a crucial element of that indignation finds expression in a historical perspective that both includes and transcends Hawthorne's personal case. A Jonathan Pue, a Chaucer, or a Burns could rely on the traditional support of his government and culture. England had a history of valuing its artists, while America did not. The recognition was not new to Hawthorne, but he experienced it now more fully and personally than earlier; and in so doing he discovered the subject necessary for the novel that had so long eluded him: the very origins of anti-aesthetic, anti-imaginative prejudice of New England. Lying at the heart of *The Scarlet Letter*, therefore, exists a fairly large measure of hostility aimed at Puritan America's conventional mistrust of art. More fully articulated than in previous works, such mistrust went hand in hand with the cultural separation between New and Old Worlds. And more fully evident than heretofore appears a division in Hawthorne's loyalties to these separate worlds because of his determination to recover an English aesthetic for himself and America. Bitterness over the circumstances of his removal from the Custom House may have been the immediate cause of his deciding to undertake a full-scale recovery,[1] and yet the substance of many of the historical tales virtually imply as much, while "The Old Manse" surely predicts the method.

Nevertheless, more cogently than in Hawthorne's previous work, *The Scarlet Letter* is about the cultural history of Puritan America, and the conflict between dominant and recessive qualities of Puritanism more or less defined by 1649. As Hawthorne sees it, the seven-year period covered by the novel's action is pivotal, not only in New England history but also, and most relevantly, in English history. With his knowledge of colonial American history, in conjunction with his considerable knowledge of English history,[2] Hawthorne again traces the growth of the dominating forces of Puritanism: severity, rigidity, intolerance, iconoclasm, militancy, and persecution. But he also explores to a far greater extent than earlier the attractive but recessive qualities of early Puritans that form a part of their English heritage: sympathy, charity, gaiety, communal celebration, respect for tradition, and appreciation of art. These qualities—personified especially by Dimmesdale, Hester, and Pearl—are posed as alternatives to the dominant traits of the Puritan majority. Linked with English antiquity, these alternatives, if they had flourished in the New World, would have given an entirely different tone and direction to New England and thus to American history as a whole.

Presenting the dominant and recessive dualism as a historical principle and using it as a structuring device, Hawthorne substantially retraces the design of his seventeenth-century tales. The gentle side of Puritanism retreats as the militant side continually advances. Moreover, Hawthorne takes up in *The Scarlet Letter* where he leaves off in "The Custom-House," allying himself with an English ancestry whose aesthetic and spiritual traditions are pitted against those of his Puritan forebears, which essentially survive among his contemporaries. While the dominant values of the Puritans are not wholly those of nineteenth-century Salemites, the recessive values in each century are nearly identical as expressed through Hawthorne's self-projected narrator. The majority parties of the seventeenth and nineteenth centuries are oppressive in their own ways, as they resist or fail to consider either the value of art or alternatives to the narrow Puritan tradition. The legacy of Puritan antipathy for artistic values survives in nineteenth-century descendants, even though religious zeal does not. When Hawthorne adopts an English ancestry and aesthetic heritage in "The Custom-House," when he creates the artistically beautiful scarlet letter and commits himself to writing a novel on the historical and symbolic importance of this artifact, he clearly takes a positive stand at once against the dominating values of his contemporaries and his ancestors. At the outset of *The Scarlet Letter,* something antagonistic figures in Hawthorne's motives in writing on a Puritanical animus for art and the individualistic spirit of artists. Perhaps he does ally himself to the antinomian tradition of Anne Hutchinson.[3]

A measure of this antagonism appears directly or implicitly in repeated parallels between English culture and the New England scene. Underlying the primary attention given to New England history in the novel, there resides a subsurface of English history that Hawthorne has carefully structured in order to examine American Puritans within a framework larger than the provincial boundaries of New England. This subsurface of English history alternately interpenetrates the condition, consciousness, and subconsciousness of that early group of Puritan immigrants comprising the Great Migration. Hawthorne's sensitivity to the tension fostered by Massachusetts's quarrel with and dependence on the mother country finally amounts to one of the novel's chief imaginative distinctions. For *The Scarlet Letter* stands alone in American literary history as the only major novel directly concentrating on the seventeenth-century historical transition between Old and New Worlds, as if Hawthorne had come to believe that native literature could have little if any foundation unless the process and results of this transition were adequately examined. Given Hawthorne's treatment of early Puritan culture, the dynamics of this shift must necessarily constitute the endowed basis of both American history and art.

References to an English heritage in *The Scarlet Letter* therefore combine to establish a rich cultural lineage available to the Puritans as part of their English birthright. Yet they try their utmost to disguise or deny this very lineage. As "The May-pole of Merry Mount" has forecast, historical continuities, communal relations, traditional festivals—all of England's hereditary customs celebrating life and community relations—are transformed or virtually rejected by Puritan emigrants. The best aesthetic qualities inextricably tied to the English church and, farther back, to the Catholic Church suffer a similar fate. Even worse, the ancient respect for these qualitites is left behind, for the most part, in the mother country. *The Scarlet Letter* thus centers on a period in American history when leading forces of Puritanism—the vanguard, to Hawthorne, of the notorious second generation of Puritans—are on the verge of totally disinheriting themselves from the richest traditions of their past. Hawthorne's evocation of these traditions, as they existed at a critical moment in seventeenth-century history when they might have been nourished, casts into relief the instituted severity and barrenness of Puritan culture.

The Puritans' confrontation with the American wilderness accounts for only a small portion of the transformation of English customs and aesthetic values. As the second paragraph of the novel suggests, the Puritans had from the outset a mistaken conception of their Utopian enterprise so admirably expressed in Winthrop's "Modell of Christian Charity." Something intrinsically uncharitable and iconoclastic lay deep in Puritanism itself. Whether in England or in America, Puritans were engaged in a process of cultural self-disinheritance. The relationship between English and American Puritans is surely not an especially obvious one in *The Scarlet Letter*. Simply by taking note of the novel's time frame (1642–49), however, one quickly realizes the connection. In light of other signal details in the book, it becomes clear that Hawthorne has purposely structured the chronology of *The Scarlet Letter* to coincide with that of the English Civil War.[4] The hyperbolic revolutionary climate of presidential elections in "The Custom-House" becomes a counterpart to revolutionary change in *The Scarlet Letter*.

The significance of this historical parallel can hardly be overestimated. For if one considers the novel with the English Civil War in mind, along with references and allusions to earlier epochs of English history, then the subject of historical alienation found in the book assumes a dimension far greater than a privileged focus on New England allows.[5] Hawthorne, adopting a sweeping historical view, suggests that this alienation includes the breach between past and present in both the Old and New Worlds. In a manner analogous to the strategy in "The Old Manse," he enlarges the provincial dimensions of his American setting with imagery attached to traditions in England, suggesting evaluative comparisons for judging American history and culture—often with ironic, paradoxical, damning, and sad reflections on American Puritanism. Hawthorne indeed becomes "the historian of the historically disinherited,"[6] but in more sweeping cultural terms than have been recognized.

The time frame of *The Scarlet Letter* can most easily be determined from the reference in chapter 12 to John Winthrop's death, which took place in 1649, and from the numerous references to the scaffold scene that opens the novel seven years earlier.[7] Since the novel begins in 1642 before news of the Civil War has reached Massachusetts, it is appropriate that when the beadle ushers Hester out of prison, he cries aloud to the crowd surrounding the door, " 'Make way, good people, make way, in the King's name' " (1:54).[8] No further allusion to Charles I appears until chapter 13, following mention of Winthrop's death in the previous chapter and thus chronologically following the execution of Charles I on 30 January 1649. Hawthorne then appropriately alludes to regicide in a passage relating to Hester and a schism in the traditional heirarchy: "It was an age in which the human intellect, newly emancipated, had taken a more active and a wider range than for many centuries before. Men of the sword had overthrown nobles and kings" (1:164). Ambiguous though the plural "kings" seems to be, no monarch other than Charles I was overthrown during the age, a fact known to a writer as widely read as Hawthorne in British and European history.

Further allusion to the Civil War and regicide surfaces in chapter 20, "The Minister in a Maze." Upon his return from the famous forest interlude with Hester, Dimmesdale—now knowing that Chillingworth is Hester's husband—must face the old physician. When the two meet, Dimmesdale has a "confident suspicion" that the old man knows about the forest interview. He therefore deduces that "so much being known, it would appear natural that a part of it should be expressed" (1:224). Something of the clever leech's enmity is indeed expressed when Dimmesdale declines medical assistance in preparation for his upcoming election day sermon and declares that he can only repay Chillingworth's "good deeds" with prayers. Chillingworth then responds, " 'A good man's prayers are golden recompense! . . . Yea, they are the current gold coin of the New Jerusalem, with the King's own mint-mark on them!' " (1:224). With this image of the coin, Hawthorne subtly revitalizes the clash of religious and political forces in mid-seventeenth-century England. As Hawthorne has already shown in *The Whole History of Grandfather's Chair,* New England did not begin to mint its own coin until Cromwell came to power. Chillingworth's mention of New Jerusalem has reference not to New England but to the English commonwealth after the regicide, the fifth monarchy promised in Dan. 7 and anticipated by many millernarian Protestants following the Reformation.[9]

Seventeenth-century Puritans especially emphasized the millenarian aspect of the Civil War. With the advent of the New Jerusalem, the fourth monarchy ends; that is, Charles I is beheaded and the crown becomes osbsolete. While Chillingworth's reference to New Jerusalem suggests these associations with the fifth monarchy, his comment is purposely tortured by the ironic presence of the king's mint mark. Coin of the realm continues to bear the seal of the defeated fourth monarchy a good while after the ostensible inauguration of the fifth. The lingering image of Charles I not only hints at this anachronism but also perverts the purity of New Jerusalem.[10] Hawthorne's knowledge of these trans-Atlantic details was matched by his awareness of circumstances in New England. In Joseph Felt's *Historical Account of Massachusetts Currency,* he would have encountered an observation whose subject and timing perfectly coincide with Chillingworth's sly banter. Felt writes in an entry dated 2 May 1649, "As specie still remains inconvenienly scarce, one reason for it is the vigilance with which authorities in England prevent its exportation hither."[11] The demonstrable point in Chillingworth's cunning insinuation is that Dimmesdale is not a good man and that his prayers are hypocritical.

By recalling customs and festivals evolved from English antiquity, and by setting *The Scarlet Letter* during the years of the Civil War, Hawthorne takes advantage of contrasting versions of England. Both versions are necessary to illuminate the historical conditions of New England upon which he most obviously focuses. With these dual versions of England in the background, several issues in *The Scarlet Letter* become especially meaningful.

By way of preface, a few additional details help to clarify the overall historical context within which Hawthorne explores such issues as the relationship between past and present, the role of art in conflict with Puritan iconoclasm, the religious conflict within Dimmesdale, the relation between Dimmesdale and other Puritan leaders, and the ironic concluding promise of a glorious future for America. In England, the religious tensions between the English Church and Puritans, along with political tensions between the monarchy and Parliament, reach a breaking point between 1642 and 1649. Puritan forces gradually assume power, overthrowing the monarchy and episcopacy. As the old order declines in England during these years, so too does it decline among the first generation of American Puritans—a generation having emigrated because of the increasing tensions in England, without altogether having denied the heritage of the mother country. The characteristics of the old orders in

England and America are certainly not equivalent, yet they do resemble each other compared to the more militant and iconoclastic forms of Puritanism that replace them. Just as the representative of the old order in England dies in the person of Charles I, so the representative of the first generation of American Puritans dies in the person of Winthrop (and, in his symbolic role in *The Scarlet Letter,* in the person of Dimmesdale). And just as Cromwell assumes command of England after Charles I, so the militant Endicott takes charge of the second generation in New England after Winthrop. The break with tradition and its patriarchal leadership is completed both between and within the Old and New Worlds.

The Scarlet Letter employs the method of characterization seen in the tales discussed in the first chapter. Separate characters embody the dominant and the recessive (but attractive) sides of Puritanism. The novel, however, far more complex and ambitious than the tales, places in the foreground the figures who are to recede from American history—Hester with her luxuriant Renaissance-style artistry; Pearl, the symbol of that art; and Dimmesdale with his influential power of sympathy. These characters are particularly anomalous in the Puritan setting of the novel; Hawthorne must imaginatively create them in order to counter the harsh historical forces represented to some degree by Governor Bellingham and, less overtly but far more importantly, by Endicott, who is almost entirely offstage yet ready to make his entrance as the action of *The Scarlet Letter* concludes on election day. As Endicott comes to power, Dimmesdale dies and Hester and Pearl remove themselves from the New World. Pearl is altogether lost to America, while Hester returns appreciably altered in character. Through these figures, preeminently, *The Scarlet Letter* dramatizes mitigating alternatives to Puritanic militancy, persecution, and iconoclasm. It is clearly no accident that these appealing figures are lost to the colony, for the same pattern of survival and loss extends to minor figures, including the gentlest of the women watching Hester's disgrace at the novel's opening: unlike the bloodthirsty "gossips," she is dead in the final scene seven years later (1:51, 246).

The qualities that recede include aesthetic sensibility, tenderness, and, on a broader scale, a sense of time-honored communal relations uniting past and present. Hawthorne had factual warrant for claiming the one-time existence of these alternatives to Puritanic extremism: the "not unkind" (1:113), sometimes temperate John Wilson is a historical figure partly analogous, in the book, to Dimmesdale; and King's Chapel, reviving English tradition in America later in the seventeenth century, does stand in modern Boston by what Hawthorne fictionally designates as the burial ground of Dimmesdale himself. But Hester's art evidently has no historical counterpart; thus, as in "The Custom-House," Hawthorne has created it without reference to an actual source. Nevertheless, his eclectic use of historical background in presenting Hester, Pearl, and, especially, Dimmesdale deserves more than passing consideration.

The Scarlet Letter places Renaissance color and love of exotic beauty, embodied by Hester and Pearl, in striking relief against the stark, joyless modes and manners of the Puritan majority. Similarly, it shows that Dimmesdale is all that the Puritan magistrates are not. While it is true that his character and actions are rendered somewhat ambiguous by his sin of adultery and especially by his failure to confess it, it is Dimmesdale who, on occasion with Wilson, tempers the severe judgments of Bellingham and others. Not only do his peers and superiors listen respectfully to him (Wilson finds him "wise beyond his years" [1:65]), but also the people respond to him with the sympathy that he alone seems able to draw from them. His inability to aid Hester and, worse, to be a father to Pearl surely troubles a modern reader—but we should note that for other parishioners he serves as a comforting confessor and spiritual advisor: "his heart vibrated in unison with theirs, and received their pain into itself" (1:142). His sympathetic powers clearly distinguish Dimmesdale from the other clergymen who are "endowed with a far greater share of shrewd, hard, iron or granite understanding; which, duly mingled with a fair proportion of doctrinal ingredient, constitutes a highly respectable, efficacious, and unamiable variety of the clerical species" (1:141). The lack of amiability characterizes virtually all the Puritan clergy, save Dimmesdale.

Just as Hester and Pearl are in continuous conflict with the entire populace, so Dimmesdale is pitted throughout the novel against more particularized forces of persecution: Chillingworth's Old World science and scholarship turned diabolic; Bellingham's outward displays of gentility but inner Puritanic intolerance; and, implicitly, Endicott's militant separatism in relation to English heritage. Hawthorne regularly surrounds Hester, Pearl, and Dimmesdale with Old World motifs—often Anglo-Catholic or Renaissance images—not, of course, to make them Anglicans but to differentiate them from the other Puritans and to emphasize positive historical and cultural continuities, once potentially available to America through them.

The Aesthetic Tradition

As Hester stands on the scaffold, feeling the "heavy weight of a thousand unrelenting eyes" staring at the scarlet *A* on her breast, her "memory" involuntarily revives: "Reminiscences, the most trifling and immaterial, passages of infancy and schooldays, sports, childish quarrels, and the little domestic traits of her maiden years, came swarming back upon her, intermingled with recollections of whatever was gravest in her subsequent life" (1:57). Similar to Hawthorne in "The Custom-House," Hester recalls her past to gain relief "from the cruel weight and hardness of reality" (1:57). She remembers her "native village, in Old England, and her paternal home; a decayed house of gray stone, with a poverty-stricken aspect, but retaining a half-obliterated shield of arms over the portal, in token of antique gentility" (1 : 58). She also recalls her marriage to Chillingworth and their initial move to Amsterdam among "huge cathedrals, and the public edifices, ancient in date and quaint in architecture" (1 : 58).

Hester's memory of her girlhood in "our old home" is no less fond or significant than Tobias and Dorothy Pearson's memory of England in "The Gentle Boy." Nevertheless, her English past and the optimism suggested in her duplication of the Pilgrim moves to Holland and America vividly contrast with "the rude market-place of the Puritan settlement" where, upon the scaffold, she stands holding Pearl, her public sin and perhaps her private shame exposed (1 : 58). Hester has been influenced with a sufficient amount of Calvinistic doctrine to feel that "the scaffold of the pillory was a point of view that revealed . . . the entire track along which she had been treading, since her happy infancy" (1 : 58). So much for sloughing the skin of Old World corruption in coming to the New World.[12] But while Hester acknowledges her predetermined reenactment of original sin, she evidently has not observed the orthodox logic of how she ought to behave as a result of it. She has clearly spent her months in prison in rather unrepentant and even heretical fashion. As Hester stands exposed before her neighbors in all the beauty of her person, dress, and scarlet letter, she reveals something quite different from evidentiary Puritan atonement, something far more in keeping with her Old World reflections.

In view of Puritan sumptuary laws prohibiting the general populace from wearing lavish dress, and from the vantage of Puritan opposition to religious images, Hawthorne describes Hester's appearance and the effects of her needlework in terms anomalous to the historical setting. He continues to associate her with the Old World and, more specifically, with its aristocratic (even ecclesiastical) art, presumably inimical to Puritanism. Hester, we later learn, has "fingers that could have embroidered a monarch's robe" (1 : 161). Through the artful stitching witnessed in the scarlet letter, she produces a "specimen of her delicate and imaginative skill of which the dames of a court might gladly have availed themselves, to add the richer and more spiritual adornment of human ingenuity to their fabrics of silk and gold" (1 : 81–82).

The beautiful artifact initially repels the colonists, who later persecute Hester and ostracize her from the community not only because she has sinned but also because she has created a distinctly non-Puritan form of beauty from the symbol of her sin. Given the Calvinistic side of her ruminations, Hester should have expected nothing less, and so it would seem that she contributes to her own alienation. She has fashioned "wild" and "picturesque" clothing, and she has also embroidered the scarlet letter with an artistic "luxuriance of fancy." Together, these products of her skill and imagination have "a splendor in accordance with the taste of the age, but greatly beyond what was allowed by the sumptuary regulations of the colony" (1:53).[13] Some of the spectators obviously make no mistake in thinking that Hester "make[s] a pride out what" the magistrates "meant for a punishment" (1:54).

From a Puritan point of view of providential signs, Hester's confinement in the dark jail should have allowed enough time for her beauty to fade and for guilt to shadow forth its physical effects. But her appearance belies these unsanctified effects anticipated by those Puritans "who had before known her, and had expected to behold her dimmed and obscured by a disastrous cloud." Instead, they are "astonished, and even startled, to perceive how her beauty shone out, and made a halo of misfortune and ignominy in which she was enveloped" (1:53). Preconceptions give way to uncomfortable perceptions; and the Puritans have every reason to be alarmed over what they see. As if illuminated by the traditional aureole in Christian art and "transfigured" by the scarlet letter (1:53), Hester appears before the crowd as if in resemblance of a once-revered icon, but now an idolatrous image of the Virgin Mary. The historical moment of transition from Old to New World is the crucial context. Like John Wilson, the assembled Puritans have been "nurtured at the rich bosom of the English Church" (1:109). They are accordingly familiar with the Roman Catholic imagery in the churches having survived destruction under Edward VI and in those having been readorned under James I and Charles I.[14] What they sense in Hester's image is partly what they abhor in the Church of England: the religious art that to their minds constitutes not only idolatrous images but threatening signs of a renewed affiliation with Rome on the part of the Stuarts.[15]

Beautiful, illuminated, and "transfigured"—her sin notwithstanding—Hester appears before the Puritans as if mocking their severe religious and aesthetic sensibilities. But at the same time, because of her sin, she poses as a shameful contrast to the traditional image her appearance suggests:

> Had there been a Papist among the crowd of Puritans, he might have seen in this beautiful woman, so picturesque in her attire and mien, and with the infant at her bosom, an object to remind him of the image of Divine Maternity, which so many illustrious painters have vied with one another to represent; something which should remind him, indeed, but only by contrast, of that sacred image of sinless motherhood, whose infant was to redeem the world. Here, there was the taint of deepest sin in the most sacred quality of human life, working such effect, that the world was only the darker for this woman's beauty, and the more lost for the infant that she had borne. (1:56)

The introduction of a Roman Catholic point of view, no more anomalous than historically resonant, temporarily completes the aesthetic resemblance Hester and Pearl bear to the Virgin Mary and Christ. Hawthorne then safely denies the suitability of the resemblance by accentuating Hester's sin. Still, we are left with uncomfortable dualisms of purity and sin, redemption and damnation, which, as it turns out, interlock in a paradoxical image symbolizing the spiritual and historical complexities at issue throughout the novel.

The Anglo-Catholic imagery associated with Hester and her art does not entirely disappear following the evocation of Madonna and Child. She exchanges her beautiful clothes for a gray robe and she hides her beautiful hair beneath a cap. Pious Bostonians, who believe in the efficacious logic of "visible sanctity," observe her "penance" and "good deeds" for seven years (1:62); and thus, by some trick of perception, memory, or Federal Theology, they come to believe that the scarlet letter has meanings other than its original designation for adultery. Even those who cannot forget the "black scandal" see with no apparent ill reflection on their divine covenant and errand that the scarlet letter "had the effect of the cross on a nun's bosom," or that it "imparted to the wearer a kind of sacredness" (1:163). Altered in luxurious beauty though it is, Hester's presence somehow manages to sustain an impression "majestic and statue-like" (1:163). And so from Madonna, to nun with a cross, to statue, Hester's metamorphosis retains a resemblance to icons, wholly anathema to the Puritan setting. Nothing inconsistent finally obtains in the fact that when Hester supports the fallen Dimmesdale in the last scaffold scene she once again evokes the Madonna; for their pose pictorially suggests the traditional pietà in Christian art, the whole scene having unmistakable overtones of a crucifixion (1:252–56).

Emphasis on these iconographical similarities further expresses the artistic side of Hester's nature, which is itself patently antipathetic to Puritan New England. There exist no religious paintings and icons in New England, and obviously there are no nuns. Before the 1640s, as "Endicott and the Red Cross" has already forecast, the Puritans effectively dispense with the cross as an idolatrous image belonging to Catholicism. Hawthorne certainly knew that these images were hateful anachronisms, but their ahistorical placement in the setting connects the early Puritans to their not very distant English past. Not that the colonists themselves are particularly conscious of the connection or that they would have approved of the connection had they possessed such consciousness. Hawthorne suggests instead, based upon a supposition speaking almost as much to the historical situation as it does to his own artistic needs, that beneath the iconoclastic level of consciousness the early Puritan mind remains somewhat receptive to symbols and images inherited from the Old World. Adhering to his consistent view that the past invariably exerts an influence on the present, and yet keeping within the historicity of the novel, Hawthorne does not place the image of "a nun with a cross on her bosom" directly in the minds of the Puritans, only the "effect" of that image. Hawthorne as historian and artist creates the image, because he needs the aesthetic tradition belonging to the very Anglo-Catholic theology renounced by his Puritan ancestors.

Conforming to his view that the first-generation Puritans were closer to Renaissance sensibility than were their descendants, Hawthorne also shows how Boston's upper classes actually come to patronize Hester's art. While the community has left behind some of the strict divisions in the social and ecclesiastical hierarchy of English culture, it has instituted its own forms of rank and status—social, civil, and clerical—still bearing resemblance to those in the mother country. Just as Hester's art is worthy of cultivated tastes of the monarch and nobility in England, so it is in demand by the higher orders of Puritan society:

> The taste of the age, demanding whatever was elaborate in compositions of this kind [Hester's "finer productions"], did not fail to extend its influence over our stern progenitors, who had cast behind them so many fashions which it might seem harder to dispense with. Public ceremonies, such as ordinations, the installation of magistrates, and all that could give majesty to the forms in which a new government manifested itself to the people, were, as a matter of policy, marked by a stately and well-conducted ceremonial, and a sombre, but yet a studied magnificence. Deep ruffs, painfully wrought bands, and gorgeously embroidered gloves, were all deemed necessary to the official state of men assuming the reins of power; and were readily allowed to individuals dignified by rank or wealth, even while sumptuary laws forbade these and similar extravagances to the plebeian order. (1:82)

Eventually Hester's needlework becomes the "fashion" among the upper ranks of Puritan society, a chief reason being that her art "really filled a gap which must otherwise have remained vacant" in the community (1:82).

The appeal of Hester's art to this first generation of Puritans that once lived in England would be less surprising were Hester's art not associated with the sin out of which the luxurious needlework first emerges for public view, and were it not, moreover, reminiscent of royal and even perhaps "papist" aesthetic forms. Hawthorne's ironic explanation for this rather egregious lapse in Puritan scruple is that "Vanity, it may be, chose to mortify itself, by putting on, for ceremonies of pomp and state, the garments that had been wrought by her sinful hands" (1:82–83). The extent of this mortification is adequately revealed in the novel's opening scene and more fully yet in the election day scene near its conclusion.

In his treatment of Pearl, Hawthorne depicts other Old World survivals in early America.[16] When, after the novel's opening scene, Hester exchanges her dress for the gray robe, she gives her striking mode of apparel on the scaffold to Pearl. The child's dresses, made of the "richest tissues," display the aesthetic range of Hester's "imaginative faculty" (1:90). Transferring the splendor of her clothes to Pearl, Hester also transfers the halo of her beauty: "So magnificent was the small figure, . . . and such was the splendor of Pearl's own proper beauty, shining through the gorgeous robes . . . that there was an absolute circle of radiance around her" (1 : 90). Such radiance surrounds her almost everywhere in the novel, most brilliantly in the forest scene when she receives the blessing of the sun (1 : 183–84). The aureole of Christian art is once again suggested here. Notwithstanding references elsewhere to Pearl's occasional impish behavior, as she stands at the brookside wreathed in flowers, she may indeed call to mind "a medieval icon for grace."[17]

Pearl's most visually impressive and historically resonant scene occurs in Governor Bellingham's splendid mansion, which specifically recalls Old World connections to the new colony. Hawthorne partly designs the scene to comment ironically on the intolerant Bellingham; but he also obviously intends to locate Pearl in a setting particularly well-suited to her. Bellingham has modeled his house upon those of "gentlemen of fair estate in his native land" (1 : 104). The descripton of the house, however, seems a purposeful evocation of ecclesiastical architecture.[18] The door has an "arched form" and is "flanked on each side by a narrow tower or projection of the edifice" (1 : 103–4). Like a cathedral, the structure has a "lofty hall, extending through the whole depth of the house, and forming a medium of general communication . . . with all the other apartments. At one extremity, this spacious room was lighted by the windows of the two towers, which formed a small recess on either side of the portal. At the other end, though partly muffled by a curtain, it was more powerfully illuminated by one of those embowed hall windows which we read of in old books, and which was provided with a deep and cushioned seat" (1 : 105). The mansion obviously cannot be a cathedral, and yet its arched door, twin towers, lofty ceiling, and vaulted ("embowed") window resonate with architectural associations beyond those of an English country house. They illustrate once again Hawthorne's purpose of transporting English forms of civilization to America in order to impart a sense of antiquity and continuity to the fledgling Boston society.

When the Reverend Wilson sees Pearl in the Governor's cathedral-like hall, dressed as she is in the red and gold embroidery of Hester's art, he immediately perceives that she reincarnates ecclesiastical art in Puritan America and asks:

> "What little bird of scarlet plumage may this be? Methinks I have seen just such figures, when the sun has been shining through a richly painted window, and tracing out the golden and crimson images across the floor. But that was in the old land. Prithee, young one, who art thou, and what has ailed thy mother to bedizen thee in this strange fashion? Art thou a Christian child,—ha? Dost know thy catechism? Or art thou one of those naughty elfs or fairies, whom we thought to have left behind us, with other relics of Papistry, in merry old England?" (1 : 109–10).

Because Wilson has been "nurtured at the rich bosom of the English church," Pearl reminds him of stained-glass imagery in England's ecclesiastical buildings, imagery to which the Puritans objected and which they were already destroying in England when this scene in the novel takes place.[19]

The plain-style severity of Puritan aesthetics and religious forms is completely alien to Pearl's figuration of Old World religious art. Through Wilson's memory, however, Puritan iconoclasm becomes suspended for a moment. England's aesthetic traditions, converging in Pearl, suddenly illuminate the dull piety and religious forms of New Jerusalem. Although a devout Puritan, Wilson is not horrified by Pearl's evocation of Catholic art. He is in fact playful and fatherly with the child, perhaps seeing in her infant form an iconographical symbol of joy and beatitude out of Old World experience too dear to want to forget. His lingering receptivity to Anglo-Catholic art does not last for long, however. Bellingham steps in to record the response we might expect from orthodox Puritanism, conflating Pearl's image with Hester's sin: " 'We might have judged that such a child's mother must needs be a scarlet woman, and a worthy type of her of Babylon!' " (1:110).

While the severe Bellingham inhabits a splendid English mansion, the interior does contain symbolic clues to his Puritanic character. In the hallway stands a suit of armor whose breastplate serves the same condemnatory function as that of the zealous Endicott in the "Red Cross" tale. As Hester sees herself mirrored in the breastplate, the polished surface only magnifies the scarlet *A*, just as the pietistic Bellingham exaggerates her sin. A harsh and insensitive man, Bellingham earnestly proposes to separate mother and child, for which reason they have come to his home. Cast as a hypocrite by objecting to Pearl's splendor while he surrounds himself with luxurious adornments, Bellingham also lacks the ability to recognize Pearl's intrinsic nobility or to sympathize with Hester's natural plea to keep her child. When influenced by the gentler Wilson and Dimmesdale, of course, this first-generation official does ultimately tolerate Pearl and Hester.

Not even this qualified tolerance exists between Pearl and her contemporaries, the second-generation Puritans charged by Hawthorne with having worn "the blackest shade of Puritanism" (1:232). Since Pearl is partly a symbolic figure, it is immensely significant that she finds herself more acceptable to the older Puritans than to their children. But her alienation from her peers causes far less damage to Pearl than might be expected, coming from Hawthorne; yet it surely redounds to the discredit of the Puritan children, Pearl's potential playmates, that she is an outcast. Some indefinable though lucid apprehension makes Pearl aware that they are her enemies on grounds deep-seated and irrevocable.

Embodying the very art of her mother, which is engrained in traditions antithetical to Puritanism, Pearl attacks the Puritan children like "some half-fledged angel of judgement,—whose mission was to punish the sins of the rising generation" (1:103). In her beauty, imaginative play, harmony with nature, and ties with ancient traditions—all the valorized qualities carefully assembled in "The Old Manse" and "The Custom-House"—Pearl represents the best values out of which American culture might be built, the very elements missing in second-generation Puritans (and missing to a great degree in the first). Even in its childhood games, the second generation forecasts Puritanic obsessions in the latter half of the seventeenth century: "scourging Quakers; or taking scalps in a sham-fight with the Indians; or scaring one another with freaks of imitative witchcraft" (1:94). That the children also play at going to church indicates with what piety they will later persecute the Quakers in the 1650s, massacre the Indians in King Philip's War, and convict their brethren of witchcraft in the early 1690s.

While Hawthorne introduces Pearl for multiple purposes in *The Scarlet Letter,* all of her functions seem to converge in the personification of art. Born out of sin and an extension of it, she nevertheless transcends her unholy origin. Indeed, she will grow up to become an artist in her own right when, having duly inherited Hester's talent, and having grown up somewhere in Europe within a milieu appreciative of art, she creates "beautiful tokens" with "delicate fingers" (1:262). Pearl therefore embodies the powers of art as Hawthorne conceives them: beauty, intuition, morality, spirit, passion, and a respect for the aesthetic forms of the past. Worldly and spiritual truth unite at once in her, "The living hieroglyphic, . . . the character of flame" (1:207). Consequently, she may indeed give human shape to the ubiquitous yet mysterious presence of the Pentacostal tongue of flame so importantly figuring in her father's concluding appearance in the novel.[20]

When Hester and Pearl leave New England a year after Dimmesdale's final scene on the scaffold, they take with them the aesthetic continuity between England and America that they have represented. They leave America, in other words, aesthetically barren—with the very "gap" that Hester once filled and that Pearl could one day fill in her turn. Their departure, coincident with the rise of the second generation of Puritans, suggests the magnitude of the historical schism evaluated by Hawthorne in *The Scarlet Letter.* England and Europe, not America, are cast not only as the cultural sources but also the ultimate repositories of art. Accordingly, after Hester returns to Boston some years later, she does not resume her needlework except in one instance: to embroider "a baby-garment, with such a lavish richness of golden fancy as would have raised a public tumult, had any infant, thus apparelled, been shown to our sombre-hued community" (1:262). Because their origins lay in England, most first-generation Puritans could accept this form of dress in Pearl and even want to possess other articles for itself evincing Hester's art. But the second generation, led by Endicott, becomes Puritanic. Unlike its counterparts in England who experience the Restoration, it retains the iconoclastic legacy of Civil War extremists. Thus, at the novel's close, Hester must send the only expression of her art back to Europe—to Pearl and her child, symbols of a cultural transmission and of a potential artistic heritage not yet acceptable in America. The ultimate logic of Puritan severity and inconoclasm leads to restrictions altogether abortive to the development of an aesthetic tradition in the New World upon which Hawthorne and other native American artists might draw. Because he inherited an aesthetic void from New England's past, while nevertheless imagining a historical situation in which Hester could defy her persecutors and create an art constituting the basis for a tradition, it became Hawthorne's task to resurrect the tradition in his own day. His too, no less than Hester's, was a magnificent act of defiance, an assertion not only of art's legitimate place in America but also of its freedom to borrow and adapt cross-cultural traditions for reasons transcending the provincial biases of any time and place.

The Oxford Puritan

Along with Hester and Pearl, Dimmesdale also has connections to Anglo-Catholic motifs that set him considerably apart from the New England clergy and make him, perhaps, a more striking anomaly in the historical setting of the novel than either his former lover or child. He has, to begin with, apparently graduated from Oxford University (1 : 120), the theological center of Episcopacy in the early seventeenth century, rather than from Cambridge, where the Puritans had acquired a strong minority in a few colleges beginning in the late sixteenth century. Since Dimmesdale is a young man when events in the novel begin in 1642, he would have had to graduate from Oxford no earlier than 1630. He would therefore have been at Oxford when William Laud was Chancellor (1630–33) or Archbishop of Canterbury (1633–40). Needless to say, it was no easy decade for nonconformists. From both positions, Laud headed a successful movement to expel Puritans first from Oxford and then from Cambridge. The chances of a professing Puritan to graduate from Oxford during these years when Laud was demanding conformity were therefore extremely poor, if not impossible.[21] The improbability would have been greater yet in the case of Dimmesdale, whose "scholar-like renown still lived in Oxford" (1 : 120), during the first years of the Civil War when Charles I was using Oxford as a temporary seat of government.

Hawthorne unquestionably knew that virtually all Puritan ministers who came to New England received their education at Cambridge. The fact was common knowledge in Massachusetts. But he also found ample evidence in his reading to support the common lore. In his *Magnalia,* for example, Cotton Mather calls Emmanuel College "that seminary of Puritans in Cambridge."[22] He also attributes a Cambridge education to more than a score of Puritan divines before Harvard began training clergymen in 1636. Only nine Puritans are said to have gone to Oxford. Of these, three seem to have graduated: Samuel Newman, John Davenport, and Samuel Eaton. But Eaton, either out of desire or necessity, first took orders in the Church of England, as the large majority of Puritans did; like Newman and others, he became a dissenting Puritan after his years at Oxford. One of the six who did not graduate, Richard Mather (Cotton's ancestor), was at Oxford before 1618, and he appears to have converted to nonconformity after that time. Another of the group, John Oxenbridge, refused to take the oath of conformity required at Oxford after Laud became Chancellor. Of the remaining four, it is impossible to tell why they left the University or whether they were nonconforming Puritans during their enrollment there.[23]

In the edition of Winthrop's *History* familiar to Hawthorne, editor James Savage explains that Newton, Massachusetts was renamed Cambridge "in compliment to the place where so many of the civil and clerical fathers of New England had received their education." He adds that in 1638 "there were probably . . . forty or fifty sons of the University of Cambridge in Old England—one for every two hundred or two hundred and fifty inhabitants—dwelling in the few villages of Massachusetts and Connecticut. The sons of Oxford were not a few."[24] Who these "sons of Oxford" were, or when they attended Oxford, Savage does not say. But he does know that Oxford was not friendly to Puritans. Mistakenly accepting the word of his sources that Roger Williams attended Oxford, and knowing the radical nature of William's nonconformity in England and Massachusetts Bay, Savage declares that "his life proves he had learned more [at Oxford] than in that day was commonly taught.[25]

Hawthorne's reading in Scott's *Woodstock* was also a source or supplement to his knowledge of Oxford's Laudian and Royalist persuasion. The novel is set in and around the ancient royal palace at Woodstock, near Oxford, in the aftermath of the regicide. The issues separating the Cavaliers from the Roundheads have not abated but intensified since the "martyrdom" of Charles I. Expressing the loyalties of Scott, the leading Royalist characters in the novel wait hopefully for a Restoration. In the meantime, they fear that Puritan iconoclasm will lead to the destruction not only of Woodstock palace but also of Oxford.[26] Because Oxford stands for historical allegiance to Laudian, High Court principles, Scott makes a point of dissociating the university from Puritanism: "the air that blew over the towers of Oxford was unfavorable to the growth of Puritanism, which was more general in the neighbouring counties."[27]

In strictly historical terms, Dimmesdale's scholarly renown would not have been alive at Oxford in the mid 1640s unless he had advocated Laudian principles during his years at the university. The friendliest town in the kingdom to Charles I was without doubt Oxford—friendly in adhering to Laudian church doctrines and in maintaining allegiance to the monarchy. For these reasons, Charles I retreated to Oxford in 1642 and continued the war against Parliamentary Independents. Hawthorne could have recalled from Clarendon's *History of the Rebellion* that in 1642 Oxford was "the only City of *England,* that [Charles] could say was entirely at his devotion; where he was received by the University."[28] He might also have remembered Daniel Neal's *History of the Puritans,* which confirms Oxford's loyal support in 1642 and its continued support of him and Episcopacy as late as 1647–49.[29] But if for some reason Hawthorne failed to recollect the information in Clarendon and Neal, he had Scott's *Woodstock* to jog his memory. One of the principal concerns of the novel is how the Laudian and Royalist party survived at Oxford after the regicide. The novel derives its tension from the intrusion of Puritans (and of schismatics born and encouraged by Puritan dissent) who contend with the traditional party.

Traditional order, of course, is as much at stake in *The Scarlet Letter* as in *Woodstock.* Hawthorne's sympathies for historical continuity are not greatly different from Scott's. Were *The Scarlet Letter* exclusively focused on the provincial scene of Puritan New England and the predominant historical influences composing that narrow focus, Hawthorne would surely have attributed a Cambridge education to Dimmesdale. By making him an Oxford graduate, however, Hawthorne points to Dimmesdale's affinity with a cultural heritage preceding and accompanying the rise of Puritanism. The implication is no different from the one obtaining in the case of Hester and Pearl: New England Puritanism cannot be understood apart from its English background.

The seemingly casual reference to Oxford therefore has a profound resonance, encapsulating the historical tensions between England and America in *The Scarlet Letter.* Dimmesdale is surely no thoroughgoing Anglican in disguise, but neither is he an unqualified Puritan. Although Hawthorne normally refers to Dimmesdale as a minister or clergyman, on five occasions he discards these familiar clerical titles for Puritan divines and calls Dimmesdale a "priest."[30] Chillingworth also designates Dimmesdale at one point as a "miserable priest" (1 : 171); and in the forest scene with Hester, Dimmesdale refers to himself as a "polluted priest" (1 : 195). The term appears four other times in the text, on three occasions applied to New England clergy and on another to a religious leader among Indians.[31] But whether Hawthorne means the term in a general, sacerdotal sense, he knew better than to apply it to Puritan clerics. The Puritans shunned the term in reaction to its use in the Church of England, since to their minds it implied a lingering and dangerous tie with Roman Catholicism. That "priest"was not the proper reference for a Puritan minister, in a positive sense, Hawthorne knew from his reading in New England history and Scott.[32]

Hawthorne does distinguish between Roman Catholic and Episcopal priesthood. Dimmesdale, for instance, refuses to select "one of the many blooming damsels" for a wife, "as if priestly celibacy were one of his articles of church-discipline" (1:125). In tireless yet futile attempts to purge his secret sin, he whips himself with a "bloody scourge," a practice "more in accord with the old, corrupted faith of Rome, than with the better light of the church in which he had been born and bred" (1:144). Failing to purify his "guilty conscience" by flagellation, he undertakes long fasts, not like "many other pious Puritans, . . . but rigorously, and until his knees trembled beneath him, as an act of penance" (1:144).

As was true of virtually all the non-separatist Puritans who came to Massachusetts Bay, the church in which Dimmesdale "had been born and bred" is the Church of England. It permitted the marriage of priests but considered repugnant the mortification of the flesh. Puritans thus had no quarrel with the Church over these matters. The dispute centered on specific points of doctrine, ecclesiastical orders, ceremonies, and objects of special sanctification or instruction. New England Puritans had none of the symbolic decor traditional in the Church of England. Nor did their ministers wear the surplice or vestment, but instead the dark Geneva cloak, the very one Hawthorne twice ascribes to Wilson and Dimmesdale (1:150, 220). On one occasion, though, Hawthorne suggests that Dimmesdale wears the traditional surplice of Anglican priests. In his act of exposing Dimmesdale's breast (and arguably seeing a stigmatic A), Chillingworth has to "thrust aside the *vestment*, that, hitherto, had always covered it even from the professional eye" (1:138; emphasis added). Hawthorne was familiar with the controversy over vestments, as he shows in "The Gray Champion," and thus it hardly seems likely that he would choose the word without purpose.

That purpose does not entail a transformation of Dimmesdale into an Anglican but it does intend to suggest a lingering substance of Anglican in his makeup. The survival of Old World ecclesiology amid Dimmesdale's New England attachments enriches the historical dimension of his clerical role much the way the "abbey" reference enriches the Manse. As a result of these dual influences, Dimmesdale and the imagined historical moment he represents acquire a complexity appreciably greater than would otherwise be the case. For Hawthorne manages to insinuate how elements of the English past withstand deliberate efforts to suppress them during the transition from Old to New Worlds. Dimmesdale's graduation from Oxford, his priestly associations, and his wearing a vestment comprise three constituents of this recessive design. Still other surviving components emerge prior to the final scene on election day. One involves the widow's house where Dimmesdale lives. Most tellingly, this house covers "pretty nearly the site on which the venerable structure of King's Chapel has since been built" (1:126). Originally constructed in 1689,[33] King's Chapel was the first Anglican/Episcopal Church in Massachusetts, located, as Hawthorne specifies, adjacent to the original graveyard in Boston—the very plot (named after another forlorn lover, Isaac Johnson) in which Dimmesdale is finally buried. The coherence is just too tight to ignore: from his English birth and education, to his home and final resting place in America, Dimmesdale is somehow or other connected with the Church of England.

Even Dimmesdale's parishioners revere him in a manner paralleling the unorthodox side of his role. They believe that he is a "miracle of holiness," that "the very ground on which he trod was sanctified" (1 : 142), and that he is a veritable "saint on earth" (1 : 144). Hence "the aged members of his flock . . . enjoined it upon their children, that their old bones should be buried close to their young pastor's holy grave" (1 : 142–43). As we have seen in "Grandfather's Chair," such a wish obviously echoes that of many early Bostonians who wanted to be buried near Isaac Johnson; and yet the reverence for Dimmesdale exceeds the bounds allowed by Puritan dogma. Even though their adoration stands in ironic counterpoint to Dimmesdale's sin and hypocritical concealment of it, they correctly see exceptional qualities in him. His extraordinary saintliness and sanctification are not entirely ill-suited to Puritan ecclesiology, as witnessed in the controversy over Anne Hutchinson,[34] but if his grave is to become hallowed, as seems indicated here, it is most fitting that the eldest Puritans wish to be buried near the enshrined bones of the saint, since they could recall the Anglo-Catholic reverence for saints from their experience in England. For centuries the cultural life of England was organized around the commemoration of saints' day in the Church calendar. Hawthorne was thoroughly familiar with the calendar and the traditions surrounding saints' days from William Hone's *Every Day Book,* a work he consulted, for at least the third time, during the last phase of writing *The Scarlet Letter.*[35]

The Anglo-Catholic design unfolds again during part of Dimmesdale's midnight scaffold scene in chapter 12. Having suffered seven years for his sin, hypocrisy, and inability to make public confession,[36] Dimmesdale fears—and rightly so—that a public exposure would lead to his being cast out, which, in 1641, actually happened to a lusting Puritan clergyman.[37] Guided by this fear, he stands on the scaffold for a "moment's peace" (1 : 146), hidden from the public eye, in a "vain show of expiation" (1 : 148). But "the agony of heaven-defying guilt" overwhelms the young minister, causing him to shriek aloud (1 : 148). Upon discovering that his shriek has not exposed him, he shortly conceives of another possible act of repentance when John Wilson walks by the scaffold on his way home from Governor Winthrop's deathbed. Wilson, after all, can be considered Dimmesdale's "brother clergyman,—or, to speak more accurately, his professional father" (1 : 150). Perhaps, Hawthorne suggests, the anxiously penitent Dimmesdale might confess to "Father Wilson," who is surrounded by a "radiant halo" and who is reminiscent of "the saint-like personages of olden times" (1:150).[38]. Here again, Hawthorne alludes to a clerical priesthood conforming to an Anglo-Catholic tradition. Specific mention of Wilson's ecclesiastical fatherhood is appropriately reserved for this scaffold scene in which Dimmesdale most demonstrably reveals his need to confess. Indeed, at one stage of composition, Hawthorne evidently planned to have Dimmesdale confess to a Catholic priest.[39] Dimmesdale's temptation to offer private confession to a fellow priest is probably as vain as the brief expiation he expects from the midnight vigil on the scaffold. If he is to achieve expiation, and if Hawthorne is to maintain the historicity of seventeenth-century Puritanism, Dimmesdale must confess in public. Pearl emphasizes this requirement when she and Hester join the minister on the scaffold, nagging her bewildered father with the persistent question, " 'Wilt thou stand here with mother and me, to-morrow noontide?' " (1:153).

Whitsuntide

Connections and disconnections between the English past and Puritan present emerge as the key feature of election day activities described in chapters 21 and 22—"The New England Holiday" and "The Procession." To understand these events, we must recognize that they are disguised and abbreviated forms of Whitsuntide festivities inherited from the English Church calendar. The time of year for election day is indisputably that of Pentecost, or Whitsuntide, foreshadowed in *The Scarlet Letter* by recurring images of the tongue of flame or tongue of Pentecost (1:141, 142, 191).[40] In his election day sermon, Dimmesdale is honored with the reappearance of the Pentacostal gift, when he converts the atmosphere "into words of flame" (1:248). While the importance of the Pentecostal image has not gone unnoticed,[41] a good deal might yet be said about the Pentecostal setting, its relation to English traditions and to the Bible, and its significance to Hawthorne's version of New England history.

The setting of Dimmesdale's last appearance in *The Scarlet Letter* does not take place on Whitsunday, or Pentecost itself, but on the following Wednesday, the traditional day for investing new magistrates in Massachusetts Bay. Hawthorne knew that election day always fell on Wednesday and that it coincided with the movable feast of Pentecost. In Winthrop's *History*, James Savage notes: "It has been too hastily thought, that our general election always came nearly at the same time as is fixed by our modern constitution. Careful readers, observing its occurrence in these volumes at different dates . . . will find the explanation in the Charter of 1629, providing that the general court be held on the 'last Wednesday in Easter term yearly' "— that is, fifty days after Easter.[42] As Hawthorne points out through a variant spelling in "Old News," election week "was the true holyday-season of New England" (11:138). The Puritans, of course, dispensed with celebrating

Whitsuntide, along with other traditional holidays approved by the Church of England. Yet they obviously adopted their own theocratic form of the Whitsuntide festivities by shifting election day from Sunday to Wednesday. Beyond the novel's clear suggestion of this ingenious transmutation of the Church calender, we have Hawthorne's testimony from *The English Note-books*. In the entry for 30 May [1855], he states:

> The two past days have been Whitsuntide Holidays; and they have been celebrated at Tranmere in a manner very similar to that of the old 'Lection' time in Massachusetts, as I remember it a good many years ago—though the festival, I think, has now almost or quite died out. Whitsuntide was kept up on our side of the water, I am convinced, under the pretence of rejoicing at the election of the Governor: it occurred at precisely the same period of the year—the same week—the only difference being, that Monday and Tuesday are the Whitsun festival-days, whereas, in Massachusetts, Wednesday was 'Lection Day,' and the acme of the merry-making. (*EN*: 114–15)[43]

Thus the Puritans carry on an English tradition, but one substantially transvalued. Hawthorne does all he can artistically to suggest the Whitsuntide season—so crucial to the religious and historical meanings of Dimmesdale's final sermon—without departing from the civil context within which the Puritans measurably confined the celebrations on election day. Being the offspring of fathers who had lived in "the sunny richness of the Elizabethan epoch," an epoch as "stately, magnificent, and joyous, as the world has ever witnessed," the Puritans would seem to copy the pageantry and festivity of their fathers, "to combine mirthful recreation with solemnity" (1:230). But, as we ought to expect after "The May-pole of Merry Mount," their copy turns out to be a pitiable "shadow," a "dim reflection of a remembered splendor, a colorless and manifest diluted repetition of what they had beheld in proud old London,—we will not say at a royal coronation, but at a Lord Mayor's show" (1:230). The degree to which the Puritans' holiday, procession, and "installation of magistrates" form a "colorless" and "diluted repetition" of Lord Mayor's Day can be seen in comparison with William Hone's description of this festival in his *Every Day Book*.[44]

Even on this one day of the year when they permit "diluted" English celebrations, the Puritans "appeared scarcely more grave than most other communities at a period of general affliction" (1:230).[45] Just as in "The May-pole of Merry Mount," this gravity is easy to understand since the Puritans have expelled the games and amusements traditionally promoting happiness in England:

> Here [in New England], . . . were none of the appliances which popular merriment would so readily have found in the England of Elizabeth's time, or that of James;—no rude shows of a theatrical kind; no minstrel

with his harp and legendary ballad, nor gleeman, with an ape dancing to
his music; no juggler, with his tricks of mimic witchcraft; no Merry
Andrew, to stir up the multitude with jests, perhaps hundreds of years
old, but still effective, by their appeals to the very broadest sources of
mirthful sympathy. (1:231)

The Puritans do not omit all English pastimes, just the ones most conducive
to a merriment reminiscent of England and the Church that promoted
them. They do retain sports that instill and encourage manliness, such as
wrestling and drilling with the quarterstaff, or engaging in contests with
buckler and broadsword. Sports such as these no doubt satisfy the "stirrings
of martial impulse" felt by Puritan soldiers, among whose ranks march
gentlemen who "sought to establish a kind of College of Arms, where, as in
an association of Knights Templars, they might learn the science, and, so
far as peaceful exercise would teach them, the practices of war" (1:237).

Surely the reference to the College of Arms seems harmless enough, but
the one to the Knights Templars, an order of knighthood beginning in
North Africa during the Crusades, has an import as malicious as any to be
found in Hawthorne's works. From what is specifically known about his
reading, Hawthorne must have relied on Scott's *Ivanhoe* for information on
the Templars. His only other likely source, William J. Thoms's *Book of the
Court,* consulted in the spring of 1849, fails to mention the Templars among
the British orders of knighthood, and with good reason.[46] Their absence
from the orders results from the Templars' having been suppressed by
Papal decree throughout Europe in 1312.[47] Hawthorne and Scott may or
may not have known about this suppression and the intricate controversy
behind it; but Scott does not have a good word for the Templars of the late
twelfth century. As a result of their nearly successful plot to usurp the
throne, Scott casts the Templars as an invidious and cruel order of
knighthood. Richard I, of course, banishes them.

Owing to Scott's treatment of the Templars, Hawthorne would not likely
associate the Puritan soldiers with this "most Holy Order of the Temple of
Zion"[48] for any purpose other than ironic. Evidently, the main English
legacy that the majority of Puritans wish to perpetuate in America is the
military. Only the military legacy still has "corporate existence" in the
nineteenth century (1:237).[49] And it is this militant aspect of most early
Puritans and their descendants—involving persecution, iconoclasm, and
rebellion—that Hawthorne invariably criticizes.

Nevertheless, Hawthorne appears intent on acquitting the first generation Puritans of responsibility for the gloominess and narrow-mindedness
bequeathed to later generations. The earliest Puritan settlers seem exoner-
ated because they are merely engaged "in the first stages of joyless deport-
ment" (1:232). Echoing his indictment in "The Custom-House,"
Hawthorne charges the second generation with having worn "the blackest

shade of Puritanism, and so darkened the national visage with it, that all subsequent years have not sufficed to clear it up (1:232). The immediate point concerns the effects of the Puritan heritage on American culture. "We have yet to learn again," Hawthorne laments, "the forgotten art of gayety," which the Puritans' fathers had enjoyed in Renaissance England (1:232). If Hawthorne's partial defense of the first generation is meant to be his last word on the matter, we are left with evidence in the novel and in the tale of how the first generation was surely joyless in its own right. By the time this holiday scene takes place in *The Scarlet Letter*, Endicott had twenty years earlier wiped out the transposed and transmuted gaiety of Merry Mount.

And yet Hawthorne does pull back, apparently intent on salvaging some respect for the first generation by virtue of the "stability and dignity" characterizing its patriarchal magistrates (1:237). These men of "civil eminence" contrast with the military escort preceding them in the procession: "Even in outward demeanour they showed a stamp of majesty that made the warrior's haughty stride look vulgar, if not absurd" (1:237). Except for the lately deceased Winthrop, the figures of Bradstreet, Endicott, Dudley, and Bellingham represent governors spanning the seventeenth-century Puritan experience under the first charter. If the welfare of New England is at stake, if its charter is threatened from without or the authority of the Puritan saints questioned from within, these leaders metaphorically stand like a "line of cliffs against a tempestuous tide" (1:238). Despite their having left "all degrees of awful rank behind" in England, "the faculty and necessity of reverence [is] still strong in [them]" (1:237). The people bestow their reverence, in other words, on "the idea of permanence" (1:238). In what seems to be a further effort to signify "the idea of permanence" and to align these gubernatorial "aristocrats" with a respectable heritage in England, Hawthorne relates them in a curious manner to English nobility: "So far as a demeanour of natural authority was concerned, the mother country need not have been ashamed to see these foremost men of an actual democracy adopted into the House of Peers, or made the Privy Council of the sovereign" (1:238).

Beyond the measurement of these Puritans by English aristocratic standards, as well as the obvious fact that Massachusetts Bay never had an "actual democracy," the significance of this passage lies in the irony that the House of Peers and the Privy Council no longer exist as institutions in 1649 when, as Hawthorne presents it, their members compare favorably with Puritan magistrates. But Hawthorne surely knew, at least from Clarendon and Guizot, that the Privy Council became defunct before the execution of Charles I in January and that, immediately after the regicide, Parliament abolished the House of Peers.[50] Consequently, within the 1649 context, the equation of Puritan "democratic" magistrates and English nobles is a torturing irony, the whole idea of permanence and reverence for traditional authority being undermined in light of the collapse of England's monarchical system. There does indeed seem to be a great tribute paid here to the noble Puritan founders and democratic "types,"[51] but Endicott's appearance in the group should in itself caution against taking the tribute at face value, especially considering the ostensibly honorific similarities shared by New England's magistrates and England's nobility and king. For, as we have seen, Endicott always serves as Hawthorne's arch-opponent to England's traditions and monarchy. Sword in hand, Endicott represents the king-defying and regicidal spirit in Hawthorne's Puritan drama. At the moment he appears in the election day ceremony of *The Scarlet Letter,* Endicott is about to occupy center stage more dominantly than ever, since he will be chosen governor for thirteen of the next fifteen years.[52] The Quaker persecutions in "The Gentle Boy" should be sufficient reminders of what ominously awaits Puritan America under Endicott's leadership.

From the foregoing discussion of the ties and disconnections between England and America, certain conclusions can be drawn. Hawthorne presents English forms and traditions as positive historical origins from which the Puritans are in the process of disinheriting themselves. The degree of disinheritance is virtually a gauge of cultural loss to New England. Since first-generation Puritans retain some measure of the customs inherited from their Elizabethan parents, Hawthorne presents it less negatively than the one to follow. The original settlers, however, are harsh enough in their own right, despite their moderation when compared to their children. The conflict with England having begun on theological grounds has come to include cultural issues at large. As Hawthorne seems to conceive it, the process of disinheritance was probably irreversible; for while the first generation of American Puritans was about to give way to the second, Puritans in England were also overthrowing the traditional order. On the other hand, by centering on this transitional phase of Puritanism, Hawthorne perhaps suggests that the "blackest shade of Puritanism" was not fated or predetermined to succeed the first colonists. Alternatives existed, not only the all-or-nothing choice between "jollity and gloom" highlighted in "The May-pole of Merry Mount" but also a choice to mediate these absolutes.

Dimmesdale becomes the fictional embodiment of mediation in *The Scarlet Letter,* paralleling the mediating roles of Williams in "Endicott and the Red Cross" and Bradstreet in "The Gray Champion." Had Puritans chosen as their leader a man of Dimmesdale's ability to unite the Puritans in a bond of sympathy, the negative qualities of the second generation, Hawthorne implies, might have been tempered. Political power was, after all, "within the grasp of a successful priest" whose "intellectual ability" distinguished him from the magistrates (1:238). Like his fellow clergymen, Dimmesdale has intellectual gifts, but his are less hardened than theirs. Who among the clergy could become a successful leader of the Puritan errand better than

Dimmesdale, since all but he lack "the gift that descended upon the chosen disciples, at Pentecost, in tongues of flame" (1:141)? Perhaps by equating themselves to Old Testament Israelites, New England Puritans chose the wrong typological models.

Such would seem to be the implication in the final scene when Hawthorne puts forward Dimmesdale as a typological descendant of the disciples who received the Pentecostal gift—he "convert[s]" the atmosphere "into words of flame" (1:248). The scene has several obvious analogies to the biblical Pentecost described in Acts 2. Irrespective of the exact meaning of his words, Dimmesdale speaks in a universal language, "a tongue native to the human heart" (1:243). The sound that comes from heaven, the metaphor of a "rushing mighty wind" in Acts 2:2, corresponds to the description of Dimmesdale's voice as Hester hears it: "Now she caught the low undertone, as of the wind sinking down to repose itself; then ascended with it, as it rose through progressive gradations of sweetness and power, until its volume seemed to envelop her with an atmosphere of awe and solemn grandeur" (1:243). Just as the multitude of believers "were together, and had all things common" in Acts 2:44, so the Puritans come out of the meeting house with a "united testimony" on the wisdom and inspiration of Dimmesdale's sermon (1:248). Appropriately, this is the only occasion in the novel when Hawthorne unifies the multiple perceptions of Puritan observers.

The content of Dimmesdale's sermon also draws from the biblical Pentecost. A decade or so too early for an Old Testament Jeremiad, the sermon adheres to the Pentecostal promise of salvation and well-being:

> [Dimmesdale's subject, it appeared, had been the relation between the Deity and the communities of mankind, with a special reference to the New England which they were here planting in the wilderness. And, as he drew towards the close, a spirit of prophecy had come upon him, constraining him to its purpose as mightily as the old prophets of Israel were constrained; only with this difference, that, whereas the Jewish seers had denounced judgments and ruin on their country, it was his mission to foretell a high and glorious destiny for the newly gathered people of the Lord. (1:249)

Were Dimmesdale's prophecy for New England true, however, and were the election day scene really a thorough duplication of the biblical Pentecost, Hawthorne would be suggesting that Puritanism was, in fact, a noble origin for American history. But such is clearly not the case. The prophecy and Pentecostal scene relate to Puritanism only in some bitter ironic sense of lost opportunity. The Puritans are not about to "save [themselves] from this untoward generation" (Acts 2:40) of which Endicott, the newly elected magistrate, will take command and which he will lead in persecuting the

Quakers. Dimmesdale's having been gifted with the tongue of flame, briefly uniting the Puritan elect with his sermon, actually indicates a beneficent power and leadership that, historically, the Puritans never had. When the congregation emerges from the church and raises "one great voice by the universal impulse which makes likewise one vast heart out of the many," Hawthorne underscores the difference between history and fiction in the *The Scarlet Letter:* "Never, from the soil of New England, had gone up such a shout! Never, on New England soil, had stood the man so honored by his mortal brethren as [Dimmesdale]" (1:250). Never, indeed. The novel casts such unfulfilled potentialities as the tragedy of seventeenth-century Massachusetts.

Paradoxically, as Dimmesdale gains a personal triumph by confessing his sin at death, the community loses his benign influence. Only a few adherents from the first generation of settlers remain to continue the gentle, recessive Puritan strain in the shadow of Endicott. Pearl, who is the ongoing representation of a Renaissance tradition and who is, moreover, finally blessed with human sympathy at her father's death, leaves America behind her; and Hester, after an absence, returns less an artist than a theorist, hypothesizing America's "coming revelation" from a woman made wise "not through dusky grief, but the ethereal medium of joy" (1:263). It is hard to tell what the source of such a joy might be. The novel seems already to have precluded the desirability of realizing Hester's dream, inasmuch as Pearl will grow to maturity with a balanced view of the world. Unlike Edith and Edgar in "May-pole," she promises to "grow up amid" both "human joy and sorrow, nor for ever do battle with the world, but be a woman in it" (1:256). At any rate, Hester's art would seem to externalize a more appealing side of her character than her speculative philosophy; but her artistic productions are eventually lost to Puritan America, while her teaching and counseling become widely propagated. They may provide solace to individuals, but their cultural influence will be negligible as Endicott assumes control over the second generation.

In the face of the ultimate failures of potential in seventeenth-century America, Hawthorne, of course, found no Dimmesdale, Hester, or Pearl in his historical sources; rather, he created them, like the scarlet letter artifact itself. He thereby established a cultural ancestry for his nineteenth-century aesthetics. While such characters never existed, the best impulses that they embody were, according to Hawthorne, at least inherent—but recessive—in early New England. Their connections to Old World continuities reveal a potential transmission of art and sympathy to a New World setting, a transmission Hawthorne resurrected for his own aesthetic foundation. The recovery of this transmission had been an implicit part of Hawthorne's critique of the Puritan tradition from the beginning, and it became a conscious intent no later than 1846 when he wrote "The Old Manse." With his dismissal from the Custom House, Hawthorne for the first time felt, legitimately or not, a persecution of himself, as artist, which he evidently equated to a legacy of Puritan iconoclasm. His reaction against his own sense of persecution, and against the Puritan legacy to which his own ancestors contributed, resulted in his adopting the aesthetic traditions of England in order to assert the validity of art and himself as artist.

6

Divided Loyalties: Politics and Aesthetics in *The English Notebooks* and *The American Claimant Manuscripts*

When Franklin Pierce appointed Hawthorne consul to Liverpool, he allowed the author to see firsthand the homeland of his ancestors—the land, indeed, whose idealized values had been, from the outset of his career, an essential part of his historical imagination and aesthetics. One can well imagine Hawthorne walking the deck of the *Niagara* in early July 1853, somber over leaving behind his native country yet full of expectation over what lay ahead in England. He may not yet have articulated to himself that he might simply be exchanging one home for another, but it seems likely that he would have felt some sense of returning to "our old home." Many years earlier, in "Fragments from the Journal of a Solitary Man" (1837), he had expressed through the figure of Oberon a yearning to return to ancestral and cultural roots in terms that would prove incredibly prophetic: "And England, the land of my ancestors! Once I fancied that my sleep would not be quiet in the grave unless I should return, as it were, to my home of past ages, and see the very cities, and castles, and battle-fields of history, and stand within the holy gloom of its cathedrals, and kneel at the shrines of its immortal poets, there asserting myself their hereditary countryman" (11:315). Such a yearning for the hereditary home accords with the young Hawthorne's ambition to create literature in no way inferior to that penned by the "scribbling sons of John Bull." Then, too, the ancient structures and layers of history available to English writers, sensible in the landscape itself, afforded the mature romance writer storied and poetical associations of rich antiquity—essential ingredients, Hawthorne would argue in the preface to *The Marble Faun*, altogether too thin or lacking in America. Within a month after stepping ashore, Hawthorne began to keep a record of his impressions of the English past and present. The journal stretched to prodigious length, concluding seven volumes later on 3 January 1858, just before Hawthorne's departure to the Continent. Un-published in his lifetime, these seven volumes have come to be known as *The English Notebooks*. Hawthorne drew upon his English experience and the *Notebooks* not only for the twelve sketches comprising *Our Old Home* but also for materials that inform drafts of a romance on an American's claim to English patrimony, *The American Claimant Manuscripts*. Examined separately in this chapter, the *Notebooks* and the *Claimant Manuscripts* complete this study's diagram of Hawthorne's lifelong attraction to cultural continuities belonging to England.

The English Notebooks

The significance of the *Notebooks* for Hawthorne's career has not been adequately assessed. The most extensive discussion of them remains that by Stewart in the Introduction to his edition of the *Notebooks*. Critics have drawn from them to show sources for the twelve essays Hawthorne eventually published as *Our Old Home*,[1] and biographers have mined them for information on Hawthorne's years in England.[2] But little analysis of developing concerns in the text has emerged.[3] Perhaps, as one reader believes, the *Notebooks* do not merit critical attention.[4] But this chapter takes issue with that position through an examination of Hawthorne's discovery that his cultural loyalties to England often compete uneasily with his political loyalties to America. The *Notebooks* are obviously "about" England—or, more accurately, about the England Hawthorne imagined and perceived. They offer a chronicle of his impressions of England that are by no means static, as biographers by and large lead us to believe. His impressions change in both slight and radical ways, and the whole may be read as an evolving record of Hawthorne's positive attitudes toward things British.

Because of its selectivity and abbreviation, as well as its having been written essentially for an American audience, the more commonly discussed *Our Old Home* gives diluted or erroneous impressions of Hawthorne's views of England. The point applies especially to materials covering the last two years of Hawthorne's stay, which make up well over one-half of the *Notebooks* but are greatly slighted in *Our Old Home*. Three of the twelve chapters in *Our Old Home* draw rather exclusively on entries written during the last two years: "Pilgrimage to Boston," "Near Oxford," and "Some Haunts of Burns." One chapter, "A London Suburb," might be said to draw equally on Hawthorne's time in England. The other eight, in which one finds examples of Hawthorne's negative estimations of English poverty and institutions, have been gleaned from the first two years' experience. Only in the *Notebooks* is it possible to trace the full development of Hawthorne's estimate of English culture. In them, we can pursue the cross-cultural themes that preoccupied Hawthorne, the evolving nature of those themes, and the sheer weight of attention he gives them that should finally count for what mattered to him most.

To begin with, we should notice the value Hawthorne assigned to the journals gathered in the *Notebooks*. He wrote to his publisher, James T. Fields, just before sailing to France in January 1858:

> I made up a huge package the other day, consisting of seven closely written volumes of journal, kept by me since my arrival in England, and filled with sketches of places and men and manners, many of which would doubtless be very delightful to the public. I think I shall seal them up, with directions in my will to have them opened and published a century hence; and your firm shall have the refusal of them then.[5]

Hawthorne then entrusted the journals to the care of a young Englishman, Henry Bright, who had become a close friend. Just before sailing to France, Hawthorne posted them, along with the following note:

> Dear Mr. Bright,—Here are these journals. If unreclaimed by myself, or by my heirs or assigns, I consent to your breaking the seals in the year 1900—not a day sooner. By that time, probably, England will be a minor republic, under the protection of the United States. If my countrymen of that day partake in the least of my feelings, they will treat you generously.[6]

Hawthorne's nationalistic jesting should not distract us from how valuable he felt the journals one day would become. Most immediately, they contained sources for "sketches of places and men and manners" that might delight the public. He had been toying with the idea for quite a while, even as he affected to dismiss publication on grounds that his critical views of the English were so frank that, should they greet the public eye, a proverbial hornet's nest of British resentment would descend on him.[7] When *Our Old Home* was eventually published, of course, his forecast of British reception was more or less borne out by the reviews.[8] Another immediate function Hawthorne may have planned for the journals was as source material for a romance involving a bloody footstep, which he was definitely contemplating in April 1855.[9]

Coupled with his economic motive in accepting the lucrative consulship was Hawthorne's desire to witness the English side of the historical tensions between England and America with which most of his historical fiction had been concerned. These tensions, both religious and political, had resulted in repeated outbreaks of violence, and, we have seen, were entangled in the cultural and aesthetic issues of personal importance to Hawthorne as an artist. He understood better than many of his contemporaries the disadvantage American writers faced from the anti-aesthetic, iconoclastic tradition of his own Puritan forebears. Thus his long-standing personal conflict over admiration for the strength of character in some early Puritans and regret over their general failure to appreciate and promote art. The historical conflict and personal conflict were for Hawthorne essentially a family quarrel between offspring and parent. Like most family quarrels, it took place at home. But in this case there were two homes, both real and imagined: the native homeland in the New World, and the ancestral home in England. When Hawthorne set out for England, he faced the opportunity to resolve conflicts between these two homes (if resolved they could be), or, in other words, to settle his lifelong tension between political allegiance to America and aesthetic loyalty to England.

For more than forty years, Randall Stewart's views have effectively guided readers' perceptions or opinions of the *Notebooks*. With his early article on the patriotic motif in the *Notebooks*,[10] his introduction to its edited text, and his biography of Hawthorne, Stewart has led the way in viewing Hawthorne's experience in England as a continuing squabble over English character, landscape, society, and politics. He was by no means single-minded in his interpretation. In fact, scarcely anyone else has been more acute than he in pointing out Hawthorne's deep appreciation for elements of English life, or in observing a division in his opinions.[11] Nevertheless, at odds with Hawthorne's increasingly favorable opinion of England as the *Notebooks* evolve, the weight of Stewart's commentary falls on Hawthorne's "American" quarrel with English society.

Stewart does offer, however, two useful categories to which we might provisionally assign most of Hawthorne's impressions of England. He finds that during the extensive travels through England, Hawthorne "was of two minds, which might be called the historical and the contemporary, or perhaps the English and American."[12] As Stewart describes this division, Hawthorne, as an American democrat, was critical of the hierarchical social and political system of contemporary England that resulted in poverty and squalor on the one hand, and in luxury, prestige, and elegance on the other; but as an American interested in history and traditional ties to the mother country, Hawthorne was drawn to artifacts and sites reminding him of bygone times. In other words, he liked what was old for the sake of its age, while despising the social system out of which the historical artifacts had issued or in which, anachronistically, they continued to thrive. Eventually, this argument concludes, Hawthorne found antiquity a repressive hindrance to democratic reform and therefore wished that it might all be swept away.

There is no denying a measure of truth in these proposals. Hawthorne does marvel at historical monuments, artifacts, surviving modes of ancient life, and he does criticize the politics, social circumstances, and people of the contemporary scene. But this convenient dualism oversimplifies a complex body of evidence. Insofar as his views of contemporary England are concerned, Hawthorne is hardly consistent in his criticism. Indeed, after the early phases of the Crimean War, during which Hawthorne was outraged (and apparently ready to go to war)[13] over British postures threatening the United States, his criticism of contemporary England comes very near a virtual halt. That is, if followed chronologically, Hawthorne's opinion of present-day English life undergoes a seemingly radical shift. Given the frequent negative opinions found in the first two years of the Notebooks, one has to look hard to find two or three in the last two years. Compliments, however, grow increasingly abundant, not only to the English past but also to the English present. The degree of Hawthorne's favorable response to England during these years can also be traced in his letters to William D. Ticknor, over the course of which he repeatedly mentions how unattractive America appears to him and how he would rather stay in England.[14]

Hawthorne does not, of course, entirely shed his negative opinions of contemporary English character and society: we must sometimes assume a critical view behind a comparatively neutral observation. But he does modify and soften his criticisms to a surprising extent, given his American political biases and the very "strangeness" a foreign country is bound to present to a first-time visitor. But the longer his stay in England, the wider the latitude of his understanding and tolerance, to the point that by the end of his visit he seems almost as fond of England in the present as he is of England in the past.

No small shift is entailed in this change of attitude. Hawthorne came to England possessing ingrained prejudices both for and against what he expected to find there. It seems quite plain that, during the first couple of years, his native prejudices often interfere with and color his perceptions. It is also plain, however, that the basic honesty and integrity of Hawthorne's mind will not rest easy with convenient stereotypes. Nearly from the outset, Hawthorne acknowledges the prejudicial filters through which he perceives England, thus alerting himself to the possibility of subsequent revisions in his views. These experiences become active epistemological exercises for him and the members of his family. Ultimately, he wanted to remove the filters altogether, to see through a clear lens. Whether he ever managed to achieve that sort of vision is problematical. Even in the most unqualified admiration Hawthorne comes to feel for England, there was a predisposition to do so that he also brought with him from America; and this leaning, involving his interest in things past and his reading in English literature, is nearly as strong as his inherited political animosity.[15] All the same, the degree of fondness Hawthorne eventually feels for England exceeds by far what he apparently came prepared to feel. The overall pattern in the Notebooks therefore involves two roughly parallel movements: while Hawthorne's inclination to favor England grows, his contrary inclination to disfavor it decreases, both finally joining in a positive opinion.

The Notebooks make it clear, however, that Hawthorne was in no immediate danger of becoming an Anglophile, readily adopting English ways while snobbishly spurning those of America. He was sufficiently proud of his Americanism to resist expatriated affectations. Moreover, his introduction to England, like Irving's and Melville's before him, was to the unattractive quarters of Liverpool's commercial and trading center, which held none of the interest Hawthorne had no doubt expected from an English city, surely nothing approaching the attractions offered by London about which he had read and heard for years. Poverty and filth met him all too often. His consular duties very quickly proved onerous. The July weather was cool—even cold.

The early unfavorable impression of England is emphasized in the third entry of the *Notebooks,* nearly a month after Hawthorne arrived in Liverpool, in an account of a visit paid to Grace Greenwood (Sara Jane Clarke), who had emigrated (briefly, it turned out) to England. Greenwood apparently extolled the merits of England far more than the chilled Hawthorne, who missed the hot New England summer, could bear. He says: "We talked about England and America; and while telling how much she loved this country, she drew her shawl about her shoulders, and looked shivery and miserable. There ought to be an extraordinary warmth in the people's hearts, to make up for the chill of such a climate" (*EN*: 5–6). During the following month, Hawthorne had not found enough warmth in his own heart to offset the cold summer, and he was obviously suffering homesickness, which prompted him to reflect not simply on his homeless condition in England, but on his unsettled life since marriage. A 2 September 1853 entry reads in part:

> It was a dismal rainy day, yesterday; and we had a coal fire in the sitting-room; beside which I sat, last evening, as twilight came on, and thought rather sadly how many times we have changed our home, since we were married. In the first place, our three years at the Old Manse; then a brief residence at Salem, then at Boston, then two or three years at Salem again; then at Lenox, then at West Newton, and then again at Concord, where we imagined that we were fixed for life, but spent only a year. Then this farther flight to England, where we expect to spend four years, and afterwards another year in Italy—during all which time we shall have no real home. For, as I sat in this English house, with the chill, rainy English twilight brooding over the lawn, and a coal-fire to keep me comfortable on the first evening of September; and the picture of a stranger . . . gazing down at me from above the mantel-piece, I felt that I never should be quite at home here. (*EN*: 23)

As such works as "The Gentle Boy," "The Old Manse," and *The House of the Seven Gables* make clear, Hawthorne placed exceedingly high value on the domestic home and hearth, and the odds are that he did so precisely because he rarely enjoyed such a setting for any length of time. The early sense of homelessness in England was really nothing new, only different, inasmuch as he was now removed from his native country too. If he was ever to feel especially good about England, then, he could hardly express it more meaningfully than through the talismanic "feeling at home." We must for a moment put aside our knowledge that Hawthorne would later entitle the published version of his English experience *Our Old Home*, in order to observe how he came to feel at home in England—not just at old Boston late in his stay, as one reader has argued,[16] but by degrees from an early date. Except for the honeymoon years at the Old Manse, Hawthorne was never to feel more at home anywhere than in England.[17] One of the first adjustments he had to make was to the weather, even to the cool English summers. By 22 June 1855, he has already made a considerable adjustment: "I suppose there is still latent in us Americans (even of two centuries date, and more, like myself) an adaptation to the English climate, which makes it like native soil and air to us (*EN*: 121–22).

Notwithstanding numerous criticisms of things English in the first third of the *Notebooks*, this sense of a latent ability to adapt to England is a major recurring idea. The idea itself involves an inherent home-feeling, a particular affinity for the English past, and it affords the means by which Hawthorne will gradually feel more at home in the present. It initially appears in the entry of 3 April 1854, wherein Hawthorne reflects on the antique village of Eastham, near Chester: "the finest old English village I have seen, with many ancient houses, and altogether a picturesque and rural aspect; unlike anything in America, and yet possessing a kind of familiar look, as if it were something I had dreamed about" (*EN*: 57). Later the same year, in an entry of 9 October devoted solely to the point of innate familiarity, Hawthorne is more specific: "My ancestor left England in 1635. I return in 1853. I sometimes feel as if I myself had been absent these two hundred and eighteen years—leaving England just emerging from the feudal system, and finding it on the verge of Republicanism. It brings the two far separated points of time very closely together, to view the matter thus" (*EN*: 92).

As the notion of historical familiarity with England takes hold, Hawthorne loses most of his sense of alienation and he criticizes far less the obvious differences separating English people and institutions from those in America. Although he learns that England is not moving toward republicanism nearly as much as he wants or affects he wants, he begins to feel at home all the same, especially when separated from the consulate and when free of social engagements required of his position. During the yuletide holidays in 1854, he is led to surmise, "I think I have been happier, this Christmas, than ever before—by our own fireside, and with my wife and children about me. More content to enjoy what I had; less anxious for anything beyond it, in this life" (*EN*: 98). It therefore strikes him as strange that, being happy, famous and (for once) prosperous, he should be revisited by a dream, recurring over the last twenty or thirty years, that he is a hopeless failure. The emergence of the dream at this time may paradoxically reflect on the measurable home-feeling Hawthorne has thus far achieved in England.

Certainly he achieves a growing ease and happiness as the months pass by. The summer of 1855 is particularly pleasant, after he has taken up family residence at Leamington Spa for the benefit of Sophia's health. Near the end of an entry for 13 July, recording a pleasure excursion to the Lake district and a visit to Furness Abbey, Hawthorne remarks: "We reached home somewhere about eight o'clock—home I see I have called it; and it seems as homelike a spot as any we have found in England, the old inn, close by the bridge, beside the clear river, pleasantly overshadowed by trees. It is entirely English and like nothing that one sees in America; and yet I feel as if I might have lived here a long while ago, and had now come back because I retained pleasant recollections of it" (*EN*:160).

The longer Hawthorne remains in England and the more he travels beyond the commercial world of Liverpool, the more his aesthetic and historical interests come to the foreground of the *Notebooks*, the entries taking on greater length and filling out with added detail. Even in the bustle of London on his first visit, he feels completely comfortable, imaginatively at home, equipped as he is with a reading knowledge of certain sites, especially those occupied by "writers of the Queen Anne age." An entry of 7 September 1855 offers a telling illustration: "Yesterday forenoon, I went out alone, and plunged headlong into London and wandered about all day, without any particular object in view, but only to lose myself, for the sake of finding myself unexpectedly among things that I have always read and dreamed about" (*EN*:204). Unlike Melville's Redburn, who unsuccessfully tries to retrace his father's tour through Liverpool from an outdated guidebook, Hawthorne does not feel at all disappointed. Everything in London is where it should be as he has imagined it. He both is and is not a stranger.

The same kind of imagined acquaintance holds true for his experience in Poet's Corner in Westminster Abbey. "Poet's Corner has never seemed like a strange place to me; it has been familiar from the very first;—at all events, I cannot now recollect the previous conception, of which the reality has taken the place. I seem always to have known that somewhat dim corner" (*EN*:247). As if feeling the spirits of the entombed writers, Hawthorne is reminded of the affection and respect felt by the English for their authors: "what portion of the world's regard and honor has hitherto been awarded to literature" (*EN*:219). Their monuments may not be as magnificent or ostentatious as those of wealthy aristocrats and merchants elsewhere in the cathedral, but they have their special place amid the incomparable beauty, commemorating England's special regard for its literary sons whom the ambitious young Hawthorne had hoped to emulate. A far cry from the situation Hawthorne knew in America, these honored stones signify not only the dignity of writers now dead but also the prestige and worth they felt, as artists, when alive.

His American patriotism notwithstanding, Hawthorne witnesses first hand what he had really sensed from the beginning of his career: England or Europe was the repository for art, however antiquated its social and political institutions might be. The point is most fully articulated in Hawthorne's imagined Boston in *The Scarlet Letter*, which underlies the significance of his trip to old Boston in late May of 1857—his "pilgrimage" as he calls in *Our Old Home*. The *Notebooks* do not cogently express the opinion found in *Our Old Home*—that Hawthorne "began to feel at home in this good old town, for its very name's sake, as I never had before felt, in England" (5:156). Comparatively speaking, this published confession may be true. As we have already seen, however, Hawthorne has by this time acquired a substantial home-feeling in England at large. Had he not, the Boston trip would no doubt have turned out to be less special than it was, as the *Notebooks* prove. "It is singular what a home-feeling, and sense of kindred, this connection of our New England metropolis gives me, and how reluctant I am to leave this old town, on that account. It is not unreasonable to suppose that the local habits and recollections of the first settlers may have had some influence on the physical character of the streets and houses in our Boston; at any rate, here is a similar intricacy, and numbers of the same old peaked and projecting-storied dwellings, some of which I used to see there" (*EN*:479).

In perceiving how old Boston's architecture corresponds to a portion of new Boston's when he was a youth, Hawthorne is, one might say, feeling "American." The American home-feeling then leads to a reflection on the historical setting in old Boston at the time his ancestor, William Hathorne, embarked for the New World. While his own ancestral roots unquestionably accounts for the warmth of his expression, another dimension of Hawthorne's experience in old Boston transcends family origins and extends farther back in history than the seventeenth century. In one scene, Hawthorne ruminates near a church in old Boston, a structure dating back to Catholic times and thus utterly foreign to the plain-style meeting houses built by Puritan settlers in the New World:

> The scene was very cheerful in the morning-sun; people going to their labor in the day's primal freshness; children with milk-pails loitering over the burial-stones; the simple old town preparing for its day, that would be like myriads of other days which had passed over it, but yet a day that would be worth living through. And down in the church-yard, where were buried many generations whom it remembered in their day, looked the stately tower; and it is good to think of such an age-long giant, connecting the present epoch with a long past, and getting quite imbued with human nature by being so long connected with men's knowledge and interests. (*EN*:475)

Reminiscent of the evocation of Indian life in "The Old Manse" and "Main-street," this passage reveals Hawthorne's inveterate habit of searching out historical continuity; and appearing along with other periodic expressions of its kind, it shows the fondness he feels for the harmonious effects produced by time upon England.

The extent of that fondness can be measured by just how much Hawthorne assimilates England's aristocratic system. Nothing in contemporary English society so perplexes or vexes Hawthorne as does this system that grants privilege to the few while withholding opportunity from the many. Overall, he believes that aristocracy can not last; indeed, during the Crimean War he feels that the system verges on collapse: "The progress of the age is trampling over the aristocratic institutions of England, and they crumble beneath it. This war has given the country a vast impulse towards democracy" (*EN*: 99). He makes this prophecy even while acknowledging that "the nobles were never positively more noble than now—never, perhaps, so chivalrous, so honorable, so highly cultivated" (*EN*: 99).

Still, no matter how strong his antipathy to the hierarchical structure, Hawthorne comes steadily under its influence, and to a certain extent he seems perfectly happy to do so.[18] As with other issues, he approaches the aristocracy in terms of the distinction between past and present. Reporting on the local low opinion of the Derby family at Knowsley-park, for instance, he draws this conclusion: "in fact, it is rather a pity to see, that, after so many centuries of connection with the soil and neighborhood, they have not the slightest hold on the affections of the country" (*EN*: 53). Even in the presence of poverty-ridden citizens, Hawthorne reflects an idealized affection for aristocracy. In front of the Liverpool Exchange on a cold day in January 1855, he notices "avenues densely thronged with people of all ages, and of all manner of dirt and rags. They were waiting, I believe, for soup-tickets, and waiting very patiently too, without outcry or disturbance, or even sour looks—only patience and meekness. Well—I don't know that they have a right to be impatient of starvation; but still there does seem to be insolence of riches and prosperity, which one day or another will have a downfall. And this will be a pity, too" (*EN*: 103).

The reason for this pity immediately becomes evident, for in the same paragraph Hawthorne reflects on estates at Otterspool and Larkhill:

. . . it is a wonder to behold—and it is always a new wonder to me—how comfortable Englishmen know how to make themselves—locating their dwellings far within private grounds, with secure gateways and porter's lodges, and the smoothest roads, and trimmest paths, and shaven lawns, and clumps of trees, and every bit of the ground, every hill and dell, made the most for convenience and beauty, and so well kept that even winter cannot disarray it;—and all this appropriated to the same family for generation after generation; so that I suppose they come to think it created exclusively and on purpose for them. And really the result seems to be good and beautiful—it is a home—an institution which we Americans have not—but then I doubt whether anybody is entitled to a home, in so full a sense, in this world. (*EN*: 104–05)

Beauty, privacy, and home—honorific and embraceable terms for Hawthorne—expose an attraction to the aristocratic system far greater than a "thorough-going democrat" would be likely to feel or confess. The elements of time and permanence associated with landed estates only add to the attraction, despite Hawthorne's occasionally enunciated belief in democratic progress. If we begin to sense a renewed evocation of values recalled in "The Old Manse," we are no doubt attuned to the deep-seated and derivative nature of Hawthorne's "English" pastoralism.

In short, Hawthorne's respect for art and tradition gradually beguiles him into seeing a positive side to the entire heirarchical structure of English society. Recalling the beautiful English countryside and the cottages of the "working poor" throughout the Lake district in July 1855, Hawthorne says:

Certainly, England can present a more attractive face than we [Americans] can; even in its humbler modes of life; to say nothing of the beautiful lives that might, one would think, be led by higher classes, whose gateways, with broad, smooth gravelled tracks leading through them (but where none but the owner's carriage, or those of his friends, have a right to enter) you see every mile or two along the road, winding into some proud seclusion. All this is passing away; and society must assume new relations; but there is no harm in believing that there has been something very good in English life—good for all classes—while the world was in a state out of which these forms naturally grew. (*EN*: 172)

No harm, indeed, so long as Hawthorne can manage to appreciate the class system as an anachronism progressively passing away and thus not forget its injustice to the English poor. That he is not immune to adopting aristocratic attitudes becomes clear even to himself, confessed in an entry of 28 November 1855: "I have grown woefully aristocratic, in my tastes, I fear, since coming to England; at all events, I am conscious of a certain disgust at going to dine in a house with a small entrance-hall, and narrow staircase, parlor with chintz curtains, and other arrangements on a similar scale" (*EN*: 269). While he concludes that his attitude is "pitiable," he does not succeed in subsequent months to reform his newly acquired tastes according to the scruples of his avowed republican conscience. A dinner with Herbert Ingram, at the House of Commons in April 1856, presents a noteworthy example. Hawthorne denies that Ingram can be a gentleman and ridicules his rise in fortunes for inventing a "quack-pill" and for establishing the *News* to advertise it. Then in summary, he says: "Mr. Ingram is a man of liberal politics, of a kindly nature, of the homeliest personal appearance and manners. He will have no shadow of influence in the House of Commons, beyond his own vote; and, to say the truth, I was a little ashamed of being entertained by such a very vulgar man, especially as I was recognized by Mr. Bramley-More, and some other Liverpool people. This was really snobbish of me" (*EN*:325). At such a point, this son of a father "in trade," this genteel American of no independent means, comes close to mimicking an aristocratic prig. Confessing his sin with a probable intent to mend his ways is one thing; actually mending them is another.

If Hawthorne falls under the spell of England's class system, the spell probably results from his confusing the attractive past, "out of which these forms naturally grew," with the not-so-attractive present. To a flexible mind like Hawthorne's, with a profound interest in England and her history, a susceptibility to the nation's customs seems almost predictable. Emerson's *English Traits* and Hawthorne's *Our Old Home* (or the *Notebooks*) provide an illuminating contrast here. Even though English institutions, writers, and "national character" receive Emerson's praise, the commendations almost solely apply to these subjects as they existed centuries ago. Their modern-day survivals simply exist as dead forms, spiritually hollow, evidence of an individual and national decline underway since the days of Shakespeare or Bacon.[19] Whatever achievement Emerson admires in England's past, he never relinquishes his categorical perception of its compatibility with a passing moment in history. Hawthorne certainly agrees with Emerson that the English are overly dedicated to ritual and overly devoted to material things for the health of both mind and body, but he clearly wavers either in his perception of or in his feeling for what legitimately belongs to the past and what might still be suitable to the present.[20] At a Lord Mayor's dinner in January 1855, for example, Hawthorne grouses about the modern-day formal dress he and others must wear. He then states:

> I should like to have seen such assemblages as must have gathered in that reception-room, and walked with stately tread to the dining-hall, in times past—the Mayor and other civic dignities in their gowns, noblemen in their state dresses, the Consul in his olive-leaf embroidery—everybody in some sort of bedizenment—and then the dinner would have been really a magnificent spectacle, worthy of the gilded hall, the rich table-service, and the powdered and gold-laced servitors. At a former dinner, I remember seeing a gentleman in small clothes, and with a dress-sword; but all formalities of this kind are passing away. The Mayor's dinners, too, will no doubt be extinct, before many years go by. What should we think of them in America! (*EN*:102–3)

Evidently Hawthorne wants as much of the old English past as he can get. Observing a procession in London during October 1855, he comments: "it put me in mind of the old times when the sovereign and nobles were wont to make a high street of the Thames, and make pompous processions on it." A gorgeous coach, along with liveried coachmen and footmen, then leads him to doubt "whether their finery can endure much longer. People will recognize that it is nearly as bad taste to bedizen themselves with gay colors and gold lace, in the persons of their servants, as to wear these gewgaws themselves. Meanwhile, I am glad the fashion has endured till my day; for I love to see it" (*EN*:249). This love for pomp and splendor, so much at odds with plainer American customs, fully accords with Hawthorne's expressed admiration for English fashions in "Old News," "Legends of the Province-House," and *The Scarlet Letter*.

No less than the monarchy itself attracts Hawthorne when he sees the beautiful interior of Hampton Court, in March 1856:

> But what a noble palace, nobly enriched, this Hampton Court is! The English government does well to keep it up, and to admit the people freely into it; for it is impossible for even a Republican not to feel something like awe—at least a profound respect—for all this state, and for the institutions which are here represented, the Sovereigns whose moral magnificence demand[s] such a residence; and its permanence, too, enduring from age to age, and each royal generation adding new splendors to those accumulated by their predecessors. If we view the matter in another way, to be sure, we may feel indignant that such dolt-heads, scamps, rowdies, and every way mean people as most of the English sovereigns have been, should inhabit these stately halls, (which, by the way, they have not for a long time past,) and contrast its splendors with their littleness; but, on the whole I readily consented within myself to be impressed for a moment with the feeling that royalty has its glorious side. By no possibility can we ever have such a place in America. (*EN*:286)

Hawthorne only mildly deprecates his appreciation here. He has been perceptively moving toward an idealization of English institutions that his down-to-earth skepticism qualifies but never really diminishes. The fact that he repeatedly mentions the brighter side of English institutions confirms the strength of their attraction and the difficulty he has in reconciling them with his own politics. What he finds especially difficult to believe is that noblemen could behave in petty or morally despicable ways while at the same time being responsible for productions evincing laudable aesthetic taste. The Duke of Marlborough might be "thinking of nothing nobler than how many ten-shilling tickets had that day been sold" to tour his estate, but Hawthorne prefers another scenario: "Republican as I am, I should still love to think that noblemen lead noble lives, and that all this stately and beautiful environment may serve to elevate them a little above the rest of us. Even a hog, eating acorns under those magnificent oaks, would be cleanlier and of better habits than common hogs" (*EN*:410).

This declaration probably reveals less about the vulnerability of Hawthorne's democratic politics than it does about his worldly idealism when confronted by exquisite beauty. Perhaps we also detect a rationalization of the class system, in which the grandeur of the upper class theoretically shines down and inspires those beneath it. In any event, Hawthorne is finally unwilling to consider the beauty cultivated and accumulated by the nobility as their sole possessions; they are, instead, national treasures redounding to the honor of and available to the whole culture. Returning to Hampton Court in September 1856, he proclaims, "How beautiful the royal robe of a monarchy is embroidered! Palaces, pictures, parks! They do enrich life; and kings and aristocracies cannot keep these things to themselves—they merely take care of them for others. Even a king, with all the glory that can be shed around him, is but the liveried and bedizened footman of his people, and the toy of their delight. I am very glad that I came to this country, while the English are still playing with such a toy" (*EN*: 424). The future democracy Hawthorne sometimes predicts for England may wipe out the grandeur surrounding the aristocratic system, but in the meantime he has considerably entered into its spirit—so utterly at odds with anything he has known in America—of unsurpassed beauty, order, and stability in time. The aesthetic delights of England, in addition to the system responsible for them, obviously oppose his American view of progress. Troubled at times by the system from which the beauty has issued and in which it still thrives, he is surely not consistently troubled and finally seems remarkably untroubled. But then his progressive notions had always been a little vague if not shaky, his opinion of reform never anything if not skeptical.

Politically, Hawthorne had always been torn between the old and the new, tradition and reform.[21] Intrigued by the Old World traditions, he was also apparently convinced of the future improvement of social relations in America,[22] even though he did not subscribe to the active progressive ideology of O'Sullivan. No mere drollery is at play in "The Old Manse" when Hawthorne prescribes an age-long nap as an antidote for the weary advocates of progressive reform. Being fixed in a forever unchanging present, however, was a prospect incompatible with his divided mind. He wanted change, but increasingly, during his years in England, he was not sure in which direction. He seemed to want to go forward and backward at the same time, eliminating the worst while retaining the best of the past. His was the familiar problem of the classical conservative, and were we to align him with any political thinker, Edmund Burke would likely come closer than anyone else to representing Hawthorne's moral and cultural politics. Granting the necessity for social change, once the impulse of reform were set in motion, where would it stop? The age had not yet recovered from its horrified reaction to the excesses of the French Revolution. "Earth's Holocaust" (1844) registers the full extent of Hawthorne's fear, but similar doubts inform most of the historical tales and all three novels written in the early 1850s. His fear may even inform the kind of romance he writes.[23] Hawthorne does not successfully "mingle" imagination and actuality in these works any more than he typically blends tradition and reform. And so in the midst of dubious change, as threatened in "The Old Manse," he discovers a temptation to stand adamantly still.

England, of course, presents Hawthorne with a much sharper contrast than America between old and new, tradition and reform. But he has discernibly more success in mediating the contrast. If at one moment he can criticize, with an American progressive's eye, "a place where no change comes for centuries, and where a peasant does but step into his father's shoes, and lead just his father's life, . . . time without end," he can in the next breath admit, "yet it is rather pleasant to know that such things are" (*EN*: 126). His evaluation of weary routine, written in 1855, recurs in similar form in 1857, but without the "pleasant" rider (*EN*: 485). By 1857, however, the qualification no longer becomes necessary, for in the intervening years he raises no doubt that his interest in what is old, his *love* for what is old, substantially outweighs his reservations on modern England. We must therefore notice, fairly early in the *Notebooks,* how a distinction between old and new helps explain this imbalance: "when one sees how much antiquity there is left, everywhere about England, and reflects how it may stand in the way of improvement, it is no great wonder that [the English] should laugh at our estimate of it. An old thing is no better than a new thing, unless it [be] a symbol of something, or have some value in itself" (*EN*: 127).

Hawthorne never spells out exactly what the old must symbolize in order to exceed the new, but in another early entry, dated 6 January 1854, he establishes a distinction that ought to be taken as the guide to his response to English antiquities for the remainder of his visit—the familiar division between head and heart: "If mankind were all intellect, they would be continually changing, so that one age would be entirely unlike another. The great conservative is the heart, which remains the same in all ages; so that common-places of a thousand years standing are as effective as ever" (*EN*: 45). Hawthorne came to England uneasily divided between head and heart; during his stay he became increasingly in favor of the heart— consciously so. Thus in the *Notebooks* he steadily aligns himself with English cultural values either present or revered in his art from the beginning of his career. He grows to love the continuing influence of the English past to such an extent that he considers never returning to America—especially as the conflict between North and South moves swiftly toward war. Peevish moods cause him to exaggerate his discontent with America, all to the benefit of his warm feeling for England—which lead in turn to his considering that were it not for the sake of his children, he would stay abroad.[24] Indeed, as his time remaining in England grows short, he begins to fantasize transporting England to some outlying region of America.[25] Such a fancy, if actualized, would provide a historical sanctuary in the midst of radical change. Moreover, it would do in a large way what the Puritans had done inadequately and hence what Hawthorne had been trying to correct for many years. Whether from heart or head, evidently he prefers a relentless past to relentless change, so long as the "commonplaces of a thousand years" keep that past vitally alive.

With this idea in mind, many passing entries in the *Notebooks* bristle with a significance otherwise ignored, such as one on old footpaths written 12 August 1855:

> These are probably the ancientest of ways—older than the Roman roads—older than towns or villages—old as the time when people first debarred themselves from wandering freely and widely, wherever they chose; and they swerve and linger along, and find pretty little vales and nooks of scenery where the high-road discloses nothing but the tiresomest blank. You can sometimes find these paths joining on to one another for miles and miles together. The right to them, on the part of the public, is highly valued and jealously guarded in England; and I saw a little while ago, a notice of a meeting of a society, in the neighborhood of Manchester, for the "preservation of footpaths." The landowners, on each side of the way, put up sign-boards, threatening prosecution to whomsoever may encroach on their premises; but they cannot abridge this liberty of the poor and landless to pass freely through the very heart of their territories; and thus the poorest man retains a kind of property in the oldest inheritance of the richest. Sometimes the stiles, over which you climb, are made of stone-steps, so worn that they are themselves a record of the antiquity of the path. I doubt whether I ever saw a dozen stiles in America—no; not half-a-dozen—not more than one or two. (*EN*: 191)

The reason for the scarcity of stiles in America, which draws this passage into added relief, appears in a previous entry for 22 June 1855: "I delight in these English by-paths, which let a wayfarer into the heart of matters, without burdening him with the feeling if instrusiveness. Very likely, many, and most, of such paths are of more ancient date than the high roads; inasmuch as people travelled on foot before they had carriages or carts. In America, a farmer would plough across any such path, without scruple; here, the footsteps of centuries are sure to be respected" (*EN*: 122). As he reflects on surviving modes of English antiquity, Hawthorne comes steadily to question the need for change. He reflects further that the English past, compared to present-day England or present-day America, does indeed symbolize timeless verities of the human heart. The present age, he feels, scarcely produces anything associated with the heart and thus has nothing to contribute to a cultural heritage: "We are likely to leave no fashions for another age to copy, when we shall have become an antiquity" (*EN*: 127).

It is beauty that most fundamentally attracts Hawthorne's conservative heart to aged things. After taking a cursory tour of the Eastern Chapels in Westminster Abbey, Hawthorne declares: "there is enough in this one section of Westminster Abbey to employ one's mind for years; and, without seeing them, it is impossible to have the dimmest idea of what beautiful things the people of the past centuries have planned and wrought" (*EN*:219). Following his first tour of the antiquity exhibits at the Crystal Palace, he feels the aesthetic impoverishment of contemporary life: "It takes down one's overweening opinion of the present time, to see how many kinds of beauty and magnificence have heretofore existed, and are now quite past away and forgotten; and to find that we—who suppose that, in all matters of taste, our age is the very flower-season of time—that we are poor and meagre as to many things in which they were rich. There is nothing gorgeous now. We live a very naked life" (*EN*:238–39). These are hardly new revelations to Hawthorne. He had suspected as much in "Old News" and "Legends of the Province-House," but more compellingly in *The Scarlet Letter* through Hester's Old-World art as it contrasts with the otherwise colorless life of seventeenth-century Boston. Seeing English treasures firsthand, however, he discovers that the actual beauty of the past often transcends his imagination of it. This discovery, as much as or more than his view of social institutions, accounts for his belief that England has lived out its life, and that, as Emerson also thought, her great beauty grew out of institutions now outmoded (*EN*:246).

Yet the discovery does not lead Hawthorne to despair or to criticize England as Emerson does; it leads instead to another two years of accelerated touring. Since the past was more beautiful than the present, he will indulge sensually and intellectually in as much of the past as possible. Nothing in England so captures Hawthorne's historical imagination and aesthetic sensibility as church architecture of the gothic period. By reviewing his experience with this form, we approach a fuller understanding of the extent to which he consents to be lured by England's aesthetic history. Three months after his arrival, Hawthorne takes a short trip to Chester with William D. Ticknor and receives an introduction to the features of England that he has long been anticipating: "it is quite an indescribable old town; and I feel, at last, as if I had had a glimpse of Old England" (*EN*:28). But he feels dissatisfied with Chester Cathedral, because it does not quite live up to his expectation: "an American must always have imagined a better cathedral than this" (*EN*:29). Nevertheless, he realizes that he needs to see it again "to better advantage," which may cause him to change his mind. Indeed, he does change his mind when, after observing gothic art during the next three years, he returns to Chester on 20 November 1856 in the company of Melville. Chester now offers everything contained in the human heart (*EN*:434–36). Clearly Hawthorne has acquired experiential lessons in how to see. In the course of his learning, he has come to love churches and cathedrals far beyond his frustrating inability to capture their magnificence in language.

By the summer of 1855, the forms of gothic architecture exceed his imagination of them. St Michael's Church in Coventry, for example, evinces "all that I could conceive of," leading to this generalization: "I admire this in Gothic architecture—that you cannot master it all at once—that it is not a naked outline, but as deep and rich as human nature itself, always revealing new little ideas, and new large ones. It is as if the builder had built himself up in it, and his age, and as if the edifice had life" (*EN*: 137–38). A gothic church is so full and rich that it comes as near as one can imagine to manifesting the ideal conception of its creator, an aesthetic opinion Hawthorne had expressed in "The Artist of the Beautiful." The ruin of Furness Abbey, for instance, has "the crumbling traces of the half obliterated design producing somewhat of the effect of the first idea of anything admirable, when it dawns upon the mind of an artist or a poet—an idea which, do what he may, he is sure to fall short of" (*EN*: 157).

When he fails to appreciate a church or cathedral at a first sighting, Hawthorne continues to admit the probable inadequacy of his initial perception, even as late as April 1857 when he first sees York Cathedral. Returning to such infrequent disappointments as York always results in a thorough revision of first impressions. From the summer of 1855 on, he gradually suggests that gothic architecture achieves a transcendence of this world. Westminster Abbey presents the first suggestion of this elevation: "Looking at its front, I now found it grand and venerable beyond my idea" (*EN*: 212). At Peterborough Cathedral in May 1857), he finds everything connected to the structure capable of transforming the real world:

> . . . everywhere, there are old houses that appear to have been adapted from the monkish residences, or from their spacious offices, and made into convenient dwellings for ecclesiastics, or vergers, or great or small people connected with the Cathedral; and, with all modern comfort, they still retain much of the quaintness of the older time—arches, even rows of arcades, pillars, walls beautified with patches of Gothic sculpture, not wilfully put on by modern taste, but lingering from a long past; deep niches, let into the fronts of houses, and occupied by images of saints; a growth of ivy overspreading walls, and just allowing the windows to peep through; so that no novelty, nor anything of our hard, ugly, or actual life, comes into these limits, through the defences of the gateway, without being modified and mollified. (*EN*: 483)

Beyond a reiteration of "The Custom-House" definition of romance art in these closing lines, the passage as a whole distills the beneficent influences that Hawthorne had imaginatively assimilated from New and Old World sources when he created the abbey-parsonage in "The Old Manse." If we fail to sense his elation over discovering the actual existence of the historical paradigm created out of longing in "The Old Manse," we will no doubt feel very little of the man's emotional and aesthetic need for England that he finally satisfied.

The fullest expression of admiration for gothic architecture, absolutely fulfilling the ideals expressed in "The Artist of the Beautiful" and "The Old Manse," appears after a return to York Cathedral in July 1857:

> After breakfast, we all went to the Cathedral; and no sooner were we within it, than we found how much our eyes had recently been educated, by the power of appreciating this magnificent interior; for it impressed both my wife and me with a joy that we never felt before. Julian felt it, too, and insisted that the Cathedral must have been altered and improved, since we were last here. But it is only that we have seen much splendid architecture, since then, and so have grown in some degree fitted to enjoy it. York Cathedral (I say it now, for it is my present feeling) is the most wonderful work that ever came from the hands of man. Indeed, it seems like a "house not made with hands," but rather to have come down from above, bringing an awful majesty and sweetness with it; and it is so light and aspiring, with all its vast columns and pointed arches, that one would hardly wonder if it should ascend back to heaven again, by its mere spirituality. Positively, the pillars and arches of the choirs are so very beautiful that they give the impression of being exquisitely polished, though such is not the fact; but their beauty throws a gleam around them. I thank God that I saw this Cathedral again, and thank Him that he inspired the builder to make it, and that mankind has so long enjoyed it. (*EN*: 544–45)

Along the way toward realizing the transcendent beauty of gothic architecture, Hawthorne has often become disenchanted—not with the structures but with his inability to express their details and his appreciation in language. His disenchantment becomes so severe that at Salisbury Cathedral in June 1856 he flirts with the notion that the gothic does not fulfill his idealized conception:

> I am weary of trying to describe Cathedrals; it is utterly useless; there is no possibility of giving the general effect, or any shadow of it; and it is miserable to put down a few items of tombstones, and a bit of glass from a painted window, as if the gloom and glory of the edifice were thus to be re-produced. Cathedrals are almost the only things (if even those) that have quite filled out my ideal, here in the old world; and Cathedrals often make me miserable from an inadequacy to take them wholly in; and, above all, I despise myself when I sit down to describe them. (*EN*: 359)

This doubt recalls Hawthorne's belief, stated elsewhere, that no aesthetic form can be translated into the language of another. He apparently arrives at this conviction after trying to describe Westminster Abbey in September 1855: "these things are not to be translated into words" (*EN*: 212). But, belief or no, he cannot rest easy with the implication. The *Notebooks* clearly suggest that the main purpose of Hawthorne's extensive tours during the last three years is to see ecclesiastical art. Time and again, upon arriving in towns, he tries to acquire the fullest impression possible of such art. Then he writes about the impression extensively, even while confessing his verbal failure to capture the effects. A gothic cathedral may be "a great stone poem," but since it possibly constitutes "the greatest work man has yet achieved," it stubbornly resists verbal expression (*EN*: 149).

Whether Hawthorne manages to render gothic architecture into language suitable to his tastes, readers are likely to agree that no American prior to Henry Adams writes so well upon the beauty or imagines so eloquently the spirit translated into the building of gothic architecture. It is easy to understand why. Not even Irving and Cooper so fully regretted the loss to America of the sensate pleasures offered by gothic art as did Hawthorne. At St. Paul's in August 1856, he exclaims: "Oh that we had Cathredals in America, were it only for this sensuous luxury!" (*EN*: 389). Before coming to England, he could only imagine this sensuous luxury as he found it reproduced in prints or symbolically expressed in gothic script, a form equated to Lincoln Cathedral in May 1857: "The West Front is wonderfully and unspeakably grand and rich, and may be read over and over again, and still be new, like a great, broad page of marvelous meaning in black-letter" (*EN*: 472). No wonder, then, that Hawthorne comes increasingly to feel at home in England; for he has found actual expressions of the historical and aesthetic features that he had tried for years to incorporate in otherwise plain American settings.

After reading such passionate tributes, we might well take note of how far Hawthorne has distanced himself from his New England heritage. The plain style aesthetic of the Puritans was designed to omit "idolatrous" religious symbols from meeting-houses in order to encourage undivided attention to sermons. Hawthorne, on the other hand, loves the ornate symbols that his forebears saw as distractions from the Word. He does not simply love them from a historical perception of how magnificent churches and abbeys are "the only kind of poetry which the age knew how to produce" (*EN*: 538). He loves them for the aesthetic and spiritual influence they produce in him at the moment. This Puritan descendant has fully integrated himself, I would submit, into the religious spirit of gothic—that is, Roman Catholic—art.

As many readers have pointed out, Hawthorne certainly appears to side with his Puritan ancestors after listening to sermons delivered in English churches and cathedrals.[26] At least two occasions can be specified: at Chester Cathedral in late October 1853, and at York Cathedral for Easter services on 12 April 1857. The latter is always the one singled out to show Hawthorne's Puritan sympathies:

> The services of Easter Sunday, I believe, comprehend more than the ordinary quantity of singing and chanting; at all events, nearly an hour and a half were thus employed, with some intermixture of prayers and reading of scriptures; and being almost congealed with cold, I thought it

never would come to an end. The spirit of my Puritan ancestors was mighty in me, and I did not wonder at their being out of patience with all this mummery, which seems to me worse than papistry because it was a corruption of it. At last, a Canon gave out the text, and preached a sermon of about twenty minutes long, the coldest, dryest, most superficial rubbish; for this gorgeous setting of the magnificent Cathedral, the elaborate music, and the rich ceremonial, seems inevitably to take the life out of the sermon—which, to be anything, must be all. The Puritans showed their strength of mind and heart, by preferring a sermon of an hour and a half long, into which the preacher put his whole soul and spirit, and lopping away all these externals, into which religious life had first gushed and flowered, and then petrified. (*EN* : 451)

Hawthorne's allegiance to the Puritans in this passage is hardly complete. He does not say that he prefers a Puritan sermon over the Cathedral. What appalls him, what disgusts him, is the sermon's failure to approach the beauty and spirit of the gothic cathedral. His response, in other words, essentially implies a comparative aesthetic judgment. The gothic structure, statuary, ornamentation—all are spiritually elevating. The Anglican sermon is not.

If only for the effects produced by aged stained glass, Hawthorne would no doubt have preferred the interior of a gothic church to the lengthy sermons of Puritan divines. The description of windows at Saint Mary's Church in September 1855, that of the Chapter House adjacent to York Cathedral in April 1857, and more fully that of the churches at York in May 1856 show that he finds their beauty and religious symbolism equivalent, if not superior, to holy doctrine itself in approaching the glory of God :

York is full of old churches, some of them very antique in appearance, the stones weather-worn, their edges rounded by time, blackened, and with all the tokens of sturdy and age-long decay; and in some of them I noticed windows quite full of old painted glass, a dreary kind of minute patchwork, all of one dark and dusty hue, or nearly so, when seen from the outside. Yet, had I seen them from the interior of the church, there would doubtless have been rich and varied apparitions of saints, with their glories round their heads, and bright-winged angels, and perhaps even the Almighty Father Himself, so far as conceivable and representable by human powers. It is a good symbol of religion; the irreligious man sees only the pitiful outside of the painted window, and judges it entirely from that view; but he who stands within the holy precincts, the religious man, is sure of the glories which he beholds. And to put the simile a little farther, it requires light from Heaven to make them visible. If the church were merely illuminated from the inside—that is, by what light a man could get from his own understanding—the picture would be invisible, or wear at best but a miserable aspect. (*EN* : 349)

There is probably no better expression than this of Hawthorne's religious faith; but along with many others, it reveals his love for gothic art as a whole and helps in turn to account for numerous journal references to Puritan iconoclasm during the English Civil War. As his appreciation for gothic architecture grows, so does the frequency and poignancy of his remarks on that iconoclasm. Most observations simply point out how Cromwell's soldiers seldom missed an opportunity to smash noses on church statuary. Later entries in the *Notebooks* spell out how these "violent and ignorant men" (*EN*:219) marred and demolished entire interiors. With these reminders of the iconoclastic nature of his own Puritan ancestors, Hawthorne sees firsthand the reason his New World heritage had been stripped bare in its very origin. Lincoln Cathedral, for example, "is not rich in monuments; for it suffered great outrage and dilapidation both at the Reformation and in Cromwell's time. The soldiers of the latter stabled their steeds in the nave, and hacked and hewed the monkish sculptures at their wicked pleasure" (*EN*:469). Peterborough Cathedral offers even more evidence of Puritan destruction for condemnation. The statue of a prelate, like so many others, has a face "obliterated by Puritanic violence." The nave has been repaired, but "this sacred vessel suffered especial indignity from Cromwell's soldiers; insomuch that if anything could possibly destroy its sanctity, they would have effected that bad end." While a few specimens of Catholic art survive, the entire "Chapter House was destroyed—no doubt by those devilish soldiers of Cromwell" (*EN*:482). Hawthorne takes in all the iconoclasm and then reflects, "It is wonderful how suddenly the English people lost their sense of the sanctity of all manner of externals in religion, without losing their religion too" (*EN*:481).

Far less committed to doctrine than his Puritan ancestors, Hawthorne apparently understands the motivation for their iconoclasm but he despises the results. If gothic artwork symbolized for the Puritans the hollow ritual and corrupt ecclesiastical orders evolving from Roman Catholicism, it is for their nineteenth-century descendant so beautiful, majestic, and elevating that it fulfills its purpose as intermediary between the substance of this world and the spirituality of the next. None of these perceptions is wholly new to Hawthorne. He had furnished Endicott with sufficient anti-Catholic sentiments to represent the iconoclastic nature of Puritanism during the important shift between first and second generations when the first immigrants lost what remaining pleasures they derived from having been "nurtured at the rich bosom of the English Church." Hawthorne believes he had inherited the barrenness of that loss, and thus he can only imagine what artistic treasures colonial America might have passed on to him had it not been for the iconoclasm and plain-style aesthetic of his grandsires. In England, he sees more fully than he had imagined to what extremes his forebears had gone to rid themselves of Anglo-Catholic art. They may not have felt deprived, but he certainly does. This message surfaces in Hawthorne's observations of a remodeled church in Linlithgow, Scotland: "I remember little or nothing of this edifice, except that the Covenanters had uglified it with pews and a gallery, and white-wash; though I doubt not it was a stately Gothic church, with innumerable enrichments and incrustations of beauty, when it passed from popish hands into theirs" (*EN*: 529).

After seeing Hawthorne's frequent attraction to English cultural traditions in his career, and after observing from several angles the growth of his appreciation for England while he actually lived there, we can now appreciate his exhilaration bursting forth in June 1857: "What a wonderful land! It is our forefathers' land; our land; for I will not give up such precious inheritance" (*EN*: 495). This is no mere sentimentality over quaint antiquity. He has just finished a tour lasting more than two months, seeing a host of curiosities and splendors. He has seen York Cathedral for the second time, becoming so deeply impressed that he will visit it again three months later. He has gone to Lincoln Cathedral for the first time, "loving it the better the longer I looked" (*EN*: 472). He has taken in Peterborough Cathedral and felt its "sacred seclusion" (*EN*: 483). In this Old World where time seems to have stood still, where all around are signs of age that nevertheless remain vibrantly alive, Hawthorne may well have identified with this own progenitors and then asked himself why he would want to leave the Old World for anything else. He surely feels by this time a fuller sense of the conviction he expressed in July 1855: "If England were all the world, it still would have been worth while for the Creator to have made it; and mankind would have no cause to find fault with their abode . . ." (*EN*: 182). England had always been "our old home" for Hawthorne, disinherited by the Puritans on religious grounds, disinherited by revolutionists on political grounds, but readopted by Hawthorne for the sake of his and his culture's need for a tradition and example of art.

The American Claimant Manuscripts

The sensitivity and complexity of Hawthorne's responses to England are crucial, I believe, to understanding why in his last years he was unable to write a romance about an American claimant to English title and estate. The origin of the project came from Hawthorne's experience as consul to Liverpool. In an *English Notebooks* entry dated 31 December 1853, four months after assuming his duties, Hawthorne writes:

> The other day, there came to me, with an introduction from Governor Crosby of Maine, a Mr John A. Knight, who had come across the Atlantic in attendance on two ladies, claimants of the Booth estate in Cheshire. His information on the subject seems to be of a very vague character; and, no doubt, the claim is wholly untenable. The ladies assume to be of royal blood, and are apprehensive that the English lawyers will be the less willing to allow their pretensions from a disinclination to admit new members into the royal kin. I think I recorded the visit, a short time ago,

of the lady who claims the most valuable part of Liverpool, including the Exchange and Docks. (*EN*: 43)

The idea of writing on an American pretending to an English legacy eventually led to three separate but related manuscripts, along with other documents, which the editors of the Centenary Edition have entitled *The American Claimant Manuscripts*. Three principal texts, "The Ancestral Footstep," "Etherege," and "Grimshawe," he wrote between 1858 and 1861, interrupted by the composition of *The Marble Faun*, his move from Italy back to England, and then his return to the United States in 1860.[27] The three drafts reveal Hawthorne's inability to resolve problems of character, plot, and theme. Inserted comments and notes to himself express struggle and frustration over discrepant and inchoate material. One of his major difficulties was indecision over the attitude his American should take toward a claim to an English birthright, suspended (though vaguely suspected) for nearly two hundred years. As he conceived the overall work in "The Ancestral Footstep," Hawthorne planned to write an autobiographical preface similar to "The Old Manse" and "The Custom-House," locating himself at the Consulate in Liverpool and presenting "the strange species of Americans, with strange purposes in England, whom I used to meet there; and, especially, how my countrymen used to be put out of their senses by the idea of inheritances of English property. . . . and then this Romance shall be offered, half-seriously, as the account of the fortunes that he [a young man] met with in his search for his hereditary home" (12:87). But the foolish presumption of American claimants that he encountered at the Consulate proves to be significantly toned down, if not completely transformed, as Hawthorne struggled through the three drafts of the *Claimant Manuscripts;* and "half-seriously" is a far cry from the gravity resulting from the struggle.

As the claimant-protagonist appears in "The Ancestral Footstep," an ambivalence toward his claim to an English birthright and toward England herself is suggested in the character's name—Middleton. Unlike the naive Robin Molineux, he is a figure reminiscent of Hawthorne's mediators in the seventeenth-century tales. Although Hawthorne plans to have this character finally reject the English entitlement, Middleton vacillates between acknowledging and denying his claim. He clearly has no interest in an English title, but he finds himself tempted by the hereditary estate occupied by one Eldredge. Because he has grown up in a progressive-minded America, Middleton looks to England exactly as did Hawthorne: "He had come hither, hoping as it were to find the past still alive and in action" (12:6). Around the ancestral home, Middleton discovers the past very much alive and beguiling. Indeed, he feels what Hawthorne confesses to feeling in the *English Notebooks:* "he rather felt as if he were the original emigrant, who long resident on a foreign shore, had now returned, with a heart brimful of tenderness, to revisit the scenes of his youth, and renew his tender relations with those who shared his own blood" (12:60).

An old almshouse pensioner who saves Middleton's life has the function of encouraging the young man to recognize that America " 'has nothing to do with England' " because a mixture of " 'Alien races' " has been introduced in England since the settlement of America (12:37–38). Middleton, however, argues for the ties between New and Old Worlds on grounds equivalent to those Hawthorne had been suggesting for many years: " 'our relations with England remain far more numerous than our disconnections, through the bonds of history, of literature, of all that makes up the memories, and most that makes up the present interests of a people' " (12:38). By contrast, Middleton feels "more than half ashamed of the dreams which he had cherished before coming to England" because the strong "sentiment that impelled him to connect himself with the old life of England" begins to assume a "strong tinge of reality" (12:38–39). Yet the influence exerted by the English setting becomes very great, to the point that Middleton later begins to imagine the presence of ghostly grandsires. Unlike the negative depiction of Hawthorne's Puritan ancestors in "The Custom-House," Middleton's English grandsires have a positive influence: "it seemed as if the merry ghosts of his kindred, a long shadowy line, held forth their dim arms to welcome him; a line stretching back to the ghosts of those who had flourished in the old, old times; the doubletted and beruffed knightly shades of Queen Elizabeth's time; a long line, stretching from the medieval ages" (12:62). This attractive lineage represents precisely what Hawthorne had lacked in America, but it obviously echoes the one imagined in "The Custom-House" when he substitutes Pue, Burns, and Chaucer for his Puritan forebears.

Hawthorne surely does not depict Middleton as the silly or deranged figure initially planned. Despite his temptation to exert a claim on the Eldredge estate, Middleton never does openly declare his intention but passively allows others to assume he is the legitimate heir. He is conscious, as an American republican, of a potential wrong in reasserting English ties. Moreover, he considers that "there was a higher and a deeper law than was any connected with any ancestral claims," which encourages his loyalty to democratic institutions of America (12:42). Lest he waver, Hawthorne provides a young woman, American by birth, who nudges Middleton toward conforming to this "higher and deeper law." Faults, weaknesses, and errors of Americans notwithstanding, Alice admonishes Middleton to cast his lot with his countrymen (12:56). At another point, however, she makes England appear so enticing (despite her strategy to argue against England's attractiveness) that her pro-American intention virtually breaks down: " 'There is much that is seductive in English life; but I think it is not upon the higher impulses of our nature that such seductions act. I should think ill of the American, who, for any causes of ambition—any hope of wealth or rank—or even for the sake of any of those old, delightful ideas of the past, the associations of ancestry, the loveliness of an age-long home—the old poetry and romance that haunt these ancient villages and estates of England—would give up the chance of acting upon the unmoulded future of America'" (12:72). Only someone like Hawthorne, attracted to "the loveliness of an age-long home," could know the special seductions of England and need to resist the compelling arguments in their favor. Omit the caveat on ambition for wealth and rank, which did not apply to Hawthorne and which hardly applies to Middleton, and we discover the cultural and aesthetic lures of "our old home" that Hawthorne refused to deny himself.

Despite the possibility that Hawthorne originally intended to explore "the differences between democratic America and class-bound England,"[28] one of the most curious features of "The Ancestral Footstep" is that all the English figures are attractive. At the onset, to be sure, the occupant of the hereditary home is cast as an English roughneck who kills himself in a scuffle with Middleton. But dissatisfied with eliminating his villain in the early pages, Hawthorne resurrects the figure of Eldredge and revives his role in a singularly transvalued way. In his next appearance, Eldredge suggests a somewhat attractive yet controlled character who suspects Middleton as the rightful claimant to the estate. Later, however, Hawthorne decides to give Eldredge foreign associations—to make him not really English although English by birth: "Mr. Eldredge, moreover, has resided long on the Continent; long in Italy; and had come back with habits that little accorded with those of the gentry of the neighborhood; so that, in fact, he was almost as much a stranger, and perhaps quite as little of a real Englishman, as Middleton himself" (12:61). The more he works with the character, the more Hawthorne creates him into a stock, gothic villain, completely alien to English culture. In a comment to himself late in the manuscript, Hawthorne says: "Eldredge, bred, and perhaps born in Italy, and a Catholic, with views to the church, before he inherited the estate, has not the English moral sense and simple honor; can scarcely be called an Englishman at all. Dark suspicions of past crime, and of the possibility of future crime, may be thrown around him" (12:79).

The problem Hawthorne has with Eldredge—his transformation from Englishman to Italianate villain—relates to the problems evident in the manuscript as a whole. Try as he might, Hawthorne has difficulty dramatizing unfavorable views of England or English people. Even though he did not have the *English Notebooks* to draw on in Italy when he wrote "The Ancestral Footstep," if his views of the English character recorded in the *Notebooks* were as predominantly negative as critics have led us to believe, Hawthorne surely could have remembered his general complaints and structured them into the narrative. But, as noted in the first section of this chapter, Hawthorne's criticism of England and of the English character radically diminished during his last two years on the island, and when he left for Italy he had a high opinion of both. It may well be that, in the glow of good feelings for England, perhaps intensified by his comparative dissatisfaction with Italy, Hawthorne was influenced to portray only the better side of England in "The Ancestral Footstep."

When he wrote the "Etherege" draft after returning to the United States, Hawthorne unquestionably drew on the *Notebooks* for the differences between the social systems of England and America. Middleton's ambivalent affection for England in "The Ancestral Footstep" is not initially apparent in "Etherege," in which the Middleton character is renamed Ned Etherege. Even though in a note of self-instruction Hawthorne says, "Early and forcibly—let the deep, unconquerable interest, which an American feels in England, its people, and institutions, be brought strongly out" (12:124), he presents Etherege's vague longing for England as a "foolish yearning for a connection with the past" (12:149). This yearning amounts to a minor part of Etherege's character, for he has been a member of the House of Representatives and, despite having lost his seat due to political intrigue, he seems to be an ardent booster of "Young America."[29] Thus he senses a necessary change incipient in the seemingly permanent social arrangement of England, reflecting an early view of Hawthorne's in the *Notebooks*. In an implicit reference to England's class system, Etherege declares, "'I am proud of [American] institutions, [and] . . . I have a feeling, unknown probably to any but a republican, but which is the proudest thing in me, that there is no man above me—for my ruler is only myself, in the person of another, whose office I impose upon him'" (12:162).

Yet greatly anomalous to his "leveling" democratic views, Etherege is depicted as having a quicker moral sense and a finer aristocratic appearance than Englishmen have. The young man himself asserts superiority of American manners over those of the English. And he receives an ambassadorial appointment to a European court (12:187), enhancing his credentials as a social equal to the English gentlemen he encounters. Such details, reflecting Hawthorne's self-justifying although contradictory adoption of English aristocratic standards in the *Notebooks,* are qualified by remarks amounting to a nineteenth-century version of the Ugly American (12:170).

Through much of the "Etherege" manuscript, however, Etherege expresses Hawthorne's more critical views of England. He looks around the vicinity of the ancestral home and feels "revolted" by the stasis and "hereditary pretensions," however much they may strike his fancy. While the rural village presents an appealing picture worth giving up his ambitions to enjoy, Etherege ultimately finds it tiresome because "the new American was stronger in him than the hereditary Englishman" (12:180). And when Etherege finds himself tempted to envy an Englishman's loyalty to the Crown, Hawthorne can enter the narrative to set him straight by providing an American perspective (12 : 240). The original purpose of ridiculing the idea of an English claimant appears safely in control.

But, in terms of plot, the major shift from "The Ancestral Footstep" to "Etherege" pivots on the fact that Etherege has no legitimate claim to English birthright, although he thinks he does because of hazy information suggested by his childhood guardian, a strange spider doctor and genealogist. Yet Etherege does have some sort of connection to the hereditary English family, the substance of which Hawthorne unsuccessfully tries to establish. In the first half of the manuscript, he casts Etherege as a descendant of the second son of the ancient family during the English Civil War. For differing proposed reasons, mostly involving conflict over a woman with his older brother, this son emigrates to America after leaving a bloody footstep on the threshold of the family hall. In another proposed version, the family—Roman Catholic supporters of Charles I—believes that the second son fought with Parliamentarians and served as the hooded executioner of Charles I, disappearing after the Restoration. Eventually, however, Hawthorne decides to elevate the importance of the old pensioner who saves Etherege when he is wounded in an assault near the ancestral home. The pensioner, not Etherege, becomes the descendant of the second son and thus the rightful heir.

Hawthorne's developing plans for the pensioner's ancestor, the second son who went to America, reveal typical preoccupations found in the historical tales and *The Scarlet Letter*. While the English family believes that the son was a "dark and fierce Puritan—with his own hand a king killer," he was really a gentle, sensitive man, a deserving follower of George Fox (12 : 303). Rather than executing Charles I, he "was on the scaffold to support and comfort the dying monarch, to die for him if possible; everywhere he was sacrificing himself" (12 : 304). Also, since this son had emigrated to New England during the time of the Protectorate, Hawthorne late in the manuscript decides that he "was hanged by the Puritans" during the Quaker persecutions (12 : 334). The reversal of this figure's political allegiance (from regicide to devout monarchist) and his fate in the Bay colony governed by Endicott suggest once again Hawthorne's criticism of the intolerant and violent Puritan spirit along with his refusal to cast the regicide in positive terms. The American heir's claim to an English patrimony becomes lost at nearly the same time that Hester and Pearl's Old World art becomes lost to the New World, reinforcing Hawthorne's view of the historical shift under way in both hemispheres at the time of the regicide.

Even though he planned to enlarge the role of the old pensioner in a revision of the manuscript, Hawthorne continues to focus on Etherege in the second half of the "Etherege" narrative. Here, Etherege's democratic principles begin to weaken as the young man increasingly comes in contact with the hereditary home and its proprietor, now named Brathwaite, whom everyone in the neighborhood dislikes because he is not English (12:173–74). An underlying reason behind Etherege's growing attraction to the estate may be resentment over a foreigner's possession of the English home. Hawthorne often stresses how Brathwaite must be "carefully Italianized," not only to help explain, in conventional gothic terms, his motive for wanting to murder Etherege (12:206), but also to instill an Anglophilic reaction against him. When Brathwaite invites Etherege to the estate, the murder plot is set in motion, as is the shift in Etherege's views as claimant.

Apparently Hawthorne did not plan to have the shift become so marked as it does, for after leading up to the point of Etherege's meeting with Brathwaite and receiving the invitation, Hawthorne interrupts the narrative with this notation: "here ensues in the Romance much description and talk about old English dwellings, and the differences between English and American social life, and how we have given up certain delightful possibilities forever, and must content ourselves with other things" (12:233). But Etherege never really takes the tack suggested here. Instead he finds himself seduced by the "delightful possibilities" inherent in English life. These delights, associated with the Brathwaite estate, reinforce his desires for the inheritance: "they had suddenly taken form and hardened into substance; and he became aware, in spite of all the lofty patriotic sentiments which he had expressed . . . that these prospects had really much importance in his mind" (12:255). When Etherege approaches Brathwaite Hall, he indeed abandons his American patriotic sentiments as he spreads his arms and rapturously declares, " 'Oh home, my home, my forefathers' home! I have come back to thee! The wanderer has come back!' " (12:260). This passage, obviously indebted to the emotionally charged tribute to old Boston in the *Notebooks*, shows that Etherege's feeling for the old English home is identical to Hawthorne's own.

As Etherege walks around Brathwaite Hall, his recognition of the venerable charm of English life involves the idea of innate familiarity also possessed by Hawthorne in the *Notebooks*. Reappearing here are the very qualities Hawthorne had imagined in the idealized Manse: "the ivy that overran parts of it; the marks of age, . . . [Etherege] wondered at the firmness of the institutions which, through all the changes that come to man, could have kept this house the home of one lineal race for so many centuries; so many, that the absence of his own branch from it seemed but a temporary visit to foreign parts, to which he was now returned, to be again at home by the old hearthstone" (12:281). Still, Etherege tries to resist the charm, the sense of the past and its stability, by thinking that, should he successfully make his claim on the estate, then " 'America has been discovered in vain' " (12:281). Despite the fact that America has nothing to compete with the "juiciness and richness" of the estate (12:282), Etherege declares to Brathwaite that England does not finally offer much happiness, for "'A brighter, healthier, more useful, far more satisfactory, though tumultuous life would await me in my own country.'" Yet, in the same breath, he exposes the extent to which his ambivalence has grown when he admits: "'But there is about this place a strange, deep, sad, brooding interest, which possesses me, and draws me to it, and will not let me go. I feel as if, in spite of myself, and my most earnest efforts, I were fascinated by something in the spot, and must needs linger here, and make it my home if I can'" (12:305–6). He, no less than his creator, cannot make up his mind. Each feels emotionally pulled in opposite directions; toward the political and social opportunities of America and toward the aesthetic, domestic, and historical attractions of England.

As Hawthorne works toward a swift, provisional conclusion, Etherege is captured by Brathwaite, imprisoned in a secret chamber of the Hall, and rescued by the old pensioner, the rightful heir to the estate. Thus, too conveniently, Etherege does not finally have to choose between America and England. Yet surely Hawthorne has gone far beyond his original motive by presenting Etherege with a troubling dilemma, a choice between New World opportunity for democratic change and Old World possibility for aristocratic grace and permanence. Never having had a home, Etherege has come alive to the old English home, the stability of which, more than the title and wealth attached to it, quickens his imagination. Hawthorne obviously reveals his own vulnerability to the attractive face England presents to sensitive American observers. Tracing the transformation of Etherege's perception of England, we actually retrace Hawthorne's own transformation in the *Notebooks*. After stressing democratic sentiments in the first half of "Etherege," Hawthorne more than redresses the imbalance by exploring the seductions of England in the latter half. He has succumbed himself, after all, and he resurrects in Etherege his own serious confrontation with the "delightful possibilities" unavailable in America but present in "our old home."

Putting aside "Etherege" before working out details for its conclusion, Hawthorne began "Grimshawe" to flesh out the American background of the claimant. The thirty-nine pages in the Centenary Edition that cover this background in "Etherege" become ninety-eight in "Grimshawe," fully three-quarters of the manuscript. They ostensibly focus on the childhood of Ned, who will be renamed Redclyffe when, as a young man, he arrives in England. But the reader quickly recognizes that Hawthorne has far more interest in Ned's guardian, the benevolent spider doctor in "Etherege" whose character undergoes an alteration for the worse in "Grimshawe." Named successively Ormskirk and Grimshawe, the doctor has found Ned in an Almshouse and, for vengeful motives that Hawthorne cannot clearly conceive or articulate, encourages the boy to think that he is somehow connected to an English title and estate. And for reasons Hawthorne again cannot explain, Doctor Grimshawe also has guardianship of Elsie, whose father may turn out to be the old pensioner, the legitimate heir in "Etherege" who does not want the estate. This figure actually makes an appearance in the doctor's household. Through him and, later, an emissary from the ancestral home, the likely existence of an American claimant is established and Redclyffe will meet both of these figures when he arrives in England.

Despite the expanded background section in "Grimshawe," Hawthorne adds nothing of significance to the claimant plot except a shift in the setting's historical period. The English setting of "The Ancestral Footstep" and "Etherege" is in the 1850s, allowing Hawthorne a few decades of American independence and development with which to compare English culture. In "Grimshawe," though, Ned's childhood occurs in the immediate aftermath of the Revolutionary War, which means that later events in England must take place prior to 1810, otherwise Redclyffe and Elsie will not be young enough for Hawthorne to create a conventional love plot suggested in the earlier manuscripts. A further implication, of course, is that the story ends on the eve of the war of 1812. Whether Hawthorne considered these matters cannot be determined from "Grimshawe" or ancillary documents of the American claimant project. He evidently hoped to capitalize on the hostility between England and America resulting from the Revolution, preliminary to subsequent tensions in the English setting and perhaps even to a foreshadowing of the War of 1812.

Yet if Hawthorne planned to use the post-Revolutionary War setting for American patriotic purposes, he went out of his way to create a hostile view of Americans in that setting. The townspeople in "Grimshawe" resent the doctor, who presumably represents British attitudes of superiority and exclusivity, although Hawthorne enunciates the doctor's low birth, natural sourness of temper, and rude manners—influenced by excessive drinking. The people become a mob, a reactivated version of those seen in "My Kinsman, Major Molineux" and "Lady Eleanore's Mantle," when they descend on the doctor as he punishes a child for throwing a mud ball at him:

Had they been created for the moment; or were they fiends, sent by Satan in the likeness of a blackguard population? There you might see the off-scourings of the recently finished war, old soldiers, rusty, wooden-legged; there sailors, ripe for any kind of mischief; there the drunken populace of a neighboring grog-shop, staggering helter skelter to the scene, and tumbling over one another at the Doctor's feet; there came the father of the punished urchin, who had never shown heretofore any care for his street-bred progeny, but now came pale with rage, armed with a pair of tongs, and with him the mother, flying like a fury, with her cap awry, and clutching a broomstick, as if she were a witch just alighted. (12:384).

Lacking the identifiable English characteristics of a Major Molineux or a Thomas Hutchinson, "Doctor Grimshawe" does not provide a clear rationale for this mob's behavior, although it seems evident that Hawthorne remains willing even at this late date to present a scurrilous portrait of Americans during the Revolutionary period.

Details of the claimant plot in "Grimshawe" basically accord with those established or anticipated in "Etherege," but the manuscript ends shortly after Redclyffe arrives in the vicinity of the ancestral estate. As a young boy, Ned/Redclyffe is endowed with refined manners, a natural grace, and poetic sensibilities. These qualities apparently spring from human nature generally and cannot be compromised either by the crass influence of Doctor Grimshawe or by the crude American townspeople among whom he grows up. Ned's refinement is meant to suggest that America can produce gentlemen of manners equivalent to those in England but without the breeding instilled by an aristocratic system. The point of view for judging manners, however, is implicitly that of the English aristocracy, for Hawthorne equips Ned with credentials obviously worthy of cultivated English taste. Even though not a legitimate heir to an English patrimony, Ned possesses innate English standards and consequently discovers his attraction to the possibility that he is an American claimant.

Hawthorne presents the claimant idea in "Grimshawe" in largely affirmative terms, for at the heart of Ned's imagination lies the condition of homelessness in America, clearly echoing Hawthorne's own belief in the *Notebooks:* "After what the Doctor had told him of his origin, he had never felt any home-feeling here; it seemed to him that he was wandering web, which the wind had blown from afar; somehow, or other, from many circumstances which he put together and seethed in his childish imagination, it seemed to him that he was to go back to that far, old country, and there wander among the green, ivy-grown, venerable scenes; the older he grew, the more his mind took depth, the stronger was this fancy in him" (12 : 422–23). When Ned grows up, becomes Redclyffe, and arrives near the ancestral home, his imaginative connection to England leads him to the same sense of innate familiarity with the mother country expressed by Hawthorne in the *Notebooks* and "Etherege": " 'How familiar these rustic sounds,' " he says. " 'Surely I was born here' " (12 : 444). But such feelings do not prevent Redclyffe from holding a more rational view: " 'My countrymen are apt to advance claims to kinship with distinguished English families on such slight grounds as to make it ridiculous, . . . I should not choose to follow so absurd an example' " (12 : 465). The "Grimshawe" manuscript concludes before Redclyffe will make a claim, or be tempted to make a claim, following his prototypes in "The Ancestral Footstep" and "Etherege."

The most difficult problem Hawthorne faced in working on the American claimant idea was how to harmonize his own divided feelings for England and America. His lifelong belief in American democracy, social equality, and economic opportunity quite naturally led to his objection to English aristocratic privilege. Like many Americans of his day and ours, however, he no doubt felt some measure of cultural inferiority to England which, by turns, caused him to idealize and even envy the manners, customs, and institutions upon which the English could so confidently rely. But no matter how much Hawthorne stood at political and social odds with England, he was drawn throughout his career to English cultural and aesthetic values. England seemed to him the mother country in these respects, not superficially but as a profound symbol of source and nurture—as a home. The English writers who served as models for his ambition to be an artist were inextricably connected to this symbol. Hawthorne believed that he shared with these writers a kinship; and upon them and the legacy of art they shared, he felt he had a legitimate claim.

It now seems obvious that Hawthorne was bound to encounter immense difficulties in writing about the American claimant. Having begun with the ideal of ridiculing Americans with foolish pretensions to English rank and fortune, he immediately faced the problem of creating a story out of a shallow motive lodged in a necessarily shallow character. His solution was to add gravity to the protagonist by hedging on whether he was or was not a legitimate claimant and, if he were, whether he would or would not assert his claim to a title and estate. The possibility of structuring the plot in terms of a temptation over which the hero struggles and finally triumphs does not appear to have clearly occurred to Hawthorne, even though ample evidence exists in the manuscripts to indicate such a strategy. But by subsequently making the old pensioner the actual heir, Hawthorne worked toward eliminating the possibility of his young American hero struggling over a genuine temptation. The hero is merely left with an illusory claim to an English birthright, as is the case of Ned/Redclyffe in "Grimshawe." This eventuality, of course, brings Hawthorne back to his original dilemma, since Redclyffe ultimately has only a foolish pretension subject to ridicule. In addition, it is difficult to fathom how Hawthorne expected to create anything but a hypocrite out of a character who espouses American democratic values while clinging to the delusion that he is a claimant. Such ambivalence ill-suits a hero, and yet, as all three of the *Claimant Manuscripts* suggest, Hawthorne wanted his American to be a noble protagonist.

No one should be surprised that Hawthorne found the materials so unworkable that he finally abandoned the claimant idea. He could not finish because of his own unresolved or poorly clarified loyalties to America and England. Like Middleton/Etherege/Redclyffe, he was an American patriot, an advocate of social democracy. Yet he was also drawn to England for reasons that may have seemed to him equivocations of American principles. Being opposed to the special privileges of the aristocracy did not, however, prevent him from admiring their lives or their beautiful country estates. He was attracted to the imagined qualities of those lives and to their settings, in the same way his American claimants are, despite their patriotic resistance. Hawthorne was too astute not to acknowledge that the seductions of England—art, scenery, domestic serenity, and evidence of historical stability—were integral to a social system that he questioned and perhaps deplored. Nevertheless, he seems to have wanted to separate the good from the bad and to balance the results. Like his dominant Puritan types in the early tales, his American claimants never attempt similar feats of discrimination and balance. They are simply enticed by the qualities of the ancestral home and are caught between feelings affiliated with England and political ideas affiliated with America. But the degree to which they are frustrated over the division between head and heart suggests uneasiness and irresolution in Hawthorne. His actual experience in England only reinforced the attractiveness of being the very cultural claimant he had been all along, and so both he and his claimants could not relinquish their lifelong hold. In this connection, a passage in the *Notebooks* bears repeating: "What a wonderful land! It is our forefathers' land: our land; for I will not give up such a precious inheritance" (EN : 495). Such a tenacious claim to the better side of English culture, reflected in *The American Claimant Manuscripts,* opposes Hawthorne's intention to have his claimant give up his birthright. Even when he finally decided that the old pensioner would be the rightful heir and would humbly refuse to take possession of the ancestral home, Hawthorne was unable to conceive of the refusal as an absolute denial of an American's claim on England. For the old pensioner, American by birth and with two hundred years of American family history, has used his name to become a member of the pension house located adjacent to the patrimonial estate. In this proximity he plans to live out his life, not entirely denying his American principles and not wholly accepting his English patrimony. He wants something of both worlds, which is precisely what Hawthorne wanted from England and America throughout his career.

Conclusion

Calling the published sketches on his English experience *Our Old Home* was Hawthorne's felicitous way of phrasing a nostalgic connection between New and Old Worlds evident in his works for more than thirty years. Because *The American Claimant Manuscripts* suggest that Hawthorne failed to resolve his ambivalence over what might be gained in claiming the lost "home" as his proper inheritance, it is fitting to conclude this study with a brief recapitulation of the significance of "home" and of the values associated with the term in Hawthorne's work. As we have seen, efforts of Puritans such as John Endicott to define themselves and their "errand into the wilderness" by excluding time-honored expressions of festivity and art appeared to Hawthorne as overreactions to the oppressive civil and ecclesiastical systems in England. Overreaction merely bred another form of oppression, revealed in "Endicott and the Red Cross" and "The Gentle Boy." In the latter, the opportunity to create a New World home worthy of the name dies a-borning; and thereafter, in works set in the seventeenth and eighteenth centuries, efforts to affirm cultural and domestic values of home are incapacitated by Puritan superstition, rigidity, and self-righteousness. In "The Man of Adamant," Richard Digby becomes obsessed with purity, while love and marriage yield to gloom and intolerance. In "Young Goodman Brown," the title character leaves his bride in order to test his faith, returning to her so filled with sanctimonious suspicion that their marriage is effectively destroyed. And in "The Minister's Black Veil," Parson Hooper sacrifices the possibility of domestic happiness to his obsession with secret sin.

By contrast, Hawthorne's historical tales often subtly evoke positive images of domestic life in England prior to emigration. Dorothy and Tobias Pearson, in "The Gentle Boy," have an affectionate "memory of their native land," which is part of the "immovable furniture of their hearts" (9:88). Hester Prynne, when she stands on the scaffold for the first time, recalls her childhood and youth in an English village and the "antique gentility" of her paternal home (1:58). Even Endicott, in "Endicott and the Red Cross," recollects "the green and fertile fields, the cottages, or, perchance, the old gray halls, where we were born and bred"—all sacrificed to the Puritan mission in the "howling wilderness" (9:438). The fond recollections of home life in England by these first-generation settlers recall similar expressions in Hawthorne's known historical sources. John Winthrop's *History*, Nathaniel Morton's *New England's Memorial*, and Cotton Mather's *Magnalia* all compare the domestic comfort left behind in England with the harsh environment of New England.

Hawthorne's use of such contrasts is not simplistic. He could admire the crude or simple shelters and houses erected during the early phases of Puritan settlement, especially if the Puritans inhabiting them could be imagined to possess a spirit of love and cheer to compensate their loss of domestic and cultural "furnishings" associated with old English homes. But as Hawthorne found it, the Puritan character was as stark and stern as its dwellings. There came to be many houses, but no homes. In a sense, then, Hawthorne's Puritans are homeless, and they hand down their homeless condition to their descendants, not the least of them Hawthorne himself.

Hawthorne experiences a special sense of homelessness, for reasons far greater than his having been raised without a father in a household composed exclusively of women—a homelessness related to his desire to be a writer-artist in a culture uncongenial and even hostile to art. In his earliest projection of himself as an artist figure—"Passages from a Relinquished Work" (1834)—he delineates the barriers raised by his homeland against an aspiring artist. The protagonist, an orphan reared in the household of Parson Thumpcushion, must defy "the stern old Pilgrim spirit of [his] guardian" in order to become a wandering storyteller, thus "keeping aloof from the regular business of life":

> This would have been a dangerous resolution, any where in the world; it was fatal, in New-England. There is a grossness in the conceptions of my countrymen; they will not be convinced that any good thing may consist with what they call idleness; they can anticipate nothing but evil of a young man who neither studies physic, law, or gospel, nor opens a store, nor takes to farming, but manifests an incomprehensible disposition to be satisfied with what his father left him. The principle is excellent, in its general influence, but most miserable in its effect on the few that violate it. (10:407)

The storyteller's "chief motives" for enacting his scheme are "discontent with home, and a bitter grudge against Parson Thumpcushion, who would rather have laid me in my father's tomb, than seen me either a novelist or an actor" (10:408). Calling upon Goldsmith, as well as Gil Blas, Don Quixote, and Childe Harold, the storyteller evokes Old World models in justification of his desire to become an itinerant artist. Although he has a place at the Parson's that he "called home" (10:414), he clearly uses the term only nominally, because of the Puritanical severity characterizing the Parson's household. Thus the storyteller must make a virtue of necessity when he says, "I have a home every where and no where, just as you please to take it

(10:414). His youthful confidence does not disguise underlying anxiety: the young man has no family and feels isolated in a culture without native traditions of art to nurture his talent. Accordingly, he turns to English and Continental authors to sustain his ambition to become a storyteller. Not coincidentally, he shares with Hawthorne a resolve to be an American storyteller, to use American materials, and to claim the Old World as a foundation, a symbolic home, to support this resolve.

The storyteller's ambition to follow English and Continental models entails an aesthetic, spiritual kinship that, on the face of it, has nothing to do with Old World political or social ties. Indeed, while it necessarily dictates a repudiation of Puritanical resistance to art, the ambition itself seems to presuppose the openness and fluidity of the American social structure. Hawthorne's treatment of Robin as a claimant in "My Kinsman, Major Molineux" offers a useful comparison. Robin leaves his paternal home in the country because he wants to rise in the world through the patronage of his English uncle in the city. In the Revolutionary climate of the story, Robin's class consciousness becomes especially ironic: his uncle will be dispossessed of the elevated position from which to bestow special privilege. No longer having an aristocratic English system upon which to make a claim at the story's conclusion, Robin must necessarily renounce class pretension if he wants to succeed in the mobile society of post-Revolutionary American democracy.

Youth and naïveté may excuse Robin's hopes of trading upon inherited British "status" in pre-Revolutionary War America. Yet no such excuse can be made for Hepzibah, in the nineteenth-century setting of *The House of the Seven Gables*. Feeling an aristocratic superiority all the more anomalous because of her penniless condition, Hepzibah feels ashamed of having to open a cent-shop to support herself. Like Robin, she hopes to gain economic status worthy of her pride. Hence she considers the possibility of making a claim on "the member of Parliament, now at the head of the English branch of the family—with which the elder stock, on this side of the Atlantic, had held little or no intercourse for the last two centuries—this eminent gentleman might invite Hepzibah to quit the ruinous House of the Seven Gables, and come over to dwell with her kindred, at Pyncheon Hall" (2:64–65). Hepzibah's fantasy is more excessive and silly than Robin's. Whereas social rank and hereditary privilege still dominate the social and economic life in mid-nineteenth-century England, such determinants of status have virtually disappeared in America. Even though Hawthorne was unable to support his own career without accepting government patronage, he generally affirms the virtues of economic opportunity and relatively fluid class boundaries in America, questionable though he finds the materialism and utilitarianism that accompany them.

Posed against the dubious "Old World" pretensions of Robin and

Hepzibah are the more valid claims of Hawthorne's artist figures upon English cultural and aesthetic traditions. The storyteller in "Passages from a Relinquished Work" is only the first in Hawthorne's canon to assert this claim. In "The Old Manse," Hawthorne's self-projected narrator evokes Old World art, the pastoral tradition, and English parsonages to create a paradigmatic home, grounded in both Old and New World continuities—a domestic, spiritual, and artistic retreat from the materialistic values and frenetic reform movements of nineteenth-century America. The Manse as home stands in opposition to the federal "home" featured in "The Custom-House." Here, far more thoroughly than in "Passages from a Relinquished Work," Hawthorne takes a stand against the philistine Yankee values of his time and the anti-art tradition of his Puritan forefathers from which they evolve; but such a stand, however moderated by his discovery of "true" artistic Fathers in surveyor Pue, Burns, and Chaucer, leaves him in a condition almost as homeless in nineteenth-century America as Hester found herself in seventeenth-century Boston.

The issues of home and homelessness are central to Hawthorne's *The House of the Seven Gables,* a work that can be seen to repeat the "Manse"/"Custom-House" counterpoint rather than develop it. A major configuration in *Gables* involves another homeless artist, Holgrave, who eventually recovers a lost patrimony. But Holgrave has no wish to claim the House of the Seven Gables, which is the house that Puritanism built in place of his ancestor's pastoral "garden-ground and homestead" (2 : 7). Like Hawthorne, he is perfectly aware that surviving Puritan traits symbolized by the house are responsible for the culturally improverished condition of America. Unlike Hawthorne in "The Custom-House," however, Holgrave does not reflect on how his presence in the house and his obsession with Judge Pyncheon, the reincarnation of the original Puritan villain who dispossessed Holgrave's family of their birthright, impede his development as an artist. Only after the Judge's death does Holgrave become fully conscious that his homelessness and reaction to the Puritan tradition have stunted his growth.

The Judge's death in the House of the Seven Gables and Holgrave's move to the Judge's country estate complete a circular pattern of dispossession and possession in the novel's conclusion. Appropriately, the Judge dies in the house because he is the rightful heir to the Puritan guilt lodged there. Similarly, Holgrave is the rightful heir to the country home, an elaborate extension of the homestead first built by his ancestor. This dwelling invites comparison with the Manse, a pastoral retreat which, after the marriage of Holgrave and Phoebe, will satisfy the same requirements of a home for them as the Manse did for Hawthorne: the slow accretion of time and a continuing opportunity for renewal. As Holgrave says, "I wonder that the late Judge . . . should not have felt the propriety of embodying so excellent a piece of domestic architecture in stone, rather than in wood. Then, every generation of the family might have altered the interior, to suit its own taste and convenience; while the exterior, through the lapse of years, might have been adding venerableness to its original beauty, and thus giving that impression of permanence, which I consider essential to the happiness of any one moment" (2:314–15).

While Holgrave finds a "home," as Hawthorne evidently did at the Manse, Holgrave's path and Hawthorne's career sharply diverge. Hawthorne left the Manse to spend several years in Salem at the Custom House, then additional years at Boston, Salem, and Lenox before returning to Concord for a year prior to "returning" to the ancestral homeland in England—which raised anew the tensions presumably resolved in the conclusion of *The House of the Seven Gables*. After his return to the Wayside in 1860, Hawthorne was frequently ill at ease, the Civil War no doubt exacerbating his discontent. In addition, he was physically unwell. For reasons of health, he left his family at the Wayside home to take several trips during his last years, walking the seashore and visiting distant places in the company of old friends. Indeed, he died away from home on one of these trips. His behavior accords with his writing over the last decade of his life, as he tried to construct and recover possible homes, but never finally discovering one that put together both sides of his American and English inheritance. The point finds lucid illustration in the conclusion of *The Marble Faun*. Kenyon and Hilda resolve to give up their expatriated existence and return to America. Their decision probably issues from Hawthorne's occasional sense while abroad that he and his children were gradually losing important elements of their birthright. But Kenyon and Hilda's choice is a comparatively easy one. Italy is not England. Italy is not the ancestral home having all the hereditary attractions to which Hawthorne and his protagonists in *The American Claimant Manuscripts* are so unavoidably drawn, and because of which they worry over compromising their Americanness. England and America possess attractions having almost equal drawing power. It is perhaps Hawthorne's fate as an ambivalent or mediating figure to be irrevocably divided.

For many years Hawthorne had tried not only to plumb the causes and results of lost cultural ties between New and Old Worlds but also to reestablish connections to an English aesthetic tradition broken off when American Puritans rid themselves of both the best and the worst of their birthright. His dilemma, in the last years, over how to treat and what to do with his American claimant was linked to divided attractions to two homelands, as well as to his identity as a writer. Thus his failure to complete the claimant romance suggests his own inability to decide, once he confronted the dilemma directly, between his life-long aesthetic claim on England and his political allegiance to America. He quite clearly felt unable to endorse an overt reclamation of trans-Atlantic ties to an American audience, even though he had subtly suggested it many times in previous works. Nor could he, at the end of his career, fully or finally ridicule the desire to reclaim such ties, any more than he could posit an irrevocable split between a connection he had done so much to bridge. Such ambivalence gave profound depth and shape to Hawthorne's career.

Notes

Introduction

1. The letter is dated 13 March 1821 and can be found in the Centenary Edition of Hawthorne's correspondence (15:138–39).

2. For this literary setting, see Neal F. Doubleday, *Hawthorne's Early Tales: A Critical Study* (Durham, N.C.: Duke University Press, 1972), pp. 32–52; and for additional important information see William Charvat, *The Profession of Authorship in America, 1800–1870,* ed. Matthew J. Bruccoli (Columbus: Ohio State University Press, 1968), pp. 5–67.

3. Concise background for all the unfinished Romances is best found in the Historical Introductions of *The American Claimant Manuscripts* and *The Elixir of Life Manuscripts,* vols. 12 and 13 of the Centenary Edition.

4. For the first and still best discussion of the importance of home in Hawthorne's works, see Roy R. Male, *Hawthorne's Tragic Vision* (1957; rpt., New York: W. W. Norton, 1964), pp. 38–53. See also Terence Martin, "Hawthorne's Public Decade and the Value of Home," *American Literature* 46 (1974):141–52.

5. See Ursula Brumm, *American Thought and Religious Typology* (New Brunswick, N.J.: Rutgers University Press, 1970); Sacvan Bercovitch, *The American Jeremiad* (Madison: University of Wisconsin Press, 1978), pp. 93–131, 176–210; Thomas M. Davis, "The Traditions of Puritan Typology," in *Typology and Early American Literature,* ed. Sacvan Bercovitch (Amherst: University of Massachusetts Press, 1972), pp. 11–45; and Mason I. Lowance, Jr., *The Language of Canaan: Metaphor and Symbol in New England from the Puritans to the Transcendentalists* (Cambridge: Harvard University Press, 1982).

6. Michael J. Colacurcio, *The Province of Piety: Moral History in Hawthorne's Early Tales* (Cambridge: Harvard University Press, 1984).

7. See Q. D. Leavis, "Hawthorne as Poet," in *Hawthorne: A Collection of Critical Essays,* ed. A. N. Kaul (Englewood Cliffs, N.J.: Prentice-Hall, 1966), pp. 25–63.

8. Michael Bell, *Hawthorne and the Historical Romance of New England* (Princeton: Princeton University Press, 1971), p. 117.

9. For a recent study supporting this configuration, based upon political oratory and similar expressions, see John P. McWilliams, *Hawthorne, Melville, and the American Character: A Looking-Glass Business* (Cambridge: Cambridge University Press, 1984), pp. 25–90.

10. Bell, *Historical Romance,* pp. 22–33, has outlined this myth in New England literature and has argued several places in his study that Hawthorne works with the myth.

11. Quoted from a letter to William D. Ticknor, 26 October 1855, in *Letters of Hawthorne to William D. Ticknor, 1851–1864,* 2 vols. in 1 (1910; rpt., Washington, D.C.: NCR/Microcard Editions, 1972), 1:111.

12. Cushing Strout, *The American Image of the Old World* (New York: Harper & Row, 1963).

13. Henry James, *Hawthorne* (London: Macmillan, 1879), p. 119.

Chapter 1. John Endicott as Puritan Type

1. The tale first appeared in *The Token* in 1835 (dated 1836). James K. Folsom, *Man's Accidents and God's Purposes* (New Haven, Conn.: College and University Press, 1963), p. 121, says that the tale was "written probably in 1828 or 1829." J. Donald Crowley leaves open the possibility that the tale "was one of the pieces which Hawthorne planned to use in a projected volume called *Provincial Tales* at least as early as 1830" (9:491). Nelson F. Adkins, "The Early Projected Works of Nathaniel Hawthorne," *Papers of the Bibliographical Society of America* 39 (1945): 119–45, believes that the tale may have been one of the *Provincial Tales*, but he does not speculate on the dates of its composition (pp. 130–31).

2. For Hawthorne's knowledge of Bradford as it filters through Nathaniel Morton and Thomas Prince, see Colacurcio, *Province*, pp. 263–69. Colacurcio rightly challenges the accuracy in the standard source study of the tale, G. Harrison Orians, "Hawthorne and 'The May-Pole of Merry Mount,'" *Modern Language Notes* 53 (1938): 159–67.

3. Leavis, p. 30.

4. This point is the main focus of McWilliams, *Hawthorne, Melville*, pp. 43–46.

5. Leavis, p. 30.

6. For the political typology in Hawthorne's rituals, see Peter Shaw, "Hawthorne's Ritual Typology of the American Revolution," *Prospects: An Annual of American Cultural Studies* 3 (1977): 483–98.

7. Bell, *Historical Romance*, pp. 119–20.

8. A number of readers see the need for mediation: Folsom, p. 121; Doubleday, p. 101; John E. Becker, *Hawthorne's Historical Allegory* (Port Washington, N.Y.: Kennickat Press, 1971), p. 28; Harry Levin, *The Power of Blackness* (New York: Alfred A. Knopf, 1958), p. 54; and Frederick Crews, *The Sins of the Fathers: Hawthorne's Psychological Themes* (New York: Oxford University Press, 1966), p. 25.

9. John B. Vickery, "The Golden Bough at Merry Mount," *Nineteenth-Century Fiction* 12 (1957–58): 203–14 (the quotation is from p. 207); and Daniel Hoffman, *Form and Fable in American Fiction* (1965; rpt., New York: W. W. Norton, 1973), p. 144. In addition to these mythic readings, see Norris Yates, "Ritual and Reality," *Philological Quarterly* 34 (1955): 56–70.

10. Gayle L. Smith, "Transcending the Myth of the Fall in Hawthorne's 'The May-Pole of Merry Mount,'" *ESQ: A Journal of the American Renaissance* 29 (1983): 73–80.

11. Bell, *Historical Romance*, p. 120. Becker, pp. 21–30, offers a historical reading of the tale. Robert H. Fossum, *Hawthorne's Inviolable Circle: The Problem of Time* (Deland, Fla.: Everett/ Edwards, 1972), pp. 59–64, reads the tale in terms of the moral burden of the fall and the historical burden of time. See also Richard Drinnon, "The Maypole of Merry Mount: Thomas Morton and the Puritan Patriarchs," *Massachusetts Review* 21 (1980): 382–410.

Three studies of the "May-pole" deal closely with Hawthorne's reliance upon and departure from historical sources: Doubleday, pp. 92–101; Orians, pp. 159–67; and J. Gary Williams, "History in Hawthorne's 'The May-Pole of Merry Mount,'" *Essex Institute Historical Collections* 108 (1972): 173–90. The last is by far the most thorough and accurate.

12. Colacurcio, *Province*, p. 254.

13. Leavis, p. 34.

14. Bell, *Historical Romance*, pp. 123–24.

15. Leavis, p. 189, notes the importance of the Oxford reference.

16. Hawthorne's reading in Caleb H. Snow would have been sufficient. See *History of Boston, The Metropolis of Massachusetts. . .* (Boston: Abel Bowen, 1825), pp. 50–53. For Hawthorne's reading in Snow, see Marion L. Kesselring, *Hawthorne's Reading, 1828–1850: A Transcription and Identification of Titles Recorded in the Charge-Books of the Salem Athenaeum* (1949; rpt., Folcroft, Pa.: Folcroft Press, 1969), p. 61. For the fullest treatment of Blackstone's appearance in the tale, and of the scholarship on that appearance, see the discussion and notes of Colacurcio, *Province*, pp. 269–77.

17. This unnoticed detail appears in a note written by James Savage, editor of the edition of Winthrop's *History* familiar to Hawthorne. See John Winthrop, *The History of New England from 1630 to 1649* (1825–1826; rpt., 2 vols. in 1, New York: Arno Press, 1972), 1:44.

According to Kesselring, Hawthorne checked out only the second volume of Winthrop's *History*, which begins with events in 1640 (old style). Whether or not he knew the first volume poses a somewhat serious problem inasmuch as many scholars have often taken it for granted that he did, such as Arlin Turner, "Hawthorne's Literary Borrowings," *PMLA* 51 (1936): 543–62. Yet Nelson F. Adkins, "Hawthorne's Democratic New England Puritans," *Emerson Society Quarterly*, no. 44 (1966): 66–72, without considering the distinction between the first and second volumes, believes that Hawthorne could not have absorbed very much from Winthrop since he possessed the *History* for "less than three days" (p. 68)—from 16 to 19 April 1828. But Adkins goes on to argue that Hawthorne had Winthrop for a source of "Endicott and the Red Cross," which depicts events in 1634 and 1635 contained only in the first volume of Winthrop's *History*.

The best evidence for Hawthorne's knowing this first volume (however he managed to read it) is contained in the biographical sketch, "Mrs. Hutchinson" (1830)—see Riverside Edition, 12:217–26. The proceedings against Anne Hutchinson, the persons present at the proceedings, and first the association and then dissociation of John Cotton and Hutchinson were facts available to Hawthorne only from Winthrop's account as first published by Savage.

18. Again, the point is made by Savage in Winthrop, 1:44n.

19. Thomas Frankland, *The Annals of King James and King Charles the First . . .* (London, 1681), pp. 31, 436–38. For Hawthorne's reading in Frankland, see Kesselring, p. 50.

As for the use of Blackstone in the tale, Hawthorne's own footnote correctly denies the presence of the one-time English priest in the Merry Mount settlement. Orians, pp. 163–64 and Doubleday, p. 97 have shown, however, that Hawthorne depended on historical sources for Endicott's charge that Blackstone quarreled with the Anglican Church. From several sources, Hawthorne would have known that Blackstone reputedly said to the Puritans: "'I came from England, because I did not like the lord-brethren'"—see Cotton Mather, *Magnalia Christi Americana*, 2 vols. (1852; rpt., New York: Russell and Russell, 1967), 1:243. Orians believes that Hawthorne knew some form of this quotation from three sources: Mather's *Magnalia*; Davis's *Memoir of Blackstone*; and Alden Bradford's *History of Massachusetts*. Doubleday properly adds Caleb Snow's *History of Boston* to the list. One might also include Thomas Hutchinson, *The History of the Colony and Province of Massachusetts-Bay*, ed. Lawrence S. Mayo, 3 vols. (Cambridge: Harvard University Press, 1936), 1:20. Hawthorne had read the first volume of the 1795 edition at least once before 1830—see Kesselring, p. 53.

20. The quotation is from Doubleday, p. 100. See p. 99 for the point on Cavaliers.

21. Joseph Strutt, *The Sports and Pastimes of the People of England*, ed. William Hone (London: Chatto and Windus, 1898), pp. 440–515. Hawthorne read the 1810 edition—see Kesselring, p. 62. He would also have found the same specified occasions in King James's *Books of Sports*—see Williams, pp. 183–85. Joseph B. Felt, *The Annals of Salem, from Its First Settlement* (Salem, Mass.: W. & S. B. Ives, 1827), p. 81, distilling the Puritan opposition to Strutt, says that Charles I, being opposed to Calvinistic clergymen, "reduced them to the alternative, either to withhold some of their opinions and read in time of public worship the Book of Sports, which encouraged an open profanation of the Sabbath; or submit to prosecutions, fines, imprisonment, and deposition from the ministry." For Hawthorne's reading in Felt, see Kesselring, p. 50.

22. Daniel Hoffman says that "Endicott's onrushing band, then, is but a public confirmation of an inner change and seals the lovers' recognition that they were born, like all humans, to an inheritance of sin." See "Myth, Romance, and the Childhood of Man," in *Hawthorne Centenary Essays*, ed. Roy Harvey Pearce (Columbus: Ohio State University Press, 1964), p. 261.

23. Doubleday, p. 101.

24. Later in his career Hawthorne points out in "Main-street" that not long after Endicott arrived in Salem, his wife, Anna Gower, died (11:57). At the time of writing the tale, he already knew this detail from Winthrop, 1:44n, as well as that Winthrop officiated at Endicott's remarriage in 1630 (1:44).

25. Bell, *Historical Romance*, p. 125.

26. The sanctions can be found in *Records of the Governor and Company of Massachusetts Bay in New England*, 3 vols., ed. Nathaniel B. Shurtleff (Boston: William White, 1853), 1:146. After the General Court delivered its verdict in May 1635, Endicott apparently took quarrelsome exception to the decision; for at the General Court session of 2 September 1635 the deputies "voted, & by general erection of hands concluded, that Mr. Endicott should be committed, for his contempt in protesting against the proceeding of the Court; and, upon his submission, & full acknowledgment of his offense, he was dismissed" (p. 157). If Hawthorne did not come across this information in reading colonial records of sundry kinds, he would not have missed it in Felt, p. 81.

27. As Doubleday has argued (pp. 101–3), Hawthorne relied mostly on Felt's *Annals*. Yet I believe that Hawthorne gleaned many of the details, missing in Felt, either from Wintrhop's *History* or Hutchinson's *History*, especially the connection between Endicott and Williams, absent in "Endicott and the Red Cross" but very much present in "Grandfather's Chair." Colacurcio, *Province*, p. 229, argues for Winthrop's account as the pretext of "Endicott and the Red Cross."

28. Hawthorne no doubt had read William Bentley's opinion in "A Description and History of Salem," *Massachusetts Historical Society Collections*, 1st series, 6 (1800): 212–88— "[Roger Williams] disapproved the connexion of the churches in Old and New England; yet he was prudent enough not to offer violence to the established forms. But all his hearers could not make the same distinctions. Endicott ventured to apply the doctrine, and cut the cross from the military standard. Endicott did it without advice; but the resentment of the magistrate spent itself upon Williams, who, though the innocent, was the real cause of it" (p. 246). For Hawthorne's reading in the *Collections*, hereafter cited as *MHSC*, see Kesselring, p. 56.

As Colacurcio, *Province*, pp. 224–25, suggests, one reason for the disunion is that "Williams is there to endure, so to speak, the bigoted seventeenth century—and to establish against it, on Hawthorne's behalf, the rightful balance of the liberal nineteenth."

29. Felt, p. 77.

30. In the account of Bentley, p. 245, Hawthorne would have noticed that Endicott was a political embarrassment to the Massachusetts Bay Company before Winthrop arrived with the main body of settlers. Approximate to the time of his Merry Mount activities, Endicott began persecuting the Browne family, whose partial allegiance to ecclesiastical orders of the Church of England ran counter to Endicott's plan for church government. "Unexperienced in the passions of men, and unaccustomed to consult even with his friends, he was resolved to admit no oppositions. They, who could not be terrified into silence, were not commanded to withdraw, but they were seized and transported as criminals. The fear of injury to the colony induced its friends in England to give private satisfaction, and then to write a reproof to him, who had been the cause of such outrages, and Endicott never recovered his reputation in England." Felt, pp. 38–39, substantiates and amends this account while trying to exonerate Endicott for sole responsibility. [John Eliot], "Ecclesiastical History of Massachusetts," *MHSC*, 1st series, 9 (1804): 3–5, supports Bentley's account and says that "Endicot's party were wrong, because they used violent measures" (pp. 4–5). Endicott's violence was in fact notorious. In Winthrop, 1:53n, Savage notes that Endicott was fined for battery [in 1631] against Thomas Dexter.

31. The best reading of Endicott as a typological predecessor is in Bell, *Historical Romance*, pp. 53–60.

32. Ibid., pp. 54–56.

33. If the Puritans were alarmed over the beginning conflict between Charles I and

Parliament, or if they felt threatened by English interference as early as 1634, they kept a prudent silence, judging from the historical sources familiar to Hawthorne. After the Civil War began, however, the Puritans could, through their inimitable logic, sacrifice their caution in favor of the Parliamentarians. Felt records that the General Court in 1644, "As divisions were taking place in reference to King and Parliament, the Court state, that Parliament were only 'against the malignant papists and delinquents,' of England, but not the King, and, therefore, they forbid any to declare themselves for the King against Parliament" (p. 163).

34. Sacvan Bercovitch, "Diabolus in Salem," *ELN* 6 (1969): 282.

35. Hawthorne commonly includes Indians in his works on the seventeenth century. Quite tellingly, they are always situated at the edge of a scene, as if on the verge of being pushed out of consideration. This positioning aptly represents Hawthorne's understanding of the Indians' removal from or destruction in the American scene. By the 1690s, the Indians no longer carry weapons in Hawthorne's treatment. The biographical sketch, "Sir William Phips," presents "a few dark Indians in their blankets, dull spectators of the strength that has swept away their race" (Riverside Edition, 12:233). "Grandfather's Chair," of course, presents the fullest and most sympathetic treatment of vanishing Americans.

36. John Halligan, "Hawthorne on Democracy: 'Endicott and the Red Cross,'" *Studies in Short Fiction* 8 (1971): 301–7, analyzes Endicott's speech techniques as those of a demagogue obsessed with power.

37. Fossum, p. 34.

38. Felt says: "Tradition relates, that when a body of Indians had come against Providence in 1676 during King Philip's War, Mr. Williams resolved to visit and strive to pacify them. Accordingly, he took his staff and went towards them. Some old Indians recognized and so solicited him to return, lest the young warriors, unacquainted with his person, should injure and kill him" (p. 91). On the other positive traits of Williams's character, Felt records the following two citations: "His views of civil policy were uncommonly liberal. A sorrowful lesson had taught him, that it was precious to enjoy equal social rights, whatever might be the difference of religious opinions" (p. 92). "His benevolence flowed to all around him. The property he had, was always ready for the relief of public or private misery. He scorned to have his soul bound to earth with the heavy shackles of covetessness. No man who ever set foot in America, more adorned the Gospel precept of forgiveness to enemies, than Roger Williams" (p. 93).

39. Like Endicott, Dudley was often a thorn in the side of Winthrop. Hawthorne probably did not need to see a negative judgment of Dudley beyond what he could detect from colonial records, but he would have seen the opinion of John Eliot, "Ecclesiastical History of Massachusetts," *MHSC*, 1st series, 10 (1809):1–37—"His temper was irritable and his mind was not expanded with the liberal sentiments and polite education of governour Winthrop, his predecessor; but he always approved himself a lover of justice and a friend of truth. His bigotry arose from his being an enemy to all disorder, heresy, and corrupt doctrine; he discovered the habit of his soul in writing his own epitaph, 'I am no libertine'" (p. 30).

40. Colacurcio, *Province*, pp. 236–37, suggests the link between Winthrop and Endicott, even while recognizing Hawthorne's "unforgiving" judgment of the theocratic union established by the Puritans (p. 238).

41. Colacurcio, *Province*, p. 236.

42. Bell, *Historical Romance*, p. 58, has suggested a similar point.

43. Colacurcio, *Province*, pp. 224–31, would disagree. He finds the historical subtext of "Endicott and the Red Cross" to reside not only in Williams's radical wish to separate from the Church of England but also in his more radical wish to separate church and state in Massachusetts Bay.

44. See my article "The Demonic in 'Endicott and the Red Cross,'" *Papers on Language and Literature* 13 (1977): 251–59.

45. Hawthorne may have been calling upon another trait of Williams recorded by Felt who says, upon Williams's death: "Thus departed a man, who was ardent in pursuing the object of

what he deemed right, whether over plains or mountains, through flowers or thorns" (p. 91).

46. For a discussion of the typological issue, see Bell, *Historical Romance,* pp. 56–59. The quotation is from p. 58.

47. The deterministic logic is Bell's, pp. 58–59.

48. For the influence of historical sources on the tale, see G. Harrison Orians, "The Sources and Themes of Hawthorne's 'The Gentle Boy,'" *New England Quarterly* 14 (1941): 664–78; and Doubleday, pp. 159–70.

49. The differences between these generations is discussed at length in the opening section of chapter 5. Hawthorne's treatment of them can be found in *The Scarlet Letter* (1 : 232).

50. Bentley, p. 256. And Felt, p. 183, notes that in 1651, William Hathorne opposed a fine on Richard Leader for defaming Endicott.

51. My historical diagram is compatible with that of Harry B. Henderson, whose particular observation on the historical context of "The Gentle Boy" no doubt implies as much as my own spells out: "None of the major characters of 'The Gentle Boy' . . . belongs to the second generation, the 'immediate successors.' Both the Quakers and the household of Tobias are recent emigrants, who bring to Massachusetts a rich experience of political and religious strife of the Old World." See *Versions of the Past: The Historical Imagination in American Fiction* (New York: Oxford University Press, 1974), p. 103.

52. In *MHSC,* 3rd series, 1 (1825):51–53, Hawthorne would have seen an undated letter of Endicott's, probably written to Lord Clarendon or the Earl of Manchester sometime after February 1860, proclaiming his hope for the king's favorable view of the colony, as well as his intent to search for the regicide judges Whalley and Goffe "and sending them over in order to their trial for having a hand in the most horrid murther of our late sovereign, Charles the First, of glorious memory" (p. 51). Endicott proceeds hyperbolically to relate how news of the Restoration was received in Boston: "to the great rejoicing of the people, expressed in their loud acclamations, God save the king! which was no sooner ended, but a troop of horse, four foot companies, then in arms, expressed their joy in their peals; our forts and all the ships in our harbour discharged, our castle concluding with * * * * * * all thundered out their joy" (p. 53).

53. See for example, Bell, *Historical Romance,* p. 111; and Seymour L. Gross, "Hawthorne's Revisions of 'The Gentle Boy,'" *American Literature* 26 (1955): 196–208.

54. According to Bentley, p. 255, "The first law against [Quakers], under the penalty of death, was in October, 1658, and Endicott was in its favor." In Caleb H. Snow's *History of Boston,* p. 141, Hawthorne had a good source for the particular severity ushered in by Endicott after he became governor. Snow says that in the early 1650s, "the scrupulosity of the good people of the colony was at its height. Soon after Mr. Winthrop's death, Mr. Endicott, the most rigid of any of the magistrates, being governor, he joined with the assistants in an association against the wearing of long hair, as a thing uncivil and unmanly." And Felt, p. 183, records that in 1651, under Endicott, the General Court "forbid dancing at taverns, on penalty of 5 [shillings]." Moreover, in 1652, the court ordered that, on a second offense, any person denying the Bible as the word of God would be put to death (p. 186).

55. For an astute treatment of the Puritans' reliance on law, of their preferring Moses to Christ, and of Hawthorne's countering their legalism with a covenant of love, see Colacurcio, *Province,* pp. 184–95, especially p. 187.

56. Henderson, p. 104, anticipated something of my own discovery when he says: "This is one of the horns of an historical dilemma, for, Winthrop being gone, Endicott is the price of stability, the price of New England's escape from the dialectics of Old English change: a 'voluptuous' Charles II for an 'ambitious' Cromwell." I would argue, however, against Endicott's being presented as the "price of stability." From a Puritan point of view, he is never presented as a disagreeable alternative to other leaders, except Winthrop. Rather, he embodies the sum and substance of most Puritans' desires—thus, in Hawthorne's lamentation, the right man at the right time.

57. William Harris, *An Historical and Critical Account of the Life of Oliver Cromwell* (London,

1762), pp. 135–54, 318–22. For Hawthorne's reading in Harris, see Kesselring, p. 53.

58. See *Woodstock* in Waverley Novels Edition (Edinburgh: Adam and Charles Black, 1852), 21:143–44.

59. Ibid., p. 496.

60. Ibid., pp. 117, 198, 498, 504, e.g.

61. Bell, *Historical Romance*, p. 114; and Crews, p. 66. Surprisingly, Colacurcio, *Province*, p. 167, leans in favor of the Puritan bias against Pearson's motives.

62. For the best discussion of the head vs. heart and of Hawthorne's distrust of Puritan assumptions to election, see Colacurcio, *Province* pp. 168–75.

63. Crews has especially argued that Pearson is a neurotic (p. 67).

64. *The Token*, ed. S. G. Goodrich (Boston: Gray and Bowen, 1832), pp. 227–28.

65. Gross, "Hawthorne's Revisions," p. 58.

66. Ibid., pp. 206, 207.

67. When the old Quaker tells Catherine that she will soon be free of "the cares of that little boy" and that "his tottering footsteps shall impede thine no more" (9:101), no parent would likely disagree with Colacurcio's sensitive response: "The chilling terror implied by the calm fanaticism of this climactic speech is, I think, unsurpassed in American literature" (*Province*, p. 182).

68. In Colacurcio's formulation, "the Quaker errand into the enduring Puritan Wilderness, undertaken on behalf of the inviolability of individual conscience, has left him as cold as the original Puritan errand itself. Tobias' nature remains as divided, as incomplete as ever. Once nature is fractured, no experience of grace seems possible" (p. 181).

69. Roy R. Male presents Pearson as a sympathetic figure caught between conflicting forces in *Hawthorne's Tragic Vision*, pp. 46–47.

70. I am indebted to Male's discussion of the search-for-home motif in the story (pp. 45–48).

71. For a discussion of thwarted childhood within Hawthorne's historical review of Puritan influence on America, see Clark Griffith, "Pearl's Green A: *The Scarlet Letter* and American History," *Australasian Journal of American Studies* 2 (July 1983): 21–33.

72. Agnes McNeill Donohue says that the deformed boy who betrays Ilbrahim has "the characteristics of the devil" (p. 164), in "'The Fruit of That Forbidden Tree': A Reading of the 'The Gentle Boy,'" in *A Casebook on the Hawthorne Question*, ed. Agnes McNeill Donohue (New York: Crowell, 1963), pp. 158–70.

73. See the opening chapters of Bell's *Historical Romance* and Doubleday.

74. The first three chapters of Bell's *Historical Romance* deal with early practitioners.

75. The argument is McWilliams's, *Hawthorne, Melville*, pp. 45–48, which is borrowed from Bell who is more cognizant of Hawthorne's irony. My disagreement with the argument accords with one of the major points of Colacurcio's analysis.

76. See Bell, *Historical Romance*, pp. 47–53; Doubleday, pp. 85–92; Hoffman, "Myth, Romance, and the Childhood of Man," p. 210; Joseph Schwartz, "Three Aspects of Hawthorne's Puritanism," *New England Quarterly* 36 (1963): 192–208; Marvin Fisher, "The Pattern of Conservatism in Johnson's *Rasselas* and Hawthorne's Tales," *Journal of the History of Ideas* 19 (1958): 173–96; and Ursula Brumm, "A Regicide Judge as 'Champion' of American Independence," *Amerikastudien* 21 (1976): 177–86.

77. Colacurcio, *Province*, pp. 208–20, enlarges upon my previous ironic reading of the tale. See my "Hawthorne's Ironic Criticism of Puritan Rebellion in 'The Gray Champion,'" *Studies in Short Fiction* 13 (1976): 363–70.

78. For the importance of Hawthorne's raising Cotton Mather's opinion of Randolph in the tale, see Colacurcio, *Province*, pp. 211–13.

79. Exodus 14:13.

80. For the history and sources of the legend, see G. Harrison Orians, "The Angel of Hadley in Fiction: A Study of the Sources of Hawthorne's 'The Grey Champion,'" *American Literature* 4 (1932–33): 257–69.

81. See my "Hawthorne's Ironic Criticism of Puritan Rebellion in 'The Gray Champion,'" pp. 368–69.

82. *Waverley; or, 'Tis Sixty Years Since* in Waverley Novels Edition (Edinburgh: Adam and Charles Black, 1852), 1:468.

83. Ibid., p. 469.

84. Ibid.

85. Ibid.

86. Ibid., p. 472.

87. Fossum, pp. 32–33.

88. Hutchinson, 1:158.

89. Hutchinson, 1:279.

90. Felt, p. 327.

91. Colacurcio, *Province*, p. 217.

Chapter 2. Puritan Typology and Democratic Ideology

1. See Michael Kammen, *A Season of Youth: The American Revolution and the Historical Imagination* (New York: Alfred A. Knopf, 1978), pp. 3–32.

2. John P. McWilliams, *Hawthorne, Melville*, pp. 25–90.

3. For a discussion of how the sacred mission of the Puritans develops into the secular mission of the War of Independence, see Bercovitch, *The American Jeremiad*, pp. 93–131.

4. Lester H. Cohen, *The Revolutionary Histories: Contemporary Narratives of the American Revolution* (Ithaca, N.Y.: Cornell University Press, 1980), p. 4. See also p. 234, note 3, for Cohen's discussion of the coverage and limitations of the few histories published from the point of view of Loyalists.

5. The fullest study of the issue is that of Blair Rouse, "Hawthorne and the American Revolution: An Exploration," *Nathaniel Hawthorne Journal, 1976*, pp. 17–61.

6. For writers who do avail themselves of the Revolution, see Kammen, pp. 186–220.

7. The most reliable study of these collections remains that of Adkins. See also Alfred Weber, *Die Entwicklung der Rahmenerzählungen Nathaniel Hawthornes* (Berlin: Erich Schmidt, 1973).

8. By my count, there are six "Puritan" tales of the seventeenth century: "May-pole," "Endicott," "Gentle Boy," "Champion," "Man of Adamant," and "Goodman Brown." There are eleven eighteenth-century tales: "Minister's Black Veil," "Roger Malvin's Burial," "Molineux," the four "Legends of the Province-House," "Old News," "Bell's Biography," "Book of Autographs," and "Battle Omen." Two others might be added to the latter, considering their important historical contexts or references: "Prophetic Pictures" and "Drowne's Wooden Image."

9. The tale, perhaps only a sketch, appeared in the *Salem Gazette*, 2 November 1830. It was not collected in Hawthorne's lifetime but appears in vol. 11 of the Centenary Edition.

10. Colarcurcio, *Province*, pp. 563–64n, suggests the tale may have been written as early as 1826.

11. The standard psychological reading that stresses the patricidal nature of Robin's oedipal search is that of Crews, pp. 61–79. For an earlier hint of this reading, see Male, pp. 50–51. For the regicidal implications of patricide, which lead to mythic and historical dimensions, see especially Hoffman, *Form and Fable*, pp. 113–25; and, best of all, Peter Shaw, "Fathers, Sons, and the Ambiguities of Revolution in 'My Kinsman, Major Molineux,'" *New England Quarterly* 49 (1976): 559–76.

12. Modern interpretations of "Molineux," whether mythic, allegorical, psychological, or historical, are indebted to Q. D. Leavis, who presents Robin as a young American in the act of defying and separating from parental England. See "Hawthorne as Poet." It is impossible and unnecessary to cite the many significant studies of "Molineux" that build upon Leavis. Other

than those cited in this section, one might also call attention to Doubleday, pp. 227–38; Fossum, pp. 26–31; Roy Harvey Pearce, "Hawthorne and the Sense of the Past; or, The Immortality of Major Molineux," *ELH* 21 (1954): 327–49; Hyatt Waggoner, *Hawthorne: A Critical Study*, rev. ed. (Cambridge: Belknap Press of Harvard University Press, 1963), pp. 57–61; Julian Smith, "Historical Ambiguity in 'My Kinsman, Major Molineux,'" *English Language Notes* 8 (1970): 115–20; John Russell, "Allegory in 'My Kinsman, Major Molineux,'" *New England Quarterly* 40 (1967): 432–40; A. B. England, "Robin Molineux and Young Ben Franklin," *Journal of American Studies* 6 (1972): 181–88; Peter Shaw, "Their Kinsman, Thomas Hutchinson," *Early American Literature* 11 (1976): 183–90; Robert G. Grayson, "The New England Sources of 'My Kinsman, Major Molineux,'" *American Literature* 54 (1982): 545–59; and James Duban, "Robins and Robinarchs in 'My Kinsman, Major Molineux,'" *Nineteenth-Century Fiction* 38 (1983): 271–88.

13. Colacurcio, *Province*, pp. 140–42, spells out the patronage and currency issues.

14. Since it has a steeple (11:219), the church is not King's Chapel, the first Anglican/Episcopal church in Boston, nor the Old South Church. It may be the First Church, as Colacurcio, *Province*, p. 146, has suggested.

15. See Colacurcio, *Province*, p. 569, note 97.

16. Although Colacurcio, *Province*, p. 141, recognizes that Boston might just as well be London in terms of its "Egyptian" corruption, he argues that the "operative point" in the tale is how "an Old English Court party has insinuated itself into the provincial life in countrified New England." It seems to me, however, that the difference between the country and city in the tale is too absolute for Bostonians to be subsumed under a countrified party. The point seems most clearly evident when the gentleman-escort admonishes Robin not to return to his paternal home but to remain in the city, as if those in the country do not (yet) know what Bostonians do.

17. That the parti-colored leader represents the devil is well established. See Hoffman, p. 119; Fossum, p. 29; and Becker, p. 12.

18. The depravity issue is advanced by Richard H. Fogle, *Hawthorne's Fiction: The Light and the Dark*, rev. ed. (Norman: University of Oklahoma Press, 1963), p. 106.

19. For an account of how New England's strategy of embracing the Act of Toleration backfired, see Perry Miller, *The New England Mind: From Colony to Province* (1953; rpt., Boston: Beacon Press, 1961), pp. 373–74.

20. Fogle, pp. 111–16, first recognized the lunacy at work in the tale as a result of the moonlit setting and the obvious allusions to *A Midsummer Night's Dream*.

21. Better than anyone else, Colacurcio, *Province*, pp. 148–50, elaborates on Hawthorne's surprising inclusion of the moon's point of view.

22. Henderson, p. 101, says that "Molineux" "affirms the outward direction of that impulse toward forceful assertion and revolutionary strength that has been transmitted to the latter-day 'Yankees' directly from Endicott."

23. Colacurcio, *Province*, p. 138, places the mob scene in the historical context of a rum riot.

24. John P. McWilliams, "'Thorough-going Democrat' and 'Modern Tory': Hawthorne and the Puritan Revolution of 1776," *Studies in Romanticism* 15 (1976): pp. 549–71, draws substantially upon "Old News," but the sketch has not received either the analysis or the search for its sources that it deserves.

25. Only Colacurcio gives a full reading of each tale, *Province*, pp. 389–482.

26. The case cannot be exaggerated, even with modern biographers, beginning with Robert Cantwell and concluding with the latest studies by Arlin Turner and James R. Mellow.

27. Disregard of the "Legends" is typified in "A Chronology of Nathaniel Hawthorne's Life to 1853," part of the introductory material to the Centenary Edition of Hawthorne's *Letters* (15:91–101). While many of Hawthorne's minor works are listed in the "Chronology" (even when not referred to in the correspondence), not one of the "Legends" is listed, despite references to two of them in Hawthorne's letters.

28. As Becker sees it, Howe's masquerade reveals an English "failure of nerve before reality," showing "Hawthorne's basic indictment of royalist British rule" (p. 44).

29. As McWilliams, "'Thorough-going Democrat,'" p. 561, observes, "In fiction as in history, Hawthorne's justification for the Revolution is the rebirth of Puritanism." Colacurcio's chapter on the "Legends" more accurately argues for Hawthorne's criticizing a resurrection of Puritanism either in the Revolution or in the Revolutionary historiography and Democratic ideology of his time.

30. Peter Shaw would argue the point. The "Merrymount tradition," he says, "has been permanently cut off by Endicott's act, so that there is no warrant for treating the Revolution as a revival of its spirit." See "Hawthorne's Ritual Typology," pp. 483–98. It seems to me improper to speak about a "Merrymount tradition" in the first place. That no such tradition of festivity ever took root in New England, even in a modified form, is precisely Hawthorne's point. The potential was cut off, similar to the way that the reintroduction of English fashion and gaiety in the eighteenth century was discarded in the Revolution.

31. See Hutchinson's *History*, 1:310–11, for Increase Mather's activity in first trying to retain the old charter and then securing a new one favorable to New England. Hawthorne would have read a fuller account of Increase Mather's efforts to retain the original charter and then to secure the privileges of the original in the new charter in "Extracts from Rev. Cotton Mather's Memoirs of Remarkables in the Life of His Father . . .," *MHSC*, 1st series, 9 (1804): 245–53.

32. Hawthorne is enjoying a historical irony here, for Byles was well known as a punster. See *Dictionary of American Biography*.

33. McWilliams, "'Thorough-going Democrat,'" pp. 562–63, persuasively identifies the seventeenth-century model for Joliffe, drawn from Hutchinson's *History*. He argues that, by "postdating Joliffe's existence seventy years," Hawthorne "links the Charter rebellion of 1689 to the taxation rebellions of the 1770's, while showing that the Puritan character, dormant in the early eighteenth century, had underlain both."

34. Fossum, p. 37, faults the English for not making history "usable" and commends Joliffe for accurately interpreting the lessons of history. As we shall see in "Old Esther Dudley," however, the English method of valorizing the past for its own sake, rather than for the sake of selected moments symbolizing the unfolding design of providence, is used by Hawthorne to subvert the complacent, progressive ideology of the 1830s.

35. See Colacurcio, *Province*, p. 402, for the anti-masque; and Shaw, "Hawthorne's Ritual Typology," pp. 494–96, for a discussion of the ritual.

36. Shaw, "Hawthorne's Ritual Typology," p. 496, observes that "challenges to authority directed against governors . . . always symbolically involved the king."

37. In Cotton Mather's chapter on Winthrop, for example, Hawthorne would have noticed that Winthrop approved a limited participation of citizens in the decision-making of the colony. It was his way of checking the people's desire for more sweeping influence, which would "run the whole Government into something too *Democratical.*" See *Magnalia*, 1:125.

38. The legend is finally nothing if not moral, both as Tiffany understands it and as Hawthorne qualifies that understanding through irony. See Julian Smith, "Hawthorne's *Legends of the Province House*," *Nineteenth-Century Fiction* 24 (1969): 31–44, who claims that "Howe's Masquerade" is "one of Hawthorne's most morally neutral stories" (p. 34).

39. Shaw, "Hawthorne's Ritual Typology," p. 495, accepts the connection between Vane and regicide as an accurate piece of history.

40. See Charles Wentworth Upham, "Life of Sir Henry Vane, Fourth Governor of Massachusetts," in *The Library of American Biography*, 1st series, conducted by Jared Sparks (Boston: Hillard Gray, 1835), 4:322–70. According to Upham, "As Sir Henry was not one of [Charles Stuart's] judges, and was known to have been opposed to his condemnation and execution, it was supposed that the Declaration of Charles the Second at Breda, previous to his restoration, would have secured him from the vengeance of that monarch" (p. 334). Also of note is the fact that Clarendon does not mention Vane throughout the trial and execution of Charles I. See

Edward Hyde Lord Clarendon, *The History of the Rebellion and Civil Wars in England,* 3 vols. in 6 (Oxford, 1707). For Hawthorne's reading in Upham and Clarendon, see Kesselring, pp. 61, 47. For a modern account, see Violet A. Rowe, *Sir Henry Vane the Younger: A Study in Political and Administrative History* (London: Athlone Press, 1970), pp. 232–38, who clearly shows that Vane was convicted of treason and not against Charles I but Charles II. The fact that he appeared at his admiralty office on 30 January 1649, the day of the regicide, did tell against Vane at his trial (p. 139).

41. Considering Howe's specific ignorance, if not his general obtuseness, in the legend, it is difficult to accept the point of Evan Carton that "Howe, sought, through masquerade, to invoke his country's past 'romance and historic grandeur' . . . in order to bolster and legitimize its present"—particularly when the quoted ideal belongs to the narrator, not Howe. See "Hawthorne and the Province of Romance," *ELH* 47 (1980): 331–51, esp. p. 337.

42. Colacurcio, *Province,* pp. 393–97, discusses the narrator's weaknesses.

43. As Julian Smith, "Hawthorne's Legends," p. 33, says, "the setting forces us to a melancholy realization that the alternative to aristocratic splendor is often proletarian shabbiness." Carton, p. 336, further observes that "As royal power is exorcised from the revolutionary past, the power of that revolutionary past forsakes the present."

44. Taking the unacknowledged lead of Smith, McWilliams, "'Thorough-going Democrat,'" p. 563, says that, "As the tale and frame continue to contrast with one another, the reader might well wonder whether Puritan principle has produced only egalitarian complacency, whether aristocratic splendor has not given way to the tawdry and the dull."

45. Hutchinson, 3:221.

46. McWilliams, *Hawthorne, Melville,* p. 75, says, "Throughout his writings of the Revolutionary era, Hawthorne's interest was in the coming of war rather than the building of a republic, in conflicting loyalty rather than battlefield victory, in the foreground of violence rather than the future of liberty." See also Colacurcio, *Province,* p. 406.

47. Lewis P. Simpson, "John Adams and Hawthorne: The Fiction of the Real American Revolution," *Studies in Literary Imagination* 9 (Fall 1976): 1–17.

48. It is true, of course, that Hutchinson knew that the charter placed the governor in charge of forts and garrisons; thus, as Bernard Bailyn says, "it was a real question in Hutchinson's mind whether he had legal right to surrender that command to another officer, even at the order of their common superior, the king." See *The Ordeal of Thomas Hutchinson* (Cambridge: Belknap Press of Harvard University Press, 1974), pp. 173–74. Given Tiffany's patriotic, anti-Hutchinsonian perspective, however, it seems doubtful that the lieutenant-governor's hesitation could suggest this historical fact. But behind Tiffany, Hawthorne may well have considered Hutchinson's quandary.

49. Hutchinson, 1:278–79, 281–85, 297–320.

50. Ibid., 3:84–106.

51. Ibid., 3:153–58.

52. Ibid., 3:157.

53. Ibid., 3:221–22.

54. Ibid., 3:222–24.

55. Ibid., 3:222. Doubleday, pp. 124–25, also notes this passage, and he provides a sympathetic discussion of the historical Hutchinson's moral dilemma.

56. The colonial Assembly's legalistic gamesmanship played with Governor Bernard and Lieutenant-Governor Hutchinson is a particular focus of Hutchinson's third volume. See especially pp. 10–220.

57. The earliest example is the painter in "The Prophetic Pictures" (9:179).

58. Smith, "Hawthorne's Legends," p. 35, treats the tale in terms of the gothic, as does Doubleday, pp. 126–28, who criticizes Hawthorne's handling of the portrait: "the ineptness seems almost contemptuous." Perhaps it is time to consider that Hawthorne's use of the gothic goes hand in hand with his use of Puritan spectral evidence. Where the one is trite and fails, the other is historically profound and succeeds.

59. Colacurcio, *Province*, pp. 410–21, elaborates the significance of the devil's relation to the Puritan errand in the legend.

60. In the third volume of his *History*, Hutchinson often singles out the Council as the group most troublesome to his and the crown's policies. Hawthorne somewhat inaccurately aligns the Council with Hutchinson because he needs representatives of the British faction to support his familiar historical paradigm involving contestants in the English Civil War.

61. Doubleday, p. 126, suggests that Mather's opinion of Randolph, stated in "The Gray Champion," served as the "germ" for the treatment of Randolph in "Portrait." That Randolph is, in New England's redaction of history, the blasted wretch Mather claims, and that Hutchinson will be equally damned form the substance of Colacurcio's chapter on "Portrait."

62. Alice seems to behave in accord with the principles of liberty belonging to her probable namesake, Sir Henry Vane, as Carton, p. 353, first suggested, although he misidentifies Vane as "royal."

63. Smith, "Hawthorne's Legends," p. 36, first noticed the possibility that Lincoln may have turned Loyalist.

64. Bailyn entitles his chapter on Hutchinson during this period "The Captive."

65. Colacurcio makes this a central point in this treatment of Hutchinson. In his opinion of Governor Burnet's administration (1728–29), Hutchinson says, "He did not know the temper of the people of New England. They have a strong sense of liberty and are more easily drawn than driven" (2:276).

66. McWilliams, "'Thorough-going Democrat,'" p. 557.

67. Historians are curiously silent on the American reception of Victoria's assuming the throne in June 1837 and of her coronation of July 1838.

68. The standard format for all pages was six columns, running the length of the page, with four to six thousand words per page for news items, depending on type size. Only the Boston *Evening Gazette*, 28 July 1838, offered a lead-in on the coronation in column six of the first page.

69. See the Boston *Courier*, 27 July 1838, p. 2, whose coverage carried over into the sixth column; the Boston *Commercial Gazette* (bi-weekly), 30 July 1838, p. 2, whose coverage occupied five columns; the Boston *Atlas*, 27 July 1838, p. 2, whose coverage occupied four columns; the Boston *Evening Gazette*, 28 July 1838, whose coverage, beginning on p. 1, carried over to five and half columns on p. 2. The Boston *Mercantile Journal*, 26 July 1838, p. 2, offered two full columns, as did the Boston *Morning Post*, 27 July 1838, p. 2.

70. See the Boston *Weekly Messenger*, 1 August 1838, p. 4, which devoted five and a half columns to the coronation.

71. For example, the Salem *Gazette*, 27 July 1838, p. 3. Covering a column and a half, the *Gazette* quotes from the New York *Sun* for the coronation's details, but concludes on its own by saying, "The effect was sublime beyond description."

72. The Boston *Courier* calls the coronation a "splendid ceremony"; the Boston *Gazette* calls it "an imposing and magnificent pageant." The Boston *Atlas* says, "the English papers are chiefly filled with accounts of the coronation; and although we agree with Earl Fitzwilliam, in holding the whole ceremony to be a very silly affair, yet as we well know the universal curiosity which prevails in republican America, touching all the details of royalty, we have devoted almost the whole of our columns to an account of the coronation." The coverage here would seem to belie the sarcastic editorial view. The otherwise glowing account in the Boston *Morning Post* includes coverage of Lord Glenley, whose coronet fell off during the coronation ceremony while he was asleep.

73. See, for example, the satire on the coronation in the *Knickerbocker New York Monthly*, September 1838, p. 1.

74. Smith, "Hawthorne's Legends," p. 41, says, "Chronologically and thematically, 'Lady Eleanore's Mantle' and 'Old Esther Dudley' are the alpha and omega of aristocratic abuse and suffering." P. L. Reed, "The Telling Frame of Hawthorne's 'Legends of the Province House,'" *Studies in American Fiction* 4 (1976): pp. 105–11, argues that because they are told in one sitting,

the last two legends "tend to indicate a still more intense fascination with the past" on the part of Hawthorne (p. 109).

75. For the fullest allegorical reading of the legend, see Becker, pp. 49–59.

76. Seymour Gross first noted this detail and argued against a simple patriotic reading of the legend. See "'Lady Eleanor's Mantle' as History," *Journal of English and German Philology* 34 (1955): 549–54).

77. Colacurcio, *Province*, pp. 427–28, discusses pride as both sin and punishment in traditional Puritan terms.

78. Colacurcio's chapter argues for the appropriateness of pox as punishment within a context of the Puritan covenant.

79. See Hutchinson, 2:207–8.

80. See William B. O. Peabody, "Life of Cotton Mather," in *The Library of American Biography*, 1st series, 6:314. In his treatment of Cotton Mather and smallpox in *The Whole History of Grandfather's Chair*, Hawthorne has Grandfather recommend the Peabody biography of Mather to his grandchildren (6:105).

81. See Kenneth Silverman, *The Life and Times of Cotton Mather* (New York: Harper & Row, 1984), pp. 336–63.

82. Ibid., p. 353.

83. This is the pharmaceutical and rhetorical argument of Mitchell R. Brietweiser, *Cotton Mather and Benjamin Franklin: The Price of Representative Personality* (Cambridge: At the University Press, 1984), pp. 117–32.

84. The quotation is from Hawthorne (6:102), which adequately hints at his knowledge of how Mather was excoriated in the press as pointedly as Perry Miller presents it in *From Colony to Province*, pp. 343–66.

85. Miller, p. 363.

86. See Hutchinson, 2:188, 200, 204. For Clarke's association with Cooke, see G. B. Warden, *Boston, 1689–1776* (Boston: Little, Brown, 1970), pp. 85–86.

87. Silverman, p. 339.

88. Ibid., p. 351.

89. Ibid., pp. 345, 353; and Warden, p. 91.

90. Silverman, pp. 355–57.

91. Miller, pp. 324–44; and Warden, pp. 85–86.

92. See Warden, pp. 90–91, for the Anglophobia, and pp. 86–89 for the plight and recovery of the clergy; and see Hutchinson, 2:244–45, for Mather's petition.

93. In the formulation of Fossum, p. 41, "Sin makes democrats of us all."

94. I am indebted to Colacurcio's discussion of pride-as-pox and of the relevance of the Jeremiad.

95. Smith, "Hawthorne's Legends," p. 38, counts five queenly references and reads them as Jervase's supplication to a king.

96. Colacurcio, *Province*, pp. 432–33, argues for London as the Puritan hell and thus for the sound-and-sense spelling. Earlier, Fossum, p. 40, had suggested the sound-as-sense surname.

97. Smith, "Hawthorne's Legends," p. 38, points out the significance of these representatively social figures.

98. McWilliams, "'Thorough-going Democrat,'" p. 551, misidentifies the origin of the cup by claiming it is "Anglican." Doubleday, p. 130n, mistakenly argues that Hawthorne inaccurately credits the Old South Church with using communion wine. But the use of fermented wine in communion did not become an issue until the nineteenth century. Based upon newspaper accounts in the 1740s, Hawthorne claims that enormous quantities of imported wines were stored in the cellar of the Old South Church. The purpose would seem obvious. See "Old News" (11:141).

99. Warden, p. 88, shows the growing success of the English Church in Boston during the 1720s.

100. Colacurcio, *Province*, pp. 434–37, nominates Clarke as the central figure because of the politics of the 1720s associated with him.

101. And yet there are critics who take it seriously. See Fossum, p. 40; and A. N. Kaul, *The American Vision: Actual and Ideal Society in Nineteenth-Century Fiction* (New Haven: Yale University Press, 1963), p. 171.

102. Sheldon W. Liebman, "Ambiguity in 'Lady Eleanore's Mantle,' " *Emerson Society Quarterly* 58 (1970): 97–101, esp. p. 100.

103. Colacurcio, *Province*, p. 457, again writing the best analysis of the tale, says that " 'Old Esther Dudley' forces consideration of the cultural loss America suffered because first Puritan and then Democratic ideologists persisted in defining the Revolution as they did." He would not, however, credit the narrator with perceiving the reasons behind the cultural loss.

104. Colacurcio, *Province*, p. 451, says, "Only in the context of the *Democratic Review*—in the midst, that is, of Bancroftian History, Jacksonian Democracy, and Manifest Destiny—can we understand the anticlimactic concluding function of 'Old Esther Dudley,' or account for the involuted complexity of Hawthorne's narrative point of view."   .

105. For a discussion of how Esther represents two distinct kinds of past, one objective and the other subjective, see Bell, *Historical Romance*, pp. 204–8.

106. Thus one must differ with Colacurcio, *Province*, p. 461, who dismisses the importance of the tales told about Esther's mirror.

107. Carton, pp. 347–50, without discriminating between the stories Bostonians tell about Esther and those Esther tells to the children, interprets the old woman and her romance as crazed.

108. Colacurcio, *Province*, pp. 462–64, elaborates on the value of Esther's stories as "the *pastness* of the past."

109. As Colacurcio puts it, "the past simply dies, unable to transmit anything to a present so revolutionary as to be interested only in the future. The party of the past has been *so* mindlessly 'faithful' to its own terms that it has rendered itself obsolescent" (p. 471).

110. It is because of the ironic fact that Hancock, rather than Sam Adams, is the first elected governor that Hawthorne must obviously delegate him to replace Esther in the Province House. Thus the answer to the question posed by McWilliams, " 'Thorough-going Democrat,' " p. 566.

111. Smith, "Hawthorne's Legends," p. 43, first derided Hancock for his "pomposity—just what one might expect from the self-aggrandizing tradesman who made his own signature the most prominent on the Declaration of Independence." Baym, p. 76, sees the lines as "unironic." Doubleday, pp. 132–33, recognizing the irony in Hancock's speech, compares it to the rhetoric of John L. O'Sullivan.

112. See Colacurcio, *Province*, p. 476, who elaborates more fully the connection between Howe and Hancock first proposed by Smith, "Hawthorne's Legend," p. 43.

113. Both Smith, "Hawthorne's Legend," p. 42, and McWilliams, " 'Thorough-going Democrat,' " p. 566, address the repeated metaphor of foot-trampling in the "Legends."

114. Hancock's final disclaimer takes us back to the phrase associated with Bostonian children. As Fossum, p. 44, remarks, "Listening to [Esther's] stories, as we do to Hawthorne's, the children of the present become for a moment those children of the past whom Hancock insists Americans no longer are."

115. Or, for that matter, as do critics who decline to take seriously Hawthorne's major interest in history and who will not recognize his ironic criticism of those who smugly or blithely dismiss the past. For example, see Baym, p. 78, who believes Hawthorne considered Esther as "antiquated, eccentric, and absurd."

That Hancock wears a gouty shoe, perhaps the one that treads on royalty, is probably another of Hawthorne's ironies on this supposedly cultivated merchant. In "The Procession of Life" (1843), Hawthorne whimsically says, "Some maladies are rich and precious, and only to be acquired by the right of inheritance, or purchased with gold. Of this kind is the gout" (10:208).

116. This dying light, in unison with the depressed moral tone of the scene, is qualitatively different from previous references to the dim atmosphere of the Province House, which bear upon the precinct of "romance" art or historical allegory. See Becker, pp. 42–43.

117. What McWilliams, "'Thorough-going Democrat,'" takes to be a positive Puritan survival (or resurrection) in the Revolutionary War, Colacurcio sees as essentially negative. Obviously, I believe Colacurcio is correct.

Chapter 3. The Typology of Violence

1. For the background of the project and publication details, see Roy Harvey Pearce's Historical Introduction in the Centenary Edition of *True Stories*, 6: 292–93.

2. John W. Crowley, "Hawthorne's New England Epochs," *ESQ: A Journal of the American Renaissance* 25 (1979): 59–70, says the *"Whole History*, then, was a children's book, but Hawthorne brought to bear on its historical content the weight of adult ideas and impressions he had been gathering for over ten years" (p. 60).

3. Baym, pp. 86–96. See also McWilliams, *Hawthorne, Melville*, pp. 36–39.

4. Frequently drawing upon the *Whole History*, Colacurcio also believes the work augments Hawthorne's critical and ironic methods in the tales. See for example, pp. 419–21, 521–22 in *Province*.

5. The conflict of these qualities is the central thesis of Crowley, "Hawthorne's New England Epochs," pp. 59–70.

6. Sir Walter Scott, *Tales of a Grandfather: History of Scotland*, 6 vols. (Boston: Ticknor and Fields, 1865), 1: xiv.

7. Richard Brodhead, "Hawthorne, Melville, and the Fiction of Prophesy," in *Nathaniel Hawthorne: New Critical Essays*, ed. A. Robert Lee (Totowa, N.J.: Barnes and Noble, 1982), pp. 245–46.

8. Hawthorne refers to Bancroft's history later in the *Whole History*. He also alludes to Jared Sparks's *American Biography*. Both of these works he drew out of the Salem Athanaeum in preparation for the *Whole History*, Bancroft in April and Sparks in September 1837. See Kesselring.

9. George Bancroft, *History of the United States, from the Discovery of the American Continent* (Boston: Charles C. Little and James Brown, 1841), 1:354.

10. This is the overall thesis of Sacvan Bercovitch, *The American Jeremiad.*

11. See Pearce's Historical Introduction to *True Stories*, vol. 6 of Centenary Edition.

Chapter 4. The Recovery of English Traditions

1. See J. Donald Crowley's Historical Commentary in Centenary Edition (9: 506), and Wayne Allen Jones, "Sometimes Things Just Don't Work Out: Hawthorne's Income from *Twice-Told Tales* (1837), and Another 'Good Thing' for Hawthorne," in *Nathaniel Hawthorne Journal, 1975*, pp. 11–26.

2. See Turner for these details in *Nathaniel Hawthorne*, pp. 126–38.

3. For critical reception and financial rewards of the *Whole History*, see Roy Harvey Pearce's Historical Introduction (6: 294–97).

4. According to John J. McDonald, "The Old Manse Period Canon," *The Nathaniel Hawthorne Journal, 1972*, pp. 19, 30. "Drowne's Wooden Image" was written between 16 February and 11 March, and "The Artist of the Beautiful" was begun immediately after on 12 March and completed 3 May 1844. This period of composition seems virtually certain, despite the effort of Doubleday, pp. 186–87, to place the tale earlier in the canon.

5. For reasons beyond Drowne's discovery of a "Romantic" aesthetic, Baym, p. 111, is correct in saying: "More than any other work of the Manse period, this story looks ahead to the long romances."

6. Apparently, critics assume the truth of the rumor that an actual woman exists. See for example Richard P. Adams, "Hawthorne: The Old Manse Period," *Tulane Studies in English* 8 (1958): 115–51, who accepts the Bostonians' explanation that a real woman "goes away" with Hunnewell (p. 138).

7. For an excellent treatment of how Owen's growth corresponds to the life cycle of a butterfly, see Veronica Basil, "Eros and Psyche in 'The Artist of the Beautiful,'" *ESQ: A Journal of the American Renaissance* 30 (1984): 1–21.

8. Critical debate over whether Owen is a successfully projected artist has been long and vigorous. For an intial review of that debate and other criticism on the tale up to the mid-1970s, see Lea Bertani Vozar Newman, *A Reader's Guide to the Short Stories of Nathaniel Hawthorne* (Boston: G. K. Hall, 1979), pp. 21–27. Additional items from 1975 to the present can be found in the Fall numbers of the *Nathaniel Hawthorne Society Newsletter*.

9. See, however, James M. Cox, "The Scarlet Letter: Through the Old Manse and the Custom House," *Virginia Quarterly Review* 51 (1975): 432–47; and Roberta F. Weldon, "From 'The Old Manse' to 'The Custom-House': The Growth of the Artist's Mind," *Texas Studies in Literature and Language* 20 (1978): 36–47.

10. I am variously indebted to several writers on pastoralism for my discussion of Hawthorne's particular formula, especially Leo Marx, *The Machine in the Garden: Technology and the Pastoral Ideal in America* (New York: Oxford University Press, 1964); and Walter R. Davis, "A Map of Arcadia: Sidney's Romance in Its Tradition" in *Sidney's Arcadia*, by Walter R. Davis and Richard A. Lanham (New Haven: Yale University Press, 1965), pp. 7–44. See also Walter James, "'The Old Manse': The Pastoral Precinct of Hawthorne's Fiction," *American Transcendental Quarterly* 51 (1981): 195–209.

11. See Thomas H. Pauly, "Hawthorne's Houses of Fiction," *American Literature* 48 (1976): 271–91, esp. 284–85.

12. The quotation is from a letter of Hawthorne's to Evert Duyckinck, 22 February 1846 (16:146).

13. See Hawthorne's letter to Duyckinck of 30 April 1846 (16:159).

14. The issue of calling New England clergymen "priests" is discussed in chapter 5 on *The Scarlet Letter*.

15. Julian Hawthorne suggests that the Raphael was *Madonna del Pasce*, in *Nathaniel Hawthorne and His Wife: A Biography*, 2 vols. (Boston: Houghton Mifflin, 1884), 1:367. The pictures of Lake Como were undoubtedly painted by Sophia. See John L. Idol, Jr., "Hawthorne on Sophia's Paintings of Lake Como," *Nathaniel Hawthorne Society Newsletter* 10, No. 2 (1984): 11.

16. Hawthorne was attracted to the idea of keeping nature inviolate amid the mechanistic utility increasingly characterizing American life as the industrial revolution became more pronounced. This passage on the Concord's refusing adaptation to utilitarian ends must have occupied a fairly important part of Hawthorne's consciousness. Three years later, in 1850, he privately raised the issue in connection with contemporary degeneration. Horatio Bridge, *Personal Recollections of Nathaniel Hawthorne* (1893; rpt., New York: Haskell House, 1968), pp. 118–19, records that his wife had the following exchange with Hawthorne:

On one of his visits, he was talking with Mrs. Bridge at twilight, while I was dozing on the sofa. With the ease of manner that precluded all embarrassment on his part, she said to him, "Now tell me a story." Looking at me—without hesitation—he said, "I will tell you one which I could write, making that gentleman [Bridge] one of the principal characters. I should begin with the description of his father—a dignified and conservative man—who, for many years, had lived in a great mansion, by the side of a noble river, and had daily enjoyed the sight of the beautiful stream flowing placidly by, without a thought of disturbing its natural course.

"His children had played upon its banks, and the boys swam in the quiet stream or rowed their boats thereon.

"But, after their father's decease, his sons, grown to manhood—progressive in unison with the spirit of the age—conceived the project of utilizing the great body of water flowing idly by. So, calling in the aid of a famous engineer, they built a high and costly dam across the river, thus creating a great water-power sufficient for the use of many prospective mills and factories.

"The river—biding its time—quietly allowed the obstructions to be finished; and then it rose in its wrath and swept away the expensive structure and the buildings connected with it, and took its course majestically to the sea.

"Nor did this satisfy the offended river-gods; for they cut a new channel for the stream, and swallowed up the paternal mansion of the young men, and desolated its beautiful grounds, thus showing the superior power of Nature whenever it chooses to assert itself."

17. A passage in the *American Notebooks* written during the Manse period suggests reservation over Concord's militant residents (past and present) compared to the Concord River: "I am not aware," Hawthorne says, "that the inhabitants of Concord resemble their native river in any of their moral characteristics; their forefathers, certainly, seem to have had the energy and impetus of a mountain torrent, rather than the torpor of this listless stream as was proved by the blood with which they stained their River of Peace" (8 : 319).

18. In his notebooks, Hawthorne expresses more blatantly his criticism of modern theology and theologians in relation to their Puritan ancestors. Perusing the library, he says that "Doctor Ripley's own additions to the library are not of a very interesting character. Volumes of the Christian Examiner and Liberal Preacher, modern sermons, the controversial works of Unitarian ministers, and all such trash; but which, I suppose, express fairly enough, when compared with the elder portion of the library, the difference between the cold, lifeless, vaguely liberal clergyman of our own day, and the narrow but earnest cushion-thumper of puritanical times. On the whole, I prefer the last-mentioned variety of the black-coated tribe" (8 : 339).

19. John C. Willoughby, "'The Old Manse' Revisited: Some Analogues for Art," *New England Quarterly* 46 (1973): 45–61, notes how the horticulture metaphors in "The Old Manse" suggest "an organic wholeness" in life and art. He sees the "artist as beneficent gardener" and "the reader as bee"; "the reader as bee—by transferring a degree of creative responsibility to the reader—is a notion which goes a long way toward reconciling the tension between the writer's coexistent needs for detachment from and close relation to his society" (pp. 51–52). It seems to me, however, that the pastoral form itself more adequately expresses the tension and the need for reconciliation.

20. Hawthorne's familiarity with the common-sense philosophers, and his use of associational aesthetics (especially those of Archibald Alison and Lord Kames), is discussed by Leo B. Levy, "The Notebook Source and the 18th Century Context of Hawthorne's Theory of Romance," *Nathaniel Hawthorne Journal, 1973*, pp. 120–29—the quotation is from p. 124; and Bell, *Historical Romance*, pp. 195–208. For the pioneering study of this background, see Terence Martin, *The Instructed Vision: Scottish Common-Sense Philosophy and the Origins of American Fiction* (Bloomington: Indiana University Press, 1962).

21. On Sunday, 7 August 1842, Hawthorne recorded in his notebook that the Concord River "has a deep religion of its own" (8 : 321).

22. For the Saturnian context of Arcadia, see Harry Levin, *The Myth of the Golden Age in the Renaissance* (Bloomington: Indiana University Press, 1969), pp. 3–31.

23. Davis, p. 38.

24. See Roy Harvey Pearce, "Romance and the Study of History," in *Hawthorne Centenary Essays*, pp. 224–31.

25. Both Hawthrone and Sophia referred to their years at the Manse, the first years of the their marriage, as "Paradise." See, for example (8 : 317, 331). Sophia went so far as to head some of her letters "Paradise Regained" and "Hawthorne Abbey." See John J. McDonald's fine essay, "'The Old Manse' and Its Mosses: The Inception and Development of *Mosses from an Old Manse*," *Texas Studies in Literature and Language* 16 (1974): 77–108; the quotations are from note 60 on pp. 106–7.

26. Samuel Ripley's sudden decision to move into the Manse ahead of the date under-

stood by the Hawthornes, along with other problems facing the writer, are reflected in the latter portion of the "Manse" and covered by McDonald, " 'The Old Manse' and Its Mosses."

27. In a passage from his notebook entry for 8 August 1842, Hawthorne says: "To repaint [the Manse's] venerable face would be a sacrilege" (8:325).

28. See McDonald, " 'The Old Manse' and Its Mosses," for a detailed account of Hawthorne's correspondence to Duyckinck on completing the "The Old Manse" in relation to his move to Salem and assumption of office at the Custom house.

29. Polk signed Hawthorne's appointment on 3 April 1846; but the announcement of his taking office did not appear in the *Salem Gazette* until 22 April—see Randall Stewart, *Nathaniel Hawthorne* (New Haven: Yale University Press, 1948), p. 79. Hawthorne sent the MS of "The Old Manse" to Duyckinck on 15 April; see McDonald, " 'The Old Manse' and Its Mosses," p. 100. Hawthorne apparently knew of newspaper accounts of his appointment preceding that of the *Salem Gazette* by more than a week—or he anticipated that there would be such newspaper accounts.

30. I first wrote on the crucial links between "The Old Manse" and "The Custom-House" in my dissertation, "The English Past and the American Scene in Hawthorne's Works" (Washington State University, 1977), without the benefit of Weldon and Cox, who were perceiving these links roughly at the same time but for different purposes.

31. Turner, *Nathaniel Hawthorne*, pp. 177–87; and Stewart, pp. 98–99, deal with the reaction of Salemites to Hawthorne's treatment of the officials. Even the favorable review of the New York *Tribune* demurs over the "too sharp touches of . . . caustic acid" in Hawthorne's portrayals. See Kenneth Walter Cameron, *Hawthorne Among His Contemporaries* (Hartford, Conn.: Transcendental Books, 1968), p. 8, upper left.

32. For the best account of Hawthorne's dismissal from the Custom House, see Stephen Nissenbaum, "The Firing of Nathaniel Hawthorne," *Essex Institute Historical Collections* 114 (1978): 57–86. Nissenbaum argues that Hawthorne was not as innocent as he and his biographers have led us to believe, that the Whigs had a legitimate case against Hawthorne's using his office in "political" ways.

33. For a perspective on Hawthorne's dismissal and his counterattack in relation to improved sales of the book, see C. E. Frazer Clark, Jr., "Unexplored Areas of Hawthorne Bibliography," *The Nathaniel Hawthorne Journal, 1972*, p. 48.

34. Matthew J. Bruccoli identifies many of the Custom House officials from a marked copy of *The Scarlet Letter* belonging to the Upton family, long-time residents of Salem. See the Introduction to "Hawthorne in the Salem Custom-House—An Unpublished Recollection," *The Nathaniel Hawthorne Journal, 1971*, pp. 113–14. See also Turner, *Nathaniel Hawthorne*, pp. 195–97.

35. David Stouck, for example, oddly contends that Hawthorne admired the old Inspector because the man was satisfied with life and because Hawthorne himself needed to balance sensuality with his intellectual faculties. See "The Surveyor of the Custom House: A Narrator of *The Scarlet Letter*," *Centennial Review* 15 (1971): 309–29. A casual reading of the notebooks during the years at the Manse and in England reveals, however, that Hawthorne was not at all lacking in sexual and culinary appetites, which he frequently and abundantly satisfied. In this connection, see James R. Mellow, "Hawthorne at the Old Manse," *Gourmet* (November 1980), p. 49.

36. Hubert Hoeltje, *Inward Sky: The Mind and Heart of Nathaniel Hawthorne* (Durham, N.C.: Duke University Press, 1962), p. 278, says that the portrayal of General Miller is one of "unflinching realism blended with an idealism showing at once the limitations and the virtues of an admirable and loving man."

37. Bell, *Historical Romance*, pp. 20–81.

38. Ibid., pp. 85–86.

39. Rudolph Von Abele bases a considerable portion of his study on this commonly accepted view of Hawthorne's guilt in *The Death of the Artist: A Study of Hawthorne's Disintegration* (The Hague: Marinus Nijoff, 1955), pp. 4–6. Millicent Bell especially advocates this thesis in

Hawthorne's View of the Artist (New York: State University of New York Press, 1962), pp. 76–77, 201–2. See also Christoph Lohmann, "The Burden of the Past in Hawthorne's American Romances," *South Atlantic Quarterly* 66 (1967): 95.

40. "Main-street" also forecasts, with "regret," General Taylor's triumph in the 1848 election (11:81), which adds a personal note of irony to the problem, considering Hawthorne's subsequent removal from office.

41. Stewart, p. 80, holds this view and it involves the central thesis of Baym, pp. 143–49. Stewart also believes that the Custom House years were happy ones for Hawthorne; but he notes that Hawthorne attended lectures given by the Concord men more often during the Salem years than during the Manse years (p. 85). The implication of the fact might well be that Hawthorne was starving for intellectual activity and companionship. This lapse in Stewart's usual vigilance is all the more surprising in light of an extract from one of Hawthorne's letters to Longfellow, which Stewart quotes: "'I find myself dreaming about stories, as of old; but these forenoons in the Custom House undo all that the afternoons and evenings have done. I should be happier if I could write'" (p. 92). The full letter may be found in the Centenary Edition (16:216–17).

42. Julian Hawthorne, "Scenes of Hawthorne's Romances," *The Century Magazine* (July 1884); reprinted in Cameron, p. 253, col. 2.

43. F. O. Matthiessen, *American Renaissance: Art and Expression in the Age of Emerson and Whitman* (New York: Oxford University Press, 1941), pp. 187–88, perhaps leads the way in taking Hawthorne seriously here. Dan McCall, "Hawthorne's Familiar Kind of Preface," *ELH* 35 (1968): 422–39, takes Hawthorne even more seriously, advising the reader not to be insensitive to Hawthorne's "despair," because "Hawthorne believed, in the introduction to his masterpiece, that he had chosen the wrong path. He really believed that 'A better book than I shall ever write was there' under his eyes if he could only see it and suffer it into his pen. But he could not do it" (p. 428). Turner, *Nathaniel Hawthorne*, p. 195, has a more balanced view of the matter: In writing "The Custom-House" and thus "reproducing 'the page of life that was spread before him,'" Hawthorne "wrote a portion of the 'better book' he had despaired of writing; and in the process he transformed his report of observation into a richly imaginative sketch." For my part, I do not believe Hawthorne despaired of writing a better book but says as much by way of acknowledging the anti-fictional biases of his audience, that audience Michael Bell presents in *The Development of American Romance: The Sacrifice of Relation* (Chicago: University of Chicago Press, 1980), which is essentially the audience ridiculed by the storyteller in "Passages from a Relinquished Work."

44. McDonald, "The Old Manse Period Canon," p. 13, says that Hawthorne wrote exclusively on "contemporaneous reality" while at the Manse. "Drowne's Wooden Image," "The Artist of the Beautiful," and "Rappaccini's Daughter" would be three important tales disproving such exclusivity.

45. Submerged to some extent in Hawthorne's satiric portraits of Salemites is a disdain boldly surfacing in a letter to his friend Bridge, 13 April 1850: "I feel an infinite contempt for them, and probably have expressed more of it than I intended; for my preliminary chapter has caused the greatest uproar that ever happened here since witch-times. If I escape from town without being tarred-and-feathered, I shall consider it good luck. I wish they *would* tar-and-feather me—it would be such an entirely novel kind of distinction for a literary man! And from such judges as my fellow-citizens, I should look upon it as a higher honor than a laurel-crown" (16:329–30).

46. Hawthorne accurately "remembered" reading "(probably in Felt's Annals) a notice of the decease of Mr. Surveyor Pue" (1:30). The reference can be found in Felt, p. 455, under the date 24 March 1760.

47. By the 1760s when Governor Shirley was in charge of New England, the Anglican Church had long been reestablished as the state church in England. The number of Anglican or Episcopal Churches in the northern colonies, of course, had multiplied since William of

Orange came to the throne and demanded that Massachusetts Bay tolerate the existence of churches other than the Congregational. Pue was buried in the graveyard of Boston's St. Peter's Church, as Hawthorne recollects (1:30).

48. As early as 1843, Hawthorne was frustrated over the paradox of publishers and readers looking forward to additional productions of his work while he couldn't make enough money from them to live on. For this basic financial reason, he allowed and encouraged influential friends to promote his name for government positions. See his letter to Bridge of 3 May 1843 (15:686–88).

49. Paul John Eakin, "Hawthorne's Imagination and the Structure of 'The Custom-House,'" *American Literature* 43 (1972): 346–58, says that Hawthorne finds Surveyor Pue "more akin to his aesthetic temperament than any of his Puritan forebears" (p. 355).

50. One month before official notice of his dismissal, Hawthorne wrote a letter to Long-fellow, 5 June 1849, in which he candidly and forcefully maintains that *because of the value of his art,* he should receive the respect and support of the government rather than be a victim of the spoils system. Anticipating that he might be removed from office, Hawthorne was already planning to use his pen against his enemies. Hawthorne's comments are worth quoting at length because they have been largely ignored (the ellipsis is mine):

> I must confess, it stirs up a little of the devil within me, to find myself hunted by these political bloodhounds. If they succeed in getting me out of office, I will surely immolate one or two of them. . . . But if there be among them (as there must be, if they succeed) some men who claim a higher position, and ought to know better, I may perhaps select a victim, and let fall one little drop of venom on his heart, that shall make him writhe before the grin of the multitude for a considerable time to come. This I will do, not as an act of individual vengeance, but in your behalf as well as mine, because he will have violated the sanctity of the priesthood to which we both, in our different degrees, belong. I do not claim to be a poet; and yet I cannot but feel that some of the sacredness of that character adheres to me, and ought to be respected in me, unless I step out of its immunities, or make it a plea for violating any of the rules of ordinary life. When other people concede me this privilege, I never think that I possess it; but when they disregard it, the consciousness makes itself felt. (16:269–70)

These lines on the "priesthood" of artists illuminate in the most explicit terms Hawthorne's high admiration for art in general and for his own art in particular. Yet for more than half a century, many of Hawthorne's readers have dwelt on the guilt he sup-posedly felt because he was an artist. One ought to suspect that Hawthorne-as-guilty-artist is a myth rivaling that of Hawthorne-the-recluse. Nissenbaum, pp. 62–63, argues that Hawthorne's use of this "priesthood" was his way of trying to disguise his anger and lack of power, which may be true but does not address the historical dimension of Hawthorne's valuation of art and his own somewhat modest sense of having contributed to a literature that might last.

Chapter 5. Disinheritance and Recovery of English Traditions

1. For other accounts of how Hawthorne's reaction to his dismissal finds expression in *The Scarlet Letter,* see Mellow, *Nathaniel Hawthorne in His Times* (Boston: Houghton Mifflin, 1980), pp. 292–308; and, drawing on his essay cited in chapter 4, Stephen Nissenbaum, Introduction to *The Scarlet Letter and Selected Writings* (New York: Modern Library, 1984), pp. xix–xxxvi.

2. Hawthorne's knowledge of New England history has received wide attention and is well-known. But his extensive knowledge of English history, especially of the sixteenth and seventeenth centuries, has been slighted. Based solely upon the books withdrawn from the Salem Athenaeum credited to Hawthorne, he was familiar with no fewer than forty-four works on British history (compared to sixty on American history), excluding biographies. See Kesselring, pp. 43–64.

3. For a discussion of the novel's potential antinomian context, see Michael J. Colacurcio, "Footsteps of Anne Hutchinson: The Context of *The Scarlet Letter*," *ELH* 39 (1972): 459–94.

4. Even though he does very little with the recognition, H. Bruce Franklin was the first to notice the Civil War context in his Introduction to *The Scarlet Letter and Related Writings* (Philadelphia: Lippincott, 1967), pp. 16–17. I was unaware of this essay when I wrote "Tradition and Disinheritance in *The Scarlet Letter*," *ESQ: A Journal of the American Renaissance* 23 (1977): 1–26. See also Larry J. Reynolds, "*The Scarlet Letter* and Revolutions Abroad," *American Literature* 57 (1985):44–67.

5. For the best discussion of alienation (indeed, perhaps the best synoptic treatment of the novel), see Charles Feidelson, Jr., "The Scarlet Letter," in *Hawthorne Centenary Essays*, pp. 31–77, esp. pp. 33–34.

6. Ibid., p. 33.

7. See Charles Ryskamp, "The New England Sources of *The Scarlet Letter*," *American Literature* 31 (1960): 257–72, esp. pp. 259–61, for the details on the novel's time scheme. In addition to the year of Winthrop's death, several other clues help establish the time frame between 1642 and 1649. See Alfred S. Reid, *The Yellow Ruff and the Scarlet Letter* (Gainesville: University of Florida Press, 1955), pp. 80–81.

8. Not until May 1643 did the Puritans dispense with the oath of allegiance to the King, which Hawthorne would have known from Winthrop's *History*, 2 : 100. In 1644, the General Court forbade taking sides with Charles I, as Hawthorne knew from his reading in Snow's *History of Boston*, pp. 98–99.

9. For background of millenarian thought in Europe and England, culminating during the Civil War, see B. S. Capp, *The Fifth Monarchy Men: A Study of Seventeenth Century English Millenarianism* (London: Faber and Faber, 1972), pp. 13–45; and P. G. Rogers, *The Fifth Monarchy Men* (London: Oxford University Press, 1966), pp. 1–27.

10. The mint mark of Charles I was not changed by Parliament until at least 1652, more than three years after the regicide. Hawthorne would not have had to know (although he may have known) the deatils on Parliament's change of mint marks to observe that royal currency continued in use after the regicide. But he must have known from his reading in Clarendon's *History of the Rebellion and Civil War in England*, 3 vols. in 6 (Oxford, 1705–6), that the Lord Keeper took the Great Seal of the monarchy to Charles I at Oxford in May 1642. Clarendon points out that Parliament had another Great Seal made in 1643, which was "Engraven . . . according to the same Size and Effigies, and nothing differing from that which the King used at Oxford" (vol. 3, pt. 1, p. 406). Parliament used this duplicate of the Great Seal for six years and then used the confiscated Seal of Charles I for about two years, not making its own seal reflecting the new order until spring or summer 1649 (vol. 3, pt. 1, p. 262). From his reading in François Guizot in 1848, Hawthorne had supporting evidence that Parliament's new Seal was made after February 1649. See *History of the English Revolution of 1640, Commonly Called the Great Rebellion*, trans. William Hazlitt (New York: D. Appleton, 1846), p. 456. For Hawthorne's reading in Clarendon and Guizot, see Kesselring, pp. 47, 52.

11. Joseph B. Felt, *Historical Account of Massachusetts Currency* (Boston, 1839), p. 29. No concrete evidence exists to prove Hawthorne's familiarity with this work. And yet, considering his reliance on Felt's *Annals* and the historical compatibility of Chillingworth and Felt's comments on the coin, the odds would lean in favor of Hawthorne's having consulted the work.

12. The point is meant to confirm the reiterated thesis of D. H. Lawrence in *Classic Studies in American Literature* (New York: T. Seltzer, 1923).

13. For Hawthorne's knowledge of sumptuary laws, see Felt's *Annals*, pp. 71, 185. Snow, p. 55, has an abbreviated version of these laws.

14. Not long after this opening scene in 1642, the Parliamentary armies began destroying objectionable aesthetic features in churches throughout most of England. In August of 1643, the Long Parliament passed the first ordinances for taking down, removing, or destroying various objects of traditional decor within the churches—see John Phillips, *The Reformation of Images: Destruction of Art in England, 1535–1660* (Berkeley and Los Angeles: University of

California Press, 1973), pp. 184–85. Hawthorne does not fail to notice the results of this destruction or marvel over the occasional lack of it in his tours of ancient churches while in England. See *The English Notebooks*, pp. 150, 219–20, 237, 369, 417, 469, 492, 578.

15. The issue of iconoclasm is discussed cogently, with extensive documentation, by Phillips, pp. 157–200.

16. Bell, *Historical Romance*, p. 129, says that "it is one of the curious features of *The Scarlet Letter* that Pearl . . . is continually associated with Europe."

17. John Caldwell Stubbs, *The Pursuit of Form: A Study of Hawthorne and the Romance* (Urbana: University of Illinois Press, 1970), p. 90.

18. Jane Lundblad, *Nathaniel Hawthorne and European Literary Tradition* (Uppsala: A. R. Lundequistska Bokhandeln, 1947), p. 115, discussing the Gothic novel's influence on Hawthorne, says that Bellingham's mansion is like a castle.

19. Phillips, pp. 184–95.

20. See Anne Marie McNamara, "The Character of Flame: The Function of Pearl in *The Scarlet Letter*," *American Literature* 27 (1956): 544–45.

21. Hawthorne might easily have recalled Thomas Frankland's *Annals,* which elaborates Archbishop Laud's successful plea to the King in 1636 to have his own power to visit both universities to determine the fitness of their students and faculty in matters of doctrine, faith, and observance of High Church forms of worship. The issue grew out of Laud's aim to visit Cambridge where there were three unconsecrated chapels. Oxford was clearly not a threat to Laud. See pp. 471–76.

William Haller, *The Rise of Puritanism* (New York: Columbia Unviersity Press, 1938), says that Laud's "election as Chancellor of Oxford in 1630 enabled him to consummate his reform of that university" (p. 230). Even Cambridge experienced reform. From the Hampton Court Conference in 1604 to the Westminster Assembly in 1643, a nucleus of Puritan preachers made use of Cambridge "as its seminary" and "built up for itself what can fairly be called a kind of Puritan order of preaching brothers. . . . A few went to Oxford, but for most of them a Cambridge education culminating in a Cambridge fellowship was the starting point of their careers" (p. 52). But by the time Laud became Archbiship of Canterbury, the strength of the Puritan preachers at Cambridge was on a decline and in the 1630s sharply curbed (pp. 294, 296).

M. M. Knappen, *Tudor Puritanism* (Chicago: University of Chicago Press, 1939), points out that Oxford shifted very slowly from Catholicism to Episcopacy in the sixteenth century. Thus there was a strong tradition militating against the likelihood of the Puritans achieving any considerable influence in the university. In the 1570s, Oxford was "not unfairly reported" to be a "den of papistry." However, "there was a slight strain of Puritanism at Magdalen . . . at Merton . . . and at Corpus. . . . But the [Puritan] movement was not able to make much headway in the atmosphere that evenutally produced William Laud. At Cambridge [in the sixteenth century] the situation was entirely different" (p. 218).

22. Mather, *Magnalia,* 1:355.

23. The nine men and the information about them in this discussion can be located in vol. 1 of the *Magnalia:* pp. 322, 429, 445–46, 480, 484, 519, 585, 595, 597.

24. Winthrop, 1:265n. In his "Ecclesiastical History," commenting on Benjamin Woodbridge's having received a Doctor of Divinity from Oxford, John Eliot says: "It must have been under the reign of Cromwell, at the university of Oxford, for under no other administration could a puritan divine receive this honorary distinction from that place" (p. 32n). Woodbridge began his studies at Oxford but emigrated and was among Harvard's first graduating class. He returned to England where he received an honorary degree; and he later served as one of Charles II's chaplains until refusing to take the oath of conformity.

25. Winthrop, 1:41n. Savage, of course, is wrong about Williams's alma mater. It was Cambridge. But Savage was not alone in his inaccuracy. Felt, p. 50, also claims that Williams attended Oxford.

26. *Woodstock,* p. 59.

27. *Woodstock,* p. 39. Writing on his visit to the chapel at Stanton Harcourt, Oxfordshire, in 1856, Hawthorne shows that he is aware of Oxford University's close ties to Charles I. The fact that the statues in the chapel are undamaged, having escaped the iconoclasm of Cromwell's army, causes Hawthorne to remark: "The complete preservation and good condition of these statues is miraculous; their noses are entire, and the minutest adornment of the sculpture. Except at Westminster Abbey, among the chapels of the kings, I have seen none so well preserved. Perhaps they owe it to the loyalty of Oxfordshire (diffused throughout its neighborhood by the loyal University) during the great Civil war and the rule of the Parliament." See *The English Notebooks,* p. 417.

28. Clarendon, vol. 2, pt. 1, p. 58. For additional treatment of the close ties between Charles I and Oxford, see vol. 2, pt. 1, pp. 31, 70. Clarendon stresses the importance Oxford came to assume for the Royalists when, in May 1644, word spread that the king had been taken and Oxford fallen (vol. 2, pt. 2, pp. 484–85). Guizot, pp. 191 and 198, also remarks on Oxford's Royalist devotion.

29. Daniel Neal, *The History of the Puritans,* ed. John O. Choules, 2 vols. (New York: Harper and Brothers, 1844), 1:417; 2:57–66.

30. *The Scarlet Letter,* 1:123, 125, 195, 196, 200.

31. *The Scarlet Letter,* 1:127, 199, 230, 238.

32. None of the earliest New England historians, such as Winthrop, Morton, and Johnson, refers to Puritan ministers as priests; nor do any of the later historians whom Hawthorne especially read—Hutchinson, Snow, Neal, and Felt. Hutchinson does quote two sources in which New England clergymen are labeled priests, apparently for the purpose of equating their power and corruption with those of the stereotypical Catholic priests imaged by many Protestants in the seventeenth century. One of these sources depicts an antinomian sympathizer venemously attacking the Puritan "priests and professors" for banishing Anne Hutchinson and causing her death (1:64n). The other presents the satisfaction of Quakers upon the sudden death of John Norton, "chief priest in Boston" in 1663 (1:191n). See also the sermon delivered by the Independent clergyman in *Woodstock,* pp. 45–49.

33. The date of construction comes from Hawthorne's main source of information on the chapel: F. W. P. Greenwood, *A History of King's Chapel* (Boston: Carter, Hendee, 1833), pp. 44–45n. For Hawthorne's reading in Greenwood, see Kesselring, p. 52.

34. See Colacurcio, "Footsteps of Anne Hutchinson."

35. William Hone, *The Every Day Book, or a Guide to the Year,* 2 vols. (London: William Tegg, 1878). This work was first published in 2 vols. in 1826–27 and reprinted throughout the century. Hawthorne read the three-volume edition of 1830, which included *The Table Book* (vol. 3), in 1835–36. He checked out vol. 1 again in late January 1850. See Kesselring, p. 53.

36. A good historical discussion of the public confession issue in the novel is that of Ernest W. Baughman, "Public Confession and *The Scarlet Letter,*" *New England Quarterly* 40 (1967): 532–50.

37. The Reverend Stephen Batchellor was prohibited from carrying on his ministerial duties at Hampton for "soliciting the chastity of his neighbor's wife." See Winthrop, 1:44–45. My essay on Batchellor and his third wife, Mary, as sources for Dimmesdale's sense of his sin and Hester's sense of her punishment, will appear in *New England Quarterly* late 1986 or early 1987 under the title "A Red Hot *A* and a Lusting Divine: Sources for *The Scarlet Letter.*"

38. "Father Wilson" appears four times on pp. 150–51.

39. James Russell Lowell, writing to Miss Jane Norton on 12 June 1860, remarked: "I have seen Hawthorne twice. . . . He is writing another story. He said that it had been part of his plan in 'The Scarlet Letter' to make Dimmesdale confess himself to a Catholic priest. I, for one, am sorry he didn't. It would have [been] psychologically admirable." See Henry G. Fairbanks, "Hawthorne and Confession," *Catholic Historical Review* 43 (1957): 38–45; the quotation appears on p. 40.

40. Ryskamp, p. 259, argues that the reason Hawthorne selects late May for the death of Winthrop, instead of the historical date in March, is that "plot complications" would result

from Dimmesdale's spending his midnight vigil in the "cold, blustery month of March." But in fact, Hawthorne has the Pentecostal season in mind for his closing scene. Since Pentecost occurs fifty days after Easter, it must necessarily take place from the middle of May to the middle of June. Thus Hawthorne most likely worked backward in setting the May date for Dimmesdale's midnight vigil and Winthrop's death.

41. Male, pp. 90–118.

42. Winthrop, 2:31n. Hutchinson, 1:10, makes the same point about the original charter's requirement of annual elections.

43. *English Notebooks*, pp. 114–15. See also a briefer discussion on p. 491.

44. Hone, 1:720–27.

45. Fogle, p. 148, says that "in this statement the tone of good-humored mockery is unmistakable." Humorous or not, the criticism still stands, in much the way Hawthorne refused to change a word of his satirical treatment of the Custom House officials when a second printing of the novel was issued.

46. William J. Thoms, *Book of the Court* (London, 1844). For Hawthorne's reading in Thoms, see Kesselring, p. 62.

47. For an account of the Knights Templars and the historical literature on them, see G. Legman, "The Guilt of the Templars," in *The Guilt of the Templars* by G. Legman et al. (New York: Basic Books, 1966), pp. 1–134.

48. Scott, *Ivanhoe*, Waverley Novels Edition (Edinburgh: Adam and Charles Black, 1852), p. 434.

49. In the first edition of the Norton Critical Edition of *The Scarlet Letter*, the editors claim that this body of soldiers which survives in the nineteenth century is "The Ancient and Honorable Artillery Company of Massachusetts." Considering the reference to the Knights Templars, it seems worth suggesting that Hawthorne may have had in mind an additional organization which had "corporate existence" in his day: the Freemasons, who trace their origins to the Knights Templars—see Legman, pp. 124–26. The quotation from the Norton edition is from p. 168n.

50. Clarendon, vol. 3, pt. 1, p. 262; and Guizot, p. 456.

51. Bell, *Historical Romance*, p. 140.

52. Bell comes close to seeing the significance of Hawthorne's selecting the election day of 1649 for the closing setting of the novel's action. He says that "Hawthorne goes out of his way, considering that what he is presenting is an election celebration, not to mention who has been elected. It is Dimmesdale's day—unless, of course, one wishes to argue that the suppressed 'truth' about Endicott's succession is intended ironically to undercut the hopefulness of Hester and Dimmesdale, to prove that it is not Dimmesdale's day after all" (*Historical Romance*, p. 141n). Bell apparently does not subscribe to such an ironic reading. But I should say that the "truth" comes closer to this: Endicott's election, his ominous waiting in the wings, is intended less to undercut the hopefulness of Hester and Dimmesdale than to subvert the idea of an optimistic future for New England, at least in cultural or aesthetic terms.

Chapter 6. Divided Loyalties

1. See William G. Carleton, "Hawthorne Discovers the English," *Yale Review* 53 (1964): 395–413; and James A. Hija, "Nathaniel Hawthorne's *Our Old Home*," *American Literature* 46 (1974): 363–73; and Austin Warren's Introduction to *Nathaniel Hawthorne*, American Writer Series (New York: American Book, 1934).

2. Newton Arvin, who used the original manuscript of the *Notebooks* before Stewart, presents an especially acute analysis in *Hawthorne* (New York: Russell and Russell, 1929), pp. 222–63). See also Stewart's *Nathaniel Hawthorne*, pp. 148–82; Turner's *Nathaniel Hawthorne*, pp. 252–318; and Mellow's *Nathaniel Hawthorne* pp. 425–80. Romona Hull's *Nathaniel*

Hawthorne: The English Experience, 1853–1864 (Pittsburgh: University of Pittsburgh Press, 1980) is by far the fullest account of Hawthorne's years in England. It should be supplemented with James O'Donald Mays, *Mr. Hawthorne Goes to England: The Adventures of a Reluctant Consul* (Burley, Ringwood, Hampshire [England]: New Forest Leaves, 1983), which offers the most detailed information on the nautical and commercial circumstances involved in Hawthorne's consular responsibilities.

3. Lawrence Sargent Hall must surely not be included in this sweeping statement. His lengthy treatment of Hawthorne's experience in England may well be the most perceptive ever written. See *Hawthorne: Critic of Society* (New Haven: Yale University Press, 1944), pp. 68–100.

4. Baym, p. 219.

5. James T. Fields, *Yesterdays with Authors* (Boston: Houghton Mifflin, 1871), pp. 81–82.

6. Julian Hawthorne, *Hawthorne and His Wife*, 2:168–69.

7. Letter of 23 May 1856, sent to William D. Ticknor and published in his *Letters*, 2:15.

8. For a sample of the reviews, see the Historical Introduction of Claude M. Simpson in the Centenary Edition of *Our Old Home* (5:xxxi).

9. *EN*, p. 107. Another reference appears on p. 397. See Claude M. Simpson and Edward H. Davidson's discussion of the inception of the *Ancestral Footstep* in the Historical Introduction to *The American Claimant Manuscripts*, 12:492–94.

If the *Notebooks* were to aid in descriptive background for this projected romance, one wonders why Hawthorne did not take them with him to the Continent, where he apparently was going to write. There exist only shaky inferences that he had written any portion of the *Ancestral Footstep* while still in England and hence would not necessarily have needed to consult the *Notebooks* further. Simpson and Davidson, pp. 496–97, also seem perplexed over why Hawthorne left the *Notebooks* behind.

10. Stewart, "Hawthorne in England: The Patriotic Motive in the Note-books," *New England Quarterly* 8 (1935): 3–13.

11. See above notes 2 and 3.

12. Stewart, *Nathaniel Hawthorne*, p. 177.

13. See, for example, p. 91 in the *Notebooks*. Turner, *Nathaniel Hawthorne*, p. 316, notes the weight of Hawthorne's patriotism being the heaviest during the Crimean War; and he offers no evidence of Hawthorne's criticism of the English beyond 1854. Hall (pp. 101–46), however, perceives numerous inferential criticisms.

14. See the letters of 24 April 1856 (2:11), 26 September 1856 (2:26), 10 October 1856 (2:29), 24 April 1857 (2:51), 7 January 1858 (2:70).

15. In their biographies, Stewart (most of all) and Turner both write on Hawthorne's anti-England predisposition in traditional political terms.

16. See Baym, p. 218.

17. Julian Hawthorne's opinion, despite the special problems it poses for a critic, is worth recording here: "Yet England, past and present, rich and poor, real and ideal, did somehow enter into him and become a part of his permanent consciousness, and he liked it better than anything else he had known." See *Hawthorne and His Circle* (New York: Harper & Brothers, 1903), p. 105.

18. Warren, p. lix, is perfectly right in observing that Hawthorne's "sensitiveness to social distinctions and gradations (scarcely characteristic of a thorough democrat) is constantly evidenced throughout the English Note-Books in the form of references to classes, applications of 'genteel' and 'ungenteel,' and mental queries whether people are or are not gentlemen."

19. The chapters on aristocracy, religion, and literature especially concentrate on what Emerson perceives as an irreversible decline.

20. Hawthorne wrote a letter to Emerson on 10 September 1856 to show his appreciation of *English Traits*; but if Hawthorne believed at the time that Emerson had fairly captured what was essentially lacking in modern England compared to the past, his notebook entries during

the period, and especially after the period, reveal an utter change of mind or heart. For Hawthorne's letter to Emerson, see Mellow, *Nathaniel Hawthorne,* p. 449.

21. Edward Wagenknect's comment might be taken to represent something of a consensus: "There had always been a conflict in Hawthorne between the conservative and iconoclast. All of his work testifies that he felt the appeal of old things, old beauties. At the same time he felt the burden of the past as an accumulation of rubbish." See *Nathaniel Hawthorne: Man and Writer* (New York: Oxford University Press, 1961), p. 116. For a more profound treatment of the issues, see Harry Hayden Clark, "Hawthorne: Tradition Versus Innovation," in *Patterns of Commitment in American Literature,* ed. Marston LaFrance (Toronto: University of Toronto Press, 1967), pp. 19–37. Larzer Ziff treats Hawthorne as a "Great Conservative" in *Literary Democracy: The Declaration of Cultural Independence* (New York: Viking, 1981), pp. 108–28).

22. This is A. N. Kaul's point of view in *The American Vision,* pp. 139-213.

23. Michael Davitt Bell, *The Development of American Romance,* pp. 175–93. This very important book is, for my purposes, especially perceptive on Hawthorne's underlying fear of revolutionary impulses—in himself and society.

24. In an early letter to his friend, Bridge (30 March 1854), Hawthorne announces that "If it were not for my children I should probably never return. . . ." The only reason given for this declaration is that "we Americans are the most miserable people on earth." See Bridge, p. 136. In letters to Ticknor, Hawthorne more frequently spoke about his disillusion with America and his growing fondness for England. See the letters of 31 August 1855, 26 October 1855, 24 April 1856, and those mentioned in note 14 above.

25. See the letter to Ticknor of 26 October 1855.

26. Stewart, Turner, and Hull all focus on the point in their biographies.

27. While full and reliable details of Hawthorne's work on the three manuscripts are not known, Edward H. Davidson and Claude M. Simpson piece together an adequate scenario in the Historical Commentary of the Centenary Edition, 12:491–506. Davidson's earlier work should also be consulted, *Hawthorne's Last Phase* (New Haven: Yale University Press, 1949), pp. 1–71.

28. Davidson and Simpson, 12:506.

29. For a discussion of Hawthorne's supposed allegiance to the young America movement, see Hall, pp. 101–28. This chapter must be read with caution since Hall freely cites from *The English Notebooks* and claimant manuscripts with no regard to chronology and little to context.

Works Cited

Primary and Secondary Historical Sources

Bailyn, Bernard. *The Ordeal of Thomas Hutchinson.* Cambridge: Belknap Press of Harvard University Press, 1974.

Bancroft, George. *History of the United States, from the Discovery of the American Continent.* Vol. 1. Boston: Charles C. Little and James Brown, 1841.

Bentley, William. "A Description and History of Salem." *Massachusetts Historical Society Collections,* 1st series, 6 (1800): 212–88.

Bradford, Alden. *History of Massachusetts.* 2 vols. Boston, 1822–25.

Breitweiser, Mitchell R. *Cotton Mather and Benjamin Franklin: The Price of Representative Personality.* Cambridge: At the University Press, 1984.

Capp, B. S. *The Fifth Monarchy Men: A Study of Seventeenth Century English Millenarianism.* London: Faber and Faber, 1972.

Clarendon, Lord Edward Hyde. *History of the Rebellion and Civil War in England.* 3 vols. in 6. Oxford, 1705–6.

———. *The History of the Rebellion and Civil Wars in England.* 3 vols. in 6. Oxford, 1707.

Cohen, Lester H. *The Revolutionary Histories: Contemporary Narratives of the American Revolution.* Ithaca, N.Y.: Cornell University Press, 1980.

Eliot, John. "Ecclesiastical History of Massachusetts." *Massachusetts Historical Society Collections,* 1st series, 9 (1804): 1–49.

———. "Ecclesiastical History of Massachusetts." *Massachusetts Historical Society Collections,* 1st series, 10 (1809): 1–37.

Felt, Joseph B. *The Annals of Salem, from Its First Settlement.* Salem, Mass.: W. & S. B. Ives, 1827.

———. *Historical Account of Massachusetts Currency.* Boston, 1839.

Frankland, Thomas. *The Annals of King James and King Charles the First. . . .* London, 1681.

Greenwood, F. W. P. *A History of King's Chapel.* Boston: Carter, Hendee, 1833.

Guizot, François. *History of the English Revolution of 1640, Commonly Called the Great Rebellion.* Translated by William Hazlitt. New York: D. Appleton, 1846.

Haller, William. *The Rise of Puritanism.* New York: Columbia University Press, 1938.

Harris, William. *An Historical and Critical Account of the Life of Oliver Cromwell.* London, 1762.

Hone, William. *The Every Day Book, or a Guide to the Year.* 2 vols. London: William Tegg, 1878.

Hubbard, William. "General History of New England." *Massachusetts Historical Society Collections,* 2d series, vol. 5.

Hutchinson, Thomas. *The History of the Colony and Province of Massachusetts-Bay.* Edited by Lawrence S. Mayo. 3 vols. Cambridge: Harvard University Press, 1936.

Johnson, Edward. "Wonder-Working Providence of Sion's Savior." *Massachusetts Historical Society Collections,* 2d series, vols. 2–4 and 7–8.

Kammen, Michael. *A Season of Youth: The American Revolution and the Historical Imagination.* New York: Alfred A. Knopf, 1978.

Knappen, M. M. *Tudor Puritanism.* Chicago: University of Chicago Press, 1939.

Legman, G. "The Guilt of the Templars." In *The Guilt of the Templars* by G. Legman et al. New York: Basic Books, 1966.

Mather, Cotton. "Extracts from Rev. Cotton Mather's Memoirs of Remarkables in the Life of His Father." *Massachusetts Historical Society Collections,* 1st series, 9 (1804): 245–53.

———. *Magnalia Christi Americana.* 2 vols. 1852. Reprint. New York: Russell and Russell, 1967.

Miller, Perry. *The New England Mind: From Colony to Province.* 1953. Reprint. Boston: Beacon Press, 1961.

Neal, Daniel. *The History of the Puritans.* Edited by John O. Choules. 2 vols. New York: Harper and Brothers, 1844.

Peabody, William B. O. "Life of Cotton Mather." In *The Library of American Biography.* Conducted by Jared Sparks. 1st series. Boston: Hillard Gray, 1835.

Phillips, John. *The Reformation of Images: Destruction of Art in England, 1535–1660.* Berkeley and Los Angeles: University of California Press, 1973.

Prince, Thomas. "Annals of New-England." *Massachusetts Historical Society Collections,* 2d series, vol. 7.

Records of the Governor and Company of Massachusetts Bay in New England. Edited by Nathaniel B. Shurtleff. 3 vols. Boston: William White, 1853.

Rogers, P. G. *The Fifth Monarchy Men.* London: Oxford University Press, 1966.

Rowe, Violet A. *Sir Henry Vane the Younger: A Study in Political and Administrative History.* London: Athlone Press, 1970.

Silverman, Kenneth. *The Life and Times of Cotton Mather.* New York: Harper & Row, 1984.

Snow, Caleb H. *History of Boston: The Metropolis of Massachusetts.* Boston: Abel Bowen, 1825.

Strutt, Joseph. *The Sports and Pastimes of the People of England.* Edited by William Hone. London: Chatto and Windus, 1898.

Thoms, William J. *Book of the Court.* London, 1844.

Upham, Charles Wentworth. "Life of Sir Henry Vane, Fourth Governor of Massachusetts." In *The Library of American Biography.* Conducted by Jared Sparks. 1st series. Boston: Hillard Gray, 1835.

Warden, G. B. *Boston, 1689–1776.* Boston: Little, Brown, 1970.

Winthrop, John. *The History of New England from 1630 to 1649.* Edited by James Savage. 1825–1826. Reprint. 2 vols. in 1. New York: Arno Press, 1972.

Literary Sources

Abele, Rudolph Von. *The Death of the Artist: A Study of Hawthorne's Disintegration.* The Hague: Maninus Nijoff, 1955.

Adams, Richard P. "Hawthorne: The Old Manse Period." *Tulane Studies in English* 8 (1958): 115–51.

Adkins, Nelson, F. "The Early Projected Works of Nathaniel Hawthorne." *Papers of the Bibliographical Society of America* 39 (1945): 119–45.

———. "Hawthorne's Democratic New England Puritans." *Emerson Society Quarterly,* no. 44 (1966): 66–72.

Arvin, Newton. *Hawthorne.* New York: Russell and Russell, 1929.

Basil, Veronica. "Eros and Psyche in 'The Artist of the Beautiful.'" *ESQ: A Journal of the American Renaissance* 30 (1984): 1–21.

Baughman, Ernest W. "Public Confession and *The Scarlet Letter.*" *New England Quarterly* 40 (1967): 532–50.

Baym, Nina. *The Shape of Hawthorne's Career.* Ithaca, N.Y.: Cornell University Press, 1976.

Becker, John E. *Hawthorne's Historical Allegory.* Port Washington, N.Y.: Kennickat Press, 1971.

Bell, Michael Davitt. *The Development of American Romance: The Sacrifice of Relation.* Chicago: University of Chicago Press, 1980.

———. *Hawthorne and the Historical Romance of New England.* Princeton: Princeton University Press, 1971.

Bell, Millicent. *Hawthorne's View of the Artist.* New York: State University of New York Press, 1962.

Bercovitch, Sacvan. *The American Jeremiad.* Madison: University of Wisconsin Press, 1978.

———. "Diabolus in Salem." *English Language Notes* 6 (1969): 280–85.

Bradley, Sculley; Beatty, Richard Croom; and Long, E. Hudson, eds. *The Scarlet Letter* by Nathaniel Hawthorne. Norton Critical Edition. New York: W. W. Norton, 1961.

Bridge, Horatio. *Personal Recollections of Nathaniel Hawthorne.* 1893. Reprint. New York: Haskell House, 1968.

Brodhead, Richard. "Hawthorne, Melville, and the Fiction of Prophesy." In *Nathaniel Hawthorne: New Critical Essays.* Edited by A. Robert Lee. Totowa, N.J.: Barnes and Noble, 1982.

Bruccoli, Matthew J. "Hawthorne in the Salem Custom-House—An Unpublished Recollection." *The Nathaniel Hawthorne Journal, 1971,* pp. 113–14.

Brumm, Ursula. *American Thought and Religious Typology.* New Brunswick, N.J.: Rutgers University Press, 1970.

———. "A Regicide Judge as 'Champion' of American Independence." *Amerikastudien* 21 (1976): 177–86.

Cameron, Kenneth Walter. *Hawthorne Among His Contemporaries.* Hartford, Conn.: Transcendental Books, 1968.

Cantwell, Robert. *Nathaniel Hawthorne: The American Years.* New York: Rinehart & Company, 1948.

Carleton, William G. "Hawthorne Discovers the English." *Yale Review* 53 (1964): 395–413.

Carton, Evan. "Hawthorne and the Province of Romance." *ELH* 47 (1980): 331–51.

Charvat, William. *The Profession of Authorship in America, 1800–1870.* Edited by Matthew J. Bruccoli. Columbus: Ohio State University Press, 1968.

Clark, C. E. Frazer, Jr. "Unexplored Areas of Hawthorne Bibliography." *The Nathaniel Hawthorne Journal, 1972,* pp. 47–51.

Clark, Harry Hayden. "Hawthorne: Tradition Versus Innovation." In *Patterns of Commitment in American Literature.* Edited by Marston LaFrance. Toronto: University of Toronto Press, 1967.

Colacurcio, Michael J. "Footsteps of Anne Hutchinson: The Context of *The Scarlet Letter.*" *ELH* 39 (1972): 459–94.

———. *The Province of Piety: Moral History in Hawthorne's Early Tales.* Cambridge: Harvard University Press, 1984.

Cox, James M. "The Scarlet Letter: Through the Old Manse and the Custom House." *Virginia Quarterly Review* 51 (1975): 432–47.

Crews, Frederick C. *The Sins of the Fathers: Hawthorne's Psychological Themes.* New York: Oxford University Press, 1966.

Crowley, John W. "Hawthorne's New England Epochs." *ESQ: A Journal of the American Renaissance* 25 (1979): 59–70.

———. Historical Commentary in *Twice-told Tales* by Nathaniel Hawthorne. Vol. 9 of Centenary Edition.

Davidson, Edward H. *Hawthorne's Last Phase.* New Haven: Yale University Press, 1949.

Davis, Thomas M. "The Traditions of Puritan Typology." In *Typology and Early American Literature.* Edited by Sacvan Bercovitch. Amherst: University of Massachusetts Press, 1972.

Davis, Walter R. "A Map of Arcadia: Sidney's Romance in Its Tradition." In *Sidney's Arcadia,* by Walter R. Davis and Richard A. Lanham. New Haven: Yale University Press, 1965.

Donohue, Agnes McNeill. "'The Fruit of That Forbidden Tree': A Reading of 'The Gentle Boy.'" In *A Casebook on the Hawthorne Question.* Edited by Agnes McNeill Donohue. New York: Crowell, 1963.

Doubleday, Neal F. *Hawthorne's Early Tales: A Critical Study.* Durham, N.C.: Duke University Press, 1972.

Drinnon, Richard. "The Maypole of Merry Mount: Thomas Morton and the Puritan Patriarchs." *Massachusetts Review* 21 (1980): 382–410.

Duban, James. "Robins and Robinarchs in 'My Kinsman, Major Molineux.'" *Nineteenth–Century Fiction* 38 (1983): 271–88.

Eakin, Paul John. "Hawthorne's Imagination and the Structure of 'The Custom-House.'" *American Literature* 43 (1972): 346–58.

England, A. B. "Robin Molineux and Young Ben Franklin." *Journal of American Studies* 6 (1972): 181–88.

Fairbanks, Henry G. "Hawthorne and Confession." *Catholic Historical Review* 43 (1957): 38–45.

Feidelson, Charles, Jr. "The Scarlet Letter." In *Hawthorne Centenary Essays.* Edited by Roy Harvey Pearce. Columbus: Ohio State University Press, 1964.

Fields, James T. *Yesterdays with Authors.* Boston: Houghton Mifflin, 1871.

Fisher, Marvin. "The Pattern of Conservatism in Johnson's *Rasselas* and Hawthorne's Tales." *Journal of the History of Ideas* 19 (1958): 173–96.

Fogle, Richard Harter. *Hawthorne's Fiction: The Light and the Dark.* Rev. ed. Norman: University of Oklahoma Press, 1963.

Folsom, James K. *Man's Accidents and God's Purposes.* New Haven: College and University Press, 1963.

Fossum, Robert H. *Hawthorne's Inviolable Circle: The Problem of Time.* Deland, Fla.: Everett/Edwards, 1972.

Franklin, H. Bruce. Introduction to *The Scarlet Letter and Related Writings* by Nathaniel Hawthorne. Philadelphia: Lippincott, 1967.

Grayson, Robert G. "The New England Sources of 'My Kinsman, Major Molineux.'" *American Literature* 54 (1982): 545–59.

Griffith, Clark. "Pearl's Green A: *The Scarlet Letter* and American History." *Australasian Journal of American Studies* 2 (July 1983): 21–33.

Gross, Seymour L. "Hawthorne's Revisions of 'The Gentle Boy.'" *American Literature* 26 (1955): 196–208.

————. "'Lady Eleanore's Mantle' as History." *Journal of English and German Philology* 34 (1955): 549–54.

Hall, Lawrence Sargent. *Hawthorne: Critic of Society*. New Haven: Yale University Press, 1944.

Halligan, John. "Hawthorne on Democracy: 'Endicott and the Red Cross.'" *Studies in Short Fiction* 8 (1971): 301–7.

Hawthorne, Julian. *Hawthorne and His Circle*. New York: Harper & Brothers, 1903.

————. *Nathaniel Hawthorne and His Wife: A Biography*. 2 vols. Boston: Houghton Mifflin, 1884.

————. "Scenes of Hawthorne's Romances." *The Century Magazine*, July 1884.

Hawthorne, Nathaniel. *Letters of Hawthorne to William D. Ticknor, 1851–1864*. 2 vols. in 1. 1910. Reprint. Washington, D.C.: NCR/Microcard Editions, 1972.

Henderson, Harry B. *Versions of the Past: The Historical Imagination in American Fiction*. New York: Oxford University Press, 1974.

Hija, James A. "Nathaniel Hawthorne's *Our Old Home*." *American Literature* 46 (1974): 363–73.

Hoeltje, Hubert. *Inward Sky: The Mind and Heart of Nathaniel Hawthorne*. Durham, N.C.: Duke University Press, 1962.

Hoffman, Daniel. *Form and Fable in American Fiction*. 1965. Reprint. New York: W.W. Norton, 1973.

————. "Myth, Romance, and the Childhood of Man." In *Hawthorne Centenary Essays*. Edited by Roy Harvey Pearce. Columbus: Ohio State University Press, 1964.

Hull, Romona. *Nathaniel Hawthorne: The English Experience, 1853–1864*. Pittsburgh: University of Pittsburgh Press, 1980.

Idol, John L., Jr. "Hawthorne on Sophia's Paintings of Lake Como." *Nathaniel Hawthorne Society Newsletter* 10, No. 2 (1984): 11.

James, Henry. *Hawthorne*. London: Macmillan, 1879.

James, Walter. "'The Old Manse': The Pastoral Precinct of Hawthorne's Fiction." *American Transcendental Quarterly* No. 51 (1981): 195–209.

Jones, Wayne Allen. "Sometimes Things Just Don't Work Out: Hawthorne's Income from *Twice-Told Tales* (1837), and Another 'Good Thing' for Hawthorne." *The Nathaniel Hawthorne Journal, 1975*, pp. 11–26.

Kaul, A. N. *The American Vision: Actual and Ideal Society in Nineteenth-Century Fiction*. New Haven: Yale University Press, 1963.

Kesselring, Marion L. *Hawthorne's Reading, 1828–1850: A Transcription and Identification of Titles Recorded in the Charge-Books of the Salem Athenaeum*. 1949. Reprint. Folcroft, Pa.: Folcroft Press, 1969.

Lawrence, D. H. *Studies in Classic American Literature*. New York: T. Seltzer, 1923.

Leavis, Q. D. "Hawthorne as Poet." In *Hawthorne: A Collection of Critical Essays*. Edited by A. N. Kaul. Englewood Cliffs, N.J.: Prentice-Hall, 1966.

Levin, Harry. *The Myth of the Golden Age in the Renaissance*. Bloomington: Indiana University Press, 1969.

―――. *The Power of Blackness*. New York: Alfred A. Knopf, 1958.

Levy, Leo B. "The Notebook Source and the 18th Century Context of Hawthorne's Theory of Romance." *The Nathaniel Hawthorne Journal*, *1973*, pp. 120–29.

Liebman, Sheldon W. "Ambiguity in 'Lady Eleanore's Mantle.'" *Emerson Society Quarterly* 58 (1970): 97–101.

Lohmann, Cristoph. "The Burden of the Past in Hawthorne's American Romances." *South Atlantic Quarterly* 66 (1967): 92–104.

Lowance, Mason I., Jr. *The Language of Canaan: Metaphor and Symbol in New England from the Puritans to the Transcendentalists*. Cambridge: Harvard University Press, 1982.

Lundblad, Jane. *Nathaniel Hawthorne and European Literary Tradition*. Uppsala: A. R. Lundequistska Bokhandeln, 1947.

McCall, Dan. "Hawthorne's Familiar Kind of Preface." *ELH* 35 (1968): 422–39.

McDonald, John J. "'The Old Manse' and Its Mosses: The Inception and Development of *Mosses from an Old Manse*." *Texas Studies in Literature and Language* 16 (1974): 77–108.

―――. "The Old Manse Period Canon." *The Nathaniel Hawthorne Journal*, *1972*, pp. 13–39.

McNamara, Anne Marie. "The Character of Flame: The Function of Pearl in *The Scarlet Letter*." *American Literature* 27 (1956): 537–53.

McWilliams, John P. *Hawthorne, Melville, and the American Character: A Looking-Glass Business*. Cambridge: At the University Press, 1984.

―――. "'Thorough-going Democrat' and 'Modern Tory': Hawthorne and the Puritan Revolution of 1776." *Studies in Romanticism* 15 (1976): 549–71.

Male, Roy R. *Hawthorne's Tragic Vision*. 1957. Reprint. New York: W. W. Norton, 1964.

Martin, Terence. "Hawthorne's Public Decade and the Value of Home." *American Literature* 46 (1974): 141–52.

―――. *The Instructed Vision: Scottish Common-Sense Philosophy and the Origins of American Fiction*. Bloomington: Indiana University Press, 1962.

Marx, Leo. *The Machine in the Garden: Technology and the Pastoral Ideal in America*. New York: Oxford University Press, 1964.

Matthiessen, F. O. *American Renaissance: Art and Expression in the Age of Emerson and Whitman*. New York: Oxford University Press, 1941.

Mays, James O'Donald. *Mr. Hawthorne Goes to England: The Adventures of a Reluctant Consul*. Burley, Ringwood, Hampshire [England]: New Forest Leaves, 1983.

Mellow, James R. "Hawthorne at the Old Manse." *Gourmet* (November 1980): 49.

———. *Nathaniel Hawthorne in His Times.* Boston: Houghton Mifflin, 1980.

Newberry, Frederick. "The Demonic in 'Endicott and the Red Cross.'" *Papers on Language and Literature* 13 (1977): 251–59.

———. "Hawthorne's 'Gentle Boy': Lost Mediators in Puritan History." *Studies in Short Fiction* 21 (1984): 363–83.

———. "Hawthorne's Ironic Criticism of Puritan Rebellion in 'The Gray Champion.'" *Studies in Short Fiction* 13 (1976): 363–70.

———. "Tradition and Disinheritance in *The Scarlet Letter.*" *ESQ: A Journal of the American Renaissance* 23 (1977): 1–26.

Newman, Lea Bertani Vozar. *A Reader's Guide to the Short Stories of Nathaniel Hawthorne.* Boston: G. K. Hall, 1979.

Nissenbaum, Stephen. "The Firing of Nathaniel Hawthorne." *Essex Institute Historical Collections* 114 (1978): 57–86.

———. Introduction to *The Scarlet Letter and Selected Writings* by Nathaniel Hawthorne. New York: Modern Library, 1984.

Orians, G. Harrison. "The Angel of Hadley in Fiction: A Study of the Sources of Hawthorne's 'The Grey Champion.'" *American Literature* 4 (1932–33): 257–69.

———. "Hawthorne and 'The May-Pole of Merry Mount.'" *Modern Language Notes* 53 (1938): 159–67.

———. "The Sources and Themes of Hawthorne's 'The Gentle Boy.'" *New England Quarterly* 14 (1941): 664–78.

Pauly, Thomas H. "Hawthorne's Houses of Fiction." *American Literature* 48 (1976): 271–91.

Pearce, Roy Harvey. "Hawthorne and the Sense of the Past; or, The Immortality of Major Molineux." *ELH* 21 (1954): 327–49.

———. Historical Introduction to *True Stories* by Nathaniel Hawthorne. Vol. 6 of Centenary Edition.

———. "Romance and the Study of History." In *Hawthorne Centenary Essays.* Edited by Roy Harvey Pearce. Columbus: Ohio State Unviersity Press, 1964.

Reed, P. L. "The Telling Frame of Hawthorne's 'Legends of the Province House.'" *Studies in American Fiction* 4 (1976): 105–111.

Reid, Alfred S. *The Yellow Ruff and the Scarlet Letter.* Gainesville: University of Florida Press, 1955.

Reynolds, Larry J. "*The Scarlet Letter* and Revolutions Abroad." *American Literature* 57 (1985): 44–67.

Rouse, Blair. "Hawthorne and the American Revolution: An Exploration." *The Nathaniel Hawthorne Journal, 1976,* pp. 17–61.

Russell, John. "Allegory in 'My Kinsman, Major Molineux.'" *New England Quarterly* 40 (1967): 432–40.

Ryskamp, Charles. "The New England Sources of *The Scarlet Letter.*" *American Literature* 31 (1960): 257–72.

Schwartz, Joseph. "Three Aspects of Hawthorne's Puritanism." *New England Quarterly* 36 (1963): 192–208.

Scott, Sir Walter. *Ivanhoe.* Waverley Novels Edition. 25 vols. Edinburgh: Adam and Charles Black, 1852.

———. *Tales of a Grandfather: History of Scotland.* 6 vols. Boston: Ticknor and Fields, 1865.

———. *Waverley; or, 'Tis Sixty Years Since.* Waverley Novels Edition. Edinburgh: Adam and Charles Black, 1852.

———. *Woodstock.* Waverley Novels Edition. London and Edinburgh: Adam and Charles Black, 1852.

Shaw, Peter. "Fathers, Sons, and the Ambiguities of Revolution in 'My Kinsman, Major Molineux.'" *New England Quarterly* 49 (1976): 559–76.

———. "Hawthorne's Ritual Typology of the American Revolution." *Prospects: An Annual of American Cultural Studies* 3 (1977): 483–98.

———. "Their Kinsman, Thomas Hutchinson." *Early American Literature* 11 (1976): 183–90.

Simpson, Claude M. Historical Introduction to *Our Old Home* by Nathaniel Hawthorne. Vol. 5 of Centenary Edition.

Simpson, Claude M. and Edward H. Davidson. Historical Introduction to *The American Claimant Manuscripts* by Nathaniel Hawthorne. Vol 12 of Centenary Edition.

Simpson, Lewis P. "John Adams and Hawthorne: The Fiction of the Real American Revolution." *Studies in Literary Imagination* 9 (Fall 1976): 1–17.

Smith, Gayle L. "Transcending the Myth of the Fall in Hawthorne's 'The May-Pole of Merry Mount.'" *ESQ: A Journal of the American Renaissance* 29 (1983): 73–80.

Smith, Julian. "Hawthorne's *Legends of the Province House.*" *Nineteenth-Century Fiction* 24 (1969): 31–44.

———. "Historical Ambiguity in 'My Kinsman, Major Molineux.'" *English Language Notes* 8 (1970): 115–20.

Stewart, Randall. "Hawthorne in England: The Patriotic Motive in the Note-books." *New England Quarterly* 8 (1935): 3–13.

———. *Nathaniel Hawthorne.* New Haven: Yale Unviersity Press, 1948.

Stouck, David. "The Surveyor of the Custom House: A Narrator of *The Scarlet Letter.*" *Centennial Review* 15 (1971): 309–29.

Strout, Cushing. *The American Image of the Old World.* New York: Harper & Row, 1963.

Stubbs, John Caldwell. *The Pursuit of Form: A Study of Hawthorne and the Romance.* Urbana: University of Illinois Press, 1970.

Turner, Arlin. "Hawthorne's Literary Borrowings." *PMLA* 51 (1936): 543–62.

———. *Nathaniel Hawthorne: A Biography.* New York: Oxford University Press, 1980.

Vickery, John B. "The Golden Bough at Merry Mount." *Nineteenth-Century Fiction* 12 (1957–58): 203–14.

Wagenknect, Edward. *Nathaniel Hawthorne: Man and Writer.* New York: Oxford Unviersity Press, 1961.

Waggoner, Hyatt. *Hawthorne: A Critical Study.* Rev. Ed. Cambridge: Belknap Press of Harvard University Press, 1963.

Warren, Austin. Introduction to *Nathaniel Hawthorne.* American Writer Series. New York: American Book, 1934.

Weber, Alfred. *Die Entwicklung der Rahmenerzahlungen Nathaniel Hawthornes.* Berlin: Erich Schmidt, 1973.

Weldon, Roberta F. "From 'The Old Manse' to 'The Custom-House': The Growth of the Artist's Mind." *Texas Studies in Literature and Language* 20 (1978): 36–47.

Williams, J. Gary. "History in Hawthorne's 'The May-Pole of Merry Mount.'" *Essex Institute Historical Collections* 108 (1972): 173–90.

Willoughby, John C. "'The Old Manse' Revisited: Some Analogues for Art." *New England Quarterly* 46 (1973): 45–61.

Yates, Norris. "Ritual and Reality." *Philological Quarterly* 34 (1955): 56–70.

Ziff, Larzer. *Literary Democracy: The Declaration of Cultural Independence.* New York: Viking, 1981.

Index

DATE DUE

PRINTED IN U.S.A.